The Daily Telegraph
BOOK OF
CRICKET

Nick Hoult has been writing for the *Daily Telegraph* since 2002 and joined the staff full time in 2006. He began his career at the *Northampton Chronicle & Echo* and now lives in London with his wife and daughter. He has also edited the *Daily Telegraph Book of Golf*, published by Aurum.

The Daily Telegraph

BOOK OF

CRICKET

edited by NICK HOULT

Aurum

First published 2007 by Aurum Press Limited
7 Greenland Street
London NW1 0ND
www.aurumpress.co.uk
This paperback edition first published in 2009 by Aurum.

A catalogue record for this book is available from the British Library.

ISBN 978 1 84513 426 6

1 3 5 7 9 10 8 6 4 2
2009 2011 2013 2012 2010

Text design by Richard Marston
Typeset in Spectrum by Saxon Graphics, Derby
Printed and bound in Great Britain by CPI Bookmarque, Croydon

CONTENTS

ACKNOWLEDGEMENTS

This book would not have been possible without the help, support and advice of many different individuals. I would like to thank Martin Smith at the *Daily Telegraph* for the loan of his cricket library and advice at the beginning of the project. I would also like to extend my gratitude to the library staff at the *Daily Telegraph*, in particular Gavin Fuller and Bill Elisha. Also, my thanks to Graham Coster at Aurum Press for help in editing this book and for his willingness to get his hands dirty, quite literally, while leafing through musty old cuttings at the *Daily Telegraph* archive. I would like to thank the writers, sub-editors and sports editors who since 1855 have covered cricket with such dedication and talent. This book is theirs. Not mine. Finally, a word of thanks to my wife Catriona for her unstinting support with this book and throughout my career.

CHAPTER I
1882—1933

INTRODUCTION

It is very easy to find the first mention of cricket in the *Daily Telegraph*. Simply flick through the first few issues of the newspaper in 1855 and there it is, and on the front page no less, a report of the match between the Officers of the 94th Regiment and the Victoria and Albert Club.

Perhaps the prominent placing of the report was an attempt by the editors of the day to gain favour with the royal household – the Victoria and Albert Club won by 37 runs – or it could have been an early statement of intent. Cricket was to be an important part of the newspaper's sports coverage and those early intentions have been followed by subsequent generations of reporters and editors.

On the 150th anniversary of that match at Home Park, Windsor, cricket was back on the front page of the *Daily Telegraph*. The regal surroundings were replaced by the raw emotion of a Test match at Trent Bridge as England took a decisive lead in the 2005 Ashes series. Cricket was big news and the *Daily Telegraph* was there to report it, adding several thousand words to the millions that have been devoted to the sport since that day on 29 August 1855.

From the small beginnings of that 60-word match report has developed a relationship with cricket that has been mutually beneficial. As the sport grew, so did the *Daily Telegraph*. By the time of the first Test match between England and Australia in March 1877, the newspaper had moved into Fleet Street, enjoyed massive publicity through its sponsorship of H.M. Stanley's explorations of Africa in 1874 and by 1876 shouted about having the 'Largest Circulation in the World'.

Newspaper habits have changed little over the generations. In the same way that in the modern era the newspaper aligns itself with the sporting heroes of the day, the Victorian editors were more than happy to buy into celebrity. Whereas today W.G. Grace would be expected to write a ghosted column in exchange for a lucrative contract, in 1895 things were simpler. All he had to do then was score runs for Gloucestershire, something he had little problem with in 1895, and watch on as the *Daily Telegraph* launched a shilling fund for his benefit.

The idea was that people who could not afford a large donation would be able to participate in the nation's gratitude for the game's greatest player. Even the Prime Minister joined in. Lord Salisbury sent £5, although it is impossible to ascertain whether it came from his own pocket or that of the Exchequer. The fund was a huge success and Grace received 100,000 shillings, a sum in today's money worth more than £300,000.

The newspaper, in turn, revelled in the publicity. A fact not missed by its rivals. The satirical magazine *Moonshine* published a cartoon of the *Telegraph* proprietor Sir Edward Lawson and Grace, a doctor by profession. 'Don't mention it doctor,' the cartoon quotes Lawson as saying. 'And thank you for what you have done for my circulation.'

Grace was the champion of his age and the *Daily Telegraph* reported his successes, and occasionally glossed over his failures. In 1900 Grace's 110 for London County against the MCC was described as 'free, excellent cricket'. We have little knowledge of his dismissal other than he was 'caught at the wicket'. The reporter did not see fit to name the bowler – that other great Victorian and creator of Sherlock Holmes, Sir Arthur Conan Doyle – and displayed perhaps the most monumental lack of news sense ever to be seen in a *Telegraph* cricket report.

But also the writer was adopting the method of the day. In the course of researching this opening chapter one theme stands out. The *Daily Telegraph* celebrated the run-makers, the gentlemen and professionals who thrilled the crowds and won Test matches with the bat. This was the age of the great batsmen – Grace, Ranji, Trumper, Hobbs and Bradman.

All five are here. Ben Bennison, in his report on Bradman's 309 at Headingley in 1930, provides a glimpse of the man with whom he would later write a book. It was only after passing Test cricket's highest-ever individual score that he 'for the first time indulged in a happy and expansive smile'.

But the *Telegraph* did not simply concentrate on the international game. County matches were reported on from the early days of the first organised championship in 1895, and the following year, in 1896, what we would now call a 'colour' writer was sent to the Oval to describe a Bank Holiday day out at the cricket.

A cricket match for the two princes Edward and Albert (the future Edward VIII and George VI) was described in literary prose in 1905, and five years later, schools cricket reached its pinnacle with the match between Eton and Harrow at Lord's. The match was a highlight of the summer social scene in Edwardian London and more than 1,000 words were devoted to the match. 'A more extraordinary finish can scarcely be recalled,' wrote the excited reporter. The importance of the match may have reflected the social structure of the day but also provided a tragic glimpse of the future. Eight of the 22 players involved would later die on the Western Front.

This chapter ends with cricket's first crisis. It would be more than a decade before the *Daily Telegraph* would send its own writers on an England tour, and the reports of the 1932–3 Bodyline series in Australia were compiled in the Fleet Street office from agency copy. But the paper reacted quickly to the furore. Prompted by the Australian board's famous cable to the MCC, which accused Douglas Jardine's team of lacking sportsmanship, the Telegraph employed the former Surrey captain Percy Fender to pen a defence of leg theory.

Under an article headlined 'This "Bodyline Bowling" is New Only in Name', Fender appeared on the comment pages of the *Daily Telegraph*. Cricket had its first major story and other news was put on hold. The City Editor, Leonard J. Reid, saw his article on the problem of war debts spiked, and the newspaper's coverage of cricket entered a new era.

---

30 AUGUST 1882

ENGLAND v. AUSTRALIA

The match at Kennington Oval yesterday ended, not only in a surprise, but also in a scene of excitement scarcely, if ever, equalised on any cricket ground.

Notwithstanding the threatening appearance with which the morning opened, such was the public interest awakened by the first day's play that by ten o'clock some thousands of persons were gathered at the enclosure, and as the day wore on the crowd increased until there were, it is believed, at the close of the match, not far from 25,000 spectators; and assuredly it may be said that all the elements were present to sustain the interest in the play from the beginning to the end.

We ventured yesterday to say that the Colonials had played an exceedingly uphill game with such spirit as to give fine proof of their quality, and that although the English team had 38 runs in hand on the first innings the issue was still an open one. How well the Australians deserved this praise was shown when they went in for their second innings. The wicket was even more decidedly against the batsman and in favour of the bowler than on the previous day. Nevertheless, our visitors nearly doubled their score, making 122. There was, perhaps, some slight falling off in the English bowling. Barlow – who bowled almost the whole of the preceding afternoon with remarkable steadiness and success, taking five wickets for only 19 runs – was less effective, and even Peate did not succeed as he had in the first innings in the long succession of maiden overs which made his analysis so striking. Still, on the whole, the bowling was remarkably good, especially in the latter part of the Australian innings. It will be seen by the score that only three of the Colonials reached double figures, including Massie's fine achievement of 55, the highest individual total of the match.

Two noteworthy incidents marked the Australian innings. The first of these showed the strictness with which the game was played. Murdoch and Jones were together, when the captain made a hit to short leg. Mr Lyttelton, the wicket-keeper, fielded, and threw in the ball, which was received by another member of the team and dropped at the wicket. The ball, however, was not 'dead' – the wicket-keeper having for the moment only acted as fielder, and Jones, forgetting this important fact, left his ground, and Mr Grace, observing the movement, instantly picked up the ball and removed the bails. There was some momentary complaining on the part of sympathisers with the Colonists, but no kind of protest was made, or was, indeed, possible. The second incident followed shortly afterwards, when Murdoch, having made a fine drive to the off, was attempting a second run – on the strength of the fact that Mr Hornby, who was fielding, would be unable to throw in on account of an injury to his arm. This calculation proved unsound. Mr Hornby passed the ball to Mr C.T. Studd, who threw it to Mr Lyttelton, and so very smartly closed the Australian captain's innings for an admirably played 29. A neater or more expeditious piece of fielding has rarely been seen.

In the end the whole Australian team was disposed of for 122 runs, thus leaving the home side 85 to win. This for one of the most perfect batting elevens the country could select seemed no great feat, and the odds were supposed to be largely in their favour. Dr W.G. Grace and Mr Hornby opened the innings, their appearance at the wickets being the signal for hearty cheering. Both played with considerable animation, but when the score had reached 15 the Lancashire captain was bowled by Spofforth for nine. Barlow, one of the steadiest batsmen in England, followed, but was immediately bowled also by 'the demon', as he is called, for 0. Ulyett followed, and for a while the spell of the Colonial bowling seemed to have been broken. Runs came with fair rapidity; 20, 30, 40, 50 were successively exhibited on the board, and the hopes of an English triumph rose high. At length Ulyett gave a chance to Blackham, who never misses one, and Mr A.P. Lucas took his place. There were thus three wickets down and 34 runs were required. But the overthrow of Ulyett was a great encouragement to the Australians, and when very soon afterwards Dr Grace was caught by Bannerman at mid-off — having made 32 out of a total of 53 — their elation naturally knew no bounds. The Hon. A. Lyttelton now joined Mr Lucas. It would be hard to name two more accomplished batsmen, but they found it hard to play Spofforth and Boyle. Both were bowling in their best style, Spofforth especially seeming to be irresistible. It was no small feat that two gentlemen guarded their wickets against 12 splendid maiden overs in succession, and shortly after five o'clock it was known that they had raised the score by the most careful play to 65.

This was the crisis of the game. Twenty runs were wanted, and to get them there were Lucas and Lyttelton still in; Read, Steel, Studd, Barnes and Peate to follow. At 66 Mr Lyttelton was bowled by Spofforth — 19 runs wanted and five wickets to fall. The excitement now grew apace. It was visible everywhere — in the pavilion, on the stands, throughout the dense ring of spectators, and in the field itself. The Australians were congratulating each other openly — meeting in groups whenever a wicket fell, and displaying an eagerness and elation seldom seen on a cricket field. On the other side every ball was watched and every single run cheered as though it had been a phenomenon. Mr Lucas had just played a four through the slips, greatly to the delight of the onlookers, when Mr Steel was caught and bowled by Spofforth. Another accession of anxiety — 15 runs wanted, four wickets to fall. Maurice Read, the hope of Surrey, succeeded. Great was the enthusiasm with which he was greeted. In previous matches with the Colonials he had greatly distinguished himself. He was bowled by Spofforth's second ball. Fifteen runs still wanted, and three wickets to fall. Barnes followed, and presently drove the fast bowler for two; then three were run for a bye; and then came another disaster. Lucas played on – and 10 runs were yet needed, and there were now only two wickets to fall. The excitement reached a pitch which mere words can hardly convey, and it was not lessened when Barnes sent a catch to Murdoch, and left Mr C.T. Studd and Peate, the last men, in face of the Australian bowlers, with still 10 runs to win. Peate scooped the first ball to leg for two, but this was the end. The last ball of the over – Mr Studd never having had a single ball – disarranged the professional's wicket, and the English team were beaten by seven runs. The Australians were warmly cheered by a vast crowd, who would rather the victory had gone the other way, but who were generous enough to admit that our visitors had fairly won, and by means of splendid cricket. And so ended the most important of the contests between English cricketers and the Australians; a contest fought out with indomitable pluck by the winners, and which will long be remembered by those who had the good fortune to witness it.

Immediately after the conclusion of the innings of the Australians, one of the spectators – who it was afterwards ascertained was George Eber Spendler, of 191, Brook Street, Kennington – complained to a friend of feeling unwell, and left the seat he had for some time occupied. Scarcely had he done so when he fell to the ground, and blood commenced to flow freely from his mouth. He was at once conveyed to a room adjoining the Pavilion, where he was examined by several medical men, amongst whom was Dr Jones, the president of the Surrey Cricket Club, who pronounced life extinct, the cause of death being attributed to a ruptured blood-vessel.

---

7 JUNE 1895

SURREY v. GLOUCESTERSHIRE

Attracted, no doubt, by the knowledge that W.G. Grace would be playing, a great crowd attended Kennington Oval yesterday, when this match commenced. The official returns show that 9,252 people paid for admission, so that the total number present could not have been far below 11,000. Surrey had a strong eleven, Maurice Read reappearing in the eleven. Gloucestershire were without Painter and Ferris, but G.L. Jessop was owing to the courtesy of Dr Hockey, his principal at Beccles College, again able to assist. The eleven was completed by C.O.H. Sewell and W.M. Brown, who, reputed a good batsman, was making his first appearance in county cricket. The weather was bright, but chilly. At the outset the wicket played well, but the Oval, like all other grounds, is in need of rain, and after lunch the ball got up very fast and several of the players were hit. Spectators who came with the idea of seeing the champion bat had to go away disappointed, for Surrey won the toss and kept their rivals in the field the whole day. They scored 366 for the loss of nine wickets, Hayward, the young professional, being top scorer with 123. This is the batsman's fourth three-figure innings for the county, but the first credited to him this season. A big total did not appear probable at the outset for Jessop bowled Lockwood at five, but on Abel and Hayward becoming associated the bowling was fairly mastered, and although, in addition to Jessop, Roberts, Grace, and Sewell were repeatedly tried, runs came at a good pace. Hayward played much the freer game and completed his 50 in an hour and five minutes, but the stroke which enabled him to accomplish the feat should have seen him caught at slip by Kitcat. The first hundred appeared on the board in an hour and a half from the start, but 14 later the partnership – which had yielded 109 – was dissolved, Abel being caught at deep mid-off by Sewell. He had played very attractive cricket for his 38. Holland came in, and at lunch time the score was 121 for two wickets. At 176 Holland was magnificently caught at square-leg by Wrathall, who was loudly applauded. On being joined by W.W. Read, Hayward completed his 100, which had occupied two hours and twenty-five minutes. He made 23 more, when he was run out owing to a very smart piece of fielding at cover point by Captain Luard. Hayward made his runs by sound and stylish cricket despite the chance he gave at 49. He was at the wicket three hours, and hit 19 4s, six 3s, and three 2s. Maurice Read never appeared comfortable, and was bowled by Jessop for 13. Key opened very carefully, but when he had settled down he made 13 in three hits. W.W. Read's score of 54 was made in quite his best style. He hit nine 4s, two 3s, four 2s, and only four singles. He left at 289, and at 293 a splendid catch at mid-off by Sewell cut short Key's career. Two later the same fieldsman cleverly disposed of Richardson; but Wood and Brockwell adopted careful tactics, and after adding 58 were still together at the end of the day. Just before the end Board, the Gloucestershire wicket-keeper, was badly hit in the face. He left the field but returned in a few minutes with his nose strapped up, his pluck in coming out again being loudly cheered by the spectators.

----

21 AUGUST 1895

YORKSHIRE v. MIDDLESEX

There was a remarkable day's cricket in this match at Leeds yesterday, and so well did the Yorkshiremen perform in all departments of the game that very little time is required today to enable them to gain a substantial victory. Monday's play had resulted in the home county completing an innings for 128 and getting rid of their rivals for 103, whilst on going in a second time for five minutes' batting at the close of the day they lost Lord Hawke's wicket for five runs. On resuming yesterday, before a large crowd, another Yorkshire wicket quickly fell, Mitchell being dismissed at 18. Then, however, a splendid stand took place by Jackson and Tunnicliffe. Playing sterling cricket the pair soon obtained a mastery over the Middlesex bowling. Webbe changed the attack, but without effect, as the pair kept together for two hours and a quarter, during which period they put on 130 runs. Jackson was the first to leave, brilliantly caught by Douglas in the long field. He was batting altogether two hours and a half for a fine essay of 76, which, without being vigorous, was nevertheless a stylish display. He hit only one 4, six 3s, and fifteen 2s. Tunnicliffe was bowled immediately afterwards, having been at the wickets a quarter of an hour less than his partner. Included in his 58 were one 5, four 3s, and eleven 2s. The home batsmen subsequently did not offer much of a resistance, the whole side being out for a total of 237. Middlesex thus required 263 runs to give them victory, and it was expected they would make a good struggle of it, no one being prepared for the remarkable collapse that occurred. It is true the light at this period was unfavourable, but this did not explain the weak resistance offered to the bowling of Hirst and Peel, who, by the time stumps were drawn, had disposed of seven men for 31 runs. The close of the day was unfortunately marred by a very painful incident, an elderly man named Thornton, of Guiseley, on leaving the field, dropping down dead.

---

18 OCTOBER 1895

DEAR DR GRACE

I have the satisfaction of presenting to you herewith a cheque for a total sum of 100,000 shillings, being the proceeds of a public subscription opened some time ago, and since carried on in the columns of the *Daily Telegraph*, under the title of 'The *Daily Telegraph* National Shilling Testimonial to W.G. Grace.'

Such a magnificent demonstration, Sir, is due in the first place to a warm appreciation felt throughout the land and the Empire for your own high and worthy qualities as an English cricketer. It comprises, however, above and beyond this – as cannot possibly be doubted – a very notable and emphatic expression of the general love for those out-of-door sports and pursuits, which – free from any element of cruelty, greed, or coarseness – serve so admirably to develop our British traits of manliness, good-temper, fair play, and the healthy training of mind and body; at the same time giving pleasure and amusement to the greatest possible number. In this aspect I permit myself to regard the progress and result of the 'National Shilling Testimonial' as a manifestation, by classes and masses alike, of their abiding preference for wholesome and honest amusements in contradistinction to sickly pleasures and puritanical gloom, thus conferring upon you the happy distinction of a substantial personal tribute, which is at the same time a public approval of your salutary example to the youth and manhood of your time.

Edward Lawson

---

16 OCTOBER 1895

DEAR SIR EDWARD LAWSON

First of all, I will thank you personally for initiating the movement and allowing the columns of your paper to be used to acknowledge contributions, and for so handsomely heading the list. To have attained proficiency in the national game has ever been a source of pleasure to me, but to be the recipient of such a recognition from my fellow-countrymen, both at home and abroad, as well as from very many not of our nationality, is an honour as unexpected as it is overwhelming, and one for which I am most deeply grateful. The expressions of personal kindness and goodwill contained in many of the letters which you have from time to time published have touched me more than I can tell you, and have, indeed, afforded me as much gratification as the practical tribute of the writers. I can only marvel at the prodigious number and generosity of my friends. I think and believe, with gratitude and pride, that I must have more than any other man ever possessed.

May the noble game, which has been such a source of happiness and pleasure to me, flourish forever, and continue to help to make our boys into good and manly men.

W.G. Grace
15 Victoria Square, Clifton, Bristol

---

3 AUGUST 1896

SURREY v. NOTTS

A Non-Cricketer

I should be sorry, indeed, to have it supposed that I am in any way lacking in proper zeal for popular sports and pastimes. Nevertheless, truth compels me to confess that although I regard cricket as ranking first and foremost of all outdoor competitive games, I am always at a loss to account for the fascination it has for all classes – from the highest to that which includes the humblest toiler, who probably has to work a couple of hours to earn the sixpence that gives him the privilege of becoming one of such a vast crowd as that which assembled yesterday at the Oval to witness the match between Surrey and Nottingham. To be sure it was Bank Holiday, an occasion when, weather permitting, open-air entertainments have special attractions for the multitude, but it is always pretty much the same. Take last Thursday, Friday, and Saturday, which were the days of the contest between Surrey and Yorkshire, as an instance. It is well understood by those who cater for the amusement of the great commonalty that the few days immediately preceding the August Bank Holiday are just those that yield least money to the exchequer. Music-halls, theatres, exhibitions, public houses, all look on it as a lean time. It is not that the working folk have less to spend on pleasure than usual. It is because they are exceptionally frugal, in view of the general holiday. But such 'natural causes' do not operate where cricket is concerned. On the days in question more than 33,000 persons passed through the 'Pay here' turnstiles at the Oval. It was an amazing sight to see them come flocking in from all directions, especially as, judging from appearances, at least one-third of their number were of the mechanic class, who must have 'lost' half a day in order to be present.

But there was no question of the working classes losing 'time' yesterday. It was high holiday with everybody, and you may be sure that the great cricket-loving community did not miss the rare opportunity offered them. There was to be a feast of cricket at the Oval surpassing any other of which that favourite place had been the scene during the present season, and a well-nigh countless multitude responded joyously to the invitation. It was good to see them come flocking in from all parts an hour or so before there was any likelihood of the game commencing. They arrived from the West in private carriages and in dog-carts and in hansom cabs, and they arrived from the East in natty, newly painted 'shallows' and 'half-carts', with Mr Coster and his good lady foremost, and with a convenient board laid athwart the vehicle as a seat for an accompanying friend and *his* good lady. Trams and buses plying between the several bridges that cross the Thames and Kennington Church brought full freights every journey, and the carriages of the Electric Railway – the Oval Station of which is within a fair stone's throw of the famous county ground – were so packed that the advertised vaunt of the deep-down tunnel being the 'coolest place in London' must have been severely tested. From nearly adjacent Camberwell and Lambeth and Walworth they came trooping in afoot in such numbers that the question 'Why half-a-dozen entrance gates?' at the place to which all were bound was answered without the asking. At the same time, there were no signs of hurry or disorder. Not being a cricketer myself, I may be the more at a loss to account for it, but it would seem that a partiality for the pastime in question bespeaks a serene temperament and a disposition towards peaceful pleasure, without tumult or noisy hilarity.

But, as the crowd came flooding in from all quarters — just at twelve o'clock, when it was at its thickest — an incident occurred that demonstrated how the most decorous proceedings may all in an instant and quite unexpectedly be upset. The street leading from the highway to the Oval is but a short one, and not particularly wide. At one end of this street, and just across the road, quite a mob were pressing to pass through the turnstiles, and in at the other end of the short street the people came thronging, when there was raised a cry of 'Mad bull!' It was not a joke, either. I have not the least idea where it came from, but there was the animal, about midway in the brief thoroughfare, with lowered head and vicious eyes, pawing the dust with its hoof, at a standstill, and evidently uncertain, in the small amount of mind it had remaining, if it should run amuck to the right or to the left. That it was not a really mad bull, however, was afterwards shown by its being amenable to coaxing and persuasion. Only that the bovine kind are notorious for their temperate habits, it might have been a dissipated Bank Holiday bull under the influence of alcoholic stimulant. It, however, appeared to be mad enough, and the approaching crowd turned and fled for their lives; but at the street's further end there was the mass of people, for whom there was no quick means of escape, and if the creature had made a headlong dash that way, the damage done would probably have been very considerable. Some men attempted to lasso it with a noosed rope; but that failed, and matters were growing each moment more alarming when there appeared on the scene a butcher, after which the mad bull calmed down, and the butcher drove him off before him, and the interrupted procession thronged its way again.

A foreigner hailing from a country where cricket is unknown, entering in at the guarded gates, would be much amazed at the spectacle presented to his gaze. Writing to his friends at home on the subject he would probably say something like this. 'There I beheld, at the centre of a vast lawn-like arena, two chief priests in snowy vestments reaching to their feet, and a baker's dozen of tall figures, all chastely attired in white, two of the number being entrusted with the arduous task of preserving the perfect perpendicularity of three slender rods stuck in the ground in a row, and a palm's-breadth apart, and in imminent peril of being swept down by a cannon-ball-like missile repeatedly hurled at them by one of the enemy. Their safety depends on the quickness of eye of the defenders and the skilled use they make of the repelling wooden implement with which they are armed. When one succeeds in banging back the swift ball, and sends it flying to a distance, both defenders celebrate the achievement by running as fast they can to and fro over the space of ground between the two sets of three upright sticks, until the nine confederates of the ball-hurlers, who scamper about, recover it. And then the "bowling" begins again, and so the game goes on.' Nor would it be needful for that intelligent foreigner to conclude his strange narration for want of further interesting subject matter. He might go on and describe how the curious conflict was witnessed, at a respectful distance, by a surrounding assemblage of cricket worshippers, numbering perhaps 25,000, many of whom had made long pilgrimages from distant parts. Completely edging the verdant and sacred enclosure, there they sit, a sloping embankment, 50 feet deep, glowing with a forest growth of human faces, and every sort of head-gear known to the hatter – excepting, of course, the black and shining 'chimney-pot'. There sit or stand the thousand score, sedate as people at church, except for an occasional salve of hand-clapping or a brief ringing cheer when something occurs to win their special approval. In the full glare of the afternoon sun they must be panting with heat and sorely athirst, but, cricketers at heart, they make light of such trifling inconveniences, and with happy faces and their 25,000 pairs of eyes intent on the game, enjoy it to the close. Viewed from the Pavilion, the spectacle was one to remember. Except when some exceptionally fine act of bowling or batting roused their enthusiasm, the vast surrounding multitude sat as still as to present the appearance of a painted picture – a picture strangely lacking in high colours. Nor could it be otherwise, owing to the almost entire absence of the feminine element. I have not the slightest idea why it should be so. One might well have supposed that even on ordinary occasions a first-class cricket match would serve as an irresistible attraction for a large proportion of the fair sex; but on a Bank Holiday, when sweethearts and wives, sisters and mothers, are as anxious for a pleasant outing as their male relatives, it is difficult, indeed, to understand why they stay away. Yet so it is. From my post of 'vantage I could make extensive observation, and I can answer for it that out of the 25,000 onlookers there were not 500 that were not in manly garb. Consequently, the general effect was not nearly so brilliant as it would otherwise have been. From a picturesque point of view, one would gladly have paid recruiting price for a score or so of soldiers to dot the sombre assemblage with scarlet.

It was the same on the Pavilion. Indeed, to my astonishment, whatever may be the rule on other occasions, the presence of ladies at that privileged part was strictly forbidden yesterday. I could scarcely believe that this was so until I heard an elegantly dressed young lady politely but firmly refused admission. As well as I could make out, she expected to meet a brother or someone there, and was altogether unaware she would be prevented from doing so. 'No,' said the guardian of the sacred portal; 'I am exceedingly sorry, madam, but I cannot permit you to pass. Ladies are not admitted today.' It seemed very hard, and one cannot help feeling curious to know the reason why. That the gentler sex are not prohibited in the less select parts at the Oval I have already said, but why, oh, why, were they not more numerous? And, what should be the most amazing part of it is that the 25,000 did not appear to be in the least cast down or dejected because of the deprivation. Indeed, throughout the whole afternoon, and until the stumps were drawn, nobody seemed to be what might be called miserable.

---

14 JUNE 1900

After the heavy scoring by the London County, the West Indians were bound to be defeated when rain spoiled the wicket to some extent; but, as Mr Warner said after lunch at the Crystal Palace yesterday, they were in no way discouraged by being beaten by an innings and 198 runs. They had come to England to learn the game, and anticipated a severe defeat when opposed to the strong London County team. These remarks of the captain of the visitors were made in response to the toast of the health of the team, proposed by Mr W.G. Grace, who earnestly remarked that some of the West Indians played good cricket. Mr W.L. Murdoch struck a happy tone in telling the West Indians that the first Australian team had a disastrous match at Nottingham to start with, but, in no way disheartened, went to Lord's and beat a strong England eleven. So, if the Colonials have begun unluckily in the result of their opening fixture, they have received kind words of encouragement, which should do much towards helping them in their efforts to become masters of the game as it is played in England.

---

26 JUNE 1900

The opening of the Notts and Lancashire match at Trent Bridge, yesterday, was marked by an incident which will assuredly give rise today to very lively discussion among cricketers all over the country. To put the matter in the fewest words, Mold was no-balled for throwing, the umpire who called him to account being James Phillips. Mold was put on when the Notts score stood at 84, and in his first over 'no ball' was twice called. There was no possibility of doubt as to what had happened, for Phillips at the time was standing at the batsman's end. He acted under Law X, which, as amended by the MCC last year, now reads: 'The ball must be bowled; if thrown or jerked, either umpire shall call "no ball".' No one who follows cricket with any attention will need to be told that up to the time of the law being altered the power to no-ball for throwing rested entirely with the umpire at the bowler's wicket. The change, which Phillips himself was one of the first to advocate, was introduced for a very obvious reason. When at last – many years too late – the question of unfair bowling was grappled with, it was pointed out that if only one umpire no-balled a bowler for throwing, the captain of a side could avoid all difficulty by only putting the offending bowler on at the end at which the other umpire was standing. We are not sure whether the law as amended had up till yesterday been acted upon in first-class matches. In the movement against throwing in the last two or three years Phillips has played a more prominent part than any other umpire. It will be remembered that during the tour of Mr Stoddart's second team in Australia he no-balled Jones, and that he was one of the first umpires to no-ball C.B. Fry. The question of Mold's delivery is a rather delicate matter to deal with, as the Lancashire bowler has been playing regularly in first-class cricket since 1889, and had never till yesterday been pulled up by any umpire. It may be argued, therefore, that it is rather late in the day to no-ball him. There is something to be said for this, but the surprising thing is that he should have enjoyed such long immunity. Personally, we have no doubt he ought to have been no-balled long ago. On such a point as this cricketers are very chary of allowing their views to be made public, but the opinions we have heard expressed in private about Mold's bowling during the last ten years by some of the most famous batsmen would make very startling reading. Here, for the moment, the matter can be allowed to rest, but a great deal more is sure to be heard of it.

---

5 JULY 1900

In connection with the match [Middlesex v. Yorkshire, Lords] the MCC have done a peculiarly ungracious thing, turning the newspaper reporters out of their accustomed seats in the Grand Stand and exiling them to the roof of the new building – put up for the convenience of the Club's professional bowlers – in a remote corner of the ground. It is understood that the same arrangement is to hold good for the Eton and Harrow match, and there has been something more than a hint of an intention to make it apply to all matches, big and small. The motive for this high-handed and altogether uncalled for proceeding it is not easy to discover. Complaints have in recent years been made of insufficient accommodation for the Press in the Grand Stand at great matches, but surely some better remedy could have been found than to place all the newspaper men further from the wicket than any ordinary member of the public who pays his shilling at the gate. On the occasion of the England v. Australia match last year, when the requirements of the Press were naturally much larger than usual, extra seats in the Grand Stand were allotted to newspapers, and everything passed off satisfactorily. One could quite understand the difficulty in the way of giving extra space in the Grand Stand at the Oxford and Cambridge match, but, so far as we know, no favour of this kind has been asked. The retrogressive step now being taken by the MCC is in curious contrast to the liberal policy of the leading counties, and is in every way unworthy of the first cricket club in the world. Mr F.E. Lacey – successor to Mr Henry Perkins as secretary to the MCC – is no doubt acting with the full authority of his committee, but one can hardly think it possible that the Hon. Ivo Bligh (president this year), Mr V.E. Walker, the Hon. Alfred Lyttelton, Mr A.N. Hornby, and Mr John Shuter – to mention only a few distinguished names – have given the matter much consideration. It would be quite unlike them to put any impediment in the way of matches being properly reported.

---

13 SEPTEMBER 1901

THE YARDLEY BENEFIT

YORKSHIRE V. REST OF ENGLAND
FRY'S SIXTH SUCCESSIVE CENTURY

The Yorkshiremen had an experience at Lord's yesterday that they will not readily forget. They were bowling and fielding for five hours, and in that time the England team – very strong in some respects, but by no means representative – scored 460 runs against them for the loss of five wickets. Nothing more startling has been seen on a London ground this season. Though successful from start to finish, however, the England batting was not at all uniform in character. Everyone who went in did more or less well, but if it had not been for Jessop, the Yorkshire bowlers might have got through the day without discredit or the slightest wound to their pride. A.O. Jones opened the innings with some brilliant hitting, but so normal was the rate of run-getting for three hours that when, at half-past three, the third wicket went down, the total only stood at 201. England, of course, had made a very flattering start, but the runs had been fought for, and the loss of another wicket or two would have been sufficient to put the Yorkshiremen on excellent terms with themselves.

Jessop, however, upset everything, and treated the 4,000 spectators to a display of hitting that even he has rarely or never surpassed. He took much longer than usual to play himself in, and for about half an hour did nothing out of the common, scoring at little more than the same pace as C.B. Fry. As soon as he felt set, however, he let himself go, and gave the Yorkshire bowlers a rougher time than, with one exception, they have had all the year. When Jessop went in at 201, Fry had already made 48, and, with such a start, naturally wanted some catching. After a time, however, he became nothing better than an interested spectator of his partner's hitting, and was passed at 79 to 78. Two or three runs later he drew level again, but then Jessop went right ahead, and there was no further competition in the matter of scoring. To cut a long story short, the two batsmen were together for an hour and a half, and added 204 runs to the score. The total was 300 at 20 minutes past four, and 400 at five o'clock. Then at last the batsmen were separated, Fry, at 405, being out to a catch at extra cover-point. He was naturally overshadowed by Jessop's amazing brilliancy, but his innings of 105 was by no means the least remarkable of the many fine displays he has given this season. Not quite happy before lunch in timing the ball, he afterwards played a masterly game, driving very hard, and making one or two beautiful strokes on the leg side. This 105, by the way, is his sixth successive hundred in first-class matches, the feat thus performed being altogether without precedent. It might be said that he and Beldam prepared the way for Jessop yesterday, their fine defence for an hour and a half doing much to wear down the Yorkshire bowling.

Jessop, at the close of play, was not out 176, the result of rather less than two hours' batting. One may say without exaggeration that no other living batsman could have played such an innings. Considering the liberties he took, the certainty with which he hit was astonishing. Once he let us see how ugly the pull looks when it does not come off, but for the most part the ball was always in the middle of his bat. Except for a very sharp chance at slip when he had made 81, one did not till late in the afternoon notice any mistakes in his innings, but with his score at 155 he had a great piece of luck, Tunnicliffe dropping the simplest of chances at slip off Rhodes's bowling. As England cannot declare before lunchtime today, Jessop will have a chance of materially increasing his score, but even if he should fail to get another run, his innings will stand out as one of the biggest things done at Lord's this year. An attendance of 4,000 was not by any means bad at this late period of the season, but having regard to the fact that the match is being played on behalf of William Yardley's widow and children, we should have liked to see a bigger crowd. The weather was not very favourable, rain threatening more than once, and the sky being nearly always overcast. Probably when they read of what Jessop did, a good many people who stayed away will feel extremely vexed that they did not journey up to Lord's. W.G. Grace would in the ordinary way have captained the England team, but one of his fingers was so badly bruised in the match at Hastings this week that he could not possibly play.

----

30 JUNE 1902

A remarkable day's cricket was witnessed at Leyton yesterday in the opening of the match between Essex and Sussex. Going in first, Sussex for a time fared very badly indeed, six wickets actually going down for 92. A total of less than 200 seemed in store for them, but once more the endless possibilities of the game were illustrated. The Essex eleven were kept in the field for the remainder of the afternoon and did not succeed in getting down another wicket. Ranjitsinhji, who had gone in fourth wicket down at 82, was joined by Newham, and the pair successfully resisted all endeavours to part them. As the result of four hours batting they added 332 runs, the score at the close of the day standing at 424. Such an astonishing change in the fortune of a game has rarely been witnessed, and a different story would have had to be told had only Russell stumped Ranjitsinhji when that batsman was 27. It was a bad blunder and a very heavy price has had to be paid for it. When 176 the Indian was missed at the wicket, but that mistake mattered little, all the mischief having then been done. Apart from those two chances, Ranjitsinhji played delightful cricket, hard square-cuts and drives being the chief features of his play. He reached his 100 in two hours, and in making his 184 he only took four hours and a quarter. From 123 he was handicapped by a strain in the right calf and had to have a man to run for him. Ranjitsinhji's 184 is already the highest individual innings scored in first-class cricket this season, just beating R.A. Duff's 182 made last week at Bradford.

---

13 AUGUST 1902

There have been many splendid matches between England and Australia, but few as remarkable as the one that finished at the Oval yesterday. England won by one wicket, and the magnitude of the task they accomplished will be understood when we state that, on going in to get 263, they lost five of their best batsmen for 48 runs. To win after that on a wicket considerably damaged by rain, may fairly be described as something in the nature of a cricket miracle. Even if the pitch had been fast and true it would have been no small thing to make 263 against the Australian bowling in the last innings, but so far from the conditions being favourable to the batsmen they were very trying indeed. Let it be said at once that in one respect luck favoured the batting side, the Australians – not often at fault in the field when there is a match to win – allowing five or six chances to escape them. Some of these had no vital consequences, but two, as events turned out, lost them the match, Jessop, whose wonderful innings of 104 turned the scale in England's favour and made victory possible, giving a chance of stumping when he had made 22, and being missed at long-off with his score at 27. When these things happened no one imagined they would seriously affect the issue, England's prospects at the time being so cheerless, but the Australians had reason to remember them when the great hitter was knocking their bowling all over the field. Still, mistakes in the field are all in the game, and must not be too strongly insisted on. If on Monday afternoon Lilley had caught Trumble at the wicket, and Hirst had caught and bowled Kelly, Australia's total would have fallen very far short of 324, and the subsequent course of the match might have been altogether different. Jackson and Jessop pulled England out of a position that had looked quite hopeless, but even after Jessop left there was a long way to go, 76 runs being wanted, with only three wickets to go down. The chances were still greatly in favour of Australia, and no one among the excited thousands on the ground could have felt in the least degree sanguine of England's victory.

The credit of winning the match belonged at the finish mainly to George Hirst, who showed immense nerve and a soundness of judgment that scarcely ever failed. He played a great game at the crisis, keeping perfectly cool, and never giving the smallest chance to the fieldsmen. Lilley did very well, and to Rhodes fell the thankless task of going in last man, with 15 runs still required. He had two or three very uncomfortable moments, but he kept up his end and had the satisfaction of making the winning hit. He and Hirst during the last few years have had many exciting experiences in the cricket field, but nothing, we take it, to quite compare with yesterday. Rhodes was in at the finish when England lost last month by three runs at Manchester, but there the tension was relieved by a considerable delay through rain just before the last wicket fell. England have lost the rubber this year, but yesterday's victory, in face of a balance of 141 runs on the first innings, is in itself no small compensation. There is nothing in cricket today comparable to an England and Australia match, and when one reflects that a single hit for four at Manchester would have given us the honours, there is not a great deal to lament over. About 16,000 people watched the cricket yesterday, and probably there would have been twice the number present if such a tremendous finish could have been in any way foreseen. A finer close to a series of test games it would hardly be possible to see.

It wanted twenty minutes to twelve when England started the last innings, the task before them being certainly harder than that of getting 400 runs on a perfect wicket. Keeping to the same order as in the first innings, MacLaren went in with Palairet, and Trumble and Saunders shared the Australian bowling. The start, from England's point of view, could not easily have been more disastrous. Five runs were scored from Trumble, but in Saunders's first over two wickets went down. MacLaren half played a ball, and had the mortification of seeing it roll into the wicket, and Tyldesley was clean bowled by what looked to be a beautiful breakback. Hayward came in, and at once scored a single that was doubled by an overthrow. Palairet then got a nice three to leg from Trumble, but on facing Saunders he was bowled, three of England's best wickets being thus down for 10 runs. The bowlers were evidently able to make the ball do a great deal, and the chance of winning the match seemed too remote to be worth consideration. Jackson followed in, and if anyone could retrieve the position he, judging from all past experience, was the most likely man on the side to do it. He began confidently, getting the ball well in the middle of his bat, and there was quite a big cheer when he drove Saunders to the boundary. It was thought Hayward had been stumped, and it was so put on the printed cards, but it transpired at lunch-time that one umpire had given him not out on the appeal for stumping and the other out to a catch. The result seemed now more than ever a foregone conclusion, the task of getting such a score as 263 seeming absolutely impossible. With Braund as a partner, Jackson continued to play a very fine game, getting runs at every opportunity, and never seeming in any way troubled by the bowling. Trumble took to bowling round the wicket instead of over it, and this manoeuvre on his part was soon rewarded by success, Braund being caught at the wicket at 48.

It was at this point, with half the wickets down and 215 runs still wanted to win, that Jessop began his extraordinary innings.

---

21 MAY 1903

An inquest was held at Gedling, near Nottingham, yesterday, on the body of Arthur Shrewsbury, the famous cricketer, who shot himself on Tuesday evening at the residence of his sister.

Mr Josiah Love, brother-in-law of the deceased, gave evidence of identification, stating that Shrewsbury, who had been staying with him for the last 12 or 13 weeks, was 47 years old. He had been attended by various doctors, but lately had become very depressed. So far as witness knew he had never threatened to take his own life, and he did not know he possessed a revolver. No letter or paper explaining his action had been left by him.

Miss Gertrude Scott, of Mansfield Road, Sherwood, said she last saw the deceased on Tuesday evening at his brother-in-law's house, when he seemed to be in a rather excited condition. About eight o'clock he went upstairs and told witness he would like a cup of cocoa. She went down to make it, and shortly afterwards heard a noise, but she did not recognise it as a revolver shot. She shouted to him to know what he was doing, and he replied 'Nothing'. A minute later she heard a shot fired, and running upstairs she found deceased bleeding from a wound in his head. On Tuesday afternoon he had said to her, 'I shall be in the church-yard before many days are over.' She begged him not to think of such a thing, but he replied, 'It's quite correct.'

The evidence of a neighbour who was called in was to the effect that Shrewsbury was found in a reclining position against the bed, and lived for about half an hour after the last shot was fired. Witness had previously noticed his depressed condition, and had said he must not give way. Shrewsbury, however, seemed confirmed in the impression that he would never be able to play cricket again, and it appeared to pray upon his mind.

A gunsmith's assistant deposed that Shrewsbury purchased a five-chambered revolver at a shop in Church Gate, Nottingham, on Tuesday of last week. He bought cartridges there, and saw that they fitted the weapon, having previously pulled out of his pocket some cartridges which proved too large. He was very exacting in his inquiries as to the precise method of loading, and did not appear to be excited, although he seemed a bit nervous.

Dr Knight, of Charlton, said Shrewsbury had become hypochondria-cal of late, and took a gloomy view of his condition. He last saw him on Tuesday morning, when he complained of pain in his head, and said his brain was going wrong. Witness tried to comfort him by assuring him there was no organic disease. The jury found that the deceased committed suicide whilst in an unsound state of mind.

It appears that the late cricketer gave his presentation watch to a relative some weeks ago to keep in remembrance of him, and told his sister, if anything happened, he should like to be buried in Gedling churchyard.

---

24 JUNE 1905

Prince Edward of Wales exhibited the true instincts of healthy British boyhood in his method of celebrating his 11th birthday yesterday. The great event of the day, which was ushered in at Windsor by the merry pealing of church bells and the subsequent discharge of cannon in the Long Walk, was a cricket match in the Home Park. Here, on the pretty ground which King Edward has lately had prepared, two opening teams of young Etonians, the one captained by Prince Edward and the other by his younger brother, Prince Albert, met to try conclusions, in perfect weather and on a perfect wicket. The Eton boys were driven to the park in a couple of shooting brakes, sent from the Royal mews, and they had time for some little preliminary practice under the elm trees before the arrival of the two young Princes, who walked down from the Castle in the company of Mr Hansell, their tutor. Dressed in grey flannel and straw hats, their approach was heralded by the strains of 'God Bless the Prince of Wales', played by the famous Besses o' th' Barn Band from Lancashire, which, smartly uniformed, was on the ground by the kindly command of King Edward. The young Etonians came forward, doffing their caps, and in a few moments the necessary introductions were effected.

The spinning of the coin gave Prince Edward the choice of innings, and the opposing team turned out promptly into the picturesque field. Little Prince Albert, donning, like his elder brother, a blue cap decorated with the Prince of Wales's feathers, was assigned to square-leg. At this time many spectators had gathered under the shady trees in the Long Walk, whence a view of the game was to be obtained. Prince Edward's team, mostly somewhat older than himself, proved to include some very promising batsmen, for although the fielding was distinctly smart, some fifty runs were put on in the space of half an hour. When five wickets were down for 74 runs, a cheer betokened the appearance of the youthful captain at the wicket. Beginning with a single off the very first ball, Prince Edward played what proved a very free game. Handling his bat in quite a workmanlike way, he stood up manfully against the over-hand bowling and punished every ball that gave him an opening. Unfortunately, Prince Edward's successive partners proved less stable at the crease, for two of them were run out, thanks to some capital throwing in, and the other three also succumbed somewhat rapidly. Thus it happened, quite in accordance with the fitness of things, that his Royal Highness carried out his bat for 17, with the total standing at 104. The young Prince's success, needless to say, evoked a cheer so hearty as to quite discount the recent theory that public schoolboys have forgotten the art of demonstration.

Queen Alexandra and Princess Victoria drove down to the ground from Windsor Castle at the tea interval, and manifested the greatest interest in the happiness of the birthday guests. The boys of both teams were presented to her Majesty, who, with the ladies of her suite, sat under the trees to watch the game when it was presently resumed. Prince Albert's side opened their innings in a very brisk fashion, for off the initial overs runs came thick and fast. Prince Edward, now in opposition, had his place in the slips. At half-past five King Edward and the Prince of Wales, returning from Ascot by motorcar, came across the ground from the Frogmore side. Both shook hands with the majority of the cricketers in the field, and his Majesty, patting Prince Edward on the shoulder, heard with evident pleasure of his grandson's success with the bat. King Edward and the Prince of Wales both proceeded to the Royal pavilion, where they exchanged their white hats for headgear more suited to the cricket field. Prince Albert, like Prince Edward, was the sixth to go in for his side, and at this time the score stood at 76. His Royal Highness showed himself a rather more deliberate player than his brother, but he neglected no opportunity, and, like Prince Edward, made a boundary hit. Surviving several partnerships, the young cricketer put together a total of nine runs before his wicket fell, and the game was brought to a conclusion with the score at 92. By this time it was nearly seven o'clock, and soon afterwards the birthday gathering broke up, the Eton boys taking respectful leave of their Royal hosts and driving off delighted with their outing.

King Edward and Queen Alexandra showed a kindly interest in the Besses o' th' Barn Band, whose members, 26 in number, were compelled to leave before the match was quite over, by reason of the fact that they were quitting London a few hours later for their French tour. His Majesty summoned Mr Alexander Owen, the conductor, to his presence, and presented him with a handsome jewelled gold pin as a memento of the occasion.

---

11 JULY 1910

ETON v. HARROW

One can never tell what will occur at cricket, but the limit of the game's possibilities must have been nearly reached at Lord's on Saturday. A more extraordinary finish can scarcely be recalled, Eton winning by nine runs after having been in such a position that the odds against their victory could not be named.

They followed their innings against a balance of 155, and when their ninth wicket fell they were only four runs ahead. Such a foregone conclusion did the result seem that only the face of the match being Eton v. Harrow kept the thousands of spectators in their seats. To use the racing phrase, Harrow were walking over. This extreme position was reached soon after four o'clock and if anyone had then suggested that after all Eton might win, his remarks would have been regarded as rather an ill-timed jest. The seemingly impossible happened, however, and at six o'clock Eton's victory was an accomplished fact.

Before the end the crowd had an hour of the liveliest excitement of which Lord's, with all its memories, has ever been the scene. Failing, as they did, when to all appearances they had the game in their hands, the Harrow eleven will no doubt be taken severely to task. Still, though their score of 45 looks dreadful on paper it is only fair to make allowance for the altogether abnormal circumstances. There is no more severe test of nerve at cricket than a change of fortune such as came over the game on Saturday.

From eleven o'clock till four Harrow played on with nothing more to cause them even momentary anxiety. It was simply a question of how soon or how late in the afternoon they would win the match, defeat not being even thought of. Then, when the apparently light task of getting 55 in the last innings was entered upon the sudden downfall of three wickets for eight runs altered the whole situation, the remaining batsmen finding themselves faced by a crisis that would have tried the most experienced players. No doubt the runs ought to have been obtained, but in such thrilling moments the best batsmen have been known to fail. In proof of this one need only look up the dismal story of two or three Test matches between England and Australia. Fowler the Eton captain, in taking with his breakbacks eight wickets for 23 runs, only played on a smaller scale the part of Spofforth or Hugh Trumble.

Many brilliant things have been done in the Eton and Harrow match, but Fowler's all-round play on Saturday will take a very high place in the records. Taking all the circumstances into consideration, it would be difficult to name anything better. As a batsman he simply led what looked to be a forlorn hope, the game being apparently as good as over when his innings of 64 – in every way a fine effort – came to an end. In praise of his bowling one cannot say too much. Only once or twice during the ten overs in which he took his eight wickets did his length fail, and he repeatedly made the ball whip back from the off. He was of course the hero of the hour when the match finished, the demonstration in his honour being overwhelming.

With the help of Steel at the other end, and a very keen set of fieldsmen, Fowler won the game, but Eton's victory was only made possible by the timely and brilliant hitting of Manners. Lest the fact be overlooked, let it be stated here that, apart from his batting, Manners is one of the finest cover-points seen in a school eleven at Lord's for many a day. No matter how hard the hit he stopped everything that could be stopped, his work being just as irreproachable during Harrow's long innings on Friday as in the exciting moments of Saturday afternoon.

---

31 JULY 1914

DEATH OF TROTT

Albert Edward Trott, the famous Australian and Middlesex cricketer, was found shot dead yesterday at his residence at Denbigh Road, Harlesden. Trott, who had a revolver wound in the temple, had been ill for some considerable time, and only recently left St Mary's Hospital. He was admitted to St Mary's Hospital on 20 July, and was placed under the care of Sir John Broadbent, physician to the hospital, who took a personal interest in the case. Trott, however, complained of the 'tedium and dreariness' of hospital life, and on Tuesday stated that he could not 'stand it any longer', and insisted on going home.

The hospital authorities endeavoured to prevail upon Trott to stay under discipline, but without avail, and as he insisted upon his discharge he was placed in a taxi-cab and his fare paid to his home at Harlesden. The deceased was born in Victoria in 1873.

AN APPRECIATION

B. Bennison

After brilliant success – tragedy. That is the story of the life of Albert Trott. A more pathetic figure of a man in later days than Trott it would be difficult to imagine. He was a broken man, young yet old, and for many months terribly conscious that he had already squeezed the best out of life. His end will come as a shock to cricketers the world over, for he was one of those players it was not necessary to see to feel that one knew him intimately. For Trott, in a way even more pronounced than his famous brother Harry, one time captain of Australia, had a personality that gave to the game an attractiveness, and a force so impelling, which nowadays are regrettably rare.

Cricket was no humdrum business with him; he insisted that it should live in a way that almost invariably made it a glorious gamble. For one never knew what he could do. He had it in him to skittle a whole side out – there was a time when he was the greatest bowler in the world, so cunning, so completely mystifying. When in the mood, and given his wicket, there was nothing he could not do; the ball to him would perform all manner of capers; as someone not inaptly put it, he could make it 'sit up and talk'. In every way he was one of the greatest cricketers Australia has ever given to us: batsman, bowler, fielder, he was everything that made for the unusual and wonderful player. With the crowd he was 'Trotter'; he belonged to them, and so long as he held on to his form – I might say so long as he was actively in the game – he enjoyed unbounded popularity.

To Lord's he was what Abel, Lohmann, Richardson, Lockwood, and others of the old guard used to be at the Oval, and when, at an all too early age, he dropped out of the Middlesex side and donned the white jacket of the umpire, the game became infinitely poorer. For Trott was a man one picks out of a crowd; his big, angular, ungainly frame, his huge hands, with which he could stop and catch anything, made him unlike any other cricketer of his time.

Trott was a cricketing genius. I am sure that Australia never produced a more wonderful bowler, not even 'The Demon', Spofforth. When he was the real Trott he never bowled two balls alike. And as a batsman he hit with tremendous power – none harder. I believe I am right in saying that he was the only cricketer who in a first-class match ever hit a ball over the pavilion at Lord's, and as a bowler, when playing in his benefit match at Lord's in 1907 against Somerset, he accomplished a feat without parallel – he took four wickets with four consecutive balls, and did the hat-trick in the same innings. And he was the only cricketer who scored 1,000 runs and took 200 wickets in one season. This he did in 1899, and in the following year, and, besides, he was one of the distinguished few to take all ten wickets in an innings.

The story of how he came into English cricket is quite one of the most interesting pages in the history of the game. Against Stoddart's first team to visit Australia in the winter of 1894–5 he was recognised by all good judges as the most promising young player in the country, and that he would be one of the next Australian team to visit England was taken for granted. He was not chosen, and in a fit of pique he took the boat for England, and became attached to the ground staff at Lord's. He played his first match for Middlesex in 1898, and it was in the two following years that he took over 200 wickets and scored more than 1,000 runs. Afterwards he began to go back, but on odd occasions he would perform remarkable feats, the greatest of these, as I have said, being in 1907 against Somerset.

---

23 AUGUST 1914

The wisdom of going on with county cricket was clearly shown at Lord's on Saturday, the match between Middlesex and Surrey proving a big attraction to the public. Over 7,000 people were present, 6,125 paying for admission. Middlesex, standing second to Surrey for the championship, the match had a special interest. P.J. Warner, who has not played since the outbreak of the war, returned to his post as captain of the Middlesex team. Winning the toss, Middlesex stayed in all the afternoon, for a total of 381. This substantial score was the reward of some very fine batting, but the game might easily have taken a different course. Tarrant, with his score at nine, gave a chance at slip, and Hendren, when 14, played a ball from Hayes on to his wicket without removing the bails. The two incidents had an enormous effect, Tarrant in the end getting 99 and Hendren 124. In first and out fourth wicket down, at 210, Tarrant was batting for three hours and twenty minutes. At his best after he had once become really set, he hit eleven 4s in an innings that left little room for criticism. Hendren, who is finishing the season in extraordinary form, gave a still more remarkable display. Apart from his one piece of luck, he was never at fault till he mistimed a ball from Fender, and skied it to cover-point. He scored his first 50 runs in 40 minutes, and was at the wickets only two hours and 10 minutes for his 124. He drove with splendid power.

———————

30 JUNE 1915

SYDNEY, MONDAY

The death, from dropsy, is announced of Victor Trumper, the famous Australian cricketer. — Reuter.

A cricket correspondent writes: For some considerable time we feared that the days of Victor Trumper were numbered, and yet, now he has been called away in his 38th year, we who love our cricket, and by common consent regarded the famous Australian as the greatest batsman reared by his country, are shocked by the news of his death. Victor Trumper did not belong to Australia alone; he was of the whole world of cricket. He was just as popular in England as in his own country. The name of Trumper will endure for all time, for though we shall probably model our cricket differently in days to come than in other times, when life was less of a hustle, and when our games were less commercialised, we shall always play cricket.

There have come to this country from Australia many men who were giants of the game — Gregory, Bonnor, Murdoch, Clem Hill,

Spofforth, Jack Lyons, Massey, Blackham, Noble, Darling, and, in more recent times, Bardsley, Ransford, MacCartney; but it is doubtful whether any batsman who has visited us ever achieved the distinction and won the popularity of Trumper. It was essentially the way he had with him that made his charm; even in 1902 – his most successful year in this country – when it became a fashion to expect Trumper to make runs under any conditions, when a failure seemed impossible, he carried himself with the modesty, the quiet of a youngster yet to win fame.

Before indifferent health – Trumper for long battled against a weak constitution – robbed him of much of his form we spoke and wrote of him as 'the Ranjitsinhji of Australia', for that was the highest and most generous compliment we could pay to him. There was magic in his bat, a run in every stroke; run-getting seemed to him a joy, a thing ridiculously easy, and it was a business he made us believe during his glorious visit of 1902 that must be all sparkle. Trumper was the champagne of cricket. His pose at the wicket at once arrested attention; all that he did was unlike what other batsmen did. Quick-eyed, quick-footed, with wrists immensely supple, he was a classic batsman. It would be easy to give a long list of his big innings; he made mountains of runs. But it is not because heavy scoring will always be associated with his cricket that his name will go down to posterity as one of the greatest of all batsmen; it is because he was the embodiment of grace and ease. Batting with Trumper was a high art; it was a something to be burnished until it dazzled. No laboured, stodgy, ultra-careful business; just so much holiday-making. Wickets could be wet with rain and then baked by the sun – Trumper was always the same.

We shall long remember 1902 as an utterly wretched summer, and yet this was the season when he won his greatest triumphs in this country. Other batsmen were easy prey for the bowler – Trumper scored 2,570 runs in 35 matches, and, bearing in mind the disabilities under which he laboured, finished the tour with the splendid average of 48. He was ever a quick scorer, but never a mere hitter, a slogger. And there was no bowler he feared; he certainly did much to kill the 'googly' when the South Africans visited Australia, for against them in five test matches he helped himself to 662 runs and enjoyed an average of 94.

Trumper visited England in 1889, 1902, 1905, and 1909, but he did not reproduce his wonderful form of 1902. It must be placed on record that during his first tour in England he played an unfinished innings of 135 not out against England at Lord's, and later made 300 not out against Sussex at Brighton. If one cared to search the records one could set out many other big-scoring performances, but we knew Trumper so intimately that it is not necessary to dig out this or that heavy score to establish his right to be described as a prince of batsmen.

His death will be keenly regretted by all cricketers and sportsmen. His countrymen two years ago showed their appreciation of his talents and testified to his popularity by arranging a match for his benefit and presenting him with some £3,000.

---

24 OCTOBER 1915

We regret to announce that Dr W.G. Grace, the famous cricketer, died early on Saturday morning from heart failure, at his residence, Fairmount, Nottingham, Eltham, Kent, at the age of 67. He had been ill for some time past.

SPECIAL MEMOIR

Lieut.-Colonel Philip Trevor

Cricket is something more than the national game of England; it is an important, even an essential, part of the national life. And Dr W.G. Grace was the greatest cricketer who ever lived. We may say of him, as Pope said of Garrick, that he will never have a rival. Some twenty-odd years ago an attempt was made to show that in George Giffen, the Australian, 'W.G.' found approximately his equal as an all-round cricketer. Such a comparison may be dismissed as trivial, and as showing a woeful lack of sense of proportion. National game though it nominally was long before his time, cricket was made by 'W.G.' It was not until as a boy of 16 he burst upon the cricketing world that the game established its general hold upon, and made its universal appeal to, English people.

Who and what then, was this man, or rather boy, who came to be better known than any Prime Minister, and whose features in the days before ubiquitous photography were better known than are those of a popular musical comedy actress today? One of the younger sons of a country doctor, he learnt, as practically all great men have learnt – that is to say, he taught himself. 'W.G.' as a pupil is unthinkable. Today we visit private and public schools, and we witness the spectacle of laborious professionals and unselfish old 'blues' teaching the youth, as the popular song says, 'where to put his feet'. At 16 he who lived to be known as the grand old man was what we should now call first-class; at 18 he was the best batsman in the world. Experience teaches? No doubt; but you can't make rules for a genius. He succeeds not because he ignores them, but because he deliberately breaks them. Towards the close of his career, when his muscles were stiff and great increase of weight had made him a compulsory adherent of the firm-footed system, W.G., no doubt, was over-cautious, and indeed, more or less stereotyped. But it was not so when he made his unique reputation. For others, no doubt, he had rules of batting; not for himself. He put the bat on to the ball by instinct; quick-footed, he moved to it by instinct. But by deliberate design did he send it in this or that direction. In the art of 'placing' he was, of course, a past master. A famous story in regard to that particular form of prowess will bear repetition. Shaw, at the height of his fame, was asked this question: 'Are you the better bowler or is Dr Grace the better batsman?' The reply was that weirdest form of epigrammatic reply – the truth. 'Oh! I put 'em where I like, and he puts 'em where he likes.'

Let it be remembered that in his toddling days, W.G. had in front of him a remarkable example of successful unorthodoxy – the batting of his elder brother, E.M. In those simple days to 'pull' was the unforgivable sin. It was assumed to be a point of honour not to hit the ball on the 'wrong' side of the wicket. Young E.M. Grace took upon himself the responsibility of saying which was the wrong side; and, doing so, he made runs by the hundred. The toddling younger brother read, marked, and learnt; then grew up and 'went one better'. E.M. was a small man, W.G. a big one; and what looked awkward when done by a 5ft 5in player acquired dignity when exploited by a hero of 6ft. Moreover, W.G. did the thing infinitely better than E.M. Again, E.M., as was well said, could not make an orthodox stroke if he tried. W.G. could make orthodox strokes better than any other man in England, and his own marvellous special strokes he had at his disposal, too. He batted by instinct, and in his best days that instinct was almost faultless. Of course, he had the proverbial eye of the hawk, but more than that, he had dauntless courage. W.G. was never half out before he was in. It is common knowledge that he was seldom quite satisfied when the umpire's decision was against him, and that he often retired to the pavilion with obvious reluctance. On the other hand, he was ever eager to go in. Facing the music had no terrors for him.

Had the champion — never was that title better deserved than in his case — been blessed with perennial youth he might have affected cricket much as the exponents of the spot stroke and the nursery cannon have affected billiards. The W.G. Grace of 1871, playing upon modern wickets and against modern bowling, would, I make no doubt, have caused us to alter the rules. The general public knew W.G. chiefly as the maker of more than a hundred hundreds, but the champion became the champion not because of his knack of compiling three-figure innings — physical capacity largely accounts for that kind of achievement — but because upon wickets upon which no one else could make 10 runs he was wont to make a score of 40 or 50 without a fluke, and often without a bad stroke. On the perfect modern wickets batsmen look reproachfully at a real or imaginary spot in the wicket when the ball gets up a fraction over stump high. W.G.'s ribs would often have suffered had he not known how to use his bat. Of course, he had no pet stroke; in other words, he never put the cart before the horse. The bowler bowled the ball, and W.G. had the stroke to meet it.

'OFFENSIVE' BATTING

One most important practical lesson the great batsman always taught. He made a point of conquering the bowler; it was not enough for him to avoid disaster. Batting with him was the art of making runs in a limited time; he was not there to do so many hours on a treadmill. He was the greatest batsman who ever lived, because he made more runs than anyone else. And he made them at a time when bowling was so superior to batting that the customs as well as the laws of the game were unblushingly on the side of the run-getter. Yet W.G., and W.G. alone, was able to profit by the fact. It would not be strictly true to speak of the champion as a great bowler. That in the '70s he was easily the best amateur bowler of the day is incontestable. He was eminently successful against young and inexperienced batsmen, especially against opponents meeting him for the first time. But personality more than actual bowling skill helped him on those occasions. The great big man, with the long black beard, and the monstrous red and yellow cap, who rushed up to the wicket, and then tossed the ball up gently, was disconcerting till you got to know him. The very slowness of the flight of the ball suggested guile and wile. Yet the break from leg was small, and sometimes non-existent. For all that some of the best professional batsmen were uncomfortable when the 'old man' went on to bowl, and that was so even in his later years of cricket. To get catches made on the leg side was the champion's main device, but he had also a keen eye for 'lbw' possibilities.

In his younger days 'W.G.' was a smart and reliable fieldsman, while even towards the end of his long career, when he was compelled by lack of mobility to stand at point, he had a safe as well as a big pair of hands. It may be that history will not acclaim the champion a great captain at any period of his brilliantly and uniformly successful career. It is certain, at any rate, that he never made field captaincy a practical scientific study. To the last he retained his boyish enthusiasm, and, valuable in the extreme as enthusiasm is in the general duties of leadership, it doubtless tends to obscure the critical faculty when a particular situation has to be met. The Old Man – even when a young man – never disguised the fact that he 'liked to have a bowl'. It was not cheap vanity that so often induced W.G. to give himself a generous turn of bowling. What he did not know about play and players was 'not worth knowing'. Knowing what should be done, and how to do it, the champion was apt to overlook the probability of finding what he wanted in one or other of his colleagues. A fine personal leader is not necessarily the best of directors.

We get back to W.G. the batsman, and there we have no reservation to make, no superlatives to tone down. Who are his nearest rivals? Few will dispute the names of Ranjitsinhji – happily still with us, though sterner work than cricket claims him now – and of Victor Trumper, that star whom we shall never see again. One might, perhaps, add the name of C.B. Fry. But in reality comparison is out of place. How would these men have fared on English wickets in the seventies? It is really mere guess-work to proceed. Ranji possibly could have adapted himself and his play to any set of circumstances. But, after all, you cannot argue about wizards, and the things which W.G. did as a batsman in conditions which the modern player would unhesitatingly call hopeless are a matter of history.

THE MARVEL OF MAY 1895

A description of the champion's batting performance would fill a book; a schedule of them would occupy many columns. The month of May is essentially the bowler's month, and conversely it is just the month which is not to the liking of the veteran batsman, who needs warmth, practice, the relaxing of stiff muscles, and the tiring of bowlers ere he can assert himself. Yet in the month of May, 1895, W.G. then in his 47th year, scored more than 1,000 runs in first-class cricket matches. This, needless to say, constituted a record, and to it, in the same month, the Grand Old Man added the other unique feat of scoring his hundredth century. The public was delighted by this marvel. From the Prince of Wales W.G. received a letter of congratulation, and when the *Daily Telegraph* started a shilling fund for a national testimonial to the champion of the national game, over £5,000 was subscribed by his legion of admirers.

It was in May, 1899, that Dr Grace played his last game for England in the test match with Australia at Nottingham. This was the year in which he left Gloucestershire to captain the London County team at the Crystal Palace – an innovation in first-class cricket which was short-lived. He continued to play in first-class cricket for several seasons, but his career practically ended with the Gentlemen v. Players match at the Oval in 1906. It was a memorable finish, for on this, his 58th birthday, he scored 74 runs. Thenceforward the golf links knew more of his company than the wicket, and his eye and hand did not fail him in the more leisurely game. For nearly forty years Dr Grace played first-class cricket, and for nearly thirty he dominated it. A great innings is over at last; such another will never be played again.

It will be recalled that the famous cricketer suffered a bereavement in the early death of his eldest son, 'the young W.G.', who got his cricketing blue at Cambridge, and played also for Gloucestershire. Dr Grace is survived by his wife and two younger sons, both of whom are serving their country, Captain H.E. Grace, RN, and Captain C.B. Grace, KFRE Dr Grace's funeral will take place at Elmer's End Cemetery, Beckenham, at three p.m. tomorrow.

18 AUGUST 1925

HOBBS EQUALS RECORD

SCENES AT TAUNTON

Colonel Philip Trevor, CBE

Yesterday morning, at Taunton, Hobbs got the hundredth run of his 126th hundred, and by so doing equalled the record of W.G. Grace. He did this amid great enthusiasm. Very early in the morning there was a long queue outside the gates of the county ground, and there was no shadow of a doubt as to why. Hobbs was 91 not out, and the desire to see a great feat accomplished found expression in a gathering of 10,000 persons. Also a special train was run from Paddington to give Londoners a chance of seeing what was likely to happen.

Not until 11.25 a.m. was the game continued. A few singles and a four (off a no-ball) brought the great batsman's total to 99, and then, placing a good length ball neatly to leg, he got his hundredth run. So the thing long expected was done at last, and no doubt in the mighty cheering that followed there was relief as well as joy. Hobbs said afterwards that he, of course, could have wished that it could have happened at his Oval home. Yet perhaps it was well that it did not. No one could accuse those 10,000 cheerers of partisanship, and it was acclamation of the right sort that they gave – good, hearty, unrestrained English cheers. There was none of that sentimentality run mad which, degenerating into excess, makes a big event either ugly or ridiculous, or both.

The Surrey captain brought Hobbs out a glass of champagne, and he raised it in toast to those who continued to cheer him. For some minutes did their applause last, and very soon after it was over Hobbs's innings was over too. He got another single, and was then caught at the wicket. But his ordeal was not over though his innings was. He had to face the concentrated frontal attack of a battalion of photographers who had been taking cover behind the pavilion. To this form of martyrdom he is probably getting used, and no doubt the pain has passed away. One hopes so. He will certainly have to go through it again when he makes his next hundred, and in consequence beats the record of W.G.

When Hobbs had made the hundredth hit a telegram was despatched to his wife, who is on holiday at Margate. The message read, 'Got it as last. – Jack.' Hundreds of congratulatory telegrams were received by Hobbs, including one addressed to 'the greatest cricketer in the world', and another to 'Superman, Taunton'.

---

5 JUNE 1926

EDITORIAL

DEATH OF A GREAT CRICKETER

Mortal things, said the poet of wistful phrases, touch the mind. The famous phrase will occur to many as they read of the death of Mr. F.R. Spofforth. We are all looking forward to the first Test match, which is due within the next few days at Nottingham, and lo! one of greatest heroes in Australian cricket passes after a long illness to the playing-fields on the other side. To the younger generation, of course, Spofforth is but a name. They never saw the 'Demon' in his prime. But the name and the nickname are as familiar as any in the whole annals of the game, and so will continue as long as England and Australian cricketers contest in friendly rivalry. For the nickname was given to Spofforth by the great Champion himself on the first day he met him – and fell to him – in that ever-memorable match at Lord's at the end of May, 1878, when for the first time England realised that her old easy superiority at cricket was being challenged in earnest. It is nearly fifty years ago, but the shock of it is still fresh to those who were boys at the time. The MCC – with what was quite a fair England team representing the club – beaten in a single day! It could not be. But so it was. All out for 33 in the first innings and for 19 in the second. Impossible, yet the thing was done, and from that instant Australian cricket entered into its own. Spofforth and Boyle shared the honours of that historic match – Spofforth with his five and a half overs in the first innings and his harvest of six wickets for four runs. There was no talk of the need of brightening cricket that day. For long years afterwards those who had seen that game described it over by over and almost ball by ball, so deeply graven was it on their memories, and so profoundly did it alter the English sense of established cricket values.

This was the first of Spofforth's many triumphs. Those that followed are too numerous to count. But a word must be said of the ever-memorable Test match at the Oval in 1882 – the first of a series which we hope will go on unbroken as long as the game is played. Many good judges of the game declare that the 1882 Australian eleven – Murdoch's first team – was the best that Australia has ever sent us. Spofforth was in his prime, and won that most celebrated of all the Test matches with fourteen wickets for 90 runs, bowling in the final agony of the struggle eleven overs for 2 runs and four wickets. 'The thing can be done,' he grimly told his colleagues as they trooped out into the field for the last innings, and he did it. What, then, was the secret of his wonderful successes! It, was not, as is so often supposed, the extreme pace of his bowling. There have been many faster bowlers than the 'Demon'. He had, it is true, a very fast ball which he sent down now and then, and hid from the knowledge of the batsman till the last possible moment, just as he had a comparatively slow ball, which he judiciously mixed up with the rest. The specially demoniac feature of Spofforth's bowling was its cunning more than its pace. No one ever bowled with his head so earnestly or so malignantly – from the batsman's point of view – as Spofforth. He was a born schemer and weaver of wiles. It used to be said that he lay awake plotting how to get rid of W.G. and 'Happy Jack' Ulyett, and the Studds and Steel and the rest of that splendid generation. It took the best and coolest batsmen to play Spofforth on his day with any confidence and keep their wickets up. It is long since Spofforth bowled his last ball, but his fame survives and will endure. May the green turf he loved lie light above him! Et sit humus cineri non onerosa tuo ['and may the earth not sit too heavily on your ashes'].

---

3 JANUARY 1929

LOST OPPORTUNITY

HOBBS'S SUMMING UP OF THE POSITION

Clem Hill

Melbourne, Sunday

It has been an extraordinary fighting match, and my congratulations go to England. They have retained the Ashes, and are three up with two to play. First one side was on top, then the other, and I really think that we would have won if there had been no rain. Our bowlers all bowled better on Saturday, showing much more fight, and they made all the batsmen play for every run. But it was too late; the great opportunity had gone.

The more one ponders over the English performance, the more marvellous does it stand out. The task was hard enough on a good wicket, but on such a bad one it seemed impossible.

When Hobbs and Sutcliffe went out to bat after lunch on Friday I was talking to Percy Chapman, and he asked me the question, 'How many will we get, Clem?' My reply was, 'It will be a good performance if you get 150.' 'Yes,' he answered, 'I shall be perfectly satisfied if we can make that, knowing how nasty this Melbourne wicket can become under the prevailing conditions.'

I considered my estimate was a flattering one. If I had had to prophesy what Australia would have got under the same conditions, I would have reduced it to 100 – and then they would have had to bat extraordinarily well to do that against England's bowlers, who would have made full use of the conditions. I shudder to think how nasty White and Tate would have been, especially considering our batsmen's inexperience of playing on a wicket of this kind.

WEAK BOWLING

I am certain the Australians thought the match was theirs on Friday morning, and that all they had to do was simply to 'fire them down' regardless of length and out the batsmen would go. They did that all right, but there was no length or concentration on hitting the stumps.

Hobbs and Sutcliffe must have come to the conclusion that the bowlers were not taking advantage of the wicket, and if they continued to bowl in the same way the batsmen might be able to stay until four o'clock, when by that time England would have a possible chance. That is exactly what happened, with the result that England won by three wickets.

If Hendry had caught Jack Hobbs off A'Beckett when his score was 3, England would not have won, for on this class of wicket Hobbs is still the greatest batsman in the world, though on faster wickets he is not so good. His cleverness of footwork and judgment could not have been surpassed on Friday. Great as was Sutcliffe's innings, it was Hobbs's summing up of the position so quickly that gave England her first glimpse of victory. After Hobbs's dismissal Sutcliffe carried on the great work, and remained there till Australia's defeat was certain. To these two batsmen England owes her success. The same pair put up a similar wonderful performance at the Oval two years ago in winning the last Test, though I consider the wicket was worse and the position of the side more difficult.

What the selectors will do for the next match I am awaiting with interest. It is a grand opportunity now to look to the future and endeavour to build up the team going to England in 1930. In Woodfull, Ponsford, Kippax, and Bradman Australia have four fine batsmen, and with Oldfield as wicketkeeper – and A'Beckett – who has come to stay – there is the backbone of a good side. It is the duty of our selectors to comb the whole country for some young material.

In Jackson and Harris there are two promising batsmen; Bettington and Ebeling are decidedly most promising bowlers. I do not for one moment suggest that all the older players should be dropped at once, but certainly two or three could be labelled 'Not wanted' on the voyage any more.

Once more, my heartiest congratulations to England on her magnificent win.

---

12 JULY 1930

TRIUMPH OF BRADMAN

RECORD-MAKING 309 AND STILL UNDEFEATED
AUSTRALIA 458 FOR 3
ENGLAND BOWLERS FLOGGED

B. Bennison
Leeds, Friday

At the close of the first day of the third Test match Australia have scored 458 for the loss of three wickets. Of this huge total Don Bradman has made 309. For five hours and fifty minutes he has defied the English bowlers, and is not out. Until today the distinction of compiling the highest score in matches between the two countries was held by R.E. Foster, who, 27 years ago, at Sydney, made 287. This is the third three-figure innings Bradman has played against England in this country, and the fifth in his career. At Nottingham his score was 131; at Lord's, in his first innings, he made 254.

His partnership with Kippax for third wicket, which realised 229, is an Australian record, beating that of W.L. Murdoch and HJH Scott, at the Oval, in 1884. Bradman already holds the world record of 452. In his score today were 42 4s. One cannot exaggerate the feat of the young man from New South Wales, or overstate the magnificence of it. As a maker of runs, he must be numbered among the phenomena of cricket.

ALL BOWLERS TREATED ALIKE

During the long hours he was at the wickets he paid no respect to any of our bowlers. Every one of them was the same to him. His perfect footwork, his unerring eye, his quick brain, enabled him to do almost what he willed.

When it suited him to drive, he did so with power and accuracy. By an almost imperceptible twist of his bat, he would steer the ball through the slips; the excellence of his strokes all round the wicket was amazing. He reached the boundary by strikingly different routes, and there were times when he seemed to revel in befooling the fielders. Now he would drive through the covers, then he would cut with such crispness, such certainty, that we were utterly perplexed as to what stroke he would next execute.

It would be unkind to contrast Woodfull's batting with Bradman's. Had it not been for Bradman we should have been appalled and wearied by the desperate care and slowness of Woodfull. Bradman made us forget it. There were eyes only for him; it was his day entirely. See him as he has carried himself in each of the three Tests in this country, and there could be no surprise at his enormous capacity to score runs. If there is room for wonder it is that he is ever out.

The wicket here, it is true, was emphatically in favour of the batsman, but to enlarge upon that would be to deny Bradman full and deserved praise. And it would be unkind to say of our bowling that it was not good enough. So long as Bradman is in this country we may build an attack as we will without the least certainty that it will triumph. Bradman, for the purpose of batting, is a whole team in himself.

The day had a dramatic beginning. Tate, with the fifth ball of his first over, got Jackson caught at forward short leg by Larwood when he had scored a single. The stroke by which Jackson got himself out was a very poor one – no more than a push, by which he sought to keep the ball out of his wicket. Jackson has yet to give us a sample of the batting by which he has become famous throughout his country.

The great shout that was roared at his dismissal had scarce died away when Bradman made his appearance to the accompaniment of a rousing cheer. He settled down at once to give a masterly and magnificent display. Neither Larwood, who opened the attack, Geary, Tyldesley, nor Hammond, who were in turn employed by Chapman before lunch, appeared to cause him a moment's anxiety. He could not have been bolder or more sure of himself had he been engaged in some cricket picnic.

It was Bradman who got the first four of the day. Thereafter, it was as if he might do as he pleased. Woodfull was just Woodfull – calm, deliberate; by comparison with Bradman he was as a tortoise is to a hare. Bradman got 50 out of 63 in 45 minutes with two consecutive hits off Geary, and in that number were included no fewer than eight 4s. He brought the 100 up after the game had been in progress an hour and twenty-five minutes. When he had scored 81 he hit a ball with considerable force to Hobbs at cover-point. Hobbs stopped it and could not hold it, but it was not a catch that Bradman offered, as many of the crowd seemed to think.

Bradman put one up dangerously in the slips, and the ball was taken by Geary, but again there was no catch. Then, amid a thunder of applause, he made his score 102 with a glorious boundary to leg off Larwood. He had batted for an hour and thirty-six minutes, and had hit fifteen 4s.

When luncheon was taken Bradman had scored 105 and Woodfull 29 – in two hours. It was not the stupendous difference in the rate at which Bradman and his captain made the runs that captured the imagination; it was the totally dissimilar way by which they crushed the very life out of England's attack.

Bradman sparkled; he was care-free, joyous. Woodfull was grim, dour, unemotional. It took Woodfull as long as two hours and forty minutes to score 50; in five minutes less time Bradman made 142. Woodfull had no sooner reached the half-century than he was bowled neck and crop by Hammond. The ball which beat him was pitched slightly short. Woodfull tried to hook it; it came in quickly from the pitch and hit the middle and leg stump. It is a great feat for any man to bowl Woodfull, whose defence is as elaborately arranged as it is strong. Woodfull and Bradman had raised the total from 2 to 194.

As soon as Hammond had completed the over in which he disposed of Woodfull he was rested and Larwood was substituted, Tate taking over from Geary. Kippax survived two confident appeals for a catch, and then Bradman banged a ball from Tate to the boundary to bring his score to 150. For a little time he was comparatively quiet, but, having indulged in a breather, he went on as merrily as ever. Driving, cutting, pulling, hooking – there was no known stroke that he did not exploit. At 254 Leyland was brought from the long field to bowl. From his first and his second ball Bradman hit a two; the third he merely tapped; the fourth and fifth he sent to the long on boundary, and he got a single from the last.

Turning his attention to Tyldesley, he completed his second hundred amid a tornado of cheers. Two hundred out of a total of 268 in three hours and forty minutes! And in those 200 runs were 29 4s.

LEYLAND'S BRILLIANT ATTEMPT

He had his first slice of luck when he had scored two more runs. He then skied a ball from Tyldesley to mid-on. A faster fielder than Tate, who ran for the ball, would have caught it. There was a great cheer when Bradman after tea equalled his Lord's score of 254, and it was renewed again and again when he had beaten the previous highest individual score in the history of Test cricket.

The enthusiasm was unbounded, and the game was held up for fully a couple of minutes so that the cheers might be prolonged. He waved his hand to express his joy, and for the first time indulged in a happy and expansive smile.

---

21 AUGUST 1930

FAREWELL TO HOBBS

F.G. Lavers

The Oval, Wednesday

A scene unparalleled in Test matches occurred this evening at the start of England's second innings.

When Hobbs came out with Sutcliffe it was realised by all on the ground that this was the last time the great batsman would be seen opening the innings for England. There was poignancy, as well as a deep affection, in the roll of cheers that accompanied him in the walk to the wicket. And then as he walked to the far end to face the opening bowler, it became apparent that the Australians themselves were not inclined to let the occasion pass. Instead of separating into their places in the field they formed, in a circle, and Woodfull brought Hobbs to the centre. Then, turning to his team, Woodfull called for 'Three cheers for Jack Hobbs.' Every man clutched his cap, waved it in the air and 'Hurrahed' lustily.

Among the concourse of spectators bewilderment gave place to astonishment and to infinite delight and gratification. They recognised that they had been witnesses of a unique tribute, accorded in the happiest and most fitting way. As the Australians scampered to their positions their kindly demonstration was cheered from pavilion and public benches. A moment later the chief actors in this episode were antagonistic again. Wall, rolling up his shirt sleeves, bowled with his last ounce of strength at his country's old foeman at the other wicket.

FINAL RECESSIONAL

Fifteen minutes later, alas came pathos and tragedy. Hobbs played a ball from Fairfax on to his stumps. Conscious of all that Hobbs had done in the past, the crowd saw to it that that final recessional lacked nothing in friendly sympathy. It might, indeed, have been a triumph.

---

24 AUGUST 1930

TEST PLAYERS

UNSETTLED PROBLEMS

To the Editor of the *Daily Telegraph*
Sir – Our crushing defeat in the fight to retain the 'ashes' will cause controversy among disappointed Englishmen.

We started the season with a victorious team, from which Mr Woodfull said he had 'little hope of regaining the ashes'. After winning the first match we try no fewer than twenty-one players, steadily deteriorate in every department of the game, and finish up the campaign completely defeated and subdued. For this sorry state of affairs the selectors must bear their full share of blame.

The whole system of selection was wrong. Tradition dies hard in this country. Our expectations that Hobbs and Tate would repeat their deeds of days gone by have cost us a big price. Every problem facing us at the beginning of the season is still unsolved. The successors to Hobbs, Tate, and Larwood on the next Australian tour should now be in their places with Test match experience behind them. Their names are not even known.

Luck has been on our side, too. Games in which we were thoroughly outplayed were drawn through the call of time, and in both matches in which we were so heavily defeated we won the toss — the toss of which we have always wept over in the past, and the winning of which, in these two instances, we were assured by the 'experts' would give us victory. — Yours, &c.

Disappointed
Hounslow, 23 August

---

31 DECEMBER 1932

ENGLAND'S STORMING START TO SECOND TEST

AUSTRALIA LOSE SEVEN WICKETS FOR 194 RUNS
BRADMAN 0: WOODFULL ALSO FAILS

White Willow

Australia's conquerors in the first Test Match go marching on. From Sydney to Melbourne they have carried the flag of old England with such magnificent confidence that at yesterday's opening of the second Test the Australian batsmen failed again, and seven wickets were lost before the close of play for only 194 runs.

England are already in an even better position than they were at the beginning of their fiery onslaught three weeks ago. Bradman is out, bowled first ball, as well as Woodfull, McCabe, and Richardson, and the only resistance to England's fast bowlers was offered by Fingleton, who scored 83, and is now regarded as Woodfull's successor. The continued failure of Woodfull and Bradman has infused the match with a poignancy that must temper the exultation of even the out-and-out Englander. Unless Woodfull redeems himself in the second innings the agitation for his retirement from the side, already pronounced, will be intensified.

As for Bradman, the position of this one-time wonder batsman has become tragic. It need not be dwelt upon, except in relation to yesterday's disaster. Before the match began he published a protest against the attitude of the Australian Board of Control towards him as a player-writer, and when he came out to bat the wild cheering that greeted him showed that he had the sympathy of the whole crowd – a world-record crowd, incidentally, for there were 63,993 spectators, and they had paid £5,577 in gate receipts.

There they sat, sweltering in a heat which, though not excessive, brought myriads of flies that players and onlookers alike were obliged to keep swishing from their faces. It was, however, no wonder batsmen that they watched this time. Bradman must have been concealing some deeply conflicting emotions by the familiar smile that, we are told, was on his face as he appeared, but they were revealed in the stroke which he made to the first ball he received. It appears to have been a stroke so careless for a match of such momentousness that his first ball was also his last, and Bowes, who bowled it, thus had the distinction of capturing as his first victim in Australian Test cricket the batsman whose downfall is every bowler's great desire.

HOW BRADMAN FELL

The manner of Bradman's dismissal appears to have illustrated how utterly his luck has deserted him. Bowes sent down a short delivery on the leg side. The batsman shaped for a vigorous hook, mistimed the ball by a split second, and pulled it down on to his stumps. His carelessness lay in the fact that he had not covered up his wicket. As Bradman returned to the pavilion he was smiling again. The crowd must have loved him for that smile.

Jardine, as the England captain, had a vital share in Bradman's defeat, as he had in the whole day's success. He reserved Bowes more or less for this one batsman, nursing his fast bowlers, indeed, with the utmost care, ringing the changes on them so skilfully that, although they bowled themselves out, they were able to maintain their storming challenge to the very end of the day.

Of course, the situation demanded such captaincy; for England had taken the field with an eleven which suggested a still more daring gamble than that of the first Test. Instead of a reduction of the shock bowlers, they were increased in number; not only was Allen retained with Larwood and Voce, but Bowes was added at the last moment to the exclusion of Verity.

JARDINE'S GAMBLE

As the weather in Melbourne seems to be uncommonly changeable just now, the risk of taking the field without a slow bowler is obvious. It will be noted that Australia have not done this. In order to keep Ironmonger in their eleven they actually relegated a batsman of Ponsford's calibre to the position of twelfth man.

Bowes for Verity was the only change in the England team, but Jardine's anxiety lest his sensational hazard should fail was swiftly relieved when the match began on a perfect wicket, which, surprisingly for Melbourne, did not once prove treacherous in the notorious pre-lunch period.

Fingleton and Woodfull batted against Larwood and Voce, and the Australian captain's present lack of confidence in himself was suggested when Fingleton faced Larwood's first over. Both bowlers exploited the leg-trap, and murmurs ran round the arena at this typical gesture of defiance on Jardine's part.

NEW BALL INCIDENT

But the general annoyance was soon replaced by surprise, for before Larwood opened his second over he drew the umpire's attention to the ball, and it was replaced. In order to give the new ball the same amount of wear as the old one, the two captains played a little 'pat-ball'! Old players in the pavilion vowed they had never seen anything like that happen before.

But the annoyance broke out afresh when Fingleton found it necessary to duck four times in one over to Larwood's 'bumpers'. Woodfull was so cautious against them that he took nearly half-an-hour to score his first run, but when Allen came on for Larwood at 17 Woodfull was unable to avoid a heavy blow on the heart. No wonder an hour was spent on the first twenty runs of the innings! Then, when 9 had been added, Jardine had the satisfaction of seeing Allen bowl Woodfull off his pads.

At lunch the score was 42 for one wicket, O'Brien having joined Fingleton, and, contrary to expectations, Hammond instead of Bowes relieving Voce. Reuter, commenting on the interval, says that the ambulance men were kept busy among the fainting spectators. About 140 had to be attended to. Soon after the resumption O'Brien was unluckily out. At 67 Fingleton gently turned Bowes to leg and foolishly went for a run. Ames gathered Pataudi's return so smartly that O'Brien was hopelessly run out.

O'Brien had batted an hour for 10 runs, and his Test debut was not unimpressive, in spite of its unfortunate curtain. He adopted what is generally regarded as the correct policy for a batting side already fighting with their backs to the wall, although a more forceful method might have been more profitable. Next came Bradman, and when he also left at 67 the demoralisation of Australia might easily have followed had not such a stalwart as McCabe filled the gap.

With Fingleton he batted until tea-time, and helped the score along to 120 for three before the break was taken. Jardine's anxiety must have returned somewhat as he saw the two batsmen stem the tide, especially as for some unaccountable reason Larwood had been so troubled by his footwear that he was sometimes obliged to slow down to half-speed.

LARWOOD'S BOOT TROUBLE

What happened to Larwood's boots is a mystery. They were badly split, and suggested the nobbling of a favourite. Moreover, he was nobbled effectually, for although he bowled well he has not yet taken a wicket.

Larwood continued bowling, but it was Voce who broke the partnership after an hour and a quarter by getting McCabe finely caught in the slips by Jardine at 131. Three more wickets fell in the concluding hour of the day, beginning with that of Fingleton at 156, bowled by Allen, who was justifying his inclusion. Fingleton had batted nearly four hours for 83, and he reached the boundary on only three occasions.

O-CHANGED BOWLING

He was the only player to be excepted from the sweeping condemnation of a famous ex-captain of Australia, who has declared over the cables that the day's batting was 'the worst I have ever seen in Test cricket!' The Australian hopes about Fingleton, after yesterday's innings, are that he will prove to be their Herbert Sutcliffe.

Richardson, another of the fighting breed, hit more boundaries than anyone before he was well caught at short-leg at 188. He batted 74 minutes and scored five 4s. Jardine was now switching his bowlers about, and at 194 Sutcliffe easily caught Grimmett at short fine-leg. Voce was the bowler, and as stumps were then drawn his average stands at three for 39, Allen having the next best figures with 2 for 41. Part of the sporting tribute paid by the crowd at the close to England's fine performance both in bowling and fielding was reserved for the wicket-keeping of Ames.

TRIUMPH OF TACTICS

'The Englishmen pinned their faith in shock troops, believing that fast bowling was the surest way to defeat the Australians,' says the *Melbourne Argus*. 'The bowlers worked to a plan which succeeded surely beyond their most sanguine expectations. It was a triumph of tactics and generalship.'

---

2 JANUARY 1933

THIS ENGLAND – AND THE TESTS

A FOREIGNER GETS A SHOCK!

To the Editor of the *Daily Telegraph*
Sir – Yesterday I arrived from Cologne, and the papers announce 'England's Great Day', 'Australia's Bad Time', 'Bradman's Duck', 'Bradman, that was', 'England on top', and from a dozen announcements only the same news, and I ask myself what can have happened to England since I left for Cologne. There is nothing seen of military movement, and in the City there is no talk of the seemingly terrible happenings.

This morning I ride to the City, and leaving the hotel I read the paper says 'Lunch Score', then 'Tea Score', further 'Close of Play'. Despair holds me as I read, 'Our backs to the wall', then 'England's Desperate Task', and utter gloom comes down on me on seeing 'England's Collapse'.

With haste I arrive to the City, and I mention it to my friends and discover it is a game. I think not it is a game, to me it is more a tragedy that the papers should find nothing else but this game to fill themselves with. Papers should a nation's thoughts reflect, and I know the British nation has not entirely lost its balance, although reading of the announcements at first sight would make it seem so. — Yours. &c.

E.M. Litvinne,
Portland Hotel, Finsbury Park, N4
31 December

---

16 JANUARY 1933

PAYNTER PROVES 'TEST' TEMPERAMENT

SHOCK BOWLERS' SUCCESSES

Thomas Moult

The pendulum still swings violently in the Test Matches. On Saturday, at Adelaide, it was Australia's turn to miss a splendid opportunity. Not only were England able to complete their batting recovery, and make 341 before the innings closed, but the Australian reply began as dismally as ours had done. Four wickets, including Bradman's, fell for 51 runs against 'shock' bowling. Ponsford and Richardson lifted the score to 109 without further loss.

England's outlook is favourable. To hide one's natural optimism behind a phrase like that seems the proper thing to do just now. Ever since the first ball was bowled at Sydney, six weeks since, this Test cricket has drifted as grotesquely as a rudderless ship through mysterious seas, in England's direction on one day, in Australia's direction on the next. Even the ancient mariners of the game are confounded in trying to foretell the next crazy turn of fortune.

The experts on the spot considered, for example, that England were unlikely to add many runs to their overnight total of 236 for 7 wickets, and yet Paynter and Verity, who had followed the heroic Leyland–Wyatt partnership, added another 96 before they were separated on Saturday. Thus the Lancashire batsman justified his inclusion in the side at the first attempt, and although Verity was brought back to it as a bowler he, too, has served England splendidly.

VERITY AS A BATSMAN

Red Rose and White Rose were in bloom throughout a morning that might have belonged to a typically English summer. The little Lancastrian batted aggressively while the tall Yorkshireman held up his end; and Verity did this so stylishly that he seems to have created as profound an impression in his way as Paynter did in another. It must not be forgotten, though, that before Verity subdued himself for his county's sake he was regarded as an all-rounder. Indeed, now that he has realised his ambition to such a fine degree as a bowler, one of his aims is a batting 'come-back.' At lunch he was 35, Paynter was 72, and the England total stood at 315 for 7.

The wicket had been easy for them, but Wall, Australia's best bowler, persisted, and took three for 15 at the end of the innings. For a long time, though, no one could shake Paynter's confidence or stop his clean cover-driving and strong hitting to leg. And on one occasion Verity made ten in an over off Ironmonger. 'You'll never get 'em out!' came a despairing wail, from the mounds. This, however, was not strictly fair to the bowlers, for Verity had been missed by second slip when 16, and by first slip at 38.

FIELDING BLUNDERS

There were other fielding blunders also, Paynter escaping easy run-outs when he was 26 and 72, and Verity once escaped in a similar way. Altogether the Australians seem to have been distinctly worried. They had not expected such stern opposition, although when Paynter, soon after lunch, was well caught at square-leg the rest of the innings was quickly finished off for only 15 more runs.

Paynter's knock had lasted three hours, and he hit nine boundaries through 'beautiful footwork, George Gunn-like', said one observer; 'as nimble as a dancer's', says another. What a pity he did not reach a century in his first effort on Australian soil! At a single stroke he has revealed his temperamental fitness for Test cricket. Verity's temperament was proved long ago. He went on stolidly and conscientiously after Voce had come and gone, and then, lashing out, was missed off O'Reilly in one over and caught in the next – by the same fieldsman, Richardson. Verity's stay lasted just over two hours and a half, and the England innings seven hours altogether.

The England bowlers began their task after an early tea. They were full of heart, and with only one run on the board Fingleton was caught at the wicket off Allen's third ball, Larwood having bowled the opening over. 'We sat back and wondered what was coming,' says an English correspondent: and they had not long to wait.

WOODFULL HURT

No sooner did Bradman arrive than he saw Woodfull at the other end receive a blow on the heart from Larwood with a rising ball. 'The thump could be heard in the grandstand. Woodfull's face was twisted in agony,' says Reuter. The crowd, recalling that he had been struck by the same bowler at Melbourne, showed great anger. For a long time every ball was booed.

Larwood had bowled with an orthodox field until then, but he was so little intimidated by the scene that he changed to leg-theory bowling against Bradman, and when only 18 were scored the super-batsman fell into the trap and gave a 'gift catch' to Allen at short-leg. At 34 McCabe fell into it also. The England attack was now dominant in a really fiery fashion, and Allen himself had the next success, Woodfull playing on at 51, after a dogged innings of an hour and a half. Later he was attended by two doctors.

The rot was stemmed by Ponsford and Richardson against bowling which was weakened by the retirement of Voce, through a recurrence of the ankle trouble which has bothered him since the start of the tour. When stumps were drawn Ponsford had batted a hundred minutes for 45, including five 4s, and Richardson an hour for 21. The fielding and bowling were all-round and consistent excellence – Hammond's failure to take Ponsford was not really a missed catch – and 50,962 spectators, a record for the ground, must have agreed, however reluctantly, that it had been a very good day for England.

———

17 JANUARY 1933

EDITORIAL

'LEG-THEORY' BOWLING

It is high time that lovers of cricket both in England and Australia should declare their impatience of the sulphurous atmosphere in which the present series of Test Matches has become involved. What the exact meaning is of the Australian complaints, official and unofficial, expert and highly inexpert, against the 'leg theory' bowling of the English team, it is impossible to estimate. The printed opinions of old Australian Test players are not in agreement. Descriptions of the play suggest possibly that unskilful batting rather than dangerous bowling was the cause of loss of wickets and personal injuries.

There is, however, evidence that good judges in Australia are convinced that the 'leg theory' attack which they have seen is not within the best traditions of the game. Of its absolute legality there can be no question, but England will heartily agree that such a defence is not sufficient. On the other hand, Australia cannot have forgotten that fast bowlers have been dangerous before now, and that the tactics of a team and a captain have in former years been criticised as unexpected and rigorous by one side without convincing the other. The strain of Test play must always tend to produce unfortunate incidents. The players and the spectators and the mass of critics should minimise them. For if such incidents were continually inflamed Test matches would be a noxious element in cricket.

———

19 JANUARY 1933

THIS 'BODYLINE BOWLING' IS NEW ONLY IN NAME

FORM OF ATTACK AUSTRALIA'S BATSMEN SHOULD FACE WITHOUT RESENTMENT

P.G.H. Fender
Former Surrey Captain and Test Player

The MCC team's tour in Australia seems to have been more productive of controversy and acrimonious bickering than any other tour on record. The main bone of contention, as officially noted in the cable from the Australian Board of Control yesterday, concerns what is described – whatever the term may mean – as 'bodyline bowling'.

It is a pity that so much time and thought have been wasted in finding new and insinuating names for something which is as old as the hills. Leg theory bowling, whether fast or slow, has been known and often used by the bowlers of both England and Australia. But never before has so much been made of it, and never has it been made the cause of such feeling.

JARDINE'S TACTICS

It would be ungenerous, and it is far from my mind, to allow that these repercussions are due to the success which has attended Jardine's way of handling leg theory methods of bowling. That his method is the only new thing about the employment of the theory is common knowledge in the cricket world.

The cricketing public usually are far more likely to admire than to denounce, in cases where novelty is the only point. These demonstrations, and the uneasiness felt by many genuine lovers of the game in both countries, are due entirely to misapprehension. For instance, the very words 'bodyline bowling' convey an entirely erroneous impression. Neither facts nor the imagination can substantiate any charge that bowlers, either of yesterday or today, bowl with the intent to maim. The bowlers are men, and their captains cannot be charged with permitting such methods. Such inventions are mischievous.

The theory which words like 'body bowling' purport to describe is a simple one, and the reasons for its employment are simple. Every cricketer knows that the majority of batsmen have their weak points. It is the business of the bowler to find out, as quickly as he can, what those weaknesses are, and to play on them to the batsman's discomfiture. Some are weak on the off side, others on the leg; some can hit and cannot defend, and others can defend and cannot hit.

'CAN'T COPE WITH IT?'

A Test bowler would not be worth his salt if he did not look for, and speedily direct his attack against, any such shortcomings. And I think that it is only fair comment at the moment to say that the Australian batsmen as a whole have a decided weakness on the leg stump.

Why Jardine's determination to play on this weakness should 'cause intensely bitter feeling between the players' one can only guess. The complaint that it is dangerous and 'makes protection of the body the main consideration' can surely not be sustained without coupling with it the admission that their batsmen are unable to cope with fast bowling on the leg stump. The answer that one could expect from a Test batsman is that, if the ball is directed at the leg stump, he would naturally expect when he makes mistakes to be hit occasionally if, as is the tendency of some batsmen today, he moves in front of his wicket for every ball. If it is directed outside the leg stump there should be, on a good wicket, runs for the asking.

Unless the Australians take the line that they cannot cope with it, and for that reason want it stopped, and the MCC agree to that for political reasons, there can be no ground for instructing our captain to discontinue this most successful form of attack. It seems that Jardine has decided that the combination of fast bowling and the leg stump, with plenty of short legs to snap up the chances offered by batsmen who are not completely in control, is the recipe for the recovery of the 'Ashes'.

BATSMEN'S WICKETS

From time to time in the past the leg-theory was exploited by such fast bowlers as Gregory and Macdonald, as well as Frank Foster, but the main difference between what they did and what Jardine is doing is that he has packed the field for that type of bowling in a manner which has seldom been done before. He has forced the batsmen to play on their weakest line, and used his troops so as to take the fullest possible advantage of any lapse on the batsman's part.

So far as the argument that leg-theory bowling by a fast bowler is dangerous is concerned, it is possible that, if the series were played in England, a case of some sort could be made out. In Australia it is a very different matter. When some of us murmured in 1920–1 at the bumpers of the two Australian fast bowlers, it was frequently pointed out to us that we had bats in our hands, and that the wickets were the best in the world. We need have no fear, we were told, about the ball doing odd things, as might be the case even on the best of English wickets. The Australian wickets were such that the ball always did the same thing, and we could depend that, given identical speed and length, the ball would always rise to exactly the same height.

WHAT 'RANJI' LIKED

Again, we were told that, if we were good enough batsmen, leg-theory bowling would only provide us with easy runs. We had it on the authority of H.H. the Jain Sahib that he and his fellows sometimes ran into it and welcomed it.

It is not as if the English bowlers were alone in bowling bumpers. Every Australian Test bowler knows that it is always worth while to bounce one at Herbert Sutcliffe when he is not expecting it. They give a little signal to the man on the deep square-leg boundary, and, in the expectation that Sutcliffe will hit the ball hard and well, they hope to get him caught on the leg boundary. During the last tour they brought it off with the last ball before lunch at Brisbane. They nearly did it at Manchester in 1930. They always have it up their sleeve.

Some people who happened to be at the Oval for the fifth Test in the 1930 series may remember that half-hour after rain when the ball was kicking. Jackson and Bradman were batting. Many, after watching the different methods with which the two men met the situation, came away with the impression that one at least of them did not like fast stuff at his leg stump. Bradman drew back and tried to cut it, while Jackson stood up and played it.

BRADMAN'S WEAKNESS

When the side was chosen for Australia this time, Bradman, and how to deal with him, seemed to be the big question. Some may have thought that they had discovered the leg stump to be the chink in his armour, and decided to attack him there, having men who specialised in that form of attack. If it was too much for Bradman, it might be for others.

Another aspect of the controversy is that which concerns age. The first necessity for a great batsman is that the telegraph between eye, brain and muscle should work with the greatest possible speed. This is essential where fast bowling is concerned. It is the older members of the side who have been hit. A bowler of any sort is faster in Australia than he is in England, owing to the nature of the wickets, even if they are slower now than they used to be. And it stands to reason that, if one's eye has lost the merest trifle of its speed, one would be more handicapped there than here.

There can be no question about the legality of attacking the leg stump, and if there were the slightest question of a bowler going out more for the body than the wicket, the umpires are there, on the spot, and would act without hesitation. They are the sole judges of fair and unfair play, and would act in respect of a bowler bowling, in their opinion, at the body, just as they would over a bowler running up the wicket after delivering the ball.

WHY THIS FRICTION?

The Press and the public, being 120 yards from the wicket, cannot see enough to warrant the belief that the success of our bowlers is due to anything more than that they have discovered a hole in the Australian batting, and are making full use of it. In these circumstances there should be no question of the friendly relations between Australia and England being affected. All Tests have been won and lost as much through play on the weaknesses of one side or the other as they have been by outstanding ability.

21 JANUARY 1933

SOME CRICKET HISTORY

INCIDENTS IN 1896 MATCH

To the Editor of the *Daily Telegraph*

Sir — In 1896 in the first match at Sheffield Park of the tour of the ninth Australian team there was a memorable stand made by Dr W.G. Grace and F.S. Jackson. Both stood up to the bowling, and hooked Jones's fastest deliveries however near they happened to go to their heads. They were both much knocked about, and F.S. Jackson was actually found on the completion of his innings to have broken a rib!

I do not recall, however, that any protests were made, or that 'W.G.' threatened to withdraw from the captaincy of the England team, although many cricketers had grave doubts as to the fairness of Jones's bowling action, and he was actually no-balled some years later by the English umpire, Jim Phillips, for throwing!

I think it is useful to recall these facts at the present juncture in view of the outcry in the Australian Press about the English fast bowlers. — Yours, &c.,

W.H. Peregrine Adams
Golders Green, 19 January

BATSMEN'S 'SQUEALING'

Sir — 'Bad workmen find fault with their tools.' Messrs. Woodfull, Bradman and Co., being unable to find any defects in their bats, have to look elsewhere for excuses for their many recent failures, and so attack our fast bowlers. I venture to say that if the above-named had piled up runs against us during the present tour, as they have been known to do hitherto, one would have heard little or nothing of the accidental knocks some of the Australians have received.

These knocks are no worse, and probably less severe, than some of those received by certain of our leading batsmen from the hands of Gregory and Macdonald — knocks which produced no squealing on our side then. — Yours, &c.

H.C.P. Wood
Junior Carlton Club, 18 January

'TRAP OR DEVICE'

Sir — Admitting the legality of such bowling, the mere fact that it partakes of the nature of a trap or device constantly to embarrass the batsman, and so encompass his early downfall, seems to suggest that regular recourse to such methods in Test matches cannot contribute in the long run to the maintenance of those sportsmanlike attributes which we rightly hold so dear. — Yours, &c.

A.E. Wyatt
Lewisham, SE13, 18 January

---

3 APRIL 1933

GENIUS OF THE CRICKET FIELD

'RANJI'S' BATTING TRIUMPHS
A MASTER OF THE LEG-GLANCE
MEMORABLE GAMES

Sydney J. Southerton

No one who saw Kumar Shri Ranjitsinhji during the great period of his cricketing career could fail to regard him as a 'genius' of the game. Versatile and distinctive in his style, he burst upon the cricket firmament like a meteor — but with the marked difference that he did not exhaust his effulgence in one sudden flash. Rather did his brilliance tend to increase.

He became a member of the Sussex County XI in 1895 — two years after obtaining his 'Blue' at Cambridge — and remained with Sussex, always as a star, until 1904. During those years cricket in England was, for the most part, of a high standard in all-round skill and ability; but no batsman stood on a more lofty pinnacle than Kumar Shri Ranjitsinhji. Indeed, it is scarcely an exaggeration to say that, by his methods and the successes they achieved, he to a large extent revolutionised the art and science of batting.

ORIGIN OF 'LEG-THEORY'

He brought the leg-glance to the pitch of perfection. While this particular stroke has since been emulated with no small success by many batsmen, nobody has equalled or even approached his wonderful skill in taking a good length ball off the middle stump with such a measure of certainty.

When Ranjitsinhji was so constantly bringing off his leg-glance, opposing captains would endeavour to cramp him by packing the leg-side with fieldsmen. The ultimate adoption of this had an unfortunate sequel in the outburst against 'leg-theory' or 'body-line' bowling during the recent tour of the MCC team. I should hazard a guess that, had 'Ranji' been playing today, nothing of this sort would have happened, for he, with his immaculate skill, almost invariably devised means of penetrating the ring of leg-side fieldsmen. But he was a master.

When we first saw 'Ranji' in England we had the impression that, although possessed of strong and supple wrists, he lacked the physique requisite for driving. This view was to a huge extent confirmed by the fact that, for some time, he made most of his runs either behind or square with the wicket, and chiefly on the leg side. As he progressed, however, he developed into a good driver, and in many of his innings showed that he could put plenty of power into that stroke.

BAD PITCH SUCCESSES

At the outset he could not, with any justification, be described as a good slow-wicket player, but as ability to drive came to him, so did his faculty for making runs under difficult conditions increase. Ultimately, he played many great innings when the state of the pitch would have reduced the ordinarily good batsman to despair.

One in particular was at Brighton in 1900, when, playing for Sussex against Middlesex on a wicket which gave bowlers considerable assistance, Ranjitsinhji hit up 202 in three hours, his strokes including 35 4s. It is rather sad to compare a display of this description with many innings by first-class cricketers in modern Test matches.

But Ranjitsinhji was primarily a fast-wicket batsman, his exceptional keenness of eye and flexibility of wrist enabling him, when conditions were favourable, to accomplish almost anything in the way of scoring. It naturally follows that, in the exploitation of his amazing strokes, he required hard and fast wickets.

IGNORED AT THE START

Ranjitsinhji was born at Sarodar, in the State of Kathiawar, India, on 10 September 1872, and learned his early cricket at the Rajkumar College, Rajkot, under the coaching of Mr Chester MacNaghten, a Cambridge man, but not a 'Blue'. When he came to England in 1888, he was a batsman of some skill, but it was not until he went up to Trinity College, Cambridge, and played in the college eleven that he engaged in any cricket of note.

That he had cricket in him and knew that he had was obvious from the fact that for two or three seasons he engaged Tom Richardson, Bill Lockwood, Tom Hayward and J.T. Hearne to bowl to him at the nets. It is a fact that, at first, little notice was taken of him. Indeed, when, in 1893, he played at the Oval for the South of England against the Australians, he wandered about the pavilion at a loss to know what to do with himself. Few spoke to him, and he confessed to me that he felt thoroughly miserable.

Ranjitsinhji was a keen and skilful fisherman. I remember the famous match with Somerset at Taunton in 1901, when, after playing cards with him until well past midnight, I was then induced to get up at five o'clock and go fishing with him. We fished for about five hours, and I thought that he would scarcely be in a fit condition for cricket. However, when he went out later in the day he played the highest innings of his career in England – 285 not out – batting all the time with marvellous accuracy, precision and brilliance.

I still think, and 'Ranji' himself supported me, that one of his best innings was in the memorable match between Sussex and Surrey at Hastings in 1902, when 1,427 runs were scored for twenty-one wickets. Ranjitsinhji made 234 not out, with Richardson and Lockwood bowling almost at their best at him, and he told me afterwards that he thought he could have stayed there for ever, for the ball looked to him as big as a balloon.

TEST MATCH TRIUMPHS

Ranjitsinhji took part in fourteen Test matches – five in Australia – and in the course of those games obtained 989 runs, with an average of nearly 45. He played an innings of 175 at Sydney in 1897–98, when a member of A.E. Stoddart's second team. His greatest Test match triumph was at

Manchester in 1896, when he scored 154 not out in superb style, and was so completely master of the Australian attack that, could he have got anybody to stay with him, he would certainly have saved England from defeat.

He ended his Test match career ingloriously in 1902, with C.B. Fry as his companion in misfortune. Ranjitsinhji in the course of three matches scored 13, 0, 2, and 0 and Fry 0, 0, 1, and 4. He was also prominent in Gentlemen and Players matches, making his first appearance in 1893 and his last in 1912, with a 121 at Lord's in 1904 as his best score. He took a team to America in 1899. A lithe, supple figure in his young days, he was a brilliant field anywhere near the wicket and especially in the slips.

----

8 MAY 1933

JARDINE'S RETURN

Thomas Moult
Glasgow, Sunday

The story of the recently ended MCC tour in Australia, as I was able to piece it together on the return home of the team yesterday, is an amazing one.

I met the players at Greenock, and although their lips were sealed on certain aspects of the tour, every member abiding loyally by the official request that they should say nothing, their very silence indicated the truth that

A body of touring cricketers have never been called upon to face such difficulties in the history of the game.

NO DISSENSIONS; 'MANUFACTURED' TALES

Here are some of the impressions I gathered during my conversations on board the liner, the *Duchess of Atholl*, by which the team reached Greenock from Canada on the final stage of their 30,000 miles journey, or before they separated for their homes in various parts of the country:

That the unparalleled difficulties of the tour were surmounted, and the Ashes regained, was a great personal triumph for one man especially

– Douglas Jardine, the captain. When Larwood's success brought about a crisis, the team were unanimous in their view that D.R. Jardine should continue to employ leg-theory bowling.

The tales of dissension among the English players were deliberately manufactured. The behaviour of the crowd during the Test matches was sometimes 'nightmarish and frightening'. There were moments when the players felt that thousands of angry people would break the fences and pour on to the field. A more friendly feeling returned as the tour drew to its close. The Australian Board of Control realised that their bodyline protest was ill-timed.

There is little fear of future tours being cancelled – unless the MCC cancel them.

UTTERLY FEARLESS

Every player to whom I spoke emphasised one thing above all – the strength of character, the utter fearlessness of Jardine in the most trying situations a cricketer has ever had to face.

Several of them, I imagine, would argue against leg-theory bowling as a principle, but when the Tests reached a critical stage and it became vitally important that Jardine should have the team behind him in continuing to use Larwood, the approval of every member of the team was unhesitating. They believed in the fairness of Larwood's method. He bowled consistently on the leg stump, never outside it, as the adverse reports suggested.

What the intimidation they met with consisted of, we in England have not been given any real idea. An eyewitness of the Tests wrote home during the winter that he feared lest Jardine – and Larwood – would break down under the strain. The Test match crowds went much further than throwing oranges on to the field and counting Larwood's strides to the crease in chorus; 40,000 out of 60,000 spectators even stood up, and, all together, roared out an offensive epithet in two syllables, again and again, until they were hoarse.

Doubtless it was to this particular epithet that Jardine wittily referred when, during the visit to New Zealand, he replied to a toast by saying: 'We have just come from a country where our parentage is regarded as doubtful but our ultimate destination absolutely certain.' A glimpse of Jardine on his journey by the 'Midday Scot' from Glasgow to London on

Saturday is characteristic. Amid the excitement of cheering crowds and the homecoming that awaited him he sat back in his carriage quietly reading the newly published Life of Lord Birkenhead.

———

CHAPTER 2
1934–1959

INTRODUCTION

As the *Daily Telegraph* grew into a newspaper with daily sales of more than 1,000,000 the need for a cricket correspondent became ever more pressing. What was required was an authoritative voice able to reflect the opinions of its readers and wield influence over the game's administrators.

Philip Trevor, successively bylined Philip Trevor, Lieutenant-Colonel Philip Trevor, Colonel Philip Trevor and Colonel Philip Trevor CBE, was the closest the newspaper had to a regular cricket correspondent but his death a few months before the Bodyline tour had left a gaping hole in the *Telegraph*'s coverage. With the Australians due to arrive in April 1934 for an eagerly awaited Ashes series, a replacement had to be found quickly.

The newspaper turned to Howard Marshall and thus cricket had its first writer-broadcaster. Marshall had pioneered ball-by-ball radio coverage of cricket for the BBC but now had also to find time to pen his often lengthy match reports for the *Daily Telegraph*. The twin callings on his time did not detract from his witty and insightful newspaper reports. Marshall had a mischievous sense of humour and introduced a levity to *Telegraph* cricket reports that had not been seen before. During the Oval Test of 1934, when the Ashes returned to Australia, Bill Bowes's performance thrilled Marshall. Despite spending a night in hospital, Bowes dismissed Bradman and Woodfull the following day. 'The suggestion was made that Bowes must surely have been operated on by Dr Voronoff,' wrote Marshall. Serge Voronoff was a French surgeon who pioneered the technique of grafting monkey testicles into elderly men in order to improve their sex drive. For the *Telegraph* of the 1930s, Marshall's reference was racy indeed.

But Marshall's reign as cricket correspondent was over by the end of the 1930s and he was soon succeeded firstly by Plum Warner and then by

Douglas Jardine. Both were short-lived appointments, but in the case of Jardine, external events played a major part in ending his *Telegraph* career. Jardine was appointed in 1939 and his early reports were perfunctory and dry but he grew in confidence as that summer wore on. With war looming, the space devoted to cricket reports shrank and in one of his final pieces for the *Telegraph*, Jardine made a mournful prediction. 'This is the last Championship match I shall see for some time ...' He was right. Jardine never wrote for the *Telegraph* again.

As Jardine sat at home in the summer of 1946 he must have wondered what he had done wrong. For the position of cricket correspondent, the *Telegraph* owners decided to pass over one of the finest cricketers of the generation in favour of Sir Guy Campbell, a golf writer and course architect, with little cricketing experience. Legend has it that a driver would pick him up at Paddington Station and a messenger would be sent from Lord's to deliver his copy back to the office. After a few months Campbell was back on the golf beat. With a gaping hole to fill and a post-war interest in cricket reaching unprecendented levels, the *Telegraph* needed to find a successor to Campbell and quickly. The man they turned to would dominate and shape the paper's cricket coverage for the next three decades.

E.W. 'Jim' Swanton had landed, in his own words, 'one of the plum jobs in Fleet Street'. But Swanton, hardened by years as POW in Burma, was not going to take the job lightly. He had a point to prove. In 1932, as a young reporter for the *Evening Standard*, he had been due to spend that winter in Australia as the first reporter to be sent to cover a tour overseas. But when he missed an edition while covering a match at Leyton, the newspaper's editor asked 'if the young fellow could not get a story from Leyton how can we rely on him from Sydney or Melbourne?'. Swanton was an envious onlooker from the *Evening Standard*'s London office as the Bodyline tour gripped the country.

His bitterness over that snub perhaps drove him to become a prodigious and groundbreaking correspondent for the *Telegraph*. He was hindered during the immediate post-war years by a shortage of newsprint, which explains why there was little coverage of Bradman's Invincibles tour of 1948. The thin and fragile newsprint from that era has left its mark today. The scratchy, grainy microfilm images are tricky to read and some of Swanton's words from that landmark summer are lost in a blur of black smudgy ink.

But by the time the 1950s began, newsprint was bountiful, giving Swanton the space to express himself and grow into the giant of newspaper cricket reporting that the owners had envisaged when he was appointed. Through Swanton's eyes we see the emergence of the West Indies, England regain the Ashes in 1953 and county cricket enjoy a prominence that it has failed to recapture. The names Cowdrey, May, Compton, Hutton and Benaud are all celebrated in Swanton's unique way.

---

23 AUGUST 1934

Howard Marshall

So the Ashes go to Australia. At six o'clock yesterday evening Oldfield whipped Allen's bails off, the players scrambled for stumps as souvenirs, the crowd swarmed in front of the pavilion, and the amazing fifth Test match was over. Australia had won by 562 runs. They have never won a Test match by so large a margin before.

It would be absurd to say that we were disappointed. The time for disappointment is long past. We were resigned to our fate. Each run that Bradman and Ponsford scored on Saturday was a nail driven into our coffin. It would also, I think, be idle to pretend that we are sorry the Test matches are over. They have been ruined by controversy which could so easily have been prevented.

Let us admit, though, that the English team chosen by the selectors has been beaten by a better side. At Leeds Australia were robbed of victory by the weather. At the Oval there was no doubt of their all-round supremacy. Now that Hammond is out of luck in representative cricket we have no batsman to compare with Bradman. Our fielding was lamentably inferior. We had no pair of bowlers capable of casting such a spell upon their opponents as Grimmett and O'Reilly. Whether this formidable pair of sorcerers should have been allowed by the English batsmen to work their magic is another matter. They did so, and we know the rest. Australia were too good for us. We may as well leave it at that.

Yesterday, as a matter of fact, the English bowlers acquitted themselves with some distinction, especially Bowes, who, like Jonathan Jo in the nursery rhyme, is full of surprises. An incalculable player is Bowes. On Tuesday night he underwent a minor operation in hospital. Yesterday morning he drove from hospital to the Oval, and with his second ball clean bowled the great Bradman. Then he had a rest, and with the second ball of his second spell he sent Woodfull's stumps flying. Altogether he took five wickets for 55 runs, and the suggestion was made that Bowes must surely have been operated on by Dr Voronoff.

Seventeen thousand people had come to be in at the death – a large crowd with the game in such a hopeless position. It was a quiet crowd, though. It could not even rise to irony until it shouted for Larwood and Voce in front of the pavilion at the end of the match. I think, indeed, that the Australians would be the first to admit that they have had a fine and sporting reception from the Oval spectators.

There is not much to tell of yesterday's play. Many wickets fell, but they fell tamely. Bradman tried a wild hook at a straight ball, and Woodfull, perhaps because it was his 37th birthday, played a stroke which, from England's point of view, can only be called generous. And the English fielders, including wicket-keeper Woolley, held their catches. So, unexpectedly, but most agreeably, the Australian innings dwindled.

The old enemies came and went – McCabe, Kippax, Chipperfield, Oldfield – and, at half-past two, Australia were all out for 327. Not that they worried about that. A team with a lead of 707 does not worry unduly. England started their second innings as if they were putting themselves out of their agony as soon as possible. Walters was bowled with one run on the board, and Woolley, unfortunate Woolley, tried to drive McCabe, and gave an easy catch to Ponsford at mid-off. Two wickets down for three runs – this was humiliation with a vengeance.

It was then that Sutcliffe and Hammond gave us at least a glimpse of what might have been. They dealt well and truly with Grimmett and O'Reilly. Here, at last, was the real Hammond, hitting anything over-pitched or short of a length to the boundary, driving O'Reilly straight for a glorious six into the pavilion. Sutcliffe went, though, tricked by Grimmett, and Hammond followed when he had made 43. That was the end. We only had to wait for the kill, and at six o'clock it came, with the England total 145.

Not only a Test match was finished, but an epoch. We shall not see many of the players who appeared at the Oval in representative cricket again. When it was all over Woodfull announced that he had played his last first-class game. A redoubtable opponent, Woodfull, a great batsman and a great captain. We wish him well.

Kippax, I suppose, and Ponsford, Oldfield and Grimmett have made their last journey to England with an Australian team. If sometimes they have chastened us they have given us much pleasure, these fine cricketers. And Woolley has bidden farewell to the Test match battlefield. He was unlucky, but we think none the less of him for that. We know our Woolley. He remains upon his throne.

So it is finished. The games of 1934 are history, but we cannot yet say, 'R.I.P.' There is still controversy ahead, and we must hope that before long the historian will be able to deal finally with the leg-theory dispute.

---

27 JULY 1935

SURREY v. KENT

Wonderful Woolley! The crowd at the Oval – over 15,000 spectators were there to give Sandham's benefit match a splendid send off – watched the tall Kent left-hander take toll of the Surrey bowling in his most majestic manner. For over three hours Woolley went on in his own grand way to crack on 229 runs. It was an innings studded with four 6s and thirty 4s – and one magnificent hit sent the ball soaring out of the ground, on to the tram lines and then, first bounce, into a nearby garden!

Here is Woolley's time schedule: 52 in 28 minutes, 100 in 80 minutes, 150 in 125 minutes, 200 in 160 minutes and 229 in three hours five minutes. But mere figures can convey nothing of the easeful grace with which the Kent batsman met the harassed – but always hopeful – Surrey attack.

Woolley's brilliance overshadowed the workmanlike hundred built up in 190 minutes by Fagg. As it was, Fagg, getting sixteen 4s, shared in two century stands: he put on 136 with Ashdown – their fourth big opening stand this season – and helped Woolley add 133 in 70 minutes. And of that second partnership Woolley made 87. After Ames had left at 297 – he is completely out of luck these days – there was still a third three-figure partnership. Yet Todd was so completely overshadowed by Woolley's hurricane hitting, that of the 106 runs added in an hour Todd's share was 38.

Some idea of Woolley's mastery over the attack may be gathered from the fact that his first 103 were scored out of 161, his 200 out of 305, and, finally, when bowled by a yorker, the famous left-hander had hit his 229 out of 344.

---

22 JUNE 1937

'ENGLAND'S NO. I FOR NEXT 20 YEARS'

SUTCLIFFE'S PREDICTION

Thomas Moult
Sheffield, Monday

The outcome of the match at Bramall Lane long since became so obvious that the attention of the great crowd has been devoted almost entirely to something else than the towering domination of Yorkshire and the ever-deepening plight of Derbyshire, who, with only eight wickets standing, need 286 to avoid defeat by an innings.

Sixteen thousand people, a wonderful crowd for Monday, watched without a moment's slackening of attention, the building up by Hutton of an innings that, without exaggeration or over-optimism, must establish this young Pudsey batsman as a giant of English cricket. He scored 271 not out, but figures were less important than his manner of reaching them.

Although he will only be 21 on Wednesday, he revealed a mastery that rendered the Derbyshire attack utterly powerless against him. He made the fullest use of a good wicket, taking all kinds of bowling alike, his footwork against spin and his fearlessness against speed, alike being extraordinary.

His stroke play in attack and defence was astonishing for so young a player, and if he has anything to learn in the years to come, it has only to do with the perfecting of his art. On the off side he is already superb; there can be few things more lovely in present day batsmanship than Hutton's drive through the covers.

Hutton's batting today might be regarded as a thanksgiving for the honour bestowed on him a few hours earlier, when the selectors included him in an England eleven for the first time. Sutcliffe who, when Hutton was a colt, foresaw him as a Test player, expressed to me his great pride that his prediction has come true. 'I am grateful', he said, 'that he has fulfilled my expectations.' And as we watched Hutton together, from the pavilion, Sutcliffe made a further prediction. 'Given good health he will be England's opening batsman for the next 20 years.'

From 10 minutes past three on Saturday until half-past four this afternoon, when Yorkshire declared, Hutton was practically invincible. At the outset he was 88 not out. He reached his 100 after batting two hours 55 minutes, and at lunch was 172 out of 330 for 3, Mitchell and Leyland having left him at 212 and 229. Leyland, by the way, was the first batsman in the match to be bowled, nine of Derbyshire and two of Yorkshire having been caught.

Hutton was missed at short fine leg when 121, a sharp chance off G. Pope. Such an escape is supposed to sober a batsman, but it did not sober Hutton. Instead, he opened his shoulders and put on 55 in the next hour. After lunch, when he was 163, Townsend only just failed to take a hard return. These were the only scratches on the glorious surface of a most polished innings. He lost his fourth partner, the sturdy Barber, immediately after lunch at 334, and then he and Turner lifted the total to 525. Turner reached 81 in two hours 20 minutes of aggression that must have made Derbyshire feel they were being hit when they were down.

The closure had been anticipated long before it came. Indeed, when Yorkshire reached 500, somebody rang the pavilion bell to call the players in, and the fieldsmen actually began to make their way home. They were sent back, and Yorkshire added 25 before the actual declaration. Weary and worn and sad though they were when they eventually found rest, the Derbyshire side were as full of praise as everyone for Hutton's seven hours' stay at the crease, during which, incidentally, he hit 27 boundaries.

---

3 AUGUST 1937

FAREWELL 100 BY HENDREN

CROWD'S TRIBUTE LASTS SEVERAL MINUTES

Thomas Moult

It hardly matters now, the result that today will bring, in the last match of the season for Middlesex at Lord's. They saved the follow-on and scored 377 for 6 against Surrey's huge total of 509, but their flickering hope of winning the County Championship guttered out like a candle's end. They have fought the good fight and failed by inches – or, rather, decimals; and they have sent their congratulations to the triumphant Yorkshire.

But when their gallant, vain endeavour has receded so far into history that all the disappointment will have gone out of it as they look back, there is one of yesterday's memories that must remain bright and, moreover, wonderful.

Wonderful, indeed, is the word the Middlesex president, Sir Pelham Warner, used to me at the close of the incident which moved nearly 13,000 onlookers in a way that has no parallel in English sport. Hendren, the well-beloved, made a century in the last match he will ever play at his beloved Lord's. The scene that occurred when, with a single past Whitfield, the bowler, he made sure of a three-figure score was spontaneous, unanimous and, although deeply moving, most happy.

Earlier in the day Hendren had been given an intimation of the affection in which he is held by cricketers themselves, for as he walked out, bat in hand, to open his innings amid a storm of clapping that lasted all the way to the crease, the Surrey fieldsmen, who were apparently standing casually near the wickets, suddenly sprang to attention and, waving their caps, gave their veteran opponent three cheers.

But this was merely the prologue to the drama of the afternoon. For the next two hours Hendren repaid Surrey by cracking the bowling about in a fashion that, more than once, recalled his heyday; and, then, immediately the crowd saw that the 170th hundred of his long career was an actuality, they clapped and cheered with such fervour that the game was suspended for several minutes.

Patsy stood raising his cap again and again. Reeves, the umpire, pulled out his watch and ticked off the moments to hide his emotion, and then, half in jest, took Hendren's arm and, as he told me afterwards, tried to make him retire there and then. The applause faded, but the episode was not yet over, for a spectator under the Father Time stand took off his straw hat and used it as a baton while he led the singing of 'For He's a Jolly Good Fellow'. The whole assembly joined in, and that of itself was unprecedented – choral music at Lord's!

'I can recall nothing like it,' Sir 'Plum' Warner told me afterwards. 'Hendren has deserved it. I am most happy about it.' The ex-president of the club, Mr. A.J. Webbe, who played for Middlesex in the 'eighties, went across to the professional's room and gave Hendren his farewell congratulations.

Asking me to publish his grateful thanks, 'Patsy' laughingly revealed that when he was caught in the deep-field five minutes after he became a century-maker, a Surrey bowler called out 'Goodbye, Dillinger!' – explaining that since Jack Hobbs retired three seasons ago Hendren had been the Bowlers' Enemy Number One!

His innings had thwarted Surrey, and, in a partnership with Edrich that put on 182 in two and a half hours, saved Middlesex from a threatened collapse and possibly the humiliation of following-on. Surrey increased their Saturday total of 448 for eight to 509, Parker and Brooks adding 77 altogether for the ninth wicket, the share of the amusing Brooks being 52; and then, when Middlesex began their reply at half-past 12, two batsmen were out for four runs.

Hart was bowled at 2 and Price, who, with a badly hurt thumb, is still hardly able to use his right hand, was lbw two runs later, Gover and Watts being the bowlers. This two-fold disaster brought Edrich and Hendren together, and it was four o'clock before Surrey had another success. By that time the threat of Gover had so diminished that the wicket-keeper was able to stand up to him, and the Surrey attack became as tired and disheartened as the Middlesex bowling had been.

Hendren was soon the complete master; he hit five of his eight boundaries in 40 minutes before lunch, contenting himself afterwards with placing the ball between the fieldsmen in a fashion that brought him apparently easy 2s and 3s. He set the pace, all the same, and reached 51 out of 94 in 65 minutes. Not until he was 84 did Edrich complete his half-century – in 110 minutes – although the younger player had batted ten minutes longer.

Edrich offered a hot return catch to Whitfield at 153, which was not accepted; but Hendren was faultless. When he was 95 he received an unpleasant knock that held up the game; when he was 96 Fishlock ignored the appeal of the ring to 'Let it go', and saved an apparent 4 on the edge of the boundary, thus halting Hendren at 99. Only for an over, though; and when Hendren was caught at 103 his end was worthy of him. He was caught while trying to hit a 6 into the pavilion.

4 AUGUST 1938

HUTTON SMASHES ALL RECORDS

ENGLAND CERTAIN TO WIN FARCICAL TEST
BRADMAN FRACTURES SHIN BONE WHILE BOWLING

Howard Marshall

Hutton making his record score of 364 in the final Test match at the Oval, Bradman being carried off the field with a fractured shin bone, England declaring at the phenomenal total of 903 for seven wickets — these were the outstanding events in one of the most remarkable day's cricket ever played. That Australia lost three wickets for 117 after tea seemed entirely unimportant. The match is over, to all intents and purposes, and all that remains is to add up the records.

Records do not make cricket, however, and we can only hope that these fresh ones will prove to be eight stout nails in the coffin of timeless Tests played on wickets which turn a great game into a farce.

First of all, though, let us praise Hutton for his tremendous exhibition of concentration, endurance and skill. He gave point and purpose to the early hours, for the excitement was intense as he slowly and surely approached Bradman's record of 334, the previous highest individual score in Test matches between England and Australia. We could almost feel the huge crowd willing Hutton to succeed, and when, with a beautiful square-cut, he hit the decisive 4 off Fleetwood-Smith, a roar went up which must have shaken the Houses of Parliament across the river.

Bradman raced up to shake his hand, and while drinks came out and all the Australians toasted him in the middle of the pitch the crowd cheered, and sang 'For he's a jolly good fellow', and cheered and cheered again. An astonishing scene, and Hutton richly deserved this wonderful ovation. When at last his concentration wavered and he was caught at cover by Hassett off O'Reilly, he had batted for 13 hours and 20 minutes, and hit thirty-five 4s, fifteen 3s, eighteen 2s and 143 singles. A prodigious effort, and if Hutton's innings was immensely prolonged, it was also logically and strictly in accordance with the conditions imposed by such a wicket and such a match.

That Bradman should have slipped and fractured his shinbone while bowling was an ironical commentary on the state of affairs. This was a tragic misfortune for Australia, who have also lost Fingleton with a strained muscle, and it is doubtful whether he will be able to bat. As it happens, even Bradman could not have hoped to stave off defeat, and while we may reasonably be pleased at England's mastery, I cannot believe that any true lover of cricket will be easy in his mind about the conditions in which it was achieved.

The wicket, so prepared that the bowlers were helpless, has completely destroyed the balance of the game. A groundsman perhaps, might conceive it his duty to prepare such a wicket, and regard the result as a triumph, but it is surely high time the authorities stepped in and made an end of such harmful nonsense.

Half-an-hour of the Leeds Test was worth a whole day of the Oval travesty. At Leeds there was life in the wicket, and the balance was held even between batsman and bowler. At the Oval, on turf completely dead, the only weapons left to the bowler were flight and accuracy, and the dice were so loaded in favour of the batsmen that winning the toss meant winning the match unless rain interfered.

It is absurd that the spin of the coin should be given such entirely disproportionate importance. It is absurd that batsmanship should be reduced to a dead level of competence. And, by the same token, it is monstrous that the lovely arts of bowling should be thus arbitrarily nullified. If the boot had been on the other leg, and Australia had won the toss, we should have thought it a serious matter indeed. It remains a serious matter with England in the winning position, serious for cricket as a whole.

It was pathetic to see a fine player like Hardstaff pottering about in the afternoon with 800 runs on the board playing half-volleys respect-fully back to weary and indifferent bowlers, but he also was a victim of circumstances. Time did not matter, runs were still important, so why should he take risks against a perfectly set defensive field? That, I imagine, is how he viewed the situation, and how a match played in such conditions reacts upon a batsman.

I hope profoundly, at any rate, that we shall never again see such a total on the scoreboard in England, and that if we are to have these matches played to a finish, it shall never be upon wickets which make such absurdities possible. At least we must pay tribute to the remark-able Australian fielding, which did not flag throughout the 15¼ hours.

Bradman set his team a great example, and it was most unfortunate that his final reward should be a fractured shinbone.

The weather had changed completely overnight, and the sun blazed down when England continued their innings. All our interest was centred in Hutton's attempt to beat Bradman's record, and he and Hardstaff proceeded quietly against the bowling of O'Reilly and Fleetwood-Smith. Hutton looked as fresh as a daisy, and extremely certain and confident, but the Australian attacked him with the utmost hostility. The runs came slowly, and when Hutton was 315 O'Reilly made him edge the leg-break, and threw back his head in despair as the ball fell safely to ground.

At 670, Bradman took the new ball, and Waite and McCabe used it accurately, but Hutton forged steadily on, and at 688 the climax came when O'Reilly returned to the attack. Hutton was 320, and Bradman moved into silly mid-off, with Brown silly mid-on. A single to Hutton, a beautiful square-cut off Fleetwood-Smith, two more singles, and the record was within Hutton's grasp.

Suddenly O'Reilly bowled, Hutton flailed mightily and missed, as if concentration had deserted him, but it was a no-ball, and four runs were all he needed. Another pause, an irrepressible murmur of excitement from the crowd, a leg-break from Fleetwood-Smith, which Hutton cut gloriously to the boundary, and a storm of scorecards fluttered in the air as the crowd roared its satisfaction at Hutton's splendid triumph. After that tremendous moment the tension relaxed. Hutton, still calm and judiciously masterful, did not alter his method, and Hardstaff stayed with him until the luncheon interval. Soon afterwards, Hutton was out, hitting O'Reilly to cover, and then Wood came in to attack the bowling most cheerfully.

At 798 Bradman himself took the ball and sent down a maiden over, but by that time all reality had left the game. The total was 876 before Wood, much to his annoyance, was caught and bowled by Barnes, and Verity kept Hardstaff company until Hammond mercifully declared.

Australia, footsore and weary, began disastrously. Badcock was caught off Bowes by Hardstaff at short-leg in the second over of the innings, McCabe went with only 19 runs on the board, and it was left to Hassett to show us the true beauty of attacking batsmanship. Hassett played splendidly, and made his 42 out of 51 runs scored while he was at the wicket, and when he left Barnes and Brown quietly played out time.

———

2 SEPTEMBER 1943

CAPT. VERITY DEAD

Capt. Hedley Verity, the Yorkshire and England Test cricketer, who three weeks ago was reported missing in Sicily, was officially stated yesterday to have died of wounds on 31 July in a military hospital while a prisoner of war in Italy. He was 38.

As reported in the *Daily Telegraph* on 11 August, Capt. Verity was last seen lying wounded in the chest, by men of the company he was leading into action in the plain of Catania. His last order to his men was: 'Keep going. Get them out of that farmhouse and get me into it.'

———

15 AUGUST 1948

E.W. Swanton

The end of the Test series against Australia is a good moment to consider briefly the broad field of English cricket, since it is to the Australians that we chiefly look to provide the yardstick of our own capabilities. Though the legions of lesser players are not directly touched by their visit the doings in the Test matches are mirrored with varying degrees of clarity in games everywhere, from the near suburban field to the rough pitch at the pit-head.

A friend not excessively imaginative was recently impressed particularly with the zeal and sparkle which were cumulatively infused into a club match he was watching as tidings came through of England's splendid showing on the Saturday at Manchester. Conversely, sad to say, there must be acknowledged the damping effect of the less admirable phases of this Test series, and, not least, the disastrous England innings at the Oval last Saturday.

In the West Indies every little black boy at the roadside was batting like Worrell or Hutton, or bowling like his own hero. The impact of Tests is felt down to the humblest levels. While this is not an article about the Australians, one must at once acknowledge the value of the splendid cricket they have shown us.

Before their tour began I wrote that the one vital and unavoidable difference between the two teams was in the department of fast bowling, and that, though the counties would not be strong enough to extend them, our best could do so. The story of the Manchester and Leeds matches is, I think, strong confirmation of the truth of this.

As it has turned out, the technical differences have mattered rather less than the contrast between the mental approach of the two sets of cricketers. The Australians regard a Test match as a fight to be waged hard (though chivalrously) but also to be enjoyed. They have all a small boy's delight in a scrap, and I never saw them happier than after that third day at Manchester, when England had brought them down with a bump, and they faced a defeat from which only the rain may have saved them.

I mention this because one finds so many normally enlightened folk who imagine the Australians to be grim, humourless creatures on the cricket field. Tough and resilient, yes, sometimes, by our standards, even over-keen, but dour, no! In truth the dourness is rather more on the English side, and in these days, when our cricketers have to last till lunchtime on a watery chunk of hotel dried egg instead of the lamb chops and plates of kidneys of their fathers, it is the hardest thing to infuse them with an ardent, combustible spirit.

The trends and temper of the times have always been faithfully reflected on the cricket field, and the play in the post-war Test matches provides a genuine sidelight on the differences between life in England and in Australia today. Beyond question our leading players tend to become jaded by playing too much – and, equally certainly, their counties would go bankrupt if they played much less. Alas! for the buoyant approach to their cricket of a Stanley Jackson or a C.B. Fry – or, indeed, of W.G. himself.

Test matches are not everything, and 'the cricket that really matters is the game that Englishmen play the world over because they can't help it, because it answers some need deepest in their blood and their hearts.' At the moment, cricket, like most other civilised institutions, must struggle in order to live, from the force of circumstances deriving from the war. From a variety of causes, many of which MCC mentioned recently in the course of its report on overseas tours, the old playing standard has not been recaptured, or even closely approached.

This is true, according to my observation, in all the different strata, from the smallest village to the county of Yorkshire. It goes even beyond the players, to the umpires and the groundsmen. For seven years ranks were not restocked. (There have been many more decisions with which neither batsmen nor fielders have agreed in this series than in the last in Australia.) The level of county play suffers especially from the scarcity of good bowling, and it is axiomatic that batting tends naturally to be only that necessary little bit better than the bowling it needs to confront. To inspect the ages of the county players is to suspect that things may easily get worse before they improve.

Consider the weakness of the truly amateur element nowadays – those who have played as a relaxation have always provided so much of the yeast to cricket – and add the loss of players in that vital year of their development to national service and the difficulty of offering wages high enough to attract them to the game as a career when they finish it, and you have a set of fairly depressing circumstances.

Yet there is a brighter prospect which, though on the far horizon, so to speak, might well, in time, dissolve our present troubles. There is no indifference towards cricket, indeed, quite the reverse. The interest probably has never been so wide, and the time is therefore surely set for a renaissance. Only in sentiment can cricket ever properly be called England's national game. It has been only the minority who have ever had a fair chance of becoming good cricketers by playing on true pitches, and receiving sound instruction.

In Australia, as has been emphasised often enough, that is the privilege of the poorest boy. We all know what Don Bradman himself derived from a concrete pitch in the Bush, but we are slow to follow the implications of the fact. Bradman has preached the value of these true pitches, just as R.W.V. Robins has done, and G.O. Allen and many other English visitors to Australia. I expect Bradman may have more to say on this subject before he leaves next month.

We romanticise village cricket, and there is nothing romantic about a concrete pitch, spread with matting. But it does enable a quick-witted boy to pick up the principles of the game with the minimum of teaching, and to enjoy it.

If this fact were generally appreciated there would surely be no lack of money forthcoming from the lovers of cricket to launch a scheme for providing such pitches on a broad scale. The coaching of the more promising local players might then indeed produce some encouraging results.

On the matter of coaching good news is already in the wind, for one hears whispers of considerable assemblages of schoolmasters to Lord's next Easter to watch practical demonstrations. Teaching cricket is a demanding art, and it is a fallacy to suppose that a man can instruct merely because he is 'a pro'. A revival of coaching would have its proper beginnings at Lord's.

The practical work of such a cricket renaissance as I envisage would naturally be delegated to counties, many of whom are making strenuous efforts already within their own limits, and by them, perhaps, in turn to districts. But it could only have its inspiration from the place which is known the world over as the home of cricket.

There is, I am sure, an abundance of affection for cricket and knowledge of the game among the older generation which could be translated into a strong practical effort if it could be mobilised and directed. The be-all and the end-all of English cricket is indeed not to produce a team to beat the Australians. If it were, our present loose system would need a complete transformation, and certainly much that makes for the charm of the game would be lost.

In a sense, indeed, it might not matter very much if England never won a Test match. But it is doubtful whether public interest, and therefore the County Championship as we know it, would survive the regular eclipse of our best players. The game in England needs strong stimulation, and the well-known diction of Andrew Lang bears repetition: 'For there can be no good or enjoyable cricket without enthusiasm – without sentiment, one may almost say; a quality that enriches life and refines it, gives it what life more and more is apt to lose, zest.'

———

I AUGUST 1950

CRICKET TEA TIME

To the Editor of the *Daily Telegraph*

Sir – The tea interval was a charming social interlude in country-house and village cricket. How did it infiltrate into county cricket? Possibly at the instigation of the catering industry? I do not know when it occurred, but I think it is not in the interests of first-class cricket. In a three-day match nearly an hour is lost. A batsman has to play himself in again, a bowler to find his length.

My cricket memories go back 80 years. 'W.G.' and the heroes of the cricket world played as hard and keenly in the '70s and '80s as those of today. True, the spin-bowler was not so much in evidence, but they played on natural wickets and the fear of a 'shooter' was always before them. Surely men in full strength and vigour could do without sustenance from two to 6.30 p.m.

Yours faithfully,
E.A. POLE
Leeds

------

30 JUNE 1950

TEAMWORK GAINED WEST INDIES WIN BY 326 RUNS

GREAT BOWLING FEAT BY TWO MEN

E.W. Swanton

Lord's, Thursday

Soon after lunch today West Indies gained the victory that had seemed theirs from the time on Monday afternoon when England's batting failed against Ramadhin and Valentine. The difference was 326 runs. Thus West Indies follow South Africa, who not only chose Lord's as the scene of their first and only success in a Test in England 15 years ago, but won by a handsome and conclusive margin.

There could be no possible question of the justice of today's result. The two young spin bowlers certainly were chiefly responsible, but Rae and Walcott, Worrell, Weekes and Gomez have distinguished deeds against their names in the scoresheet. Indeed: every member of Goddard's team contributed, not least the captain himself, who made several shrewd assessments, in the field as well as setting an admirable lead by his performance at silly mid-off and short-leg.

From first to last the England batting was thrown completely back on trepidant and unconvincing defence, whereas the West Indies, faced by spin bowlers whose performance certainly could be expected to lose little or nothing by contrast with their own, declined to be dictated to at the wicket.

The delightful innings of Worrell and Weekes on the first day had a significance not properly expressed in the score. When this game is looked back to it may always be used as the model illustration of the ancient axiom that bowlers bowl as well as they are allowed to. I would not seem to detract from the merit of Ramadhin and Valentine. The former, especially, bowled magnificently, using the arts and subtleties of a spinner in a way extraordinary in one who had had not a scrap of experience before this tour. But more than one wise critic hit the ball on the head when they said they would like to see those two bowling to Worrell and Weekes. To find the ideal pair of batsmen among Englishmen of the last generation one need not go beyond Hendren and Ames. If they, or their like, had been playing it is quite certain that Valentine would not have bowled 116 overs without being hit over his head.

The most significant of all the statistics connected with the game, even making allowance for the fact that England were latterly playing for a draw, is that in the two innings West Indies received from England only 11 overs more than they bowled themselves and they scored 326 more runs.

From the English angle it is fair to add that the side was considerably weakened beyond the expected absence of Compton, who has been the focal point of all our post-war Test teams, by the injuries to Simpson and Bailey. The rubber is all square now, with two matches to come, and it would be a foolish prophet who plumped very strongly for either side finishing with a clear lead.

The analyses of Ramadhin and Valentine set many wondering what new 'records' could be unearthed to underline their performances. Alfred Shaw inevitably came to mind and Cleary and J.C. White. In 1880 Shaw bowled 116 four-ball overs against Gloucestershire, and five years later W. G. Grace, who never liked to be outdone, returned the compliment against Notts with 120 overs, what is the equivalent of 80 today. So the 72 and 71 overs of Ramadhin and Valentine in this second innings are not beyond compare. But it is safe to say that Valentine's 116 overs are the most that ever have been bowled in a match in England and that their combined score of 231 out of 298 is assuredly unique.

No summing up of the game is complete without a special word about the wicket, which was as near ideal as can be imagined. In spite of the receding rain it was reasonably quick, always took a sensible amount of spin and it lasted just about as well could be imagined. I hope Martin has many applications for the recipe.

The onus of spinning out the game when it was restarted this morning was really dependant on Washbrook giving a repeat performance. He began by surviving six maiden overs from Ramadhin, who mostly was attacking his legs with, of course, a close field. Washbrook seemed to have got the measure of this when he apparently struck his boot and was bowled by a ball that pitched about leg-stump and hit the middle. He had been in for five and a half long hours, fighting bravely.

Yardley alternated moments of difficulty with some clean hits off Valentine into the covers, but he lost Evans after 25 minutes from a half-hit sweep which Rae caught at the second attempt about mid-way between square-leg and the Mound. Then Yardley, who played Ramadhin better than anyone but Valentine rather more sketchily, snicked the ball hard to the wicket-keeper, off whose gloves it bounced to slip.

It was now a matter of whether the end would be before lunch or afterwards. Thanks to Wardle, who seemed to find little difficulty in the two young heroes now both flagging slightly, one wicket remained at half past one. Wardle hit four rousing fours off Valentine which had the effect of causing the runs scored against him slightly to outnumber his overs, and it was Worrell who finally despatched him, to the unbridled joy of his countrymen.

Some of them, armed with impromptu instruments, saluted the great occasion with strange noises, and a handful with their leader swayed round the field to give a faint reminder to those who know the West Indian Islands of the bands at carnival time. One felt sorry that the august dignity of Lord's and perhaps the sight of many helmets and uniforms so subdued the rest. But, for them at least, it was a victory unforgettable.

I MARCH 1951

BEDSER, HUTTON AND SIMPSON THE HEROES

E. W. Swanton

Melbourne, Wednesday

At last! England's victory by eight wickets in the fifth Test here this evening has altered the whole aspect of the tour as it will be remembered by the players taking part and by those both at home and in Australia who have been following the fortunes of the series.

Moral victories, near-things and unlucky breaks are all very well, but each reverse in the three series since the war has made it harder for the English side to break through. Now the reproach is past, and when the comedy of a last over by Hassett, and three premature stump-grabbings by the players, had culminated in Hutton making the winning stroke, one sensed much the same emotion of relief and pleasure among the spectators as had marked a more domestic occasion just before the war when Harrow for the first time in 40 years beat their rivals from Eton.

The crowd here was more orderly and self-conscious than that at Lord's in 1939 but they would not leave before Brown and Hassett had said their brief, well-chosen words from the grandstand balcony. As England's captain observed, it would have been even nicer if this had been the match that had decided the Ashes. But at least the manner of victory made it clear that if things had run differently it could have been, for England won inside four days of playing time on a wicket that played true from first to last and, which is the crux of the matter, after losing the toss.

I confess that when Australia won choice of innings last Friday I felt a surge of pessimism which there was no point in passing on to those at home. Since MCC sent their first team to Australia under P.F. Warner in 1903 Australia had failed only twice to win the Fifth Test, in 1912 and 1933. Normally a touring side is at its peak, as Brown's team was, about the second and third Tests. But this apart, it was hard to visualise the present batting side, dependent as it has been on one man with only occasional and uncertain outside help, making a sizable score in the last innings.

Thanks to Simpson, England gained a three-figure lead yesterday after all, and thanks to Hutton, though the runs had to be fought for, there was no breathless, palpitating struggle this afternoon for the 95 which were needed to win. But while these two heroes are being applauded for their part another name must be added, and it is a matter of personal judgment whether he occupies the chief post of honour.

When Bedser got the last Australian wicket today he brought his number for the series up to 30. If the bare fact does not sound sufficiently impressive it should be enough to quote that Richardson took 32 wickets in an Australian Test series in 1894–5. He was followed in the course of years by Rhodes, J.N. Crawford, F.R. Foster, Barnes, Tate and Larwood. Thus Bedser makes the eighth of an illustrious line who have captured 30 or more. All were great bowlers, and that overworked adjective can certainly be applied to Bedser – at least on Australian wickets.

In the whole series he was never collared. And in case any may have assumed he has concentrated mainly on the in-swinger, which to some is an unpalatable form of attack, it may be as well to point to the number of wickets he has got with slip catches. When the shine was on he frequently made the ball go the other way, and afterwards his chief weapon of destruction was the ball that he cut away towards the slips.

This is hardly the occasion for a lengthy treatise on the features and the implications of the rubber. The scoring has been lower than in any Anglo-Australian series of the last 60 years. Nor has a rubber of five been completed in modern times without the scoring of more than five centuries.

An inspection of the statistics suggests many pertinent thoughts, but the one that looms most vital from the English viewpoint is that if Hutton, in the batting, had had the support that Bedser enjoyed at one time or another in the bowling from Brown, Bailey and, in spite of adverse figures, from Wright, the battle might very easily have swayed the other way.

To make a final and significant comparison with history it will be noted that England have now put an end to a run of eleven Australian victories in three series. An exactly similar number were scored by Australia in the period after the first First World War, and the success by A.E.R. Gilligan's team at Adelaide in 1925, paved the way for England winning the Ashes on Australia's next visit to England. If the right deductions are made from the results in 1950–1 the pattern might continue to run the same way.

Before today's play began the bulk of the Australian Press, which in cricket matters does not deal much with undertones and qualification, had more or less awarded the game to England. Considering that Hassett and Hole were to be followed by three batsmen who with them could easily be capable of setting England at least 200 or 250 in the last innings, this seemed to give quite a false picture.

In retrospect the bowling of Hassett by Wright was probably the vital incident. Hassett had held the fort for three hours and 20 minutes in all and Hole had suggested he might well proceed in an aggressive counter-attack, as in fact he did. Since the new ball was due in eight overs Brown himself began the bowling with Wright and it was after 25 minutes of quiet play that Wright's beautifully pitched leg-break got past Hassett's bat. In the same over Johnson essayed an ambitious straight drive and was caught at deep mid-on by Brown, who as he waited had plenty of time to reflect on the possible consequences of a miss.

Wright up to this point had bowled dangerously and not expensively, but now Lindwall, with a lofty drive for 3, and Hole, with three 4s, took 15 in the next over. Wright, one felt before this over, might have swept through the remaining Australian batting. Those four strokes persuaded Brown to take the new ball and Bedser and Bailey bowled until the innings ended. In fact, the shine was off before, in the last over before lunch. Lindwall played too late at Bedser.

Hole, meanwhile, had shown his nerve and his quality, and if Australia had gone in with three wickets standing in addition to his there would still have been the prospect of a longish score to chase. Afterwards, as it was, the stand of 50 between Hole and Lindwall had given England something to go for.

Brown still persisted with Bailey, who was economical without looking especially dangerous at the other end to Bedser, and soon Hole was bowled as in the first innings, aiming an on-drive. That was that, and it took Bedser the minimum time to pick up the last two wickets. Hutton and Washbrook scored 32 for England's first wicket, mostly against Lindwall and Miller before they were replaced by Iverson and Johnston. Washbrook cocked an easy catch to short-leg, whereupon Simpson, now of an entirely different stature after his first innings, played easily and well with Hutton. Just before tea Simpson was surprised by the exceptional speed of Harvey in the covers and was thrown out.

The advent of Compton inevitably made for more tension, and another half-hour's struggle was needed before Hutton fittingly scored the final run. He, as ever in this series, had been the master, and perhaps the fact of Compton's being with him at the end was the sign of better things to come against South Africa this summer.

---

21 JULY 1952

TRUEMAN FIRST ENGLAND FAST BOWLER TO TAKE 8

E. W. Swanton

England won the third Test and the rubber, to be precise, at 20 minutes past five on Saturday, but India's defeat was as certain as anything could be the moment the Manchester weather changed for the worse the night before the match.

The 1902 Test at Old Trafford, which Australia won by three runs, was not only the last Test that England lost on this ground, it was the last Test England lost anywhere on a wicket wet from the first ball to the last. The handicap is too great for visiting sides from sunny countries, whether Indians or South Africans, New Zealanders, West Indians – yes, or Australians.

The remark most commonly heard when the Indians were filing monotonously in and out was: 'How I wish it were the Australians.' These thoughts bring one to a consideration of the true merit of England's performance. To what extent was it flattered by unworthy play? Would other Test sides have been likely to do substantially better?

I would say, taking the wicket, the bowling, and the fielding into consideration, that while 347 would nearly always be a winning score, a reputable Test batting side should have been capable of a much longer and more productive resistance in the first innings. The second innings was inevitably much less significant. When a side follows on 289 behind, having been bowled out for 58, and there are two and a half days to go, the only prospect of a prolonged counter-effort depends on a successful start.

Once again India's first two wickets fell before the board showed double figures, and though the faithful Hazare, with his vice-captain Adhikari, stood in the breach for an hour, Hazare was dislodged at last. Thereafter the last defences crumbled and dissolved. The irresistible pressure of events submerged the Indians so swiftly that they were bowled out a second time in the day, an indignity that has not happened to a Test side since the '90s.

That was only one of a fistful of facts and figures that zealous mathematical experts unearthed while the slaughter was going on. The scope of international conflict at all games is so greatly enlarged that most modern 'records' become entirely irrelevant. The mention of them is agreeable chiefly because it revives memories of the giants of old.

Thus, no England bowler has taken eight wickets in an innings, as Trueman did, since Verity bowled out Australia at Lord's on the sticky dog. And though everyone remembered how from Richardson, heroically unavailing in one of the classic pieces of fast bowling, took all seven Australia wickets that fell in the Old Trafford Test of '96 no one could quote a case of an English fast bowler getting eight.

If it came to the point, nor could anyone remember such suicidal batting in a Test match from accredited batsmen, as that of Umrigar and Phadkar. So bowling comparisons, on the strength of figures, if not odious, are at any rate valueless. Nevertheless, make whatever reservations you like and Trueman still performed an impressive and highly encouraging feat. He bowled down a strong wind, blowing from about mid-off, and he had the stimulus of the occasional ball that kicked.

It was certainly not a thoroughly spiteful wicket: nothing like that, for instance, on which Hutton and Ikin stood and took a battering from McCarthy this time a year ago. However, it had enough life to raise apprehension and worse in several of the batsmen, and such a state of mind causes only one sort of reaction in the fast bowler.

Trueman bowled faster than at Headingley, when the wind also blew stiffly behind him, and he bowled straighter. Furthermore, thanks to the combination of a native shrewdness and the quiet advice of his captain, he bowled very sensibly. Trueman knows that to the batsman whose legs stray to the width of the return crease the best of all balls is a fast half-volley. He has the good sense to vary his pace, and so conserve his energy, and he also has the most useful of all balls for a fast bowler, the yorker. All comparisons with famous fast bowlers may be discounted at the moment. For all his 24 wickets in this series the real testing is yet to come. In these two respects, however, he does distinctly resemble Lindwall.

The remaining factor in the day's sensations, and in some respects it was the most satisfying as well as the most spectacular of all, was England's close fielding, which was the best I remember seeing in a Test match. Not only was every one of 14 chances taken but there were a great many thrilling stops, wide, one-handed by the slips, by gullies, and short-legs that encircled the bat. The ball adhered in the most uncanny way, as though each man was trying to outshine his neighbour. Lock, standing at short-leg almost square, set the standard with a beautiful catch taken very close and an inch or two off the ground from a fast hit. Hutton followed with a high catch at first slip, the ball again travelling at a most uncomfortable speed. Next, Sheppard, in the gully, picked up off his toes a full-blooded cut that was going like a rocket.

Then if not before India must have realised that the fates were quite relentless. The fourth important catch was that of Laker which gave Roy his 'pair'. It was taken ankle-high at close Victorian point off Trueman from a firm forward stroke to a ball well pitched up. One was unreservedly sorry for Roy, who had given no ground and had batted staunchly enough for the first half-hour of the second innings.

As to the England bowling, apart from Trueman, Bedser began by taking, with Lock's aid, the most important wicket of all, that of Mankad whom he snared also in the second innings. Apart from this ball, and a deadly leg-cutter that bowled Hazare, he was not very dangerous until after tea, when for the first time he had the advantage of the wind.

Previously, as was not surprising, he was inclined to be short. When he changed ends, relieving Trueman, he swept up like a galleon in full sail, and at once became a menace. The Indians, now near demoralisation, had no answer either to him or to Lock, who bowled his left-arm spinners sometimes at almost medium pace at the other end. It is a pity that this game has afforded no proper trial of Lock.

The kindest comment on most of the Indian batting is silence. Hazare sold his life dearly in both innings, young Manjrekar batted estimably in the first and Adhikari (despite a hit in the face that caused a temporary retirement) in the second. Manjrekar was one of the only batsmen whose dismissal could be attributed directly to the wicket. He and Hazare had taken the score from 1 for five to 45 when a ball from Trueman lifted abruptly to his glove whence it lobbed gently into one of half-a-dozen pairs of hands that could have caught it.

---

6 SEPTEMBER 1952

GRAVENEY AND MAY HIT YORKS FOR 187

YORKSHIRE V. MCC

E.W. Swanton

Now and again in the season's varied scene 'a day's cricket has everything'. Such an occasion was this, whereon some 15,000 of us basked in the sunshine and watched Peter May, with two others from among the younger school of English batsmen, play a stream of strokes of a brilliance quite unusual.

Most county bowling would have wilted much as Yorkshire's did under the concentrated power of the attack launched first by May and Graveney, and then by May in company with Cowdrey. The first partnership accounted for 187 in an hour and three-quarters, the second for 106 in three-quarters of an hour, and the hitting was cool, precise and beautifully executed.

Those who have seen Yorkshire all the summer say it is only remarkable that the bowling has not had such treatment before. At all events, if some of it, and notably that of Close, grew sadly ragged, the fielding vied with MCC's yesterday, and Yorkshire lightened their labours with occasional moments of exquisite foolery. Wardle here seems to be the licensed jester, feinting to do all manner of things, and in fact, fielding quite flawlessly. Once he put the cap on a moment of comedy by catching a return from the wicket-keeper with both hands behind his back; and when May made his first and last mistake Wardle conveyed so realistically the illusion of having dropped the ball that the batsman himself was deceived.

To perform this drollery and yet to try to the utmost all the time is an art indeed, and on this occasion it no doubt made the chastisement of their bowling much easier for honest Yorkshiremen to bear.

May was simply magnificent, and if there has been an innings better designed to suit the Festival setting I have never seen it. Canterbury and the peerless batsmanship of Frank Woolley come to mind – a century off the Notts bowlers there one August morning, a blaze of easy hitting against Sussex at Tunbridge Wells.

To have written of May in such a context even a month or two ago would have seemed quite incongruous. He has, however, progressed distinctly as a stroke-maker in recent innings, and the lazy power of his hits over the infield, first bounce and occasionally full pitch, into the crowd, could have belonged to a Woolley playing right-handed. There was the same lack of superfluous movement and mannerism, the same swing of the bat, smooth, full flowing, and straight, yes, and a similar slightly stiff-kneed jaunt between the wickets. Until the bowling was subdued May kept the ball along the floor. Later, on this true and easy wicket, he hit it safely and surely on the rise.

He batted for three hours and there were 25 4s and three 6s in his innings. His first 50, begun when the first two MCC wickets had fallen for 17, took nearly an hour and a half, the second 50 scarcely more than three-quarters of an hour, and the last 74 the same time. Between lunch and tea he made 140. Although he went faster and faster, there was hardly the vestige of a mishit. It was, indeed, an afternoon of pure delight, the memory of which will warm many a winter's evening for those who were there.

Graveney, during the third-wicket partnership, ran May a close second. He, too, played handsomely and forcefully, making his runs mostly by driving. Graveney is celebrating the beginning of his honeymoon, and a century was its deserved and rightful send off; but when he was 12 runs short he hooked a long hop very hard but very straight to Lowson on the edge of the square-leg boundary.

Yardley was lucky in this, and it was also a short ball that Edrich hooked into Hutton's hands at mid-wicket. Yet he was generally the most dangerous as well as (with Wardle) the steadiest of the bowlers. He beat Simpson with a beauty, and floated one in late to Insole for a leg-slip catch. He had taken all six wickets when Robins destroyed any possibility of what might have been a worthy and glorious fluke by declaring in order to give Yorkshire half an hour's batting. This last period passed off without mishap, although Bedser's venomous first over to Hutton could well have had its reward.

There remains just a brief congratulatory line to Cowdrey. Things have not run altogether kindly for him this summer, but he is finishing in a style in keeping with the best opinions as to his promise. There is a sort of collected leisureliness about his play that in a 19-year-old is remarkably impressive.

---

9 SEPTEMBER 1952

BATTING IS SO SIMPLE TO HUTTON

Michael Melford

Hutton to May, May to Hutton – the honours at Scarborough this year have been volleyed from one to the other like a shuttlecock. Even without them this supremely easy wicket, protected from the weather throughout, would hold little comfort for the bowler.

On Saturday it was Hutton's turn, though this time his performance ended on a note of tragedy. He was run out at 99 when trying for a single which would have given him his fourth century in successive innings. With not the least need for hurry, he played the ball gently towards a close cover point and set off. His partner, Wardle, with justification, declined, and the mighty roar of acclamation which a Yorkshire crowd reserves for a Hutton 100 dissolved abruptly into a shocked silence. He stopped, turned, and started back, but Cowdrey's under-arm throw hit the top of the stumps and he was well out.

For nearly two hours the ball had scarcely been away from the centre of the bat in a perfect display against bowling which stayed reasonably steady, despite its lack of variety. Batting is a wonderfully simple business to Hutton at the moment. His partner in a fourth-wicket stand of 156 was Tompkin, who applied himself to the arc between square-leg and mid-off with a vigour and forthrightness that made a nice contrast with Hutton's graceful ease. He too failed on the threshold of glory. After making 98 in just under three hours, he played on off the inside and under edge, much as Graveney had done before him.

Early in the Players' innings of 321 for 7 declared, there was a magnificent catch by Insole in the gully, and one not much easier by Cowdrey towards long leg. Later Smith became the sixth player this summer to achieve the double, something he has accomplished twice before.

Yet for all the pleasant strokes that graced the last two hours' play, there was no escaping the shadow which Hutton's misfortune had cast over the proceedings. These things are not borne lightly at Scarborough.

---

20 JANUARY 1953

SOCCER RISKS BY TEST CRICKETERS

YORKSHIRE ADVICE TO TRUEMAN AND CLOSE

Should Test cricketers endanger their cricket prospects by playing serious football during the winter? Mr T. Taylor, president of Yorkshire CCC, speaking of Close and Trueman, had this to say at the annual meeting of the club in Leeds yesterday: 'The risk of injury that would adversely affect their bowling is so great that I feel sure they would be well advised to take the long view and concentrate upon their cricket.'

Close, who plays centre-forward for Bradford City, has been on the injured list since 20 December, when he hurt a knee against Port Vale. He is now back in training and took part in a practice game yesterday. Trueman, who is at an RAF station in Lincolnshire, played three matches, as an amateur, for Lincoln City reserves before Christmas. He said yesterday: 'After playing in those three games I received so many letters advising me not to risk injury in big football that I had a long talk with my father. We came to the conclusion that if my future in cricket might be as big as many people seemed to think I would do well to concentrate only on the one game.' He added that since then he had played in a few station team games. That would be the only type of football he would play in future.

Close, on the other hand, is hoping to play both cricket and football for a long time. He said yesterday: 'Professional football is as much my life as professional cricket. As for the risks involved, I do not think professional Soccer is as dangerous as a good deal of amateur Soccer, particularly as we get the best possible treatment afterwards. The amateurs often have to look after their injuries themselves. In any case I do not want to be wrapped up in cotton wool.' Close also said that if he did not play Soccer in the winter he would start putting on weight quickly.

Other England cricketers who have been playing football this winter include P.B.H. May, who has turned out regularly for Old Carthusians, and T.E. Bailey. The last-named, a member of the Walthamstow Avenue eleven which won the FA Amateur Cup last season, is out of action at the moment, but through shingles and not injury.

In his speech Mr Taylor specifically mentioned bowling and made no reference to the case of W. Watson, the Yorkshire and England batsman who plays football for Sunderland. In fact, most of the players who have gained outstanding success at both games – among them E. Hendren, J. Arnold, D. Compton, A. Ducat, L.B. Fishlock, C.B. Fry, H. Hardinge and H. Makepeace – have been mainly batsmen. Bailey is one of the few exceptions.

E.W. Swanton writes: Mr Taylor raises a point which will stimulate many a sporting conversation. His views will be respected as coming not only from the Yorkshire president but from a distinguished all-round games player of days gone by. One can well understand the Yorkshire club's anxiety regarding two of their most promising young players, but, as one of them observes, football is his job in winter just as cricket is in summer. It is, so to say, the jam on his bread-and-butter. Apart from the financial aspect, Close is striving, no doubt, to follow in the footsteps of many another all-rounder who has played both games well.

As regards Trueman's case, two points particularly strike one: first, that he seems the type who might become far too heavy if he did not take a good deal of hard exercise – there were those who diagnosed his spells of cramp last year as being due to not getting enough fast bowling; second, that if Service games are what they used to be, he is no less likely to crock himself than in playing League football.

I wonder if one of his contemporaries at the meeting thought to remind Mr Taylor with friendly gentleness that in his University days he was apparently not so fearful of harming his cricket for Cambridge and Yorkshire that he steered clear of hockey. I note that he helped Cambridge to four victories over Oxford in the '90s – and surely Victorian hockey was a pretty robust form of exercise!

10 APRIL 1953

FILM REVIEW

STARS SCORE WELL IN CRICKET COMEDY

Campbell Dixon

Many a footballer has made a fool of himself for 10 minutes and still ended the day a hero. Cochet regularly lost the first two sets. You may hook a golf drive round your neck, find a beautiful lie on the wrong fairway, and still confound your faultless opponent by wickedly winning hole and match.

The cricketer must be made of sterner stuff. One freak ball, a wonder catch in the slips, and he's a spectator for the rest of the match. Only in fiction does Baxter always have a second innings. Sam Palmer, in Terence Rattigan's story, *The Final Test* (London Pavilion), is unlucky off the cricket field as well as on. His son, an aspiring poet, misses one day's play in Sam's last Test because he is scribbling verse. Then he chooses to miss the next because he wants to meet an eminent poet, as if the poetic gift could be picked up by contagion. Such – as Dean Farrar said of Eric when he uttered the expletive 'Dash it' – such are the depths to which this miserable boy had descended.

A good subject for a short story, one might suppose; but a film? Not likely. The initiate, of course, recalls that at a famous Oval Test one spectator dropped dead while another, an eminent player himself, absently gnawed pieces out of his straw hat. But how can this thrill be communicated to the uninitiated?

It can't. Wisely, Mr. Rattigan doesn't try. Instead he shows the impact of the game on other people – the veteran batsman's son, whose loathsome character has already been (inadequately) indicated; the nice little barmaid at the Kennington local, growing impatient with Sam's sentimental stonewalling; the eminent poet whose affluence can only be attributed to his plays; an American doing anthropological fieldwork among the British Islanders, and those star actors, Hutton (L) and Compton (D).

'Wasn't it smashing, seeing Denis?' exclaimed a poet's 14-year-old friend as the audience fled out. And indeed it was – or would have been, if we had seen a little more of the great man in action. What wouldn't we give now for a film of Ranji glancing the fast ones off his eyebrows, and Victor Trumper making that wonderful hundred at Manchester before lunch, and best of all, perhaps, a shot of the Old Man (with soundtrack) squeaking, 'What the hell are you doing, Jonah!' when Ernest Jones sent that terrific bouncer whistling through his beard?

It's a very human and delightful film that Mr Rattigan, Mr R.J. Minney (producer) and Mr Anthony Asquith (director) have made between them. The dialogue is natural and amusing, there is hardly any cricket to bore the soulless, and the acting is very good indeed. Jack Warner plays the veteran whose swansong is cut so very short by an Australian fast bowler. Ray Jackson is the boy poet who never rose above the third eleven, and George Relph, Stanley Maxted and Joan Swinstead are all seen to advantage. Alec Bedser, Godfrey Evans, Cyril Washbrook and Jim Laker are seen, but only just.

---

12 JULY 1953

E.W. Swanton
Lord's, Tuesday

There are excellent cricketers, and there are excellent Test match cricketers, and sometimes there is a great gulf dividing them. It was England's fortune today that there came together in the crisis two men who seemed to grow in stature with the fame of the opposition.

Watson, of Yorkshire, and Bailey, of Essex, became joined on this last morning of the second Test at 20 minutes to one, after Watson and Compton had withstood the Australian bowling for 70 minutes. Despite all the bowling variety that Hassett could call upon; despite the inevitable wear in the wicket, which operated particularly against the left-hander Watson, they declined to be separated until 10 minutes to six, by which time the prospect of an Australian victory, which had seemed when they became joined almost a matter of detail, of margin in time and runs, had receded almost to nothing.

In fact, the second hero, Bailey, followed Watson, the first, quickly into the pavilion, and so it needed another half-hour's resistance by

Brown and Evans, who had waited all day in their pads, with feelings that are not difficult to imagine, to make the door almost, almost safe. When Brown was caught at slip at 27 minutes past six, four balls of Benaud's over remained. An over once begun must be completed, and so technically Australia could still win without even recourse to a hat-trick. Wardle played those last four balls, or rather, he saw them out of harm's way, and so a great Test match ended.

The adjective I submit is admissible because though the level of the cricket waxed and waned, sometimes below the level to be expected of a Test between England and Australia, the match proceeded on a plane of interest and level grappling that was sustained over almost the entire five days.

The only period in which is seemed that one side must win was when England's first three second innings wickets toppled over one another last evening. Even then something suggested that this remarkable game could not end in capitulation and I hope to be excused from saying now that your correspondent did not leave his readers altogether without hope this morning.

It is not the least satisfactory part of the occasion that the spectators who have much to endure in these days had ample value for their money from first to last. There were 137,915 of them in all, and the takings of £57,716 are by some £13,000 the largest at any cricket match anywhere.

There was plenty of leisure during the day to examine the deeds of Watson and of Bailey in the context of Test cricket and the result is illuminating. Watson has played previously in six Tests, Bailey in 16. Watson has made his mark every time and Bailey has scarcely missed in one capacity or another. Each now averages around 45 with the bat, and Bailey has also taken more than 40 wickets.

The scorecard might possibly suggest that England's ambitions need not necessarily have been limited to a draw. But I think the most that the most optimistic patriot allowed himself was the occasional moment of regret that that estimable aggressive innings by Lindwall after tea yesterday had put victory out of reckoning.

Seen in retrospect but for that England could, indeed one might say probably would, have won. As it is a draw will be held by both sides as a fair result, and for England to have achieved it after losing the toss and seeing Australia 190 on the first day before the second wicket fell should be satisfaction enough.

In the Australian camp they may well be asking themselves what more could have been done. Well, they have no reproaches in the field, for there seemed only two half chances in the whole English innings, each off Ring, to a backward short-leg standing within such closeness to the batsman's legs that his grab could have been no more than a reflex action.

When Brown and Evans had the last half-hour to face one's thoughts turned inevitably and fearfully to Lindwall. Hassett must be wondering whether he should have given him a last fling. For myself I feel he should certainly have done so.

Nevertheless it has to be said that it was Ring, bowling down wind from Lindwall's end, who had sent back both Watson and Bailey. Of course, if Australia had had Grimmett, that industrious gnome, to exploit the worn patches it must have needed even more than a Watson and a Bailey to have survived; but there is no end to speculation. If he [Grimmett] by some magic could have been summoned back England must have called for Hobbs and Sutcliffe to assist them!

Whichever of the two possible objectives England might later choose there was from their point of view only one beginning to the day. The collection of runs was unimportant as compared with survival. The first attack came from Lindwall, Johnston assisting, and Lindwall bowled fast and with all the subtlety that differentiates him from other great fast bowlers.

Compton had some fast balls on the body which he thrust down safely off his ribs. Watson one or two outside the off stump which he was lucky not to touch. This was the particular peril of the left-hander, that outside his off stump there lay a stretch of rough ground made by the bowlers' follow-through.

The batting proclaimed with every stroke that in the English camp the watchword was defiance. Yet no reasonable scoring opportunities were lost. When the leg-spinners, Ring and Benaud, appeared the temperature dropped and the spectators enjoyed the luxury of applauding three 4s in an over by Compton, the last an off-drive of the best 1947–8 vintage.

The narrowest squeak for England in the first hour was when Watson padded up and the ball falling rolled back towards the stumps.

Watson kicked it away with only an inch or two to spare. The first hour brought 51 and for the erratic Benaud came back Johnston who at 20 minutes to one broke the partnership with a ball that skidded through to hit Compton's pad at ankle height. From the moment of his taking Hutton's place last evening Compton had not put a foot wrong.

The situation was hand-made for Bailey who expresses his true nature in a long defensive vigil. Never has the dead bat stroke, both forward and back, been played hour after hour with more evident relish. In some stages of his innings Bailey seemed to accept a single with reluctance, as though unwilling to be deprived even momentarily of the bowling. Bailey fitted straight away into the gap left by Compton.

Miller had a spell down wind, including one soaring bumper, and Davidson bowled one very good over just before luncheon to Watson. The two hours' play had fetched 96 runs, from 20 for 3 to 116 for 4. Behind the playing-in period after luncheon lay the fundamental importance of both batsmen being still there when the new ball became due at three o'clock. Hence, 13 runs only in the first half-hour, 20 in the next 20 minutes, then Lindwall and Miller in full onslaught.

Watson and Bailey faced this test as they faced all else, with rigid composure, broken only twice when Bailey was hit painfully by Lindwall on the right hand. I cannot remember when a crowd so revelled in defence for defence's sake. As Bailey got right behind the ball immediately following those that hit him, the crowd applauded with a fervour that in difference circumstances might have greeted a 6.

Lindwall and Miller bowled for 40 minutes, and if any super-sanguine person this afternoon had ever presumed to think in terms of victory their expectations must have been finally quenched when this period was withstood at a cost to Australia of only 12 runs. The hour between three o'clock and four produced 23, including just five singles. At tea the score stood at 183 for four, or 160 short of the target. Afterwards Watson and Bailey proceeded with the composure that had marked their whole stand. Temperamentally it seemed the ideal partnership. Hassett tried everyone and it was his least considered bowler, Davidson, who came nearest to making the separation.

When Watson was 88 he snicked only just short of Hole at slip, and the next ball, pitching in that dangerous area outside the off stump, beat him. In golfing circles it would have been marked off as Ground Under

Repair. At 25 past five Watson went to his hundred sweeping Ring lustily to long leg and it was a sign of zeal and skill that the young Australian fieldsmen had shown throughout this game that Benaud leapt instinctively in to try to conjure a catch out of a ball going like smoke that pitched well in front of him and went smack against the railings in front of the Tavern.

The stand of four hours and 10 minutes ended when Watson apparently snicked a ball from Ring that he seemed not to play at, and which bounced off his pad to slip. A few minutes later Bailey, in his one departure from self discipline, cover-drove a widish ball into the hands of Benaud standing at cover point.

Ring now bowled to Brown and Evans with three slips, but Brown sensed that for him at least the best defence was attack and the rich forcing strokes he made on the off-side served to give the pent-up crowd something indeed to cheer. Further, it took time to fetch the ball back from the boundaries.

Thus no lapse from discretion marred the ending. England's performance all through the day had been alike full of spirit and of character.

---

20 AUGUST 1953

ENGLAND WIN ASHES

At long last the Ashes have come back to England, and the sackcloth has been returned, with suitable compliments, to Australia. The Australians will find it uncomfortable wear, but more bearable in time. Let us hope that they have plenty of time. For the moment it is enough for all true-born Englishmen that the last decisive game has been won with eight wickets in hand. Yet it is not quite enough. If Sir Len Hutton (is this an error?) had not tried to snatch a second run against all possibility and even reasonable hope, England's opening pair might have marched off the field, with their bats tucked under their arms like brief cases, and the game won with not a single wicket down.

It must be a particular satisfaction to Sir (or Mr Len Hutton) that whatever he did was declared by the critics to be wrong, and what he failed to do was declared by the same gentlemen to be obviously right.

In spite of the most determined critical attack, aimed at the on and the off stump, with an occasional bumper, Captain Hutton has produced victory. He may well be pleased. But he must not and he certainly shall not discount the unforgettable contribution of Mr Trevor Bailey. When the clouds darkened for England he was there, like the sun slowly breaking through. 'Slowly' is perhaps the barely operative word for Mr Bailey. He scored runs as a glacier gains inches, with no excitable hurry, but with the inevitability of Nature. There were times, particularly at Trent Bridge, when Mr Bailey appeared to be Nature herself, with pads on and all the time in this world and the next to spare.

As for the Australians, it must be said that never has that Continent sent a more unassuming and more cheerful captain than Mr Hassett; never a more Tennysonian batsman than Mr Morris (though he is tempted to lift his bat too high); never a greater scourge of England than Mr Lindwall; and never a man who so endeared himself to the small boys in the ranks of Tuscany as Mr Keith Miller. Fielding far out, he would have a mouthful of orangeade from the bottle of some small boy. We have been glad to see the Australians and will be glad to visit them in 1954. But we will leave the Ashes at home. That is where they belong.

---

1 MARCH 1954

ENGLAND HAVE CHANCE TO SWING TEST RUBBER

BOTTLES THROWN WHEN WICKET FALLS

E. W. Swanton

Georgetown, British Guiana, Sunday

At half-past two yesterday afternoon, when West Indies were 296 runs behind in the third Test match, their eighth wicket should have fallen and there would then have been only Ramadhin and Valentine, in company with a crippled Holt, to hold up the England bowlers. The easy catch offered by McWatt was dropped, and he and Holt stuck together undeterred by many near things until just after five o'clock.

As the game now stands West Indies are 194 behind and the last pair are together. Thus it is easy to say England's position might have been vastly better. At the same time it is a notable performance on a wicket of such excellence to have got out nine for 241. While on the subject of catches it might be added that two of the major West Indies batsmen fell to brilliant ones which chanced to go to men who had the unusual agility to grasp them.

Tomorrow it may be taken that, barring accidents, Hutton will make West Indies follow on. I do not believe the wicket will go, and it follows that England have a very considerable job on hand to bowl them out again. Still they have now seen that their opponents, when struggling, are different players from when all is plane sailing. Thanks chiefly to Statham tomorrow offers to Hutton's team at least a prospect of swinging the fortunes of rubber.

Unfortunately yesterday's exciting cricket did not end without an outburst of disorder which was not only disagreeable in itself but also, by holding up play for ten minutes, very likely prevented England from capturing the last wicket. The crowd here has a habit of clapping softly and rhythmically when one or two runs are needed to reach a round figure of some kind. When the partnership between McWatt and Holt had added 98 the applause started and it rose to a crescendo as McWatt went for the second run that would have made 100.

It was a hazardous run and a fast pick up and throw to the top of the stumps by May enabled Evans to run out McWatt by perhaps a couple of yards. McWatt, having seen the umpire's signal that he expected, just went on running to the pavilion. There was quite a pause and Ramadhin had got to the wicket before a row in one of the public stands behind square-leg was followed by a rapid barrage of soft drink bottles hurled on to the field behind Menzies, the square-leg umpire. Within a few seconds there were hundreds of them. A few isolated missiles landed on other parts of the field near the boundary and the uproar became such that there was no question for the moment of the game being continued.

The chairman of both the Georgetown Cricket Club and the British Guiana Board of Control, Mr Stanley Jones, came on to the field as mounted police went to ring off the section from which the trouble had come. After a parley with the chairman, Hutton waved his team back to their positions and indicated that, bottles or no bottles, play would go on. This decision undoubtedly saved further disorder which, so a stranger felt, might have led to more serious things, so easily are West Indian feelings roused.

Two derivations offer themselves in explanation of something the like of which has not happened for many years in a Test match, one, to which certain signs undeniably point, is that the demonstration had political origins and was professionally controlled. The other is that it was the culmination among the crowd of the disappointment with the umpire of the uninitiated following who go only to Test matches and know nothing of cricket.

It so happened that earlier in the day Christiani, a great local hero, and Weekes, when he had made 94, remained at the wicket, the one when caught the other when bowled. Both, of course, had a perfect right to wait for the decision which, in each case was given by Menzies. I have no doubt whatsoever that he was correct each time. Whatever the true origin of the trouble one had much sympathy for the sporting community here, who, in all ways, are trying so hard to keep the flag flying in difficult days.

The crowd on this fourth day had that mixture of fortune and incident that is always calculated to make the occasion memorable: thrilling batting by Weekes, extraordinary collapse, and the brave recovery by McWatt with the injured Holt keeping up his end. When Weekes and Christiani continued the West Indies innings at 31 for 3, Weekes took care to play himself in while Christiani soon launched into his strokes, heedless of an occasional missed connection. Statham and Wardle were the bowlers, the latter entering upon a spell that ended only 10 minutes before luncheon. Christiani was twice beaten by Statham, whose sting was slightly less venomous than yesterday, though once he brought a ball back and hit Christiani painfully on the thigh.

Weekes as soon as he warmed up began looking for runs off the back foot. When Laker appeared he lay back and square-cut him gorgeously for four. Wardle kept a good length but now and then was hooked hard through the leg-field. Once again one wondered that Hutton persisted with an inner circle only. Neither Wardle, nor Laker, nor Lock at any time in the day had a man on the boundary, either straight or square, or at deep mid-wicket, or at extra-cover.

After 42 runs had been added Christiani hit the ball back to Wardle slightly to his left but not very hard. Wardle got both hands to the catch and dropped it. For once, though, the batsman's luck was quickly rectified, for next moment Christiani made a crisp on-drive off Laker only a foot or two off the ground. Watson threw himself forward at mid-wicket and made a beautiful catch, rolling over as he completed the dive. Thus West Indies were 78 for 4.

Gomez is sometimes a rickety starter, but today he middled the ball from the first, while Weekes carried on, always giving the bowler cause for hope, but plastering anything short, and now and then thrusting forward into a powerful straight drive. He flashed and missed a time or two, and once played Statham down to Evans with the bottom of the bat. When the 100 went up in two hours a distinguished local commentator remarked that West Indies were 'slightly behind the clock'. Delightfully naive fellow! he should be condemned to watch a few Tests between England and Australia.

---

11 MAY 1954

OBITUARY

GEORGE HIRST

A GREAT ALL-ROUND CRICKETER

George Hirst, the former Yorkshire and England cricketer, who has died, aged 82, was one of the greatest all-rounders in the history of the game. He was born at Kirkheaton, near Huddersfield, and was playing for Yorkshire by the time he was 18. He continued to play for them until 1929, when he was 58.

E.W. Swanton writes: Cricketers of several generations, back to the very small band of his near-contemporaries that survive him, will be saddened by the news of George Hirst's death. He was a magnificent all-round player, one of the best, on the evidence of indisputable figures, who ever lived.

But he was also in the estimation of all who knew him, a great and good man. It was George Hirst and the likes of that generation from whom derived that most over-worn and over-done of all sporting phrases: 'It isn't cricket.' There was a gentle steadfastness, and yet at times a clear outspokenness, about Hirst that proclaimed his honesty and integrity. There was surrounding him a naturalness that made him equally beloved at Eton, where he taught the game for 18 seasons, retiring in 1938, and with such good effect; and among the young men from mine and mill who came, spring after spring, to the Yorkshire nets to try their skill for the county of their birth.

Hirst was in at the first real flowering of Yorkshire cricket. In the early '90s Surrey were supreme. The Yorkshire elevens, for all their native talent, were not much better than a crowd of ill-disciplined roisterers. Lord Hawke's assumption of the captaincy coincided with the arrival of Hirst, Brown and Tunnicliffe. In the 10 years from 1893 Yorkshire won the championship six times, and it is true to say that from that moment Yorkshire cricket has never looked back.

Hirst was an integral member of the side and of most England elevens intervening at any rate on English wickets, until after the First World War. He achieved the cricketer's double of a 1,000 runs and 100 wickets 11 times. Three times he scored 2,000 runs in a season, and once, in his crowning year of 1906, he scored 2,385 and took 208 wickets. That is an all-round feat that has never been approached.

His speciality as a bowler was a fastish left-arm in-swerve, described by one of his victims as being 'as though one was thrown up from cover-point'. Those who lament the change in the law this year, whereby the new ball has been made available only after 200 runs, may be reminded that in Hirst's day there was only one new ball per innings.

Stories cluster round a man held in wide affection. The one of his comment to Wilfred Rhodes as the latter joined him for the last wicket in the famous Jessop Test against Australia at the Oval in 1902, 'We'll get 'em in singles', is plainly apocryphal. A Yorkshireman, if he made any such remark, would have said that they'd get 'em in 'ones'. But the idea of grafting for victory without heroics is, of course, completely in character.

When a young Eton captain, a much better batsman than bowler, sought to obtain from Hirst a post-mortem on a defeat, all he got was, 'Ye bowled too long, and ye bowled too bad.' But he knew, as did all who ever met George Hirst, that it was the plain talk of a man whose soul was in cricket, and who knew no deceit.

---

27 AUGUST 1954

SURREY'S HISTORIC WIN OVER WORCESTER

LOWEST TOTAL IN CHAMPIONSHIP MATCH

Michael Melford

Surrey brought the County Championship to the Oval yesterday for the third year in succession with an historic win over Worcestershire. The match occupied only four hours 50 minutes of actual playing time and Surrey's score of 92 for three declared was enough to give them victory by an innings and 27 runs.

Worcestershire's second innings total of 40 made their tally for the match 65 for 19 wickets (one batsman retired hurt) and meant that only 157 runs were scored in the whole match. This is the lowest aggregate for a completed match ever recorded in the County Championship. It is the lowest in England since 1878 when MCC (33 and 19) lost to the Australians (41 and 12 for one). It is the lowest this century anywhere in the world.

Thus Surrey reached the climax of a wonderful run of devastating cricket and, as they will be the first to admit, good fortune. The run began on July 28 when they stood eighth in the table, 46 points behind Yorkshire with two matches in hand.

On the wet wickets that have persisted since, they have won eight out of nine matches. They have won the toss when it most mattered, suffered less than their rivals from the floods, yielded only the most junior of their four illustrious bowlers to the Test match and enjoyed a remarkably easy fixture list.

If one enumerates the smiles of fortune first, it is not to decry what on the soft wickets of the last month must have been the most powerful county side of recent years. In August alone they have won five matches in two days. In the bowling has lain the most obvious strength. It has been the ability of Bedser, Laker, Lock, Loader – and on one notable occasion Surridge himself – to work quickly in what little play there has been that has told this month.

Only 10 days ago at Cheltenham Surrey seemed to be foiled when at lunch on the last day it was raining hard. Derbyshire had already won and Surrey had not even first innings points until then. But there was a break in the rain for an hour and a half, Surridge strode forth to take most of the last eight Gloucestershire wickets and the 12 points were won with half-an-hour to spare.

To their bowling prowess Surrey have been able to add greatly improved fielding and solid batting right through the order. Stewart and Barrington, too, have brought in a new agility and considerable catching powers. In the few times I have seen him, Barrington has run three batsmen out.

The batting successes of these young men and of Clark and Constable have made up for the comparative shortage of runs recently from May. Further down the order the side has owed much to some invaluable contributions from Laker, one of which won a close match at Kettering, and the consistent good form of McIntyre.

The hour which Surrey needed to finish off Worcestershire yesterday was an eventful one. It began with Richardson being caught at the wicket off Laker's second ball which turned and leapt up as he tried to withdraw his bat. This was followed by a curious incident in which Umpire Cooke refused an appeal thinking it was for a catch at the wicket, called over and walked away. His colleague, Lee, at square-leg had seen Hughes hit his wicket and after a pause informed Cooke who at once changed his decision.

For the rest the story was as on Wednesday, of fine bowling, this time by Bedser and Laker (Lock was not needed), of an unpleasant but not impossible wicket and of thoroughly bad batting. There was also a difficult slip catch which Laker made look easy. Devereux, one of the few batsmen to cope adequately, had to retire with a suspected fractured finger, and the last pair came together at 26. At this point Loader was given a chance to become the fourth Surrey bowler to take 100 wickets this season.

After Yarnold had hit the only two fours of the innings and earned glory by becoming the only Worcestershire batsman in either innings to reach double figures, the chance was taken. Just after half-past 12 Bedser at first slip held an awkward catch with majestic calm and the Championship was won.

There followed much cheering, a speech to a crowd of 3,000 by Surridge, whose leadership has been as effective and ebullient as ever – and then the Oval was left deserted, ironically in glorious late summer sunshine.

I AUGUST 1956

LAKER TAKES 19 WICKETS FOR 90 RUNS

AUSTRALIA BEATEN BY INNINGS

E. W. Swanton

Old Trafford, Tuesday

For many nervous hours since last Friday evening it had seemed that England would be robbed of victory in the Fourth Test match. But Manchester expiated its sins of weather this afternoon, and it was in bright sunshine tempering the wind that the game ended in an innings win, which meant the safe-keeping of the Ashes until MCC next sail in their defence two years from now.

The only proper formal announcement of the result is that J.C. Laker defeated Australia by an innings and 170 runs. Unprecedented things are always happening in cricket because it is so charmingly unpredictable a pastime. But now and then occurs something of which one feels certain there can be no repetition or bettering.

Laker followed his capture of 9 first innings wickets with all 10 in the second. What is left in the vocabulary to describe and applaud such a tour de force? It is quite fabulous. Once at Johannesburg on the mat, S.F. Barnes, still happily with us at a ripe 83, took 17 for 159. That analysis topped the list in Test matches until this evening – when Laker, wheeling relentlessly on, left the statistical gentry without another comparison to make or another record to be knocked down.

Hedley Verity took 15 for 104 after the thunderstorm at Lord's in '34. Wilfred Rhodes, another old hero still listening to the play, even if he cannot now see it, got a like number at Melbourne half a century ago.

In the recent past, Alec Bedser got out 14 Australians for 90 at Trent Bridge on their last visit. Great figures. Great deeds. But Laker in 51.2 overs has added a 10 for 53 to his 10 for 88 against this same Australian side for Surrey. And in this Test he has actually taken 19 for 90. Laker's first innings performance was phenomenal enough, but its merit was perhaps clouded by the deficiencies of the Australian batting, as also by the palaver over the condition of the wicket.

There was no room whatever for argument regarding his bowling today. He bowled 36 overs, practically non-stop except for the taking of the new ball, all the time attacking the stumps and compelling the batsman to play, never wilting or falling short in terms either of length or direction. Nor was he mechanical. Each ball presented the batsman with a separate problem. Laker never let up and neither for an instant could his adversary.

It is, of course, scarcely less remarkable that while Laker was building up new heights of fame at one end Lock was toiling just as zealously, albeit fruitlessly, at the other. On a wicket on which one famous cricketer captured 19 wickets the other, scarcely less successful and dangerous, taking one day with another, in 69 overs had 1 for 106.

Of course if the gods had been kind Lock could have taken more. He was not, in cold fact, at his best, and if he is suffering the reaction now from all his hard bowling in Pakistan it is not to be wondered at. Still, the comparison between the figures is in one sense unarguable evidence of Laker's great performance. If the wicket had been such a natural graveyard for batsmen it is inconceivable that Lock, even below his peak, even with the other arm tied to his side, would not have taken more than one wicket.

Applause for Laker, and applause also in a scarcely lesser strain for McDonald, who, in his long vigil, rose to the occasion for Australia and fought as hard as any man could do to win his side the respite of a draw. So long as McDonald was in the odds were still fairly balanced. When he was beaten at last directly after tea the latter-end batsmen carried on in the same spirit, and there was a bare hour to go when Maddocks, the number eleven, played back and slightly across to Laker, fell leg-before and advanced up the wicket to shake the hero by the hand.

One of the Australian party summed up the day, as the crowd that massed round the pavilion dispersed and Laker, glass in hand, had turned from the balcony to the dressing-room by saying: 'Well, it was a good scrap after all.' There was relief in his voice, just as there was jubilation in the surrounding English faces.

The captains having formally disagreed, there was a delay of 10 minutes before play was continued this morning. The wicket was just about as sluggish as yesterday. McDonald and Craig, by high-class defensive play, withstood the session of an hour and 50 minutes without many moments of difficulty. They played themselves in against Bailey and Laker, who were subsequently relieved by Lock and Oakman.

Runs being of no object, except possibly to get the two batsmen to the ends they preferred, and the ball being hard to force away, the Test became one of the batsmen's concentration and judgment as to length. In this neither was found wanting, and it cannot be said that England much looked like breaking through. May gave Oakman a try, probably because from his unusual height he might get an off-spinner to lift. He kept the ball well up on the off-side and induced some strokes off the front foot into the covers. Oakman, however, is not a digger-in, and is a relatively better bowler on a hard wicket.

May took the new ball as soon as he could, which was at a quarter to one, Bailey brought back one or two and found Craig's inside edge, and Statham and he perhaps held out slightly more hopes than the spinners. Just before lunch Evans and Lock, those tireless propagandists, when the latter was bowling tried their hardest by expression and gesture to suggest that the dormant pitch was stirring. But McDonald and Craig came in calm and unscathed, having, incidentally, added 28 runs.

There were early signs after lunch that the batsmanship might be more severely tested. Craig was twice beaten by lifting balls from Lock, who naturally enough was sharing the bowling with Laker. After a quarter of an hour Craig went back to the latter and was lbw to an off-break. Thus he retired full of honour after an innings of four hours and 20 minutes, in which his stature had grown surely and steadily. The breaking of the stand was the signal for the second Australian collapse of the game. Within half-an-hour Mackay, Miller and Archer had all followed Craig, all to Laker, and all for ducks.

Granted the ball was doing a little more during this phase in answer to bursts of sun, these batting failures underlined the worth and value of the third-wicket partnership. Where before the judgment of length and direction had been good enough to ensure a smooth, well-considered defensive stroke, now the new batsmen were floundering about and either using their pads or offering a last-minute jab.

Mackay was surrounded by slips, silly mid-off, and short-legs, six in all within a five-yard radius. One could hardly see how he could survive, for in going forward he plays so far in front of the front leg. This had been evident against the slow bowlers even while he was putting up his celebrated resistance at Lord's. Now, Mackay probed out, and edged a short sharp catch to Oakman, the middle of the slips. I have never seen a batsman whose value rose and fell so abruptly according to the state of the wicket. On a good one he wants blasting out. When the ball is doing anything it is hard to see how he can last five minutes. As it was, Mackay today, like Harvey on Friday, bagged a pair.

One expected Miller to try to shift Laker's close-leg fieldsmen as he had done at Leeds. Instead he seemed intent on fending away with the pads, using the bat only as a last resort. It was this manoeuvre which undid him, for he decided at the last moment he must put the bat to a yorker on the leg stump, missed it, and was bowled. It was an innings singularly out of character. Laker had Archer pushing out at an off-break and steering it round the corner. McDonald, at the other end, steady and more or less serene, thus saw Australia's barometer drop from the healthy regions of 114 for 2 to 130 for 6.

He himself, it so happened, during this phase was almost exclusively opposing Lock, who was giving him the chance to indulge his feelings every now and then with a short ball which was usually hit for runs. Benaud now got stuck with McDonald, determination in every line, fastidious care also, for he took guard sometimes once or twice an over as though suspicious that Evans might have surreptitiously moved the position of the stumps. Benaud also gardened assiduously, which was prudent enough, seeing that the ball was taking turf. It earned him a little mildly derisory applause.

May did his best to scotch the threat of a McDonald–Benaud stand by changing round his main spinners, introducing Bailey and giving Oakman another spell which he was scarcely able to justify. Benaud was nearly yorked by Bailey. However, that was as near another wicket as anyone could come. McDonald was seemingly impervious, immovable, and this pair came in to tea, having stayed together an hour and 20 minutes. Australia were still breathing.

But McDonald did not take root afterwards and it was the inevitable Laker who got the most valuable wicket of all. This was a sharp off-break which for once went too quickly for McDonald, who edged it to the sure hands of Oakman in the middle position just behind square. So ended a valiant effort lasting without a chance for more than five hours and a half.

Lindwall made a steady partner for Benaud and at five o'clock these two looked ominously settled and determined: there was still Johnson and Maddocks to come. It was not yet 'in the bag'. But Benaud now went back where he might have gone forward and was bowled middle-and-off stumps or thereabouts. Twenty minutes later Lindwall, like so many before him, fell in the leg-trap. Then, with Johnson looking on, Maddocks made his entry and speedy, gracious exit. So the game ended. The post-mortems no doubt will linger on. But whatever is added one thing cannot be gainsaid: Laker was magnificent.

---

8 SEPTEMBER 1956

OBITUARY: C.B. FRY

Harry S. Altham, Treasurer, MCC

Had Charles Fry, who has died aged 84, been born half-a-century later, he must surely have been for some years a focus for all the resources of modern sporting publicity. As a boy at Repton, he had, before he was 17, played for the Casuals in the FA Cup, had captained both cricket and football teams and had twice won the personal athletic trophy.

At Oxford he had set up a world record for the long jump, made a century in the University match, played four years against Cambridge in Association football and had been prevented only by injury from gaining still a fourth Blue as wing three-quarter in a very strong Oxford XV. A few years later, in 1902, he played for Southampton against Sheffield United in the final of the FA Cup on a Saturday in April and on the following Monday made 82 runs at the Oval for London County against Surrey.

Most of these runs were made in partnership with W.G., with whom three years earlier he had opened the innings for England against Australia in what was his own first Test match and 'the Old Man's' last. In 1912 he captained England to victory in the only Triangular Tournament ever played against Australia and South Africa.

These years have been called the Augustan age of English batting; certainly as a spectacle the game can never have been more worth watching; nor have there ever been, before or since, so many batsmen who could without serious criticism have been chosen to play for their country, or who, if they played and made runs, would have been more certain to give pleasure to those who watched them.

Among these Charles Fry was one of the elect. He could not rank with his great friend 'Ranji' for wizardry, with Jessop for sensation, or with MacLaren, Jackson, Spooner or Johnnie Tyldesley for ease and brilliance of stroke. But in the making of runs — after all, the primary function of batting — and in making on all wickets, the bowlers opposed to him look, to use a phrase of his own coining, 'plainly playable', he could hold his own with any rival.

In advance of most of his generation he relied for defence almost entirely on back play rather than on the 'bridge-building' forward stroke which had for so long been *de rigueur*. He was therefore, especially on turning wickets and against the best bowling, far more secure than his fellows. In attack he could play all the strokes, but he was above all a driver, hitting the over-pitched ball past or over mid-off, the bowler and mid-on with certainty and truly formidable power.

In all first-class matches he made over 30,000 runs with an average of over 50 and it must be remembered that he did not play so long or so regularly as many others. His greatest season was 1901, in which he scored 3,147 runs and made 13 hundreds, six of them in succession. But Fry's athletic distinction, unparalleled in its versatility, reflected only one side of an astonishing endowment. Elected senior scholar at Wadham on a roll that included F.E. Smith, later Lord Birkenhead, he gained a first in Classical Moderations, though later a variety of distractions denied him similar distinction in 'Greats'.

After a short spell on the staff at Charterhouse he spent some years in Fleet Street, first as athletic editor to that admirable boys' magazine, the *Captain*, and later as creator, director and editor of *C.B. Fry's Magazine*. Two of his books, written in collaboration, *Great Batsmen* and *Great Bowlers and Fielders*, though now more than 50 years old, not only present an incomparable and fascinating gallery of a great generation of players in action, but still constitute the most acute analysis of cricket mechanics ever achieved. His later study on *Batsmanship* carried that analysis to still greater depths.

In 1930 he initiated a new style in cricket reporting, in the form of a running commentary, which made him within a month the most eagerly read and most widely acclaimed of cricket journalists. But it was neither in his writing nor even in his athletic achievements that he found the chief interest of his own life and made the greatest contribution to the lives of others. In 1908, on the death of Charles Hoare, the banker who founded it, he took over, as an act of faith and in circumstances of great uncertainty and indeed hazard, the control of the training ship *Mercury* on the Hamble.

There, until his retirement a few years ago and in perfect partnership with his wife, who died in 1946, he devoted all his great resources of mind and personality to developing its establishment and to the training of generations of boys for service in the Royal and Merchant Navies. He was an honorary captain in the Royal Naval Reserve. Surely the long retrospect of his *Mercury* command must have given him the best of all reasons for the title which he chose for his lively and challenging autobiography – *Life Worth Living*.

---

30 MAY 1957

WEST INDIAN SPECTATORS

E. W. Swanton

A last word on spectators, the West Indian variety rather than the home grown. We saw and heard quite a lot of them when the last team was here seven years ago. Since then many more thousands have come over from the islands, settling especially in London and Birmingham.

There was more fun and gusto in cricket at the time Englishmen introduced it to the West Indian colonies. They have retained what we have tended to lose. There have been suggestions, I see, that there is something indecorous in this West Indian enthusiasm. Personally I find it enlivening and so I believe do the majority of their fellow spectators.

The West Indians will have plenty to say for themselves in these Tests, and if anyone thinks them over-exuberant at the fall of an English wicket let him note also how generously they applaud a fine English stroke, or a piece of brisk fielding. The West Indian only wants to see plenty of action. My goodness, do not we all!

ENGLAND V. WEST INDIES

E.W. Swanton

Edgbaston, Tuesday

This has been a fabulous Test Match. Writing a few moments after watching Goddard and young Smith fighting for their lives against Laker and Lock, with the English fieldsmen clustered round them like bees round a honeypot (and with the steel calypso band performing with smiles of relief on their faces in front of the pavilion), I cannot summon the memory or the knowledge of any previous game wherein the fortunes have changed with such utter completeness from one side to the other.

At noon yesterday May and Cowdrey came together, as they did at Sydney three years ago, knowing that only a day-long stand or thereabouts could bring England back into the match. A day and a half later West Indies surveyed a scoreboard showing 62 for 7, thanking their stars for an escape from defeat which could surely be measured only in terms of minutes.

Laker and Lock did not have the sort of wicket to bowl on which filled the Australians with dread last summer. Each is a master of using what little help a wearing wicket affords. They set the West Indies batsmen indeed a testing problem enough. The root of the collapse this evening was, however, psychological. The change in events, catastrophic from their angle combined with the long weary spell in the field, made them always likely victims. In such circumstances two hours and 40 minutes can seem an eternity.

The scoresheet will make it seem that England declared too late and I believe they could have come in with complete safety half-an-hour earlier than they did, in fact when Cowdrey was out. At this point West Indies could have been asked to bat for just over three hours, with 237 runs standing between themselves and victory. Yet in retrospect a draw seems perhaps the fairest answer, bearing in mind the various West Indian injuries which dislocated them so seriously at the crucial time.

For instance they bowled with the same ball for more than seven hours since they had no one left to use a new one. In any case no one who has any conception of the strain imposed by an innings of 10 hours will be disposed to blame May himself for not declaring earlier. With him I daresay times and figures were a blur in the mind. May's batting, taking all the circumstances into consideration, deserves all the superlatives so sadly overworked which are part and parcel of a modern Test. It was an excellent innings from the technical viewpoint, an exemplary one in point of responsibility. This is the aspect, of course, which merits most praise.

George Geary at Charterhouse taught May the basic things of batsmanship and so made the sound foundations of his cricket. But the self-discipline which schools and directs his play is something he had to develop himself, albeit with the example of others to help. Here the name that suggests itself naturally is Hutton on whom May has based not only his batting on these occasions, but to a considerable extent his uncompromising philosophy of Test cricket.

It may be added that only four Englishmen have played bigger Test innings than this 285: Hutton, Hammond, Sandham and R.E. Foster, the latter by two runs. As a captain's effort, needless to say, it stands alone. As to Cowdrey's innings, it had all the attributes of his captain in an only slightly less degree. His qualities have been known and his potentialities realised ever since his notable exploits in Australia.

Now that this remarkable innings has come in a Test at home he must surely take the unquestioned place in the England side for which his talents qualify him. English prospects in the series are that much the better for his success. When the morning began the point of consuming interest was, of course, what effect the rain would have on the wicket. There had not been a great deal, but it was enough at any rate to persuade May to use the heavy roller before the start.

Goddard started with Sobers bowling an exploratory over to see whether the left-arm spin would bite and the ball lift. However, after he had bowled a harmless over outside the off stump and Atkinson from the other end had suggested that the odd one might cause trouble, Ramadhin took over from his usual end into the breeze.

In successive overs Ramadhin beat both men with leg-breaks. And when he turned the off-break he several times found the inside edge of the bat. However, since Ramadhin had neither a gully on the one side or any short-legs either in front on behind on the other, the batsmen were spared the dangers of the cocked defensive stroke. Atkinson did have a slip, a backward short-leg and a short mid-on, the latter not dangerously close. Of course Ramadhin and Atkinson were both desperately tired men when the day started and their bowling gave signs of it, even if their accuracy still demanded respect. At both ends the performance was almost mechanical.

The several moments of difficulty which both May and Cowdrey encountered were a mere fraction of what a fresh Laker and Lock might have achieved with the faint vestige of help from the wicket, which is all they ever need. May and Cowdrey both settled in as though they were simply continuing their great effort of yesterday, apparently quite fresh; two remarkably fit, strong, temperate young men. The only difference in the picture was that now Cowdrey played at least an equal part in the scoring.

To be precise he went slightly the faster. In the first half-hour, which might have been such a nervous time, they scored 20; in the second half-hour 20 more. In the second hour the speed was slightly stepped up. All the time Ramadhin and Atkinson bowled. By now the former's field consisted of a circle of nine men. All more or less equidistant both from the bat and from each other. It was just after one o'clock when Cowdrey reached his hundred. May immediately went up to him and presumably either propounded or agreed to Cowdrey pushing along faster.

We now had some handsome off-side strokes from Cowdrey, in celebration of his first Test hundred in England and his third in all. Before lunch the stand exceeded the 338 which Worrell and Weekes hammered out of a precisely identical England attack on the jute mat of Trinidad three years ago. When lunch gave everyone pause to examine the situation of the match England were 179 runs ahead with the same number of wickets intact as they had had at noon yesterday. In other words it was a question of when May would cry 'Enough'.

A general estimate seemed to be around three o'clock, if not before, leaving the England bowlers a full three hours' work and the West Indies out of any practicable hope of getting the runs. But May wanted a lot yet. In fact England batted a further 70 minutes, until twenty past three, thrashing 116 runs in this time of which the captain himself summoned the energy to hit 54. Ramadhin still went through the motions of bowling, floating about for all the world like a sleepwalker. Cowdrey arrived at 150, May at 250, the 500 appeared, the partnership became 400. At last, soon after Ramadhin had handed the ball to Smith, Cowdrey on-drove the latter into the hands of one of Goddard's three substitutes, Asgarali, at deep mid-wicket.

Thus ended the partnership for England's fourth wicket, 40 runs short of the 451 that Bradman and Ponsford picked up off England at the Oval in 1934. If May and Cowdrey had been interested in such things they could have buckled to and eclipsed this particular figure without trouble. They had been in together eight hours and 20 minutes; 500 minutes wherein supreme concentration, good judgment and strength of purpose had never wavered.

Evans was promoted now and he and May did more or less what they liked with the flagging bowlers. May's activities included two long, soaring sixes to wide long-on off Sobers. Evans cut and carved and ran for everything, and hard though the West Indies still strove in the field they could not staunch the flow. Just before he declared May hit a stinging chance off a long hop to Alexander, fielding substitute at square-leg. Apart from a half-chance which flew off deep mid-on's fingers just after lunch this was only the second catch to go to hand from May's bat, a difficult catch behind the wicket when he had made 119 being the other.

The West Indies second innings started on a note of disaster and continued in suspense and uncertainty. Where a sober start was necessary both openers were back before the shine was off the ball. Kanhai got a bouncer in Trueman's first over which he tried to hook. He hit the ball high towards long-leg and Close, coming in fast, made a very good catch about knee high. Immediately Trueman hit Pairaudeau amidships with fast full-toss. Pairaudeau took a moment to collect himself, but in the same over was bowled by a fast yorker.

One could not dissociate the one happening from the other. Trueman down wind was bowling with speed and hostility, but he soon gave way to Laker, Lock having already taken over from Statham. Having been beaten twice by Lock, Sobers clumped him twice bravely for four. He at least was prepared to keep trouble at arm's length. But Sobers is young in this sort of situation and presently he was caught at short-leg off bat and pads. Tea came at 26 for 3 after 50 minutes' batting, with Weekes undefeated and looking resourceful and determined.

In turn he saw both his distinguished colleagues depart. Each fell to the bristling short-leg field which only Weekes from now onwards sought to disperse. Both Worrell and Walcott were lame and the batting of each naturally suffered. Smith, the hero of the first innings, now joined Weekes and for half-an-hour the sixth wicket stood. Then at 10 minutes to six Weekes got a brute of a ball from Lock, pitching in the footmarks of the follow-through.

Weekes tried to whip his bat away from one that spun viciously across him only to see Trueman make a fine catch within three yards of the bat in the gully. Now came Goddard to face Lock, his left-hand-edness helping him in that Lock was spinning in to him and by going forward he could stave off a lot of trouble with his pads. There was much appealing. There were also two chances in one over, Smith being missed off Laker at deep mid-on high up by May and very close indeed by Trueman in the middle of the leg-trap.

It was almost 25 past six when young Smith tried his tactic once too often. He had batted over an hour for 5, an innings less glamorous than his first, indeed, but of infinite value. Atkinson, in what must have been the last over, relieved his feelings with a four to long-on off Laker and a few moments later walked in with his captain, the latter after 40 minutes still not out.

If the result was appropriate it was fitting, too, that the West Indies captain should be there at the death.

---

18 JANUARY 1958

INNINGS DECLARED

Mr Len Hutton has decided to call his innings closed, and retire from first-class cricket. The news comes as a rude shock, until one recalls that he will be 40 in June, and that the life of an international cricketer is too strenuous now to prolong it into middle age. Another summer or two might dim the lustre of his fame; it is typical of his prudent and realistic outlook that he should prefer to go now. He has left a profound mark on the game, and not only as one of its most accomplished batsmen. As the first professional cricketer to captain an England team in Test matches, since the almost primeval days of Arthur Shrewsbury and Alfred Shaw, he has conducted a social revolution, and has done so with such success and good-humoured dignity that there can never be again serious opposition in principle to the choice of a professional captain. Not, of course, any professional, any more than any amateur. Mr Hutton's captaincy, like his batsmanship, was exceptional in kind. It was, so to say, highly professional captaincy; lacking something in dash, in inspiration or even imagination; but infinitely knowledgeable, resourceful, and prudent, so that (with the disastrous exception of the Brisbane Test) his errors gave very little away, and his successful strokes were relentlessly pressed home. It was not a method to make for easy popularity; yet he was a popular captain, too. His own integrity and personal modesty and Yorkshire humour shone through the chain mail which he put on for the battle, and won him friends as well as matches.

---

19 JUNE 1958

YORKSHIRE STRUGGLE TO LEAD SURREY

MAY TOP SCORER WITH 34:
MATCH COULD REACH DEFINITE RESULT TODAY

E.W. Swanton

The Oval, Monday

J.C. Laker deserved better all round than he has had so far in his benefit match against Yorkshire: better of both sides, whose cricket with few exceptions was scarcely worthy of the occasion, better of the crowd which was relatively thin, and, not least, better of the weather prophets, who announced that rain 'would' affect the London area during the day.

They are very positive, these forecasts, and, not for the first time, they were today positively wrong, to the detriment of Jim Laker, who might well maintain that many more would have come if they had been given any prospect of a fine day. Yorkshire in the person of their acting-captain, Watson, put Surrey in, and after a protracted dog-fight this evening struggled to three figures and so gained a first innings lead.

As the game stands there is nothing in it, and a full day tomorrow could see the result go either way. At least, so long as the two sides do not grow mortally afraid of the other taking twelve points, there should be an interesting and full day. The wicket today was no bed of roses. Now and then the ball lifted steeply, and it could be turned regularly enough, though the spin did not often work quickly.

Runs were to be had if they were worked for, or if a hitter had a slice or two of luck and was prepared to hit straight. By the standards to be expected of champions and aspiring champions the batsmanship, however, lacked judgment and stature. The early cricket did little to make up to the crowd for their lost first day. While the wicket was not much use to the faster bowlers it was difficult to force the ball away. Moreover one of them, Platt, as his field and action proclaimed, was a purveyor of what has been well described as in-slant.

Platt propelled the new ball at medium-fast pace from the outside edge of the crease, with only three fielders on the off-side. Delivered at this angle the good length straight ball that pitches on the line of the leg stump passes outside the batsman's body. With various leg-slips deployed in a semicircle behind his shoulder there is little positive the batsmen can do. A good deal of what passes for in-swing bowling is merely of this dreary, straight, slanting kind.

At length, after 20 minutes, Platt did bowl a ball right up, starting outside the off-stump; Fletcher still not off the mark, made to drive, the ball swung in, and Fletcher hit over it and was bowled. There was more than one moral to be drawn from this piece of cricket. With both players and spectators in mind I hope that with all the distinguished coaching resources at their disposal Yorkshire may take this young man's method to pieces, assuming they think there is enough natural ability to work on, and start him off again on different principles.

Trueman's spell at the other end was more interesting in several respects, especially in view of Thursday's Test match. Hitherto, since his return after injury a week ago, I gather Trueman has bowled a few overs only, at medium-pace from a shortened run. This morning his spell of seven overs was delivered from a full run, and was pretty accurate. There was little response from the wicket and there was no point in pressing for extra pace. So far as it went this was a promising bowl. With greater events in mind one was sorry it could not have been repeated two or three times.

The Yorkshire catching, at the wicket and round the bat, was not as clever as usual, and the second wicket, thanks to certain escapes, lasted for an hour before Clark was caught at short-leg from a ball he would probably have negotiated if he had gone forward. Clark had played better than anyone was to do, apart from May. Constable, after a run of good fortune, hit one back very hard into the pit of Appleyard's stomach, whereupon May, monopolising the bowling, saved Surrey from further misfortune before luncheon.

In the afternoon the last seven wickets went down for 40 runs in an hour and a quarter. Only May could claim that he had been undone by the wicket. Eric Bedser pushed one back to Illingworth, the bowler. Swetman, with pads half as large as himself, was lbw missing a half-volley. Laker, failing to connect with another, was bowled off his pads. On Surridge's arrival at 68 for six, May launched forth. His judgment of length had been so sound and his stroke-execution so admirable, that he had scarcely been in difficulty.

The Surrey innings, with the hand of death upon it, lingered for a further 15 minutes after May's departure. Yorkshire had not needed to bowl particularly well. Indeed, the arch-critic of their bowling opined that Appleyard and Wardle bowled either too fast or too short, or both. The batting indeed, for a championship side, looked for the most part thoroughly undistinguished. The first few balls of the Yorkshire innings were alarming, despite the heavy roller, for Bedser made them stand up and bite great chunks out of the wicket.

Whether or not on this account, Close began at once to swing at anything well up to him, and with an odd slice or two of luck got Yorkshire away to a fair start. When Lock appeared Close apparently farmed him and hit cheerfully with the spin. In 50 minutes before tea Surrey took one wicket for 36, the beneficiary appropriately enough collecting it in his first over. Afterwards Eric Bedser, simulating Laker in method and manner, had Close caught by Swetman from a ball well pitched up that the small wicketkeeper took shoulder high.

This was a very nasty one, but by this time the horrors at first envisaged by Alec Bedser had proved largely illusory. As to Close, his innings was worth more than face value. He remains what he has always been, an interesting enigma, potentially an England cricketer every day of the week. Potentially.

Watson and Taylor fell almost together, and at 71 for 5 the first innings lead could still have gone either way when Wardle arrived. Inevitably came another light episode for the crowd: Wardle v. Lock. The first ball missed the stumps by a coat of paint at roughly the moment Wardle was finishing his swing to square-leg. The next he swept for 4. A single took him against Laker. Wardle clove the air five times successively and connected with the sixth.

Wardle now began to bat aggressively, but rationally, aiming over mid-off instead of behind his ear. Every now and then he decided, before the ball was out of the hand, to run out and drive, and two or three hits flew over the soft, lush outfield like a shot from a gun. After his beginning, Wardle used his judgment as well as his fine eye. Why he begins so clownishly is a mystery. Yorkshire in retrospect won their lead by the fraction of an inch by which his first ball missed the stumps.

---

20 JUNE 1958

D.R. JARDINE DIES AT 57

Michael Melford

Douglas Robert Jardine, who has died aged 57, captained England in the 'Bodyline' Test series in Australia in 1932–3.

The general public will remember him mostly for his share in that England victory, for his austere approach and his uncompromising use of the fast bowling of Larwood and Voce, but he was also a cricketer of outstanding ability, the leading amateur batsman of his day. He made 35 centuries in first-class cricket.

Jardine evolved the bodyline policy himself and in Larwood had the perfect instrument to implement it. He did not himself agree that short bowling at the body constituted physical intimidation of the batsman. In a book later he described such charges as 'stupid and patently untruthful'. When he himself was confronted with it he did not flinch. One of his most famous innings was his 127 for England at Old Trafford in 1933 against the West Indian fast bowlers, Constantine and Martindale.

However, the later matches of the 1932–3 tour were played in an atmosphere of unparalleled tension and hostility which induced a series of cables between the Australian Board of Control and MCC. The first Australian cable stated that bodyline bowling had assumed such proportions that physical defence of the body was becoming the first consideration. MCC replied that they had all confidence in Jardine.

They confirmed their confidence not only by appointing him captain in India but by congratulating him when he returned from Australia on his able and determined captaincy. In time, however, official and public opinion began to change until bodyline was generally accepted as having been a pernicious influence on the game.

The son of M.R. Jardine, of Oxford University and Middlesex, Jardine was one of the few Scots to reach the highest class of cricket. Born in Bombay, he was educated at Winchester, where he was three years in the eleven, and at Oxford University. Six feet tall and strong of wrist and forearm, he was a graceful, thoroughly sound batsman, particularly fluent on the off-side.

He won his Blue at Oxford as a Freshman in 1920 and played against Cambridge in 1921 and 1923. A knee injury kept him out of the side in 1922. After he began to play for Surrey, Jardine improved steadily and played for England for the first time against West Indies in 1928. In all, he played 22 times, the last 11 times as captain.

In Australia in 1928–9 he averaged 61, scoring centuries in his first three matches, but in the next two English seasons played little first-class cricket. The MCC team which Jardine led in Australia in 1932–3 curbed Bradman at the height of his power, played some of the best cricket ever shown by a touring side and won the series 4–1. Yet the bitterness surrounding the tour robbed the victory of much of its sweetness.

Jardine returned to England a figure of controversy. He had succeeded P.G.H. Fender as captain of Surrey in 1932 and he led them again in 1933. But while in India next winter captaining another MCC side he resigned and dropped out of first-class cricket. In 1939 he was appointed cricket correspondent of the *Daily Telegraph*, but by September of that year was on active service with the Royal Berkshire Regiment. He had been an active Territorial.

In recent years he had been President of the Oxford University CC. He had played for the Authors in the annual match in Vincent Square against the Publishers.

Jardine was a barrister and a director of several companies. He was taken ill with a tropical fever while visiting Salisbury, Southern Rhodesia, to inspect land he owned there. He married in 1934 Miss M.I. Peat who survives him with a son and three daughters.

———

9 DECEMBER 1958

122 RUNS IN DAY EQUALS THE SLOWEST EVER

CRICKET LIKE THIS POSES QUESTION: HOW LONG WILL PEOPLE WATCH?

E.W. Swanton

Brisbane, Monday

On the point of half past five this evening, with the ground seemingly emptying at the rate of thousands a minute, Mackay bowled the most innocent of innocent maidens to Bailey.

It was the sixth such maiden Mackay had bowled in seven overs, and it had its own macabre significance, for it ensured that this third day of the First Test would at least equal, in point of runs scored, the slowest in history. Rather more than two years ago at Port Elizabeth, with the South Africans batting virtually all day, we saw five hours 50 minutes go by while 122 runs found their way into the scorebook.

The wicket then was difficult, with the ball keeping extremely low. Here the conditions were ideal for batting. But the day's play in Australia is restricted to five hours, so it is a moot point in which continent the 'record' morally lies. At all events, those at home will need little persuading that what we watched here today was no skylark.

The position of the game at close of play, as compared with this morning, has shifted somewhat towards England, who now, with eight wickets in hand, find themselves 40 runs on. Someone should attempt a parody of the famous Harrow song – with due apologies, of course, to the school.

After one has complimented the England team for fighting back with their usual tenacity, it remains a solemn thought that in all the 173 games between the two countries, going back to the very first meetings in 1876–7, there has never been such a day. All the evidence seems to show that Test matches, even where the run scoring is as slow as this, retain the interest of those following them from afar. What concerns anyone watching from the spot is whether they will continue to attract people to come and see for themselves. For it is on this that the continuance of Test cricket depends.

The conclusion of the Australian innings this morning followed the pattern of Saturday right through to the last. England did better than they could have hoped in getting the remaining four wickets so cheaply, and as one watched Davidson, with no. 11 at the wicket, still reining in his well-proved powers of aggression, one came to wonder which player of which side will first try and cut loose from the shackles imposed by the bowlers.

I examined yesterday some of the difficulties of doing so against the present England attack. That was in Saturday's context, when there were always two recognised batsmen in together. This morning Davidson saw Benaud and Grout go. He might, of course, have established a fruitful partnership with either; and in any case he needed time this morning, no doubt, to get set.

But with Meckiff and Kline at the other end, Davidson's tactics for the last 45 minutes only changed in that he sometimes refused to run his own singles early in the over and his partner's towards the end. Inexplicably, he committed the most extraordinary form of suicide. With ten minutes to go before lunch, May brought on Laker for what could not have been more than a couple of overs.

This, one felt, was what Davidson must have been waiting for. On May's part it was no doubt a calculated challenge. Statham, who, with Loader, had been bowling for 80 minutes, was finished. May, rather than turn to his trusty change bowler, Bailey, took the risk with Laker. And what happened? Laker's first ball was almost half-volley length and drifted in slightly: an inswinger to the left-hander. Davidson's answer was to raise the bat aloft, pad the ball off and watch the umpire give him out lbw.

One cannot spend long in the company of the present generation of cricketers without their remarking very earnestly that the game has become so 'scientific' that it is becoming more and more difficult to make runs. The margin of error, as Lindwall and Miller reminded us in the England first innings, is essentially small, but the ball that pitches on the leg or middle stumps, of the right-hander, and flies towards the slips is as dangerous as anything an opening batsman has to contend with, especially if there is any accompanying lift or swing.

Milton had a nerve-shattering time in the early overs, especially against Davidson, and the ball several times whistled over the shoulder of his bat. A fine glance to the boundary and a cover drive or two got him going at length. Richardson placed a few short singles and showed signs of getting established when Benaud, who had recently relieved Davidson, caught and bowled him. Richardson seemed to decide to drive, then propped and saw Benaud make a characteristically good catch very wide with his left hand.

Milton had earlier withstood Davidson, who at this stage replaced Meckiff, and Milton now followed a riser and got a touch. It was noticeable that, although the wicket was playing as true as could be, the fast bowler with a whip in the action and a loose wrist could still make the slightly shorter ball rise hip high.

With both openers out England were still 18 runs behind when Graveney joined Bailey. The arrival of Bailey had been the signal for concentrated Australian pressure. Benaud bowled to him with four men forming a close square, slip, silly point, silly mid-on and backward short-leg. Bailey, of course, does not mind the pressure.

————————

CHAPTER 3
THE 1960s

INTRODUCTION

A momentous decade of social and political change was reflected in the world of sport and, to a certain extent, the way the *Daily Telegraph* covered cricket.

The libertine mood of the 1960s even crept into some of E.W. Swanton's reports. 'Everyone seemed to be "with it",' he wrote from Lord's as Sussex won the first ever one-day domestic trophy in 1963. One-day cricket had found its niche and Swanton was surprisingly receptive. 'This "instant cricket" is very far from being a gimmick and there is a place in it for all the arts of cricket, most of which are subtle ones.' Swanton perhaps sensed the changing times and just eight years later he would be in Melbourne to report on the first ever one-day international.

But the changes on the field were insignificant compared to the upheaval and confrontations off it. The 1960s were dominated by race, and cricket was sucked into its greatest crisis. The Bodyline affair affected just England and Australia; the issue of race and the participation of South Africa in international cricket would split the game across the world.

It was a problem identified and insightfully summed up by R.A. Roberts in 1962 during a piece written for the newspaper's Op-Ed pages. Roberts, a much-travelled freelance journalist, wrote, 'For unless the South African issue can be satisfactorily overcome, the solving of throwing, dragging, time-wasting and other domestic problems will be rendered meaningless in the eyes of world opinion.' By the end of the decade, world cricket had unravelled and Basil D'Oliveria had become the game's first *cause célèbre*. Roberts, though, would not live to see his prediction come true. He died of cancer at the age of 38 in 1965.

In 1961 the *Daily Telegraph* had a sibling rival to contend with. The *Sunday Telegraph* was launched nicely in time for the cricket season on 4 February 1961 and was soon providing extensive coverage of the game at international and county level. Through the eyes J.J. Warr we are painted a picture of a fascinating decade. Warr was a Cambridge undergraduate when he was picked for two Tests on the Ashes tour of 1950–1 and his bowling average of 281 remained the worst in Test cricket until the late 1990s. He later captained Middlesex and was the butt of one of Brian Johnston's favourite jokes. He would say, 'Warr's declared, whereupon an old woman in the crowd wakes up and enquires, "Who against?"'

Warr's self-deprecating humour stood him in good stead. When Fred Trueman took his 300th Test wicket he wrote, 'As Honorary President of the Fast Bowlers Union, he can put his feet up now with a momentous achievement behind him. Another 299 Test wickets and I could have done the same.'

Witty and perceptive, Warr had a playful style and was perhaps at his best away from the big international matches. Here we have some of his best sketches from the Scarborough Festival to Arundel Castle and a creaking Jim Laker bowling at Ilford. He also revelled in nostalgia. It is easy to imagine him with a mischievous smile across his face as he sat down to write his reports from matches between Old England and the Lord's Taverners.

The 1960s can perhaps also be seen as a decade of farewells. Goodbye to some of cricket's old traditions as well as some of its greatest names. Jack Hobbs is the only man to be granted two tributes in this book. First we have E.W. Swanton's appreciation followed by his batting partner Herbert Sutcliffe's piece which appeared the next day in the *Sunday Telegraph*. The lives of Frank Worrell, Bill Woodfull and Sydney Barnes are also celebrated.

But it is the end of the decade and the scandal surrounding D'Oliveria that would leave its mark on the game. It was an issue which exercised not only the newspaper's cricket correspondents, but also its readers. Letters flooded in to the Telegraph supporting and criticising D'Oliveria, some of which probably would not be published today. We hear from D'Oliveria himself and the chapter closes with a piece by the Reverend David Sheppard. His message is simple. Cricket can heal but first it must endure some hard times.

15 DECEMBER 1960

FIRST TEST — LAST DAY

WEST INDIES FORCE TIE IN AMAZING FINISH

TWO RUN-OUTS IN LAST OVER DENY AUSTRALIA AND MAKE HISTORY

R. A. Roberts

Brisbane, Wednesday

An historic cricket match flared into a stupendous climax here this evening when Australia lost their last three wickets in the last over and were held to a tie by West Indies. It is the first tie recorded in Test history.

Strong men, heroes themselves of countless Test matches, were on their feet shouting themselves hoarse as Solomon's throw hit the stumps and ran out Meckiff off the seventh ball of Hall's final over to end Australia's innings with the scores level.

Benaud and Worrell agreed they have never known a greater game. Certainly it was the finest match in my experience. The light of battle burned brightly throughout, almost blindingly at the climax. Yet not once did the exchanges lose their good humour. It was a match of genuine chivalry as well as gripping entertainment. Benaud felt this game has done more than provide a tremendous boost to this series. It has ignited a torch of hope for Test cricket the world over.

Test matches cannot always produce the exciting tempo achieved here and I don't suppose there will ever be another finish like this, yet some illuminating lessons have been provided. The most significant I feel is Hall, whose magnificent fast bowling early in Australia's second innings paved the way to the most exciting finish in Test match history that though England can feel proud to have given this game to the world, there should be no loss of pride in the fact that two Commonwealth countries have shown the way for the future.

The ebb and flow that characterised the game was to the advantage of West Indies in the first two sessions today. Hall and Valentine unexpectedly prolonged the West Indies innings by 40 minutes and, equally important, by 25 runs. But Australia still looked to have the better chance with 233 needed in 310 minutes and the pitch still playing well.

Before lunch, however, Simpson and Harvey were both victims of a Hall altogether more accurate and hostile than in previous spells here. Afterwards he struck deeper by dismissing O'Neill and Favell, while at the other end McDonald was bowled by Worrell. Half the side were out for 57 and one felt hereabouts that if Hall had had adequate fast bowling support, Australia would have been demoralised. With genuine speed at one end only, however, the effort could not be sustained and Australia fought back with characteristic heart and vigour.

Mackay helped to turn the tide before being deceived by Ramadhin's leg-break and Davidson, after a quiet period, reached the fulfilment of a wonderful all-round display. Now his batting, for the second time in the match, revealed high quality. And this time Benaud's was just as good.

At tea, Australia needed 124 in two hours. In the first hour afterwards, instead of playing for safety, Davidson and Benaud added 64 by judicious hitting blended with smart cunning. Now they were up with the clock and maintained the pace until, with eight minutes left, eight runs were needed. At this point Benaud called Davidson for a single but Solomon's pick-up and aim were too good. So Hall began the last over with Australia six short of victory.

Off the first ball Grout scrambled a leg-bye. Benaud went to hook the next and was caught at the wicket. Six balls left and four to win with two wickets to fall. Meckiff played his first ball firmly and ran a bye off the next as the fielders went through a series of agonised acrobatics to run him out. Four balls left and three to win.

Grout swung again and the ball went high on the on-side. Hall claimed the catch himself and dropped it. Meckiff pulled the sixth ball high to leg and with Hunte in hot pursuit, the batsman ran two and went through for a third that would have won the match. Hunte's return, however, was fast and true to Alexander and Grout was run out.

So the scores were level with two balls left. Kline came in and played his first ball to mid-wicket. Meckiff charged down the pitch, but, glory be, Solomon for the second time in minutes picked up swiftly and threw down the stumps direct. The small crowd made their voices heard far and wide and they will have something to tell their grandchildren about even if they find it hard to make their story believed.

28 MAY 1961

RALPH IS STAR OF 'CIRCUS'

J. J. Warr

Ilford, Saturday

The Essex travelling circus pitched its tents in Valentine's Park and gave a superb day's entertainment. The ringmaster Trevor Bailey was soon bowling against a weakened Surrey side who batted patchily so score 238. In reply Essex have gone for their shots and scored 142 for 2 in 27 overs.

The wicket was prepared by the LCC, in the absence of the groundsman, who five weeks ago met with an accident hardly envisaged by Mr Marples. He was knocked down by an alsatian dog and broke his leg in the process. However, despite the wicket's doubtful origins, it had pace and bounce and provided lively cricket today.

The Surrey innings owed most of its steam to the Chelsea footballer Tindall, who was probably relieved to be away from the tramping feet of managers, agents, lawyers and Pressmen at Stamford Bridge. He scored 85, mainly by magnificent running between the wickets with Willett and then Swetman, and a series of scorching cover drives. All the while Essex bowled tidily with Ralph held back as their secret weapon.

This was his first match of the season and the local influence was working for him powerfully to the tune of 5 for 43 including a final spell of 3 for 0. At the age of 41, his first overs were vague and elastoplastic, but once the embrocation had sunk in, then Surrey were done for. He had Constable caught behind the wicket just before lunch and trapped Lock in a similar manner just before tea. After tea, which must have included pep pills, he lured Tindall to his doom at mid-wicket, bowled Gibson who was hypnotised into playing no stroke and finally Loader.

Essex really batted well and 100 runs were scored in 18 overs of scintillating stroke play, Smith and Milner both scored 50s and gave the enthusiastic crowd something to warm their rather chilled bones.

25 JUNE 1961

LORD'S WICKET IS UNFAIR TO MAESTROS

J. J. Warr

Lord's, Saturday

Throughout the cricket-speaking world the Lord's Test match between England and Australia is the supreme moment in the sporting calendar. Grandmother has her fifth funeral since Ascot and club ties and cricket ties are given a rare run in the sunshine. However, against the pleasant social background, many critical eyes are assessing the state of the modern game.

It is a pity that the wicket in this match has not given the contemporary maestros a great chance to show their various considerable skills. The bounce of the ball has always been uneven and the pace of the wicket as difficult to sum up as any politician's speech. This has been the pattern for the Lord's Test for some years now and batsmen have been faced with two widely differing methods of playing.

One alternative is the frenzied, all-out kill or be killed innings that Weekes, McLean and Benaud have played for their respective countries. The other is the long vigil of graft and grind – which Lawry played to perfection on Friday and Mackay to a lesser extent today. The sensible middle course seems fraught with danger unless the bowling falls below Test match standard. Ridgemanship has been added to brinkmanship and gamesmanship as gambits for the more sophisticated captains.

The cricket today until tea demonstrated most powerfully the tremendous part that luck plays in the game. If Statham had been given a fiver for every Australian wave at his bowling in their innings he would have his feet up on the French Riviera tonight.

When England batted both Subba Row and Puller got the fatal nick almost at the first attempt and Dexter suffered even more grievously, dragging on a long hop with his pads. In fact Cowdrey's joust with fate started when he won the toss only to get the doubtful privilege of first innings on a moving wicket.

However, this cannot detract from the general air of purpose and determination about Australia's cricket in this game. The old lion, Davidson, was due to be put down before this game according to the pundits, but he has looked the most dangerous bowler on either side. Another old lion, Lock, when he entered the dressing-room on Thursday, was greeted by: 'Tell me, are you the son of the old Lock who used to play for England?'

---

2 SEPTEMBER 1961

SHACKLETON GIVES HANTS THE CHAMPIONSHIP

SUPERB USE OF SEAM ON DOCILE PITCH
BREAKS DERBYSHIRE RESISTANCE

A. S. R. Winlaw

Bournemouth, Friday

In an atmosphere of much tension, excitement and then rejoicing, Hampshire became County Champions for the first time in their history by beating Derbyshire here today by 140 runs.

There could be no more deserving or fitting player to have brought them the Championship than Shackleton, and in a quite magnificent spell of bowling he took six wickets for 39 runs. He moved the ball away to the slips, brought the ball back, and on a pitch which had hitherto given the seamers no encouragement he bowled a number of really difficult deliveries.

Derbyshire were set to make 252 to win in 193 minutes, and it was obvious that if they were to get them their first four batsmen would have to succeed. None of them did. Shackleton dismissed all four, and although Taylor and Rhodes batted well at the end Derbyshire were all out for 111. Hampshire batted until just before one o'clock, and although they lost wickets the runs came quickly and they were able to declare at 263 for eight. In the two hours they scored 138, with the chief contributions coming from Sainsbury and Barnard.

When Derbyshire went in Shackleton had Lee caught behind on the forward stretch in the third over, and immediately after lunch Gibson was lbw. The breakthrough really came when Shackleton bowled first Oates with one that left him and then Johnson off his pads. This was the important wicket Hampshire wanted, and Derbyshire's shaky middle order never threatened to hold on for long.

Shackleton at this stage had taken four wickets for nine runs. At the other end Wassell again bowled his left-arm spinners with considerable variation in flight. Millner, after a nervous start, played a couple of good shots, but Wassell caught and bowled him brilliantly from a drive which hardly rose from the ground. This made Derbyshire 52 for 7, and Richardson was then bowled without addition. The scene was all set for the celebrations, but there was a short and agreeable breathing space while the wicket-keeper Taylor and Rhodes batted soundly for 40 minutes while adding 52 for the ninth wicket.

Taylor at 19 is certainly a promising prospect as a wicket-keeper and he is the type of player likely to develop with experience into a pretty useful batsman. He swept and pulled very effectively and Ingleby-Mackenzie was committed to give Shackleton his overdue rest after 24 overs. Sainsbury came on, and Rhodes obligingly hit a long hop straight back to him. Taylor, having made 48, tried to drive Sainsbury for his 50. The ball went in the air for an agonising length of time, but Livingstone held the catch at long-on and history was made.

An enthusiastic scene followed with the Derbyshire players coming from the pavilion to meet the new champions, and the crowd flocked on to mob the players.

Ingleby-Mackenzie made a typically humble and charming speech, and Shackleton said it was his greatest and proudest moment – a sentiment loudly and deservedly cheered.

---

3 SEPTEMBER 1961

FOR THE BEST IN CRICKET GO TO SCARBOROUGH

J. J. Warr

Prince Philip has honoured the 75th Scarborough Festival by accepting the presidency for this year. What is there about this unique cricket occasion that seems to evoke such fond memories and to provoke such keen anticipation? The simple answer is that the cricket and the social aspect have been perfectly blended over the years to give the maximum pleasure to both players and spectators alike.

From the cricket angle, the Festival has always attracted the best contemporary players, and touring sides love to appear there. It has always been policy to play the matches straight and allow the infinite variety inherent in the game to do the rest.

There is no formula for rigged festival matches. The knowledgeable Yorkshire crowds can smell phoney cricket a mile away, and the lovely Scarborough ground would now be a bingo hall if that were the case. There is a relaxed, holiday flavour about the play, but that frequently improves its quality, rather than the reverse.

This is not the opium of modern Test cricket, but rather a shedding of inhibitions and a freeing of the soul. Wilfred Rhodes in his day would indulge in 'fancy cuts' unknown in his repertoire until September, Sir Leonard Hutton would show that batting is an art, having spent the whole previous summer trying to turn it into a science, and even Trevor Bailey has hit sixes which would have meant a ducking for witchcraft in earlier days.

Scarborough has been the stage for some of the greatest batting in the history of cricket. To have seen Hobbs's centuries in the '20s, Bradman's hundred before lunch in 1934, and May's century against the West Indians in 1957 is the equivalent in cricket of witnessing Sir Edmund Hillary plant his flag on Everest's peak.

But mixed with these great feats has been a rich vein of humour. Hendren before the second war, and Wardle and Evans afterwards were ideal festival cricketers, never overplaying the role of clown, but skilful enough to entertain, and play first-class cricket at the same time. If a little fun mixed in with good cricket is not to your taste, then stay away from Scarborough.

However, there is a social side as well. Families and friends from all over England and Scotland gather at this seaside town year after year. Father can go to the ground, 'have a taste' and watch the game, the children can collect autographs, take photographs, or play their own games as the mood seizes them, and Mother has got the band, the sunshine and the cricket. Some of the notes that the band strikes do not figure in Western music but the tunes are played with gusto, and are greatly enjoyed.

The atmosphere at the ground and in the town is welcoming and friendly Yorkshire people have a reputation for knowing how to enjoy themselves. Well, the Scarborough Festival is proof enough for me.

---

13 MAY 1962

LAKER FINDS THE WAY BACK IS NOT SO EASY

J. J. Warr

Ilford, Saturday

Come-back week in cricket ended on an appropriate note with the appearance of those two young Essex amateurs Insole and Laker. At 4.10 p.m. penitent Jim played his first shot for his new club: a rustic top-edge slog that just cleared the fielder. At 6.30 p.m. he bowled his first ball which lifted and turned. From then on he was treated to some old-fashioned stick.

It is hard in the circumstances to avoid a note of cynicism, but at least Essex can plead that they are short of players; even Dalton, the masseur, takes flannels to the ground with him just in case. However, most of the day's thunder was stolen by Jackson, who took 6 for 25 out of the Essex total of 139, and barely worked up a thirst in the process. Derbyshire have replied vigorously and intelligently with 104 for 2.

Jackson is now nearly 41 and as yet there is no autobiography on the stocks. In this match he had his luck and Rhodes looked consistently more hostile. But the old maestro was always doing enough with the ball to make any miscalculation fatal. The wicket was wet and gave some help, with the odd ball lifting enough to be physically unpleasant.

The Essex innings began ominously at 12.45 p.m. with a pair of ducks circling round the ground. Shortly afterwards Barker hit the ball hard on the wicket. Then Taylor left a gate through which Rhodes duly bowled him. Douglas Insole, an England selector, came in at an unenviable moment – the score was one run for two wickets. He played bravely and well for 24, removing much of the steam from the Derbyshire attack which at one point had Essex 47 for 7.

Both Bear and Spicer were caught behind the wicket by the young deputy for Dawkes, Taylor by name. He is a lively performer who should do well in the first-class game. Greensmith played a very useful innings for 45, watching the ball closely and driving it hard when it was up to the bat; tactics later adopted successfully for Derbyshire by Lee and Johnson.

Trevor Bailey has become infected with the stroke-playing virus, offering a drive at Jackson just before lunch with fatal results. It won't happen again for another five years. From a very poor position, when it looked as though Essex were unlikely to reach three figures, they did well to score 139.

The Derbyshire batsmen had the advantage of an assessment of the wicket. They all went for their shots, particularly Johnson. He charged Laker and was particularly severe on anything over-pitched. At 7.15, as an appropriate indication of an overcast day, the umpires went off for bad light.

---

28 APRIL 1962

CRICKET'S COLOUR PROBLEM

R. A. Roberts

International cricket in the 1950s became laboriously involved in controversy, largely of its own making. Now, just when a brighter, gayer era seemed to have been ushered in by the wonderful series of matches between Australia and West Indies last year, cricket has found itself caught up, quite innocently, but quite irrevocably, with outside political factors.

'It isn't cricket' for the game that gave this everyday expression to the language to mix with politics. But at a time when cricket, for all the domestic twinges that come and go, is being played on a wider front and before more people than ever (2 million saw MCC's recent tour on the Indian sub-continent) this unfortunate, uncompromising fact has to be faced.

I am just back from a 40,000-mile journey which, one way or the other, took in all the major cricket communities. Though it proved resoundingly that the players of all these diverse parts can and do get along perfectly well together when left to themselves, the tour also shed some significant light upon the complicated multi-racial issue that blocks cricket's natural development in a truly international sense.

The reason is that the sport, in spite of itself, has become entwined in the tentacles of apartheid. Cricket's problem is South Africa's problem, and vice versa. South Africa is the third most senior of the cricket nations, and so the contribution to the game there has been, and is, considerable. Its Government's policy, alas, has precipitated a crisis within cricket, the full consequences of which are only now beginning to reveal themselves.

For cricket, at Test-match level, is bound up with Commonwealth membership, and South Africa's departure meant its cricketers were automatically expelled. It is in efforts to come back into the fold that the complications have arisen.

Cricket is well able to generate its own conflicts without these outside forces being brought to bear. Blood pressures naturally rise whenever England meets Australia and feelings have recently simmered between West Indies and India on the use of short-pitched bowling. Contractor, India's captain, hovered between life and death after being struck on the head by a bumper in Barbados.

Yet cricket has learned to live with its quarrels, and magnanimously to forgive and forget. The Indians have even invited four of the fast bowlers, who helped to rout them, to coach in its country next season. Contractor is now recovering after a series of blood transfusions, one of them promptly supplied by his West Indies opposite number, Worrell.

Some years ago, when the border between India and Pakistan was opened on a mass scale for the first time after the cruel days of Partition, it was for a Test match at Lahore; and Sikhs once again were welcomed in the bazaars of the teeming Muslim city.

One can fairly deduce from all this that cricket has healing properties; as it certainly has an uncommon power to bring together people of different backgrounds, countries, creeds, and colours. My recent tour supplied a cheering example, especially in places where the indigenous population is not particularly interested in the game. It is often forgotten that cricket in Africa exists solely because of European and Asian enthusiasm; while in Hong Kong we found that although the

Portuguese participated the only Chinaman involved was a local secretary, and *he* spoke with a Queensland accent.

The companionship that developed on this tour between all players, South Africans included, was surely significant. Between Weekes, who travelled 50,000 miles from Barbados and back, and the Springbok, McLean, a warm friendship easily blossomed, strengthened if anything on the joking that followed a run-out between the pair.

Cricket's saving grace is its humour. When Weekes, sharing a Sydney taxi with Adcock and McLean, was asked by a driver if they were members of the South African cricket team, he replied: 'Man, are you colour-blind?'

In Bombay, we were a little concerned how Adcock and McLean, who were not playing there but had to pass through in transit, would be treated; after all, there is one hotel with a sneering notice: 'Dogs and South Africans not allowed.' So Benaud, as fine a skipper of an international team as of Australia, went along with me to the airport at midnight to see the South African pair through the various transit formalities. Instead of having their baggage turned upside down, however, we found they were able to satisfy Customs with a supply of autographs.

Unfortunately, the wider issues are no longer as easily resolved. Pakistan provides a sharp reminder on this point. In many ways Pakistan has an enlightened approach. The Pakistanis work hard there on behalf of cricket and, for example, are proposing at the next meeting of the Imperial Cricket Conference at Lord's in July that a type of second division be formed at international level.

They have circulated a list of countries that reads like a UN assembly – and even received an affirmative from the United States and a *oui* from France to their broad proposals. The Pakistan Cricket Board would also have welcomed the South African members of the International XI, but for an eleventh-hour embargo by President Ayub Khan's Government.

Yet this same cricket voice can be expected to speak up firmly against South Africa's official position when it is discussed at the ICC meeting. Pakistan will make clear the view that unless South Africa participates in multi-racial cricket, then on moral grounds alone England, Australia and New Zealand should join with the West Indies, India and Pakistan in not playing against them. In this day and age this may be a powerful moral argument, but blood ties, tradition and sentiment are also strong, and New Zealand for one readily admits that its recent tour of South Africa was the 'best ever, anywhere'.

Thus, whether we like it or not, this becomes a straight colour issue, with the European and non-European countries ranging themselves on opposite sides and regarding the South African problem through entirely different eyes. It is an issue that no one wants to divide the Imperial Cricket Conference, but it could well do so.

What, then, is the answer? One is for MCC and Australia, still the twin major powers of cricket, to come straight out and say political factors must not be allowed to disrupt the game. Far better, however, if South Africa made some bold gesture in the face of Government disapproval.

Rhodesia has started multi-racial sport. The Federation, indeed, was the springboard for the International tour, and many South African Test players, McGlew, the captain, among them, actively supported it. A Rhodesian Colts' team, known as 'The Fawns', arrives in England next week. In the touring party is an Asian – only one, it is true, but this is a start.

The South African Cricket Association could use Rhodesia, which is affiliated to it just like Transvaal or Natal, therefore, to ease its present predicament. It could seek to play West Indies, for example, in an official Test in Salisbury.

Alternatively, one of the non-European countries could seize the initiative and invite South Africa to send its best team – which might well include a coloured or two, such as D'Oliviera, if form justified their inclusion. I have heard this idea mooted in Pakistan.

Even if South Africa could not repay the compliment, its acceptance of a tour would surely be sufficient evidence of good faith for it to be re-elected to the Imperial Cricket Conference and resume its proper place in Test matches. Without some gesture, somewhere, however, the Springboks will be in a wilderness far lonelier than their own karoo. There is bitter irony here, when Rugby in that country goes along unmolested.

Nothing like the wave of anti-apartheid hysteria struck the 1960–1 Rugby team here that was encountered by the cricketers a few months earlier (McLean and company still smart, in private, from the memories of actual manhandling suffered in silence in England that sad summer of 1960). Nor will there be the moralising fuss about the imminent departure of the Lions for South Africa that will accompany MCC's next visit there.

The explanation simply is that while Rugby is an international sport in its own right, it does not attract the non-European communities in the same way as cricket.

It would not fall short of a sporting calamity, therefore, if cricket, having done so much to serve the cause of multi-racialism, should be baulked in the fact of this latest, and much the trickiest, of its problems. For, unless the South African issue can be satisfactorily overcome, the solving of throwing, dragging, time-wasting and other domestic problems will be rendered meaningless in the eyes of world opinion, to which cricket still stands out as the sport epitomising fair play.

---

5 OCTOBER 1962

HENDREN – THE MOST POPULAR PLAYER

E. W. Swanton

It is probably safe to say that no more popular cricketer ever played than E. Hendren (christened Elias but universally known as 'Patsy'), who died yesterday, aged 73.

His technical record with the bat between 1907 and 1937 was remarkable enough, with 170 centuries and a total of more than 57,000 runs, figures which rank only slightly behind those of Sir Jack Hobbs and Frank Woolley. But though his deeds for England and Middlesex can be read about in books, the statistics of his career convey no impression as to the kind of man he was.

His short figure, his happy and sometimes wistful smile, his most obvious likeableness, and his facility for enlivening even the most serious situation with some perfectly timed and never overdone piece of clowning – all these endeared him to everybody, as much as did his flashing square-cut, his favourite lofted on-drive, his mighty hook off the fast bowlers, and his nimble footwork against the slow ones.

Everywhere he went he was persona gratissima – in the West Indies the affection for him developed almost into a cult – and West Indian streets and children were christened 'Patsy'.

Nobody who was present will ever forget the scene, when in his last match at Lord's in 1937, he scored a century against Surrey. As soon as he got his hundredth run the crowd of some 17,000 rose to its feet and after repeated cheering sang 'For he's a jolly good fellow!' There has seldom been a more genuine tribute.

Hendren did not burst with sudden brilliance on the cricket world. He was 24 when, after a long apprenticeship, he became indispensable to Middlesex. Only then began his famous association with J.W. Hearne – 'young Jack' – that meant so much to the county for so long. He was equally slow to develop as a Test cricketer, and until his middle thirties was in danger of being regarded as a first-rate county player rather than an essential part of the England eleven. He was not the only one to fail against Gregory and McDonald, the Australian fast bowlers, in 1921, but the parrot cry of 'temperament' arose.

A century against Australia at Lord's in 1926, and an even more valuable one at Brisbane for A.P.F. Chapman's team in the winter of 1928, showed how wrong his detractors were, and he became indispensable to England too. Altogether he played 48 innings against Australia, 18 against South Africa and 17 against the West Indies. He made 3,525 runs in Tests with an average of 47. As a member of a touring side his personality counted for almost as much as did his performance on the field.

Among his great feats may be mentioned his 301 not out for Middlesex against Worcestershire in 1933, the scoring of more than 2,000 runs in every season between 1920 and 1929 including a total of 3,311 in 1928, a third-wicket partnership of 375 – still an English record – with Hearne, his colleague in many a productive stand, against Hampshire in 1923, and his 206 at Trent Bridge in 1925, when Middlesex, who were set to make 502, got the runs in six and a quarter hours. Hendren and F.T. Mann hit off the last 271 in 195 minutes.

In his prime he was among the best of outfields, and later became an adept at short-leg, where his work on the 1928–9 tour in Australia was invaluable. His opinion on any matter was always worth asking, and the younger Middlesex professionals, especially Compton and Edrich, owed much to his advice and guidance. In his last playing years he was an invaluable lieutenant to the youthful R.W.V. Robins.

His own contribution to the 'bodyline' controversy was the typical one of providing himself with a specially made helmet, which he occasionally wore at Lord's when the wicket was bumpy. When he retired from first-class cricket in 1937, at the age of 48, he was appointed coach at Harrow in succession to Wilfred Rhodes.

In 1939 Harrow beat Eton for the first time since 1908, and in the rejoicings afterwards Hendren was called out to the balcony and cheered again by the Lord's crowd. He retired from Harrow in 1947 and was first coach to Sussex and then scorer with Middlesex until 1959.

In his younger days he was a good Association footballer, and as outside-right for Brentford played for England against Wales in the 1919 'Victory' series.

---

26 NOVEMBER 1962

E. W. Swanton

Brisbane, Tuesday

In the context of history the 535th Test match (as I judge to be), which in a day or two will be making quite a stir in these parts and at home, must seem a small matter compared with the news contained in my break-fast-time cable this morning.

'Amateurs abolished', it announced laconically, and behind the words one saw 'finis' written to the oldest of all the traditional rivalries of the cricket field. Not only that, of course. The evolution of the game has been stimulated from its beginnings by the fusion of the two strains, each of which has drawn strength and inspiration from the other.

English cricket has been at its best when there has been a reasonably even balance between those who have made the game their livelihood and those who have played it, with whatever degree of application and endeavour, basically for relaxation and enjoyment. It is easy to wax romantic over the disappearance of the amateur, and I imagine the change will be regretted instinctively by all with any knowledge of the background.

On first thought, it is perhaps hard to separate sentiment from practical reality. I can only say, having made the effort, and having regarded the possibility of the decision for some while, that the change strikes me as not only unnecessary but deplorable.

Cricket professionalism has been an honourable estate ever since the first-class game took more or less its present form in the middle of the '90s. But it is, of its nature, dependent, and the essence of leadership is independence.

To some extent one must see the change in terms of leadership. This is not to say there have not been some admirable professional captains. Tom Dollery showed the way with Warwickshire, and all know how much the 1962 champions and their runners-up owed respectively to J.V. Wilson and D. Kenyon.

Equally, there have been some indifferent amateur captains, and anyone can elaborate this remark according to taste. Yet other things being roughly equal, there are obvious advantages, especially to the players themselves, in the control of an independent agent with only a season's tenure. The alternative is control by a player from a staff whose members have served their apprenticeship, and graduated, together.

A county club have always been able to sack their amateur if he has not given satisfaction, as we have seen. It is by no means so easy to demote a professional captain, as we have also seen. It has been said, of course, that the word amateur is an anachronism, that to preserve the status is mere humbug. I wonder.

As soon as the broken-time principle was sanctioned, and advertising restrictions removed, a distinction was created between the few who cashed in on various perquisites of their fame, and the Simon-Pure amateur. But the latter category was far from extinct. What services in this last decade and more have not D.J. Insole and J.J. Warr rendered respectively to Essex and Middlesex! Each preferred to make a personal sacrifice in order to maintain his independence.

It is doubtful whether either would have been elected a county captain when he was, under the new dispensation. It is equally unlikely that a friend, henceforward to be known as Mackenzie (A.C.D. Ingleby-) would have emerged at the age of 24 to captain Hampshire. He would have been lost to the City and if half the personal tributes to him are to be believed, Hampshire would never have enthused the cricket world last year by gaining their first championship.

I recall a young schoolmaster cricketer who, a summer or two ago, got a term's leave and travelled the country with his county in a battered old car. He gave pleasure alike by his play and by his company.

The spirit of the adventure would surely have been lost if he had been paid for it.

In future, such a man might opt out: but who will be the odd man? Is not the pattern likely to be only of the suppression of individuality in favour of a somewhat colourless uniformity? Counties will be inclined to take the safe course when vacancies occur and appoint the senior man rather than run the risk of jealousies.

With the disappearance in due time of such characters as I have named will there emerge some system of non-playing managership in order to sustain the captain and help impose discipline? This could happen, and it might even work well. But one is apprehensive of the effect of more control from the committee room.

Again, although I disliked the amateur anomalies as much as the abolitionists, the time when the future structure of the first-class game was precariously in the balance was surely the wrong one to introduce a classless society on the cricket field. If a six-day-a-week championship is on the way out, might not the future pattern have involved smaller staffs and an inflow of unpaid talent operating mostly at weekends? The amateur can scarcely be revived now. That section of the history book is closed tight for ever.

---

26 JUNE 1963

ENGLAND v. WEST INDIES

E.W. Swanton

Lord's, Tuesday

Writing as one whose lasting regret is that he was not at Brisbane for the tie, I have never seen a more exciting culmination to a Test match than this. Durban in 1948, when England won by two wickets off the last ball — and with a leg bye at that — was, I suppose, a close parallel.

When the last over started with Shackleton receiving from Hall, Allen at the bowler's end and Cowdrey plastered from left wrist to elbow waiting in the pavilion, eight runs were needed. Shackleton swung prodigiously at the first ball and missed, and took a single for a little tap for the second. Allen played a third nicely to long-leg for one.

The next ball was decisive so far as an England win went. Shackleton missed a widish one which Murray took and, as Allen charged down to sneak a bye, threw underhand at the stumps.

Shackleton was slow to respond and so we had Worrell taking Murray's throw at the near stumps, and these two senior cricketers racing towards the bowler's end, Worrell with ball in hand. It was a tight thing with Worrell the winner. If Shackleton had made his ground Allen, having crossed to the batting end, would have had two balls in which to make five with two wickets standing. As it was Allen, with six to win in two balls unable to do more than defend, played them quietly and that was that.

So ended a classic game and perhaps some neutral arbiter (if there were any such cold-blooded being present) would say that this was the right result. Obviously but for a little, a slip here an edge there, some quickening of the over rate giving more time, the score in the rubber might tonight be either one all or two nil.

In today's cricket there were two heroes, one on either side. For a physical feat comparable to that of Hall, who, apart from the tea interval, bowled non-stop fast and furiously from 2.20 to six o'clock, cricket history shows no parallel, so far as I know, since Tom Richardson slaved away unrelieved for much the same sort of stretch at Old Trafford in 1896.

Richardson saw Australia scrape home narrowly in the end. As for Hall, he must know that but for him England in all probability would have won. For England, Close batted with courage and versatility, first withstanding the fast onslaught while he played himself thoroughly in, and in the later stages taking the battle into the enemy camp in the most exciting way. Certainly he gave his own side and their supporters agonies of anxiety as he chanced his arm and his eye after tea.

But the West Indies must have been equally at their wits' end knowing that if the luck held and Titmus stayed firm they faced defeat. Lucky for the West Indies that they had such a cool head in charge. There was not an overthrow, scarcely a miss of any kind in the field. Every chance was taken.

The only qualification I must reluctantly make is that even with fast bowling holding the stage the whole time, apart from five overs by Gibbs, an over-all rate of 14 overs an hour is tedious. This brings me to Griffith, whose support of Hall, into the wind for 19 overs with only two brief breaks, was of the utmost value to his captain.

From breakfast there had been a waiting queue outside but in the dismal weather most had melted away before at twenty past two it became clear enough to start. After the crowded tiers of the first four days, the off-white expanse of vacant stands induced an anti-climax, which for a long time the cricket did nothing to dissolve.

Worrell began with Gibbs, but although the wind had so dried the turf that neither he nor the fast bowlers needed sawdust, Worrell removed Gibbs after a single over and relied on Hall down wind from the Pavilion end, Griffith from the Nursery. Both batsmen naturally took time to settle in and in due course Close seemed fairly acclimatised. Barrington by contrast had seemingly used up all his virtue yesterday and looked wretchedly ill at ease.

When he did make a good hook that was worth four it was finely fielded. At last after three-quarters of an hour Barrington got an involuntary single off his glove from a ball from Hall that flew wickedly. Barrington raised hopes with a nice four off his legs, but was then caught behind trying to make room to cut.

At this point in 52 minutes today 14 runs had come from the 13 overs bowled. Hall, very fast, variable both in length and direction and straying quite often to leg, was desperately hard to score from and Close took most of him. Indeed, when the tally was counted up at tea, out of Hall's 14 successive overs Close had received 65 balls – all but 11 of them. When Hall was short and on line Close often preferred to take the ball on the body anywhere between the top of the pads and the shoulder, doing his best to ride the blow. As an example of pluck it could not be improved on.

The only respect wherein Close fell short was in failing to take a number of safe short runs. Since time was obviously likely to be a factor, this disregard was irritating to watch. Parks is a facile scorer by nature, and with him we saw runs coming off the front foot. Parks twice coverdrove Griffith handsomely for four, but immediately after the second stroke aimed to force Griffith to leg off the back foot, was beaten by the break-back and went lbw.

The advent of Titmus led to a much greater sense of urgency in the running, perhaps in response to captain's order. The over rate at the interval worked out at 14 per hour, and the score of 171 for 5 meant that if the same rate obtained to the end England would need to score a full three runs an over to make the 63 they needed.

So far as Hall was concerned, Worrell was stony-hearted – or perhaps who knows? Hall would not countenance the idea of coming off. After tea Griffith, having bowled two overs more, was rested in favour of Gibbs. But Hall kept on, and at long-leg still had the suppleness and energy to make an amazing swoop and stop of a hit that looked four runs all the way.

Close after tea grew freer, while Titmus played staunchly and sensibly giving Close all the bowling he could. Close swung the ball for four with a fine flowing hit, then missed a hook. An appeal for lbw rent the heavens in vain. Close rubbed his thigh vigorously, which indicated the ball was going over the stumps. But I would not be prepared to swear it.

At five o'clock 48 were needed. A few moments later Close reached his 50 with his favourite stroke then repeated it off Gibbs, who had now relieved Griffith. At this point England were in their best situation: 50 minutes left, 31 needed and five wickets still in hand. But a fine catch by McMorris at short-leg changed the picture. Titmus thrust the ball firmly off his body yet McMorris, not much further away than Stewart yesterday, when he caught Worrell, clung on at the first attempt.

What now would Hall serve up to Trueman? Would the cause of the brotherhood survive so volatile a situation? Hall's first ball was an extremely fast, good length one, just outside the off stump. Trueman groped, tickled and was gone: another good catch by Murray. Joined by Allen, Close grew bolder to the extent of walking down the pitch at Hall who, puzzled, ran on to meet him without delivering. Close did this twice more without either being killed or causing Hall a thrombosis or indeed making contact.

Close interspersed improbable strokes with several brilliant hits until with 20 minutes to go and 15 only wanted he swung to leg for the last time. Little Murray made a good catch and this talented but hitherto ill-starred Test cricketer walked in with the applause of the crowd making no doubt the sweetest music in his ears.

There was a peculiarity now in that though the new ball was due Worrell preferred the old one. There were to be five more overs. Allen and Shackleton batted coolly and picked up singles where they could. There was never more than one to be had with the field either up to catch or back to save fours. Seven runs accrued or were scrambled in four overs and then came the final one.

What palpitations! What a pulling at the heart-strings! And at the close the best sight ever to be seen on a cricket field, the crowd besieging the pavilion and its heroes coming out, tired but happy, to make their bows.

---

8 SEPTEMBER 1963

SUSSEX WIN COMPLETES CHAPTER OF HISTORY
WORCESTERSHIRE MERIT PRAISE FOR WELL–BALANCED APPROACH

E. W. Swanton

A new chapter of cricket history was given an exciting and altogether worthy climax at Lord's on Saturday. Sussex won the first Knock-out Cup and all credit to them; but credit, too, in fully equal portion for Worcestershire, who over the seven hours of the game fought an even fight and lost finally with a mere over and four balls to go, by 14 runs.

Where so much has been mediocre this summer, and the weather most of all, it is almost miraculous that both the Test series and this experimental competition should have passed off so well. Often during Saturday's play one feared that the rain or the light or both would necessitate the game dragging on until this morning.

The atmosphere could not have been recaptured. However, though Sussex had a wet ball for their last seven or eight overs and Worcestershire a shocking batting light, the umpires were never called upon to make what would have been an unpalatable and highly unpopular decision.

Perhaps on a cold analysis the luck more or less evened out, for the pitch, which never flattered stroke-making, seemed to grow somewhat easier for batting as it dried. Runs always had to be earned against generally accurate bowling and a uniformly high fielding standard. In the broad aspect this no doubt is to the good. Nothing is better to see than the ball hit hard and often when the conditions allow; but this 'instant cricket' is very far from being a gimmick and there is a place in it for all the arts of cricket, most of which are subtle ones.

That is why the day was so enjoyable, not only for the patriots with their banners and their rosettes 'up for the Cup', but for the practising cricketers, past and present, of all ages and types, who seemed to form the bulk of the crowd. Everyone seemed to be 'with it', and the only regret perhaps was that the weather uncertainty decided MCC (reasonably enough) against allowing in the extra 5,000 who could otherwise have been accommodated on the grass.

I say one regret, but it could be remarked by anyone looking objectively on the scene as it reflected county cricket in 1963, that it would have been preferable for victory to have gone to the side with a balanced attack (conspicuously well organised and handled by Kenyon) rather than to a lopsided array of fastish and medium-paced bowlers, all individually admirable, such as *en masse* make the modern game so dull and stereotyped to watch.

Sussex represents so much that is best in English cricket – and it is so important that it should go on doing so – that I must risk the further wrath of those who thought I did them scant justice in some recent remarks on the championship by saying this. Let them take the excessive grass off the Hove pitch and produce something like the old surface there, and if they cannot find enough reputable slow bowling on the staff, let them attract some from elsewhere while their own young men are developing. With Dexter leading, they would then be a proper team and, incidentally, they might well become for the first time in their history real champions.

And now, without apologies for the diversion, back to the play. The Sussex innings was built on a steady foundation by Langridge and Oakman, supported by Parks in the best batting of the day. Langridge was both safer and more fluent than Oakman until they both fell in successive overs to the left-arm spin of Gifford.

When Dexter, after looking uncomfortably taut and fallible, was well caught by Broadbent falling forward at slip, aiming a stroke against the spin, there was some despondency among those who were thinking in terms of the sort of scores Sussex had made on the hard wickets of the earlier rounds. But this was much tougher work against some excellent slow bowling, by Slade as well as by Gifford, both of them keeping the ball well up in the traditional way with a long-on and a deep extra-cover.

Parks announced himself with a cover-drive of high pedigree down to the Mound. His was the one six of the day, a beautifully clean, wristy hit over long off, and after commanding the middle batting he only lost his wicket with no. 10 at the crease.

In reply Worcestershire really needed an innings of 50 or 60 from one of their four Test batsmen, but it was never quite forthcoming. Kenyon went early, and Horton after playing very well was magnificently picked up, left-handed, inches from the ground by Buss off his own bowling: a match-winning effort. By this time Headley was finding it desperately hard to score, especially against Oakman.

If Headley had seen that short pushes could produce singles at all angles, and had thereby dislocated the field, Graveney, who batted as pleasantly as Parks had done, would not have needed to take the risk which enabled Dexter to make the running catch at deep mid-on that almost sealed Worcestershire's hopes.

Almost: but there was still perhaps the most intelligent piece of batting of the day to come from Booth, who with the Sussex fielders spread on the boundaries, barely visible in the murk and drizzle, came so near to rescuing a lost cause.

And so to the final enthusiasm: the MCC President, Lord Nugent's presentation of the Cup and the medals, the presence of Frank Woolley and Herbert Sutcliffe on the rostrum in front of the Pavilion, and their naming of young Norman Gifford as 'the man of the match'.

---

22 DECEMBER 1963

JACK HOBBS – COMPLETE MASTER OF HIS CRAFT

THE LINK BETWEEN OLD AND NEW

E. W. Swanton

Sir Jack Hobbs, who died on Saturday, aged 81, was the greatest English batsman since W.G. Grace, a supreme master of his craft, and the undisputed head of his profession. Born on 16 December 1882, the son of the groundsman at Jesus College, Cambridge, he made his way to the Oval at the age of 20. Half-a-century later, long after his retirement but when his name was still a household word, he accepted the honour of knighthood.

John Berry Hobbs learned his cricket as so many Cambridge men have done before and since, on that sublime stretch between Fenner's and the Town, called Parker's Piece. Tom Hayward was his mentor there, and it was Hobbs's luck, after Hayward had persuaded him to qualify for Surrey, that he should serve his apprenticeship at the Oval as opening partner to that great batsman.

There have been three men, as one surveys the history of cricket as a whole, whose genius and influence have transcended all others; W.G. Grace, Jack Hobbs and Don Bradman. Like most of the truly great – it was the same with Hutton and Compton, Hammond and Woolley – Hobbs proclaimed his promise beyond all argument more or less right away.

He made 155 in his second match for Surrey, scored 1,300 in this first season of 1905 and improved considerably on that in his second. The next year he was chosen for the Players and also won a place in the MCC side to Australia of 1907–8. It was then already said of him that there was no better professional batsman in England bar Hayward and Johnny Tyldesley.

It was the second of his five visits as a player to Australia that brought him right to the top of the tree. In that series he averaged 82, scored three Test hundreds and with Wilfred Rhodes made 323, which is still the longest opening partnership for England against Australia.

Noting the consistency of his scoring and the speed with which the runs generally came in those days, one can appreciate the remark of Frank Woolley's: 'They can say what they like about him, but only those of us who saw Jack before 1914 knew him at his very best.' However that may be, he was and remained the world's premier batsman until when nearer 50 than 40, his gradual decline coinciding with the advent of Bradman.

The long span of Hobbs's career made it probable that he would corner most of the aggregate records. Thus no one can match his number of runs, 61,221, any more than they can compete with his 197 centuries. No doubt he was lucky in his opening partners – compared with, say, Hutton. Nevertheless, his figure of 166 stands of a century or more for the first wicket sets an almost unassailable target.

Even more conclusive may seem the consistency of his performances. He averaged just under 50 in England over his whole time, stretching from 1905 to 1934. In Australia his average was 51, in South Africa 68, and in Tests alone it stood at 56.94.

Hobbs had two great Surrey partners, Hayward and Sandham, two even more famous for England, Rhodes and Sutcliffe. It was he and Sutcliffe who decided the Oval Test of '26 that brought back the Ashes, after many crushing defeats, by their wonderful partnership of 172 on a bad wicket.

In the next series in Australia these two paved the way to the victory that kept the Ashes safe by scoring 105 together on a Melbourne glue-pot – one of the classics of bad-wicket batsmanship. On A.E.R. Gilligan's tour of 1924–5 Hobbs and Sutcliffe, going in against a score of 600, batted the entire day for 283.

If one summer marked his peak it was perhaps 1925, when, at the age of 42, he scored 3,000 runs, including 16 centuries, and with two hundreds in the match against Somerset at Taunton, first equalled and then surpassed the 126 hundreds made by 'W.G.'

Early recollections of Hobbs are confined in my own case to inessential things like the frequent spinning of the bat in his fingers before he settled into his stance, and the way he pulled down the peak of his cap, so that it slanted almost parallel with his slightly beaky nose.

Before I knew enough to admire his batting it was his fielding which fascinated most. He would walk about at cover in an innocent preoccupied sort of way in between times, hands often deep in pockets. If the ball were pushed wide of him, and the batsmen made to run, he would usually move at a quite leisurely speed to cut it off.

Then suddenly an apparently identical stroke would be repeated, and this time the relaxed figure would spring into action with catlike swiftness – there was a dart, a swoop, and the quickest of flicks straight at the stumps, with the batsman pounding to the crease as if for dear life. Australians as a rule are good between the wickets, but on one tour Hobbs at cover point ran out upwards of a dozen of them.

It has been written of him often enough that he was the bridge between the old batting and the new. When he entered the scene it was the age of elegance, and the best professionals absorbed and were caught up in the classical style based on the swing of the bat from the shoulders, driving, and the off-side strokes.

There were, of course, strong back players, notably Fry, and more and more men came to practise the art of working the ball to the on-side.

Hobbs was quickly identified with this school. Then, when he was still climbing to the top, came the revolution in technique that was made necessary by the arrival of the googly and the advance of the wrist spinner. At the same time the faster bowlers were exploring the possibilities of swing.

Neville Cardus has described him as 'the first batsman really to master the new bowling'. He combined with the classic freedom of forward play and full swing of the bat the necessary adaptation to defeat the googly and late swerve – legs and pads over the wicket with the hands held loosely on the bat in order to scotch the spin and bring the ball down short of the close fieldsmen, virtually in the crease.

But enough of technique. In the last resort of the difference between talent and mastery is a matter of character. Hobbs brought to his cricket an ascetic self-discipline which in tight corners expressed itself perfectly in his play.

He was a man of conspicuous personal modesty, but his pride in his position as – in every sense – England's no. 1 gave to his batting an aura of serenity equally communicable to his opponents and to his fellows. No one ever saw Hobbs rattled or in a hurry. And if he was anxious it never showed.

There was a quiet dignity about him which had its roots in mutual respect: for others as for himself. He had the natural good manners of a Christian and a sportsman, and the esteem in which, in his day, his profession came to be held owed much to the man who for the best part of a quarter of a century was its undisputed leader.

---

22 DECEMBER 1963

JACK HOBBS, MY PARTNER

Herbert Sutcliffe

The joint author of many an opening stand for England pays tribute to Sir Jack Hobbs, who has died at the age of 81.

The Test match at the Oval between England and the West Indies in August reminded me vividly of a Test match on the same ground played against Australia in 1926 – 37 years ago – long before every player taking part in the last Test was born, with the exception of Frankie Worrell, who was, in 1926, two years old.

At the end of this match, which was won by England, who also won the rubber for the first time in many years, the huge capacity crowd flocked across the ground to the pavilion and there the pent-up feelings of the spectators were let loose in a wave of terrific enthusiasm.

The idol of the Oval and English cricket, Jack Hobbs, was in great demand and amidst a storm of love and affection he appeared on the pavilion balcony. He had, in that match, on a vile sticky wicket, scored a classic century, an innings which he thought was his best ever, an innings which paved the way for victory.

It was typical and characteristic of Jack Hobbs that he should, under adverse conditions, display his wonderful skill. Every stroke was a technical masterpiece; feet, body, shoulders, wrists and fingers working in perfect unison, the whole controlled by a keenly alert brain which enabled him to make a speedy decision against all fast bowlers. His quickness in perceiving the exact spot of the pitch of the ball was a near miracle for it meant that he could position correctly with rapidity and ease, and as a result of this he had much more time than most people to play his shots.

I was his partner on many occasions when we were called upon to operate on extremely bad wickets and I can say this, without any doubt whatever, that he was the most brilliant exponent of all time and quite the best batsman of my generation on all types of wickets.

I do wish that the modern batsman – who is so prone to ducking frequently when facing bouncers – could have seen Sir Jack Hobbs facing up to the Australian fast bowlers Gregory and McDonald. All risky shots were reduced to a minimum so that with his great skill, resolution and fighting spirit he rarely looked like getting out.

I had a long and happy association with Sir Jack and without hesitation I can testify to his fine character. A regular churchgoer, he seldom missed the opportunity to attend church service on Sunday mornings both in England and abroad. He was a man of the highest integrity who believed in sportsmanship in the dignified sense, team work, fair play, and clean living. His life was full of everything noble and true.

14 JUNE 1964

TEST TALENT – IF IT'S A ONE-DAY TEST

J. J. Warr

Lord's, Saturday

Old England were 69 short with three wickets and 50 minutes left against the Lord's Taverners' total of 305 when rain and rheumatism finally prevailed. The ground staff had dashed out during the innings in the heavy rain to place a plastic cover over the precious Test wicket.

Reg Simpson scored a century for the ancient internationals when the wind and muscle of some of his colleagues was cracking under the strain. Surridge scored 50 for the Lord's Taverners in 23 minutes, including five sixes.

Despite a pessimistic weather forecast this annual lap of honour for old heroes attracted some 8,000 people to the ground. It was like old times when Denis Compton took the field well after the start of play. He missed some sparkling overs from the 54-year-old Voce and from Alec Bedser, OBE. In both cases, the engine was still ticking over nicely.

The preliminary sparring finished, we had a long fascinating spell from Laker at the Nursery End. He only tried to spin the ball in spasms. Benaud, Carr and Insole all scored runs against him, with the Test selector taking the honours with 60 in 68 minutes including some runs not on the leg side. Compton was showing rare dash at third man, saving many runs by turning fives into fours. Eventually Benaud was deceived by his speed over the ground and Compton took an easy catch off Ikin. Carr was bowled by Laker playing a shot that might affect the circulation of the MCC coaching book.

Roy Castle, probably the most versatile of British entertainers, came out to bat in the unenviable position of last turn before the interval. He can tell his grandchildren that he cut Bedser and hooked Voce in his total of 18, which is at least the equivalent of a month's booking at the London Palladium.

The *pièce de résistance* of the Taverners' innings came from Surridge, the captain. He sprayed the ball into the Mound Stand five times and the bat he was using was obviously not the worst one to come out of his factory. The innings finished at 2.55 with the score 305. The old internationals started badly when Robertson was stumped off Gover, an entry in the scorebook which Gover would not have appreciated in his youth. Parkhouse was well caught in the gully and Denis Compton came to the crease in another crisis.

Benaud soon came on to bowl with a radio-microphone so that tele-viewers could hear him nominating each delivery to Compton. Before the experiment really got under way Compton was bowled by Eric Bedser.

After tea the rain started to fall heavily but the players went bravely on. Godfrey Evans, whose wicket-keeping had given such joy, contributed only two shots. The first went for four and he fell flat on his face. The next went gently into Benaud's hands at mid-wicket.

With the total 236 for 7 the elements proved too much.

There were three England selectors present on the ground. Perhaps the team for the Lord's Test will come from those present in this match. They could do worse, but it will have to be a one-day Test match.

---

16 AUGUST 1964

IF ONLY THIS WAS LEEDS!

J. J. Warr

The Oval, Saturday

At 2.44 p.m. today Freddie Trueman took his 300th Test wicket. This bald statement cannot convey the extraordinary climax to one of the most colourful careers in cricket history.

Always a paradox, in his final spell he took 4 for 8 when earlier he had seemed innocuous. Given a standing ovation as he left the field, he would have been driven from the middle at Headingley in a coach and four. The applause at Kennington was warm and heartfelt, but in the North it would have rebounded off the Pennines. This rugged Yorkshireman has sweated, grunted, bowled and gestured his way to become one of the legends of the game. A cartoonists' idol and columnists' delight, he has felt controversy perpetually at his elbow. The toss of his mane and his pigeon-toed walk are as familiar to television viewers as Dr Kildare's smile.

He is to cricket what the Rolling Stones are to pop music – always in the headlines and always in the public eye.

His career started in 1949, and I was playing at Cambridge when this explosive character first swept down on to the bowling crease. The high arm and the predominant outswinger marked him as a fast bowler in the classical mould. From that moment he went on to bowl in all parts of the cricket-speaking world. Beloved by the crowds everywhere, he has only to raise an eyebrow to get a laugh.

But behind the clown's mask has lurked a burning desire to see all batsmen back in the pavilion as quickly as possible. He became universally known as 'Fiery Fred'. His activities this season are typical of the man. Starring in his own TV show, he has also been widely billed as a living example of the benefits of beer drinking.

Somewhat inconsistent this year with bat and ball, he was dropped at Manchester when Australia went on to score a mammoth total. No doubt Fred saw the funny side of that. The selectors had toyed with the idea of dropping him from the Third Test at Headingley, but were prevented when Yorkshire threatened to secede from the Commonwealth. Coming back here at The Oval he has taken four wickets with conditions right against him.

Renowned for a virility of phrase, he knows that a professorship of Anglo-Saxon awaits him at Oxford when he retires. As Honorary President of the Fast Bowlers Union, he can put his feet up now with a momentous achievement behind him. Another 299 Test wickets and I could have done the same.

---

23 AUGUST 1964

ESSEX THRASH AUSTRALIANS

J. A. Bailey

Southend, Saturday

Since the war Australian sides have approached this game as a hungry lorry driver approaches his eggs and bacon. The precedent for using Essex as whipping boys is well established.

Bradman's team — who needs reminding? — scored 721 in a day on this ground. But today the boot was on the other foot. By the time rain and bad light stopped the play at 6.15 Essex had scored 425 for six — 175 of these being scored before lunch, Barker and Fletcher running to a century partnership in 67 minutes during this time. Altogether these two added 184 in 140 minutes. Both reached excellent hundreds and with a spirited unbroken partnership between Wilcox and Edmeades adding 83 in under the hour, the Essex innings was topped off to a nicety.

Essex lost two wickets in the morning. Bear will be kicking himself for missing the boat before the gangway was even up, but it was Taylor, the other victim of Connolly, who set the tone for the innings. He scored 29 in 20 minutes. Barker and Fletcher carried on where Taylor left off. Barker, pugnacious in every movement, punched the ball to all parts, cuts and pulls bringing him the bulk of his 16 fours.

Between them these two dissected the Australian attack. Booth shuffled his pack of bowlers with a regularity borne of desperation, but failed to come up with a trump card. After Barker had left — his 100 took only 10 minutes over two hours — it was soon seen that even Bailey had caught the fever. He scored 22 in 30 minutes. There was, however, no truth in the rumour that repeated calls from the pavilion for a doctor were in any way connected with this event.

Fletcher went from strength to strength. His century came in a little over three hours, and when his beautifully compiled innings came to an end the crowd roared and, with the Australians, applauded him all the way home.

---

4 JULY 1965

SUSPECT BOWLERS SHOULD FACE PANEL

Colin Cowdrey

The sad story of Harold Rhodes all began when he joined Derbyshire at the age of 17 in 1953 as a promising batsman who bowled off-spinners.

Then, one afternoon his captain threw him the new ball because there was no one else to bowl. He hit upon a quicker ball, which proved effective and helped him to earn a place in the Test against India at

Headingley in 1959. The great Trueman of those days had difficulty in extracting any pace from a slowish pitch. At the other end young Rhodes looked half as fast again in taking four wickets for 50.

This brought a little extra out of Freddie, but hard as he tried he could not match Harold's pace. I believe that this was the first time that any suspicions were aroused. After all, here was Trueman with a magnificent physique at the height of his powers being outmatched for pace by a tall, wiry young lad who seemed to achieve everything from a whippy wrist action.

In 1960 with the cricket world buzzing about the action of South African Griffin, Rhodes's action came under the spotlight. When Derbyshire played South Africa it was with some tension that players and spectators watched to see Paul Gibb's reaction to Griffin, but to everyone's astonishment it was Rhodes who was called.

Since then Derbyshire have been to no end of trouble trying to eradicate those aspects of his action which gave rise to concern. For Rhodes this has been a tantalising spell in the wilderness, playing yet only partly playing. This year he has turned in one outstanding performance after another and for some while has headed the bowling averages. Some of the old doubts about his action have been revived. A county captain has lodged objections.

How frustrating it must be for Rhodes. If I were in his shoes I should want to bowl exhibition overs where every umpire and expert in the country could come to judge me and make up their minds for good and all. In fact, isn't this the answer? Hasn't the time come to set up a panel of five experts (three umpires and two ex-players) who can act with all speed in an emergency such as this?

If such a jury had been in operation in 1960 Paul Gibb could have referred his doubts to them and they could have moved into action. They could study extensive films. They could ask the player to bowl for them in private and they could study him from a few yards range and from every angle. They could demand to see certain types of delivery – the fast bouncer or the fast yorker, which may be the only two deliveries to break the law.

The panel might say that X throws every ball, and must be taken out of the game. In most cases, I think, they would say that X bowls fairly most of the time but that certain deliveries – the bouncer, perhaps – must be cut out, or the bowler be prepared to expect the umpire's call.

Just as valuable, this working panel would remedy the situation which arose over White of Hampshire. A few years ago an umpire was not entirely happy with the way he delivered his bouncer. This brought the odd call – quite groundless – yet the stigma has surrounded White for several seasons. A panel could have cleared White's reputation at once and, incidentally, saved umpires from further worry.

Certainly the onus of judgment would be lifted from any single umpire, and this must be a welcome move. The first-class umpire, more often than not a retired first-class cricketer, is devoted to cricket and not over-anxious to be involved in having to knock a fellow player.

For two people this week cricket has turned very sour indeed. Everyone has sympathy for Rhodes. Not so many understand the plight of Buller, one of the best umpires that the game has ever known. By doing his duty he has walked straight into a hornet's nest. He has received a swarm of stinging letters from the crowd – and others.

An umpire should never be put in this position and I hope he will soon be relieved of the fear of finding himself in it. A panel could prevent all this unpleasantness.

---

6 AUGUST 1965

ENGLAND v. SOUTH AFRICA

E. W. Swanton

Trent Bridge, Thursday

An innings was played here today by Graeme Pollock which in point of style and power, of ease and beauty of execution, is fit to rank with anything in the annals of the game.

Pollock came in when after 50 anxious minutes South Africa's score stood at 16 for two. Between this point and lunch he batted easily and without inhibition or restraint while two more wickets fell, and his companions struggled in every sort of difficulty against some very good swing bowling by Cartwright.

When the afternoon began the scoreboard showed 76 for four, Pollock 34. An hour and 10 minutes later it said 178 for 6, and Pollock was walking back with 125 to his name, and the crowd standing in salute to a glorious piece of batting which must have carried the minds of the older ones among them to Stan McCabe's great innings here against England in '38.

In cold fact this young man of 21 had made then 125 out of 162 in two hours and 20 minutes, and in the 70 minutes since lunch 91 out of 102. In his whole innings were 21 fours, and the two of these that came off the edge from Cartwright's bowling were the only false strokes of any kind that I saw. The other 19 were either hit with a full, easy-swing of the bat, or glanced or cut to every point of the compass. No one could find any way of containing him because (like E.R. Dexter, G. Sobers and R. Kanhai, perhaps alone among modern players) he uses every stroke.

He saw the ball so early that if it were of good length or more he met it with an almost leisurely movement, and drove off the front foot with a freedom and certainty that left the field standing. When the length faltered, as it did of course under such assault, he lay back and clipped the short stuff with a crack that must almost have echoed the other side of the river. It may perhaps be said by anyone trying to evaluate this innings that to have deserved the label of greatness it would have needed to be confronted by bowling of a higher quality than much that was seen.

Well, when South Africa were at their worst pass, at 43 for 4, with Bland just gone, he made three strokes to the cover boundary inside a few minutes, two off Cartwright and one off Titmus, and all three from balls that would have looked a good length to anyone else, with a precision of timing and consequent speed over the field that had everyone gasping.

With these strokes the moral balance shifted dramatically, and South Africa must have begun to see the vision of recovery so long as their young hero could stay. It may be that after lunch as his assault reached its climax the bowling began to look somewhat ragged.

The fact is, though, that until Pollock got into his stride almost anyone on the ground would have estimated South Africa's probable total at around 120, and there would have been a great many words spilt about the difficulty of getting modern bowling away, the impossibility, indeed, in conditions which allowed the ball to move as much as it did today.

Pollock has been spoken of in the same breath as Frank Woolley, and so far as the multitude of admirers of that great man are concerned such words are close to blasphemy. There is no one who holds Woolley in greater esteem than myself, and I believe that he would have been proud, at his best, to have played as well as Pollock did this afternoon.

Indeed, in the left-handedness, in the height and reach, and in the clean-cut simplicity of his striking of the ball, the comparison with Woolley is the obvious one that applies. And if any young cricketer asks how the very best of the pre-war players batted he could be safely told: 'Just like Graeme Pollock did against England at Trent Bridge'.

South Africa must have been happy to win the toss on a fine if blustery morning, for yesterday's sun had taken most of the moisture from the pitch, and there was an uncertain forecast of weather ahead. But they were in straits from an early stage against Larter and Snow, and as soon as Cartwright came on (Rumsey and Jones having been omitted from the bowling battery assembled) uncertainty gave way to disaster.

Cartwright wobbled the ball about and occasionally deviated it off the wicket. Lance fell first, and Lindsay directly afterwards. Pollock struck Cartwright for his first four through the covers as soon as he arrived, and Barlow once drove him straight to the sightscreen. But Barlow, having had to work mighty hard for 19 in an hour and a half, was caught low down by a combination of Parks and Cowdrey, the wicket-keeper managing to flick up the ball for Cowdrey to fasten on to. Parks then got rid of Bland by a most unusual piece of stumping. Bland, going forward to drive Titmus, trapped the ball with the bottom of the bat, and before he could regain his crease Parks swept the ball into the stumps. There was some question as to whether Bland was run out or stumped, but the law is quite clear in the case of a wicket-keeper who takes the ball in front of the wicket after it has hit either bat or pad.

Pollock's next partner was Bacher, who made some good strokes until, directly after lunch, from a rather less worthy one, he dragged a ball from Snow into his stumps. Van der Merwe followed to play a quite anonymous, but of course highly valuable role. He was in just over an hour with Pollock and made 10 of the 98 they added for the sixth wicket.

Pollock was caught at slip by Cowdrey chest high, and did not seem to realise he was out, having no doubt made contact with the ground at the precise moment of the ball shaving the bat.

They say, by the way, that Graeme Pollock's innings was of less merit than his 175 against Australia at Adelaide last year. I can only add I am mighty sorry I was not there.

---

8 AUGUST 1965

CAVALIERS AND ROUNDHEADS

J. J. Warr

Trent Bridge, Saturday

It has always been possible to divide cricketers into Roundheads and Cavaliers. Roundheads approach the game bristling with dourness and determination, while the Cavaliers ooze all that is devil-may-care and debonair.

There are no prizes for guessing what allegiance is held by Barlow, Bacher and Boycott. Their noses are permanently to the grindstone, and their shoulders are never far from the wheel. Among them they dominated the first two and a half hours play and their entertainment value was strictly for the connoisseur. Barlow batted with a bottom-handed belligerence and the sound of his teeth being gritted was audible in the Press box. Bacher was the prototype for all those who believe in the principles of watchfulness and nose over the ball. With Boycott bowling to these two it was almost like a summit meeting of the Exclusive Brethen of cricket. Nothing was conceded by any of the parties involved. It was all craft and counter-graft.

Oddly enough, the appearance of a prime Cavalier in the shape of R.G. Pollock ended the stalemate. Boycott's length went to pot and the cricket took on a new dimension. There are not many superlatives left to do justice to Pollock's batting. All I ask is that if he appears anywhere in the vicinity make an effort to see him. If necessary, leave the lawn unmown, the hedges untrimmed and give up the unequal struggle with the weeds.

It need hardly be added that M.J.K. Smith is firmly in the Roundhead camp as a captain. His distrust for slow bowling has been discussed at length and I believe his prejudices are based on his own preferences as a batsman. Somewhat vulnerable to the quick stuff, he thinks that all other batsmen are the same. As a very good player of slow bowling, he finds it hard to see how spinners can take wickets. This does not brand him as necessarily defensive or negative.

And this small flaw in outlook does not mean that I am against his appointment as captain in Australia. The ideal man for that job would be a combination of Billy Graham and W.G. Grace: one to lead a crusade and another to play the cricket. As they are not jointly or separately available, M.J.K. Smith is our best man for the job.

---

12 AUGUST 1965

W. WOODFULL DIES AT 67

E.W. Swanton

William Maldon Woodfull, who has died, aged 67, was a famous Australian cricketer of the inter-war time, an opening batsman who was nicknamed with good reason 'the unbowlable' and a successful Test captain.

In his 14 seasons of first-class cricket he made 13,392 runs and his average of 65 over his whole career has been exceeded by only the barest handful of the great batsmen: Bradman, inevitably, Ponsford, his equally illustrious partner for Victoria and for his country, Headley, of the West Indies, and Merchant, of India. That completes the list.

I give this illuminating fact first because it stresses a quality not perhaps generally recognised. Woodfull was anything but a spectacular player. He used an extremely short back-lift, and presented an astonishingly placid front which bowlers found none the less frustrating when they recalled that after the blunting work was done, Bradman and McCabe were probably waiting keenly with their pads on.

If no one went into rhapsodies about Woodfull as a batsman he equally failed to excite them as a captain. Yet his unassuming manner and quiet commonsense served Australia wonderfully well in a difficult era of Test cricket. Only one other Australian, Joe Darling, has captained two Ashes-winning sides in England. In between the victories of 1930 and 1934 was the Bodyline tour of 1932–3 in Australia. Then he led his country with less success. Yet for his calm demeanour in the torrid atmosphere of that disastrous episode the game of cricket was equally in his debt.

Woodfull's appointment as captain of Australia for the 1930 tour of England, over the head of his state captain, J.S. Ryder, was a sensation in its day. He was given a young side whom few people expected to regain the Ashes lost just previously to A.P.F. Chapman's team. That they did so owed much to this shy, quiet and most likeable schoolmaster. In England four years later, with the scars of the bodyline row still fresh, his tact was of equal value, and the results from Australia's point of view similarly satisfactory.

The nearest he ever came to letting his feelings get the better of him was when he had been hit grievously over the heart by Larwood in the notorious Adelaide Test of 1932–3 and the MCC manager, in an atmosphere of general bitterness, ventured into the Australian dressing room to express his sympathy.

'There are two sides out there, Mr. Warner,' he said. 'And one of them is playing cricket.' When Woodfull retired from all first-class cricket after the 1934 tour, at the age of 37, he had led his country in 25 of the 35 Tests he had played in and had made seven Test hundreds, with an overall average of 46.

But probably none of these hundreds could be matched with his second innings after the injury in the Adelaide Test already referred to. When physical courage in an opening batsman and captain was never more needed he carried his bat throughout for 75 out of the total of 193. Nothing could have expressed his character more fittingly.

---

20 MARCH 1966

HONG KONG WANT FIVE TESTS!

Michael Melford

Hong Kong, Saturday

When you find yourself watching a cricket match on the mainland of China and listening to the *Archers* through a pair of transistorised spectacles, you realise that an MCC tour is ending somewhat unusually.

On this last day MCC rattled up 266 for 6 in two and a half hours and bowled out the Colony eleven for 193. Today's opposition should have been stronger than yesterday's but their bowlers were struck for 111 in the first 50 minutes by Russell and Boycott, Russell making 59 with much brilliance. Boycott reached 100 in 95 minutes before lunch and the secretary of MCC, who plays about once a year nowadays, shared in a stand of 45 with Cowdrey.

Most long tours end in a whisper with every one counting the days, but the complete change of environment and the massive hospitality here have meant that this one is going out with a bang. There is a strong feeling, held without any disrespect to Australia and New Zealand, that next time the programmes there should be severely pruned to allow five Test matches in Hong Kong. All that will be needed then will be players of sufficient stamina.

I MAY 1966

SUNLIT DEBUT FOR WEST INDIANS

J. J. Warr

Arundel, Saturday

The West Indians began their 1966 tour at the home of the Duke of Norfolk in the incomparable setting of Arundel Castle. The weather, bad-tempered only a few days ago, was all sweetness and sunlight.

On Monday the ground itself was under water. Today the sky was Wedgwood blue and the grass was a rich and delicate green. It was estimated that 15,000 people turned up in this natural amphitheatre to see the fun. Picnics flourished on all spare patches of grass. Small boys got lost, mum forgot the salad cream and dad couldn't find the bottle-opener.

The Duke of Norfolk made a speech and the band of the Grenadier Guards played in the intervals. The West Indians blinked in the sunshine but, suspicious to the last, they kept their sweaters handy. The Duke's team had no local personalities playing because Sussex were engaged in the knockout cup at Taunton. The visitors were without Charlie Griffith: a little like watching Red Riding Hood without the wolf. He was in bed in London with gastric 'flu. His medicine drinking arm is reported to be ominously bent.

At 11.30 sharp, Graveney opened with Stewart and the Surrey captain was out for nought surprised by Hall's lack of pace. Cohen opened the other end and it must be recorded that his length was nothing like as short as many of the skirts.

Graveney and Barrington showed all their mature skill. The queues grew longer for the ice cream. Nearly poleaxed by the heat, the locals tried that smug expression to indicate that weather conditions were quite normal for the time of year.

Mike Smith was out to a shot that nearly earned him a night in the ducal dungeons. Barrington made 73 until ambition outstripped ability. The Duke's XI declared with their total at 221. The West Indians had shown all their lithe skill in the field, with the slow bowlers having the lion's share of the work.

Controversy and the burning tension of Test matches had been many light years away. When the West Indies batted, McMorris, like Stewart, also made nought, proving that it was more than just a social occasion.

The wicket was too slow for most of the spectacular strokes of our Caribbean visitors. Strangely enough their own supporters seemed unusually subdued. Perhaps the sun was too much for them.

---

10 MAY 1966

John Reason

Hove, Monday

His burly shadow undiminished by a winter in the South African sun, Milburn of Northamptonshire struck 104 before lunch here today. Admittedly it was a long morning, two and a half hours, but no doubt it seemed even longer to the Sussex bowlers. Milburn went on to make 137 out of 194. This was his second century in five days, the second time he has stumbled while in the 130s and his third hundred in successive championship matches. The only 100 he made last year was in the last match of the season.

Northants did not take full advantage of the wonderful start Milburn gave them. Oakman cut away their middle after a long spell of accurate off-spinning and they were all out for 289. Milburn hit two sixes and 20 fours. Most of these were to the short boundary on the Pavilion side, no more than 60 yards, but one was a whistling blow for six that carried nearly twice that distance over mid-off.

Another was a very testing four, all run, into the grassy distance on the other side. Except for a small patch where some rain got under the covers over the weekend, the wicket was a beauty. No one would have dreamed that it had been relaid in the winter with 9,000 square feet of new turf being moved 60 yards up the hill.

The damp patch was just about where a 6ft 4in off-spinner would want to plant the ball and Oakman plugged away at it without a rest for most of the day. He did not exactly rip through the opposition at first, but fortunately neither he nor his captain lost patience and 30 overs later they had their reward.

Oakman turned the ball quite a bit whenever he homed on target and there were one or two occasions when even Milburn was only sustained by his pads and his inside edge. Even then he had to stretch forward as far as he could. Mushtaq tried this for three balls when he came in but he made such erratic and doubtful contact that he resorted to the charge to kill the spin. Mushtaq batted patiently. He played some lovely shots with his wrists but when he had made 38 he sallied forth against Oakman once too often. Far as he travelled he did not travel quite far enough to get to the pitch of the ball and he was caught by Langridge at short-leg off the inside edge.

One run earlier Oakman had clipped the top of P.J. Watts's off stump rather easily as the batsman offered a horrible mow at the ball and one run later he had Crump caught at deep square-leg. Northants then fell apart at great speed and Buss picked up the last three wickets.

---

19 JUNE 1966

SWINGING, HUMMING, HELPING ...

J. J. Warr

Lord's, Saturday

I read that London is a swinging city. Well Lord's has certainly staged a Test match to capture that mood. The ground was humming with excitement from the first ball. It did not need mini-skirts, Rolling

Stones or even Billy Graham to convey that this was a 'with-it occasion'. 'House Full' notices were up 35 minutes before the start and a West Indian flag was fluttering bravely in the free seats.

From 11.30 onwards every incident was greeted with the extremes of rapture or gloom. Voices in various Caribbean accents kept up a constant running commentary. The umpires were helped with their decisions, the bowlers were advised on their length and direction and the batsmen had a vocal coaching manual at their disposal. When Sobers yorked Barrington at least 10 spectators were seen cart-wheeling or doing handstands. When Graveney was caught behind the wicket, the uproar was sufficient to wake up nearly every MCC member in the place.

In the afternoon Titmus provoked them into some well-organised slow handclapping that would have done credit to Rentacrowd. Sobers's opening spell was something for the connoisseur to savour. It was a rare event for the batsmen to middle the ball. Every edge was greeted with a sharp intake of breath in the free seats.

D'Oliveira seemed naturally at ease in the tense atmosphere of Test cricket. If he has a thousand nightmares he will not dream of an unluckier way to get out. Graveney's innings cast serious doubts on the selectors' sanity over the years. I am sure it is nothing that a good psychiatrist could not cure.

Overwhelmingly the day was a triumph for all those campaigning for cricket to be left alone. There has been so much meddling with the game in recent years that it needed the supreme occasion of the Lord's Test to remind us that there is life in the old dog yet. With cricketers prepared to play shots and bowl aggressively, the excitement flows naturally without cooking the books or bending the rules.

Incidentally, I think there must be a good chance that an army of photographers can rest easy in their beds. Charlie Griffith, on his form here, may not play in the next Test.

The offbeat moment of the day was the paging of jockeys Terry Biddlecombe and Josh Gifford in the heat of the afternoon. Was there a good thing running in the 3.45 at Worcester?

22 AUGUST 1966

SNOW'S TEST 59 EARNS CHURCH £34

Daily Telegraph reporter

A local bookmaker called on the Vicar of Bognor yesterday with a cheque for £34, not payment for a 'clerical flutter', but the honouring of a promise made 24 hours earlier.

The vicar is Dr William Snow, father of John Snow, the England and Sussex pace bowler and tail-end batsman. At lunchtime on Saturday, when Snow was at the Oval wicket with Lancashire's Ken Higgs and had 11 runs to his credit, the bookmaker, Mr Peter Gordon, telephoned his congratulations. Dr Snow told him that he had promised John an incentive bonus of 10 shillings for every run he scored in the match. Mr Gordon said: 'I will give you £1 for every run he scores over 25.'

He thought he was on to 'a good thing'. But Snow, whose previous highest Test score was three, shared in a 10th-wicket partnership of 128, Snow's share being 59 not out. At the Vicarage yesterday Mr Gordon said: 'I have never been so pleased to lose so much on what I thought was a perfectly safe bet.'

Dr Snow said: 'The £34 will go to church funds. The £29 10s that I owe to John to date will have to come from my own pocket. And may the good Lord help us if England have to bat again and that shrewd man Close decides to open with John.'

---

15 MARCH 1967

OBITUARY

SIR FRANK WORRELL –
A GREAT ALL-ROUNDER

E. W. Swanton

Sir Frank Mortimer Maglinne Worrell, who has died with such tragic suddenness at the age of 42, will be remembered as a cricketer of the highest attainments, as a great captain and not least as an outstanding citizen of the West Indies.

Born in Barbados on 1 August, 1924, his cricket came to light in the war years. He made 308 not out against Trinidad at the age of 19. When the West Indies re-entered the Test scene in 1948 he was a natural choice along with the other members of the trinity of 'W's' from the same island, Clyde Walcott and Everton Weekes. Thereafter the achievements in concert of these three are legendary. Walcott and Weekes had, however, retired from Test cricket when at the age of 36 Worrell was faced with his sternest trial.

In 1960 he assumed the captaincy of the West Indies in Australia for what turned out to be in all respects the best, as well as the most exciting, series of modern times. The climax of it was a motorcade through the Melbourne streets amid a cheering throng of half a million people. Three years later he led the West Indies to their famous 1963 success in England.

Announcing his retirement at the end of this tour, he was knighted the following year. By this time he had assumed high responsibilities first with the University of the West Indies in Jamaica and then as a worker in social fields with the Trinidad Government.

However, he had one further contribution to make to West Indies cricket. When in 1965 Australia visited the Caribbean, Worrell undertook the management of the West Indies team, now under the captaincy of Garfield Sobers. Thus fortified and advised, Sobers led his men to success in the rubber. Thanks to the pair of them, for the first time the West Indies now indeed bestrode the cricket firmament as undisputed champions.

Worrell was a magnificent cricketer, as elegant a batsman as ever walked to the wicket, and on his day a dangerous bowler, but it was as a leader of serene temperament who commanded the loyalty and affection of his men to an extraordinary degree that his name will shine with a special lustre in the game's history. It was, of course, his high personal qualities which gave him such a valuable influence with young people.

In the developing countries of the West Indies he seemed to have a special part to play and I believe nothing was more certain than that a Governor-Generalship would have been offered him had he lived to full maturity.

Worrell's rise as a cricketer, remarkable though it was, is simply the story of a man of much natural talent making the most of it. His development in the broader sense is even more interesting. As a young man he was considered too outspoken for the local cricket authorities of the day and on this account his services were not utilised for the first post-war West Indies tour, that to India in 1948–9. Worrell, however, set his sights on other targets besides cricket.

He forthwith began a long career in the League, first with Radcliffe and latterly with Norton, making his home in Lancashire and when not pursuing his living as a cricketer preparing for his degree at Manchester University. It was his experience of living in the north that made him such a strong anglophile and so generous a host to English visitors to the West Indies. He was a hero in Jamaica and also in Trinidad. Strangely and sadly, he was slightly less of one in his native Barbados, where there is so strong a pride of island.

Frank was a federalist who saw the many diverse elements of the West Indies as a homogeneous whole. It was this outlook that led to his frowning on what he took to be the presumption of Barbados challenging the rest of the world. Time no doubt would have brought a complete rapprochement, for he had bought land in Barbados with an eye to his distant retirement.

Turning back specifically to his cricket he made 3,860 runs in 51 Test matches with an average of 49 and took with his left-arm bowling 69 wickets at 38 apiece. These are all-round figures that only Sobers among his countrymen can exceed. He made nine Test hundreds, six of them against England, who almost invariably found him at his best.

As a batsman he was conspicuously correct in method, his bat as near to the vertical as the stroke made possible. Sir Neville Cardus has written of another and earlier great batsman that he added a bloom to the orthodox. The same could be said of Worrell. He was slim and lissom, a stylist who could not do an ugly or ungainly thing in any department.

---

20 AUGUST 1967

SECOMBE CAPS IT ALL!

J. J. Warr

Swansea, Saturday

There was indeed a welcome in the Valleys for Harry Secombe, playing for the Lord's Taverners here in their annual match against Old England. He had interrupted his holiday in Majorca for this lap of honour in his own home town. After a hostile spell of nine overs before lunch he was awarded the Swansea Cricket Club cap in the luncheon interval. He barely had enough breath to express his thanks.

Peter May, the old England captain, won the toss and Jack Robertson and Harold Gimblett took the field amidst sighs of nostalgia and a smell of mothballs. Wilf Wooller and Alf Gover, totalling well over 100 years between them, opened the bowling. The grunts would be heard for miles. The masseur in the pavilion braced himself. His services were not required, indeed the opening spell was tidy and difficult to get away.

Soon Robertson was bowled round his legs for nine, Harry Secombe was brought on to add weight to the attack. He appealed in Welsh for lbw against Spooner. Ivor Rees, the local umpire, had no hesitation in raising his finger. Harry did a cartwheel and his brother, the Rev. Fred Secombe, nodded approvingly. David Frost took over that end after lunch, and Gimblett was stumped on the leg side for a typical 57 by Ben Barnett, formerly of Australia.

Peter May scored 44 with class written on every run. He was stumped off Surridge, which should prove a fruitful talking point in Surrey circles. Allan Watkins, now coaching at Framlingham, proved that he was fitter than most, scoring 50 in 46 minutes. Trevor Bailey convinced himself that a score of 225 for 5 was a crisis and played a rugged innings, and Old England closed at 268 for 7. The Taverners' innings of 266 for 7 left them two runs short. It was dominated by a stylish 50 from Arthur Phebey, a hard-hit 49 from Barry Knight and some sensible strokes by David Frost for 39. There was also a good flourish at the end by a local player, Phil Clift.

Harry Secombe added some good lyrics to the proceedings. Indeed, the game was voted one of the best heard in these parts for years.

---

27 DECEMBER 1967

OBITUARY

S.F. BARNES – GREATEST BOWLER OF THEM ALL

E.W. Swanton

Sydney Francis Barnes, perhaps the greatest bowler of all time, died yesterday at Chadsmoor, near Cannock, Staffordshire. He was 94.

In one of his most vivid images Mr Neville Cardus has written of F.R. Spofforth that his bowling 'let in one of the coldest blasts of antagonism that ever blew across a June field'. If there is one man to whom 'The Demon's' countrymen would not have denied a similar tribute, it must surely be Sydney Barnes.

Indeed, between the two men there was a striking resemblance: both began as fast bowlers pure and simple, but soon adjusted their pace into a mere reinforcement of their great bowling art; both were tall and wiry, long-armed and strong-fingered; both had something of Cassius's lean and hungry, indeed predatory, look and both commanded alike the physical presence, the personality and the sustained intent to dominate the batsman opposing them.

Born at Smethwick in 1873 and graduating in the Birmingham League Barnes appeared in three matches for Warwickshire in the seasons of 1894–6 with singularly little success. Migrating to the Lancashire League, he still failed to make his mark in the few games which he was given for that county during the seasons 1899–1901.

Therefore his selection by A.C. MacLaren for the team which he took to Australia in the winter of 1901–2 was something of a nine days' wonder. But the insight of that great judge of cricket was triumphantly justified when in the first two Test matches Barnes took 19 wickets for 15 apiece; an injury to a knee then put him out of action.

There followed two full seasons for Lancashire in which he took a total of 213 wickets, but he then committed himself finally to the Leagues and Staffordshire, emerging into first-class cricket only to play in Test matches and for the Players against the Gentlemen. It says much for the wealth of bowling talent open to the selectors that, though he went to Australia with the side captained by A.O. Jones in 1907–8 and took 24 wickets in the Tests on that tour, he had only played in four Test matches at home when his third visit to Australia, with Warner's side in 1911–12, set the decisive seal on his fame.

On that tour with F.R. Foster as his brilliant partner, he took 34 wickets in the five games and was universally acclaimed as the greatest bowler ever to have visited that country.

But before war came still greater heights were to be scaled: in the three Test matches against the South Africans played in the Triangular Tournament of 1912 he took 34 wickets for eight runs each and then, for the MCC side that toured that country in 1913–14, he took in four Test matches 49 wickets for an average of under 11. His 17 in the Johannesburg match has since been surpassed by Laker's feat at Manchester, but no bowler in history has ever averaged 12 wickets a match in a Test series nor can any man rival his figures in Test cricket, and that against our strongest opponents, of 189 wickets at a cost of 16.43 each.

After the war he played in only some half-dozen first-class matches, but for Wales against the West Indies in 1928 his analysis was 12 for 118 and in the next year against the South Africans he took 18 of their wickets in two matches for 7 each; he was then 56 years old!

Had Barnes been born 50 years later how would he have appeared in action on the television screen to the millions for whom his name would have been a household word? Two steps and then a few long springy strides, a long arm swinging high over and past an intensely concentrated face, and then the final whip from wrist and fingers of steel, the pace would be lively, verging on fast, the length superbly controlled; above all there would be a dominating impression of sustained hostility directed by a calculating mind.

A typical over: first, perhaps, two very late out-swingers straight enough and well enough up to force the batsman to play off the front foot, then two penetrating off-breaks, the fifth ball a fast leg-break – and a leg-break it was rather than a leg-cutter – and finally such a delivery as on his great Australian tour clean bowled Victor Trumper at the height of his powers, a ball swerving from the leg stump on to the off and then breaking back to hit the leg. 'It was the sort of ball', said Charlie Macartney, 'that a man might see when he was tight.'

------

21 MARCH 1968

ROUGH JUSTICE SERVED BY ENGLAND VICTORY

SOBERS TO BE APPLAUDED

E. W. Swanton

Port of Spain, Wednesday

Colin Cowdrey's MCC team fly off from Trinidad this morning to their final games in Guyana with thankfulness in their hearts, mingled perhaps with some sense of incredulity, that the luck should have turned with such a vengeance in their favour.

Let us look briefly at the background to their victory by seven wickets. Here at Queen's Park Oval in the first Test they were the moral winners without question, having been the aggressors throughout. At Sabina Park, the bare scorebook paints the picture of a narrow English escape, but the fact is that Cowdrey was on the verge of victory when the riot occurred on the fourth afternoon. I must be excused for repeating the view that that sad event gave the West Indies breathing space, and deflated the England side correspondingly at the moment when they were poised for the kill.

At Bridgetown, England led by 100 on the first innings after losing the toss and, whereas with a little more time they might have won, there was no stage when the West Indies could have done so. But here, in their first innings, the West Indies completely mastered the English bowling from start to finish and scored at a speed (measured in runs per over or per 100 balls) that has rarely been exceeded in modern Test cricket. The figures are four and 65 respectively.

They led on the first innings by 122 by a quarter to five on the fourth day, despite the loss of four hours play thus far, including 100 minutes on Monday, but for which they ought to have been in a position to declare very early yesterday and give themselves most of the last day wherein to bowl England out a second time.

There is no precedent, so far as I know, for defeat in a Test match suffered by a side that has declared twice with a total loss of only nine wickets. There are remarkably few precedents for one declaration being followed by defeat let alone two. So there it is, England have won the one Test of the four that they least deserved to win. Yet it may be said, I hope and think with fair-mindedness and charity, that a certain rough justice has been served. In the series so far a good case can be made for the view that England deserve to be one up.

Test captains should never be held too closely to what they say in the moment of victory and defeat and one, therefore, accepted with strong mental reservations both Cowdrey's comment that he considered Sobers's declaration a 'shrewd one', and also Sobers's remark that if you have two sides playing defensive cricket you don't get a game at all.

Sobers's implication here was justified maybe up to a point on the evidence of this fourth Test, but scarcely on the series as a whole. As to the shrewdness, there were many West Indian Test cricketers in the pavilion afterwards who used other language though there were warm and general congratulations on the English win.

What Cowdrey went on to suggest was that if two or three English wickets had fallen quickly in the chase for runs, the West Indian wrist spinners might then have capitalised on any uncertainty in the English ranks as to the prime objective.

Many readers will recall how this tactical vacuum, as one might call it, helped Australia to win when they were a half-beaten side at Old Trafford in 1961.

I believe that Sobers, a gambler by nature, slightly misread his hand, under-estimated the English capacity to make runs against the clock when they really see the green light and perhaps took too little account of his own weakness *in defence*, with Griffith unavailable to bowl. Otherwise, there is no feasible explanation for his not having insisted on an all-out assault on the English bowling yesterday morning, irrespective of the irritation that the West Indians must have felt at an over rate of 11 an hour.

English sides, for that matter, have been frustrated by this sort of thing when Hall and Griffith were in their heyday, but two wrongs can never make a right. In the final analysis all followers of cricket must applaud Sobers for snapping his fingers at the tradition of Test cricket that maintains one must never give the enemy a chink of a chance of winning: and they will note, too, with warm approval that, as the end approached, he brought no gamesmanship to bear in the way of a 'go slow'. Nothing became either Sobers's team or the Trinidad spectators better than the manner of their losing.

Lastly, but not least, there will be a wide feeling of satisfaction that Cowdrey, for whom things have so often gone wrong at the decisive moment, was, with cool-headed help from Boycott, the chief architect of success.

Not even Sir Leonard Hutton or Peter May, the two great post-war English batsmen-captains, have made bigger personal contributions to a victory than his 148 and 71 in this match.

24 AUGUST 1968

TEST CENTURY PUTS TOUR IN JEOPARDY

All who detest the intrusion of politics into sport, will be sad at the possibility, which would seem to exist, that Basil d'Oliveira's fine innings at the Oval yesterday may imperil MCC's tour to South Africa in the autumn, **writes E.W. Swanton.**

The situation is this. On 12 April last year Mr Vorster, the South African Prime Minister, announced a relaxing of apartheid principles insofar as they affected teams from overseas countries 'with which we have had traditional sporting ties'.

MCC have inferred, naturally enough, that this policy declaration covered cricket, since official teams have been visiting South Africa for something like 80 years. One English side actually sailed out towards the end of the Boer War before the peace treaty was signed at Vereeniging.

While the New Zealand Rugby Board have had specific assurances that their Maori complement will be received, MCC officially at any rate, have not sought confirmation in the case of what perhaps until today was a hypothetical situation regarding d'Oliveira, who is a Cape coloured by birth and now of British nationality.

After d'Oliveira's 158, it is hardly conceivable that he will not find a place on merit when the party is named next Wednesday. When I checked the position with the secretary of MCC, S.C. Griffith, earlier in the week he merely said: 'We assume that any side we nominate will be acceptable.' If it is not MCC would have no alternative but to decline to go, notwithstanding the great disappointment that this would cause in South Africa.

One sincerely hopes that their team will be acceptable. Yet there is a persistent rumour from South Africa, the source of which is however elusive, that their government have had second thoughts, and that d'Oliveira would not be persona grata. This for many was the vague shadow that overhung an otherwise cloudless day at the Oval. Let it be hoped that it may prove a mirage induced by gossip and the heat.

---

30 AUGUST 1968

END OF MY GEATEST DREAM, SAYS BASIL D'OLIVEIRA

As the controversy over Basil D'Oliveira's omission from the MCC team to tour South Africa grew yesterday, the Cape Coloured all-rounder expressed his bitter disappointment in this special article

Basil D'Oliveira

When I said yesterday that I was bitterly disappointed, that still sums up the whole situation. My first thought was to say nothing at all while I sorted out the turmoil in my own mind. But I have been so moved by the messages of encouragement and understanding that I feel I must grope around for something to say.

However, even now, I can't reach any conclusions. As I am trying to put everything into perspective, the events and the emotions come driving back. For instance, strange though it seems, I can, at this moment, still see the ball going off the bat as I turned Gleeson for a single to get my Test century at the Oval last Friday.

I can't lie about that innings. I played it with only one thought in mind. It was the one great chance, the one opportunity and I was going to take it. I knew that not even 99 would be enough. It had to be a hundred. As I scored that 100th run I kept saying to myself: 'I've done it. I've done it. I had my chance and I've done it.'

Going back to South Africa was a dream – a dream I dearly wanted to come true. It is still hard for me to realise that the dream has been shattered. This dream of going back to my homeland has been in the forefront of my mind ever since I gained my first Test cap against the West Indies at Lord's in 1966. From that moment friends kept reminding me about the tour to South Africa this year.

This is what I had lived for. The chance to be going back. To go there knowing I would play on grounds where before I could only sit with my sandwiches in a confined area. Just to walk on to the grounds at Newlands, The Wanderers, Kingsmead and to others as a member of the MCC and to know that I was there, chosen as a cricketer.

I made no other plans for the winter although I had been offered coaching jobs. Several new offers have come during the past 24 hours, but at the moment I am trying to concentrate on my cricket and finish the season with Worcestershire. At least I do not feel the same despair as I did 10 days ago just before I was recalled to the Oval Test.

I did not mind so much when I was dropped after the first Test at Manchester because I accepted that, if England were to get equal with the Australians, they probably needed a stronger attack and I had to make way for another front-line bowler. I did hope to get my place back so that I could earn a ticket to South Africa.

As one Test followed another and I was still rejected my despair swarmed over me, and although I did not realise it my cricket suffered. Not considered for the final Test, little county form with the bat and not a hope of a tour place, last week I went to London to discuss my future with a friend. I was despondent. I was thinking of League cricket. The selectors seemed to have lost faith in my ability to play at Test level. I knew I could. I wanted to prove it and, unbelievable as it may seem, at the moment I learned I was to be given the chance my despair disappeared.

I know that many in South Africa will be sharing my disappointment. There are reports that some will demonstrate. I hope they do not. They love their cricket; they have every reason to look forward to the MCC players – a great bunch of players. MCC will give immense pleasure and I send them my sincerest wishes for a happy and successful tour, especially to skipper Colin Cowdrey and my own county captain Tom Graveney, two men to whom I owe so much.

If I can't be with them in the dressing room I shall be very near to them on the field.

---

14 SEPTEMBER 1968

SELECTORS SHOWED THEIR COURAGE

PROTESTS ON D'OLIVEIRA

Sir – I wonder whether there has ever been so much nonsense talked about any cricketing matter as about Mr D'Oliveira's non-selection for the team to tour South Africa.

Like countless others I have the utmost sympathy for him in his failure to achieve what was perhaps the dearest wish of his life. I admire the dignity with which he has accepted his disappointment.

I do not support apartheid. I took part as a sympathiser in the great March on Washington in 1963, led by the late Dr Martin Luther King. I deeply regret that it could not be publicly demonstrated in South Africa that those with white skins can live and play happily on equal terms with one whose skin is darker.

However, there is no reason to believe that the tour would not have taken place had Mr D'Oliveira been selected, especially since the South Africans have agreed to accept a New Zealand rugby team in 1970, whether Maoris are included or not.

The claims made for him rest on two admirable innings, both in Test matches, one of which, helped by Australian fielding, enabled England to draw the series. Otherwise, however, he has had an undistinguished season following a tour in the West Indies when his bowling was ineffective, his batting was an almost unbroken succession of failures, and his fielding lapses possibly cost us victory in at least one Test match.

The omission of a British-born cricketer with this record would probably have passed with little comment, as has that of Mr Milburn. The selectors have been criticised and called cowardly for supposedly bowing to political pressures. They should instead be congratulated on their courage in backing their judgment in spite of the protests they must have foreseen.

They are men of integrity, and all were good or great cricketers in their time. Their collective experience of overseas tours and knowledge of conditions likely to be encountered far exceeds that of any of your correspondents. They deserve more support than they receive, and our gratitude for the countless hours throughout the season spent on their usually thankless task.

Yours faithfully,
R.T.M. LINDSAY
Sherborne, Dorset

16 JUNE 1969
PARADISE LOST

Sir – Shade of Wordsworth watching England's pedestrian scoring:
> '*Milburn, thou shouldst be batting at this hour!*
> *England hath need of thee ...*'

C.A. Norrington
Plaistow, Sussex

---

13 APRIL 1969
MCC MUST STATE A POLICY ON RACE

David Sheppard *says it is time cricket stood firm against South Africa*

Last week's addition to the D'Oliveira file ought to put back into the melting-pot the question of South Africa's tour to this country next year. When the subject was discussed at the special MCC meeting last December some vital information was kept back from the members; the MCC Committee chose to conceal the fact that Lord Cobham had passed on Mr Vorster's warning to him last March that D'Oliveira would not be acceptable as a member of the MCC team.

As one of the committee's critics I had known from Lord Cobham about his conversation with Mr Vorster three days after the non-selection of D'Oliveira. This fact had quite a lot to do with steeling myself to going through with my part in our criticism of the committee's handling of the matter. But I was unable to use the knowledge because I had been told in confidence. The tangled web of disclosures should not distract us from the central point at issue.

The real villain of the piece is not the MCC Committee but the all-pervading South African policy of all things separate in which the South African Cricket Association has always so lamely acquiesced. Men of goodwill at Lord's have been pushed into positions they have felt they must conceal, because they have tried to compromise with a set-up which is basically wrong.

Instead of bumbling from one crisis to another, we need to declare a public policy in which we really believe and insist that those who want to take part in international cricket should abide by it. I hope that the International Cricket Conference will shortly have the preparation of such a statement on its agenda.

The immediate issue is whether South Africa should be invited here in 1970. Consider five relevant points of contact between the two countries since January, 1968.

First, on 5 January 1968, MCC wrote to the South African Cricket Association, in a friendly cricketing country, asking them to 'confirm that no pre-conditions will be laid on the selection of the MCC team'. The letter has never been answered.

Secondly, on 13 March 1968, the South African Prime Minister told Lord Cobham that a particular England cricketer, D'Oliveira, would not be accepted.

Thirdly, during last summer, as I have been told by several people at Lord's, Mr Arthur Coy, a former President of the South African Cricket Association, attempted to tell the MCC Secretary and others that it would be better if D'Oliveira were not selected. Billy Griffith, the MCC Secretary, refused to listen to him at all. Griffith has been in the most unenviable position. He is not the policy-maker, but as Secretary the servant of the committee. He has loyally, and in my opinion with great integrity, tried to work out the unworkable policy, or 'non policy', which has been handed down to him.

Fourthly, it is plain that there is truth behind last week's other story that a large sum was offered D'Oliveira in July/August from a South African source (not an official source) to accept a coaching contract which would have made him unavailable for the MCC tour.

Fifthly, when MCC finally selected their team it was rejected by the South African Government.

The MCC Council has invited South Africa here as though nothing had taken place in the last year. They propose to entertain a team sent by the same South African Cricket Association without any sign of the change of heart or of progress towards non-racial, non-political cricket. We ought not to play against South Africa again until evidence can be given of concrete progress by South Africa towards non-racial cricket.

Some are saying that if we insist on adhering to such principles all international sport will come to an end. This is not true. It underlines the need for the International Cricket Conference to produce a written statement which member countries should adhere to. We have come a long way since Archie Maclaren asked a few cricketers he knew to go to Australia with him. That may or may not be something to regret, but the modern situation has to be faced.

We need a policy. This has never just been the 'D'Oliveira Affair'. What is at stake is that we play non-racial cricket and we believe in it. When we play white South Africa we force our own players to take part in a racialist situation. Much was made in the committee's defence of the value of sport as a 'bridge' between different peoples. That is exactly what I believe sport can be.

On a tiny scale locally in East London we have a Canning Town cricket club. Its members are about equally immigrants (largely Indians and Pakistanis) and English natives. Instead of sitting self-consciously in a room and talking about race relations we have met on the common bridge of cricket. The same thing happens in a thousand other localities, but how is it 'building bridges' to play against a South African team from which over 80 per cent of their population is excluded? And if English cricket commits itself to such racialist situations what damage does that do to the good bridge-building between races that our game can provide?

We have our own racial problems in this country and we are not doing very well at them. Sport can be a great help and we need to strengthen every helping hand that is available.

CHAPTER 4
THE 1970s

INTRODUCTION

E.W. Swanton always considered the 1970s as the 'Changing Years'. From the international isolation of South Africa, the inception of the first World Cup through to the Packer affair of the late 1970s, it was tumultuous time for the game.

But the 'Changing Years' were not just confined to cricket. For Swanton, his time as cricket correspondent ended with retirement in 1975. Of course, his prolific output continued. His column appeared in the *Daily Telegraph* until shortly before his death in 2000 and his shadow lurked over the newspaper's cricket coverage up until the late 1990s. Swanton regularly contributed obituaries of friends and players and here we see him fondly recall the careers of Learie Constantine and Frank Woolley – a man whom he would later vote as one of the five best cricketers of the twentieth century. Swanton, was, of course, a man of his age and some of his phraseology would not be printed in the *Telegraph* of today. It is important we read these articles with that in mind, and so his pieces have not been changed for this book.

Swanton's retirement allowed Michael Melford, for many years Swanton's able deputy, to step into the job. Melford had honed his talents as cricket correspondent of the *Sunday Telegraph*, and the subsequent reshuffle opened up an opportunity for the former England captain Tony Lewis to join the *Telegraph* team full-time.

Lewis replaced Melford at the *Sunday Telegraph* and his appointment as cricket correspondent sparked a change in direction. The Sunday newspaper cricket feature was born. The lengthy chronological details imparted by Swanton were largely dropped by the *Sunday Telegraph* partly perhaps because of the spread of television, which had rendered the long reportage of previous cricket reports fusty and old-fashioned. Lewis was not afraid to let his opinions roam free and combined them with a readable and droll turn of phrase.

He initially combined his position with that of rugby correspondent, which precluded him from covering overseas tours. But by the end of the 1970s Lewis was on the road and through his words we are given a ringside seat at Packer's Circus – World Series Cricket.

The Packer affair dominated the late 1970s coverage and the sacking of Tony Greig as England captain in 1977 was front-page news in the *Daily Telegraph*. A quick flick through the *Telegraph* archives predicts little of the future controversy. In his yellowing and faded clippings folder, an early cutting sees Kerry Packer named as Terry. It would not be long before the Australian magnate's name would be all too familiar to the *Telegraph*'s news and sports writers.

Packer's High Court case against the Test and County Cricket Board – who were attempting to ban players who signed up with WSC – had everything a newspaper could wish for. The tall, dashing Greig provided a touch of glamour but also possessed, much more importantly, a brilliant ability to manipulate the media. Coverage was often on the front page and the subsequent ruling in favour of WSC was greeted with a plethora of letters to the editor. Packer was a master at spinning a story and here we see him defend his actions in an interview with the *Sunday Telegraph*'s Alan Lee.

But cricket was also united in the 1970s as England hosted the first-ever World Cup in 1975. The tournament took place over just two weeks but that was long enough for the sceptics to be proved wrong. The *Telegraph* took its time to assess how to cover the tournament and it was only as the World Cup became a success that they threw their support behind it wholeheartedly. 'This summer extravaganza of cricket', wrote Lewis after the West Indies won the Lord's final.

On many occasions Lewis wrote affectionately of Lord's and in May 1975 we see him at his playful best. The decision to allow women to play at cricket's headquarters was a subject he could not resist: 'Lord's has fallen; hitch up your skirts, ladies, Mecca cannot be withheld from you any longer.' Sadly, it was. The first female member of the MCC was not admitted until 1990. The club's president? A.R. Lewis.

6 JANUARY 1971

FIRST EVER ONE-DAY INTERNATIONAL

E. W. Swanton

Melbourne

Melbourne's consolation prize, the one-day 40-over match between fully representative English and Australian teams, turned out wonderfully well. Australia won deservedly enough with five overs and five wickets to spare, but only after a day of sustained interest with the arts of the game in full display.

Lawry therefore accepted $2,400 (£1,120), the winner's share of the cheque provided by Rothmans, but the $200 (£93) man of the match, nominated by Charlie Elliott, the English umpire out here, thanks to the Winston Churchill Fellowship, was John Edrich, a choice that could scarcely have been in dispute.

The only cloud on the day was that at the end of his fine innings Edrich stretched a tendon in the thigh, and though the strain is not thought to be very severe there must be some doubt whether he will be right for the fourth Test starting at Sydney on Saturday. The authorities thought that on a working day 25,000 would be a pretty good crowd. In fact 46,000 sat sprinkled thickly round the great bowl enjoying the sunshine and lapping it all up: a glad sight after the frustrations of the past week.

Lawry put England in and the innings was upheld by Edrich from its start until he was out in the 32nd over at 156 for seven. He played particularly well, timing the ball better than others whose strokes are held in higher repute and hitting five of the eight 4s — 95 yards to the sight screens and 93 yards square — of the innings.

Thomson, with his width on both sides and the number of short ones that bounced head-high, was hard to score from and Boycott had managed only eight in as many eight-ball overs before he hooked downwards and connected well, only to see Lawry make a fine catch close at square-leg. The next stand, between Edrich and Fletcher, saw England get to terms with the situation. By good strokes and fast running they made 66 together in 12 overs, being specially hard on Connolly as the analyses reveal.

The moment had come for the introduction of Mallett, the slow off-spinner. His first over yielded seven but in his next Fletcher, going for the straight hit, skied over the deep mid-off and Greg Chappell took an excellent catch running back as the ball came over his head. D'Oliveira kept up the momentum until the senior Chappell, Ian, made a brilliant left-handed stop in the covers and D'Oliveira, the non-striker, could not regain his ground. At 124 for 3, with 16 overs to go, England were now well placed but the middle subsided, entirely to the spin bowling.

Hampshire succumbed to a very good running catch at long-on, Cowdrey was caught at the wicket cutting, and Illingworth was bowled behind his legs essaying the sweep. Worse still, Edrich flicked Mallett into long-leg's hands, leaving only Knott and three bowlers, and eight overs to go. Knott was full of life and strokes, but one felt at the end that England had needed another 30. Stackpole, with Brisbane behind him, was an obvious danger but in the fourth over Shuttleworth took a capital right-handed caught and bowled. If Underwood, substituting for Edrich, could have hit the bowler's stumps from mid-on Australia's openers would both have been back cheaply.

Ian Chappell was not particularly happy but Walters soon looked as though he were going to snatch the game for Australia. One was reminded of his early Test innings with all their promise as he straight drove Illingworth for two lovely 4s and off-drove Lever for another. Walters had made 41 out of 60 in 12 overs before he was caught at the wicket off D'Oliveira, cutting: 117 for 3, 74 to make and 16 overs to get them.

It was at this point that Ian Chappell, almost as though in desperation, cut loose and in two overs, one each from Illingworth and D'Oliveira, the result was settled and sealed barring something quite sensational. There was one magnificent six off Illingworth, a carry of well over 100 yards, and several other hits of much violence in differing quality.

Illingworth, continuing the slow bowlers' tally of wickets, persuaded Redpath into a dreadful cow-shot, and in a subtle piece of co-operation with Knott had Ian Chappell stumped on the leg-side. However, by now there were overs and wickets to spare, and some elegant strokes by Greg Chappell brought a memorable day to a close.

15 FEBRUARY 1971

EDITORIAL

NOT QUITE CRICKET

Australian cricket-lovers should know that what happened on Saturday evening in the Test match at Sydney leaves just as nasty a taste in our mouths as in theirs. They may be disturbed to see a fast bowler who has just felled a lower-order batsman with a bumper standing coldly aloof as though the matter were no concern of his. So are we. They may be annoyed by that bowler's rudeness to the umpire who cautions him. So are we. They may be shocked to watch an MCC captain loudly complaining to that umpire, and accompanying his complaints with insolent gestures. So are we. They may be flabbergasted to see that captain shortly afterwards petulantly marching his whole team off the field just because of a minor fracas in one corner of the ground. So are we. No, of course, beer cans should not be thrown (nor for the matter shirts tugged). Yet, with some of the 'entertainment' which has been offered on this tour, it would be a hard heart which denied to the spectators even the solace of beer.

We knew we had not sent the most scintillating or star-studded or well-balanced team in Test history. Well, Comptons, Dexters, Barbers and Milburns do not grow on every tree; but even lesser mortals can at least be polite and patient. Umpires may well complain that the present law against intimidatory bowling is vague and subjective: perhaps it ought to be changed. Until it is, it is their unenviable duty to enforce it as best they can, and the duty of players, and of captains above all, to obey without beefing.

---

16 FEBRUARY 1972

In a Press interview yesterday when he tried to explain why he had led the England team off the field on Saturday evening, Ray Illingworth said: 'So far as I am concerned the incident is finished.' The captain may hope that this is the case, but of course the reality must be otherwise, **cables E.W. Swanton in Sydney.**

This is the 209th Test match between England and Australia, and though there have been many occasions of tension no side has ever left the field without reference to the umpires and been subsequently warned by them that if they refused to play they would forfeit the match.

Whatever the Australian Board of Control may do the English Cricket Council, as the ruling body, must expect from the Test and County Cricket Board the results of a full inquiry into the whole affair. That elements in the crowd behaved in a thoroughly disorderly way there is no argument and this poses a problem in control in these permissive days that might well make Australian cricket authority particularly apprehensive with the South African tour coming up later in the year. That is their problem.

What their English counterparts have to concern themselves with is the provocation to the crowd's misconduct by the chief characters on the field from the moment that Jenner was hit. As millions of English viewers as well as Australian could see for themselves Illingworth expostulated angrily with umpire Rowan after the latter had warned Snow under the intimidation law.

Before any cans were thrown the captain apparently cocked his thumb in the direction of the dressing-room as though indicating that he might take his men off. Snow, meanwhile, glowered at the umpire, and in case anyone should be in any doubt as to his feelings in the matter he snatched his hat rudely from him when the over ended a moment or two later.

Illingworth, before the game was continued, was also to be seen gesturing to his own players with one finger, maintaining that Snow had bowled only a single bumper in the over in question. All this was adding insult to injury with the spectators. They had watched Snow peppering their batsmen throughout the series. He had just injured one of them with a blow on the head.

There were all the elements of explosion as Snow then walked down to and beyond his place at long-leg right up to the pickets and with one foot in the drain seemingly prepared to continue the argument. This was too much for some, and the tangling and the tins followed. It was the signal for Illingworth immediately to march off to the dressing-room. Some of his side followed at a reluctant pace and the batsmen stood firm, as at first did the umpires.

The latter, quite rightly, may not be interviewed but I suspect that if Lou Rowan were to be he would say that the offence of bowling to intimidate is cumulative. While possibly he was somewhat hasty in invoking the warning when he did (there were two bumpers in this particular over), he might certainly have done so during the morning's play.

Whatever one's interpretation of the law, however, acceptance of the umpire's verdict is the first lesson that is drummed into every young cricketer, and by his openly questioning it Illingworth has shown a singularly bad example to cricketers everywhere as well as putting a superfluous strain on cricket relations between England and Australia. Illingworth's defence of his action on Saturday was that he considered one of his players was in danger of serious injury and that his taking his side off was in the interest of a quick resumption of play.

My own view was that his doing so was precipitate, and that with a modicum of tact and self-discipline all round the situation would never have arisen.

---

18 FEBRUARY 1971

E.W. Swanton

Sydney

The Ashes, after 12 long years in Australia's keeping, were recaptured with the minimum of excitement in Sydney yesterday after an hour and a half's cricket with more than a day of the seventh Test to spare.

Australia's middle and tail never looked like achieving what their chief batsmen, Stackpole excepted, had failed to do, which was to wrest the initiative from the English attack. The victory is all the more conclusive when it is recalled that England had been put in on a pitch that was helpful to bowlers at the start and grew progressively better, that they began the match without Boycott, their best batsman, and concluded it without Snow, whose injured hand allowed him to bowl only two overs in Australia's second innings.

If anyone had had any doubt that England were the better side the course of this game should have persuaded them. After the first day of the first Test they have looked to be so more often than not. That the Ashes have been retaken at a heavy and wholly unnecessary cost in terms of sportsmanship should have been evident enough to those who have followed the tour in these columns.

But such considerations apart, it is all to the good so far as the ancient series is concerned that at the sixth time of asking the supremacy should have changed hands, and Ray Illingworth is to be congratulated on his tactical handling of the side and also on the useful part that his own contributions have made. To average 37 with a top score of 53 argues an admirable consistency and the only criticism of his bowling has been that as his second innings figures suggest he has not bowled himself enough.

Snow, of course, has been the chief bowler of the series just as Boycott has been the outstanding batsman, while Knott's wicket-keeping has given almost more pleasure than any other item of the cricket. Add the batting of Edrich, Luckhurst and D'Oliveira and the bowling support provided at various times by Lever, Underwood and Willis, and the sum of it all is a solid all-round performance which Australia could not match.

The state of Australian cricket is indeed mystifyingly moderate. More people play the game than have ever done so and the public support, considering the relative lack of glamour in the two sides, has been satisfactory enough.

Players possessed of authentic Test technique seem, however, extraordinarily scarce and while Greg Chappell and one or two more have shown promise, the season has not thrown up any new players who one can be sure will be carrying the Australian standard with distinction in the decade ahead.

The limitations of Bill Lawry's side were strikingly apparent in England in 1968 when they would certainly have surrendered the Ashes if they had not been saved by the weather. In South Africa, again under Lawry, Australia were beaten a year ago 4–0, and this season, under Lawry still until this last Test, the series in all human probability would have been decided at Adelaide had England enforced the follow-on.

Of the seven sides that have confronted England in Australia since the war this, in my view, is much the weakest. When before this tour started and conscious of the lack of balance in the MCC side I said I thought the odds were fractionally on Australia, I took insufficient account of the South African evidence, supposing the Australians had been hopelessly jaded after their visit to India.

Perhaps they were, but the fact is that so far as the playing of fast bowling is concerned such men as Walters, Ian Chappell, and even Redpath, have gone back while Lawry, the stalwart for so long, has seemingly lost his attacking strokes.

Though I suspect that the Australian players as well as the public may have welcomed Ian Chappell's accession to the captaincy for this Sydney Test, there is little doubt that in a Test of six days with time a minor consideration Lawry would have made things much more difficult for England. With an average of 40, to find himself displaced by an older man new to Test cricket, Eastwood, was indeed a galling blow — which it might be added he has borne in a buoyant, uncomplaining spirit.

Australia's slim chance yesterday of making the further 100 they needed from their last five wickets was for Greg Chappell to carry the show with aggressive bats like Marsh and Jenner playing their natural game. There was a little turn to be had from the pitch which Illingworth judged to be better suited to spin than speed. Apart from one over from Lever, the captain, Underwood and D'Oliveira controlled the matter and took the wickets. Only 8 runs had been added to the 123 before Marsh offered a sadly crooked swing at Underwood and was bowled. Illingworth, though, posed the greater problems, tying young O'Keeffe in terrible knots and at least once having him perilously near lbw.

Chappell was disposed to come to meet him and succeeded for a while until he launched forth at a quicker ball that went with the arm, missed and duly became Knott's 24th and final victim. The figure incidentally is a record for an Anglo-Australian series but the playing of an extra Test nullifies all comparisons with the past. With five Tests played Knott, with 20 wickets, stood equal with Tallon and Grout.

Chappell's dismissal sealed the result. O'Keeffe swept D'Oliveira to Shuttleworth, the substitute, Lillee was taken first ball in the slips, while Jenner, a natural forcer, having attempted not a single stroke in 45 minutes, was caught off bat and pad to bring the game and the series to a curious but not wholly inappropriate end.

LORD CONSTANTINE, FIRST NEGRO LIFE PEER, DIES

E.W. Swanton

Lord Constantine, who has died, aged 69, built a life of noted public service in several fields on the original base of his fame as a cricketer.

Welfare officer, civil servant, barrister, minister in the Trinidad Government, High Commissioner for his native island in London, member of the Race Relations Board, of the Sports Council and of the General Advisory Council of the BBC. Such were the distinctions that came to him when his playing days were over.

Finally in 1969 came the life peerage, in regard to which he said: 'I think it must have been for what I have endeavoured to do to make it possible for people of different colour to know each other better and live well together.' Learie Nicholas Constantine took the title of Baron Constantine of Maraval in Trinidad and Tobago and of Nelson in the County Palatine of Lancaster.

He announced last month that he must leave Britain. He had asthma and had been warned by his doctor that another winter in this country would kill him.

He was the first coloured life peer. The first non-European to become a member of the House of Lords was Lord Sinha, an Indian, who became an hereditary peer in 1919. In his public and other capacities Lord Constantine made his mark, but in the memory of those who saw him play, or merely read of his exploits, his cricket has a place apart.

There have been many all-rounders with better records on paper with both bat and ball; but it is hard to think of one who made a more sensational impact, in either department, and above all impossible to imagine his superior as a fielder anywhere. So far as the English public were concerned, he was the first of the great players from the Caribbean islands.

Fast bowler, hitter, and performer of every sort of lithe, juggling acrobatics in the field, he indeed personified West Indian cricket from the first faltering entry into the Test arena in 1928 until the post-war emergence of the trinity of Worrell, Weekes, and Walcott.

Born into a sporting family in the cricketing hot-bed of Port of Spain — his father L.S. had come to England on the second West Indian visit of 1906 — he toured here first as a young man of 21 in 1923, making no real mark except in the field. His second appearance five years later was a different story from the moment when in early June he brought about a single-handed victory over a powerful Middlesex side to which the history of cricket has few parallels.

He reached the double of a thousand runs and a hundred wickets on that tour — one of nine overseas cricketers only to have ever done so — without however distinguishing himself in the Tests. And the plain fact is that though Constantine achieved several spectacular things in his 18 Tests his record of 641 runs, average 19, and 58 wickets, average 30, is a poor reflection of his talent.

Though general impetuosity (and poor West Indian slip-fielding!) cost him dear in the highest class Learie Constantine was, need it be said, the ideal Saturday afternoon League cricketer, a magnet without compare before or since.

From 1929 onwards until the mid-50s he made his home in Lancashire. In the war he did a Civil Defence job there until called to London by the Ministry of Labour. Small wonder that in his maturity the town of Nelson bestowed upon him its freedom.

Like Sir Frank Worrell after him, he furthered his own education while making his living as a cricketer, being finally admitted to the Bar after various diversions at the ripe age of 54.

None could call Lord Constantine a modest man, but gifts of warmth and friendliness as well as a shrewd brain and ready tongue helped to make him one of the personalities of his time. Back now in Trinidad, he became Minister of Works and Transport in the first party government, and on the granting of independence in 1962 he was knighted on taking up the new post of High Commissioner in London.

He married in 1927 Norma Agatha Cox, of Port of Spain, Trinidad, and had a daughter.

————————

4 JULY 1971

CALL HIM BOYCOTT THE INEVITABLE

Michael Melford

Lord's

Yorkshire in recent weeks have lived and died with Boycott and their innings yesterday followed the pattern faithfully right down to the almost inevitable run-out. Throughout the innings of 320 Boycott batted with magnificent infallibility and when the last wicket fell at half-past six he was still unconquered with 182, his sixth hundred in 13 innings this season.

The Yorkshire captain, already averaging 109 before yesterday, had made scarcely an error, apart from the call for a single which added Leadbeater to a long and distinguished list of sufferers. Of his other partners, Sharpe made 36 out of 53 in the first 55 minutes, but the rest found problems, mainly against Titmus, who in 42.5 admirable overs took 6 for 92 and turned the odd ball enough to raise Yorkshire hopes for later on.

On a hazy day, the ball swung more than is usual at Lord's, but nothing disturbed Boycott, who entrenched himself carefully in the first hour before tucking in with perfectly timed off-drives and a pull for 6 off a long-hop from Latchman in the half-hour before lunch.

After lunch, Hampshire, sweeping, was lbw – Titmus's third success – and Leadbeater arrived for his short and ill-fated stay. Boycott pushed the last ball of an over from Price to the right-hand of the agile Featherstone, moving in from cover-point, and made haste down the pitch. If Featherstone picked up cleanly and hit the stumps, Leadbeater would clearly have to go. Featherstone did both and Leadbeater went – to a considerable ovation for one who had made nought.

Shrugging off this mishap and a score of 121 for 4, Boycott continued at his very best until he spent half an hour in the upper nineties. This was partly involuntary, for after Woodford had driven across a ball from Parfitt, Hutton came in and took a single off the last ball of three successive overs, amid widespread merriment not shared by a partner lodged at 97.

In time, Boycott cut Parfitt to the Mound to reach 102 out of 187 in three hours 40 minutes. That he might be out for less – or indeed out at all – always seemed as improbable as daffodils in autumn.

Yorkshire's alleged vulnerability to leg-spin was not tested between lunch and tea, and when Latchman came on after tea, he yielded 12 runs in an over, mostly to Bairstow, who was within three runs of earning a fourth bonus point when he pulled Titmus to deep mid-wicket.

Ideally, an innings of great skill and value such as Boycott's should have had a rousing climax. This one had no climax at all, and after Bairstow's departure, only 55 runs were scored in the next 85 minutes off 25 overs.

Middlesex bowled to Boycott with widespread defensive fields which did not help the afternoon's entertainment, but were depressingly effective. Boycott himself regularly took a single off the first ball of the over. His partners, palpably under orders, defended sternly through the rest of it.

It satisfied a weary Middlesex who did not have to bat. It did not satisfy many others.

———————

25 AUGUST 1971

NERVE, COURAGE AND VISWANATH SEE INDIA THROUGH

INDIA REACHED 174 FOR 6 TO WIN A TEST, AND A SERIES, IN ENGLAND FOR THE FIRST TIME

E. W. Swanton

The Oval

After all but 40 years, and at the 22nd time of asking, India have won a Test in England. Nor can anyone possibly begrudge their success, however much it may have owed to the disastrous England second innings of batting.

Allowing that, it still needed an effort of nerve and courage on India's part to make the 173 they required in the fourth innings. When the last day began with the score 76 for two, India still required 97. The runs came after three hours of the tensest possible cricket.

England, as was to be expected, made every run a struggle, and had nothing with which to reproach themselves so far as their outcricket was concerned. The bowlers simply had not sufficient runs to bowl against on a terribly sluggish pitch. Sardesai played very well in the crisis for India, while Engineer supplied a robust, experienced front when it was most needed.

But the most important innings was the 33 made with the utmost calmness in almost three hours by little Viswanath (at 22 the second-youngest player on the field after Gavaskar). As if the drama intrinsic in the situation when play started was not sufficient, the first event of the morning heightened it vastly by dealing India a blow they could least afford, and doing so in the way calculated most to depress them. Without a run added Sardesai chopped Underwood to short third man, and there was a second's hesitation before both batsmen embarked on the run. D'Oliveira's throw was straight and hard to Knott's gloves and Wadekar narrowly – oh, so narrowly – failed to make his ground. The decision was a difficult one and umpire Rhodes must be relieved to know that the TV playback supported his verdict, by the smallest margin.

After his excellent innings on Monday, Wadekar seemed the linchpin of his side. What now? Against the accuracy of Illingworth and Underwood, Sardesai and young Viswanath for a long while found it hard to squeeze more than the odd single.

When Illingworth switched Underwood round, and brought on D'Oliveira, Viswanath cut uppishly and Hutton flung up an instinctive hand to what was perhaps a technical chance from which the batsmen took two. Otherwise Viswanath and Sardesai were rectitude itself, not tempted to rashness by the bristling field. Illingworth himself replaced D'Oliveira, and until lunch the two spinners thereafter performed in harness, apart from six extremely accurate but unmenacing overs from Snow.

The pitch was even slower than hitherto: Snow could bang no response from it. It was immediately on Underwood's returned instead of Snow that the stand of 48, that had stretched over one and three-quarter hours, ended when Sardesai was brilliantly caught wide right-handed by Knott. Sardesai was playing defensively to a length ball that straightened.

With the cool and experienced Sardesai out of the way, England put all the pressure possible on Solkar and Viswanath. After staying 20 minutes for a single, the left-hander seized on an uppish length ball but drove it within reach of Underwood who caught it easily left-handed: 134 for 5, 39 to win.

But thenceforward Engineer kept his head and took what chances came to punch the ball off the back foot, while his little partner continued to bat according to the text book. In the 20 minutes before lunch the sixth wicket ticked up 12 precious runs, so that when they came in India at 146 for 5 needed 27 more.

These had all but arrived when with three only needed Viswanath tried to finish the thing in one blow, and was caught behind off Luckhurst who had been brought on as a last despairing gesture. A square-cut by Abid Ali was swallowed up in the surging crowd, and all was over. India deserve the warmest congratulations for their double effort this year, victory over the West Indies followed by this.

Chandra's fine bowling on Monday had made the vision possible, but it was indeed a team effort, wherein Wadekar's cool, shrewd handling on the field played a crucial part.

---

20 JUNE 1972

TEST CRICKET WITH A BIASED LOOK

Sir – Mr E.W. Swanton has lent his eminent authority to the statement that the selectors of Test teams have never shown any kind of 'prejudice' – least of all a 'Southern bias', which he describes as a 'tedious jibe' ('Cricket Commentary', 31 May).

As someone without any 'Northern bias' ('a very aggressive condition', in his words), but with a pride in the feats of cricketers from the Huddersfield district, where I was born, and other industrial centres of the West Riding, such as Pudsey, I wish to record the following chain of events, all happening within my personal recollection.

In 1921, Holmes, joint holder of the record opening stand of 555 (made in 1932), and of the record number of 68 other such partnerships, scored 32 out of a total of 112 in his first and only Test against Australia, when England collapsed against Gregory and Macdonald at Nottingham.

After that he was not even included in an Australian tour. After the same Test, Rhodes, the only bowler to take over 4,000 wickets and the scorer of about 40,000 runs, was also dropped, although in that year he topped the bowling averages, as usual, and also hit his highest score of 267 not out. He was finally recalled to play a notable part in winning the Ashes at the Oval in 1926.

Sutcliffe, who heads the averages against Australia with 66 (10 more than anyone else) had his Test career ended in 1934, when he was 39, although his form was still good enough for him to score four successive hundreds in 1939. Verity, Yorkshire's No. 10, opened the innings in the series in Australia in 1936–7, lost by 3–2. Among alternative openers left behind was Hutton, who in the following season scored 2,885 runs, including his first Test century and a highest score of 271 not out.

Leyland, whose record against Australia is unique for a left-hander (seven centuries in 20 Tests, against two in 33 by Woolley), was dropped after the tour of 1936–7 (two centuries) but recalled to the Oval in 1938 to make 187 and share with Hutton in a record stand for any wicket, 382.

Hutton, scorer of the record 364 and 18 other centuries in Tests, was replaced by Emmett (who made 0 and 10) for the Old Trafford Test of 1948, after scoring 94, 76, 122 not out, 3, 74, 27 and 13 in his seven preceding innings against Lindwall, Miller and Co.

Also, after regaining the Ashes in 1953, he returned from a drawn series in the West Indies in which he had averaged 96 to face the ordeal of long suspense while the selectors considered his replacement as captain in Australia by the then Rev. D.S. Sheppard.

Boycott, the recognised leading run-maker in the game today, was dropped after making over 240 in a Test.

Other leading players from the West Riding to be affected by 'Southern bias' include Mitchell, Trueman (the only bowler to take over 300 Test wickets) and Close. Illingworth, a Pudsey man, perhaps shrewdly, now prefers to play for Leicestershire.

HUMPHREY BROOKE
London, SW7

E.W. Swanton writes: Mr Brooke has certainly instanced omissions which retrospectively seem to have been mistaken. But did geography come into the matter? Tom Graveney, of Gloucestershire, was often mysteriously passed over, and how about Frank Woolley, of Kent, who made 3,352 runs in 1928 and was not chosen to go to Australia that winter? John Langridge (Sussex) scored 34,380 runs and took 786 catches, yet never played in a Test match. I could continue.

24 JUNE 1972

MASSIE HOLDS COURT

ENGLAND, WITH ONE SECOND-INNINGS WICKET
REMAINING, LEAD AUSTRALIA BY 50 RUNS

E.W. Swanton

It is hard to think of a match within recent memory as rich as this in terms of excitement and drama.

In all respects, there's no place like Lord's for a Test match. The crowds know more; are more generous in acknowledgement; and the players react to the setting and its unique feel and spirit. It is all this that makes it a breeding ground for heroes, the stage for great deeds.

The present game has been swung into Australia's lap by two young men, Bob Massie and Greg Chappell, whose achievements at Lord's have in three pulsating days shifted, for the moment at least, the whole moral balance of Anglo-Australian cricket.

Until the play took its violent and decisive turn on Saturday afternoon, there were many Englishmen who either hoped for, or were at least complacent about the prospect of an Australian victory, for the simple reason that this would ensure a marvellously tight-fought series, whereas if England won again their position would be impregnable. But their thoughts ran thus because at the back of their minds they had the comfortable feeling that England all through were the stronger side, and would win the rubber in the end.

By close of play such complacency seemed a particularly foolish illusion, as Massie was leading Australia back into the pavilion with such a triumph to his name as none of his countrymen has ever achieved in Test history. The Demon Spofforth's 14 wickets in the Oval Test of '82 has been left behind. In Tests between England and Australia Massie stands now with Rhodes and Verity, both of whom have taken 15 wickets – and Massie may this morning match his eight in the first innings with eight in the second.

Only Jim Laker's 19 for 90 at Old Trafford in '56 lies – no doubt for ever – out of reach and, of course, rain came to his aid as it did also to Rhodes and Verity, to say nothing in Laker's case of a spot of dust. At Lord's, let it never be forgotten, the pitch has been fast and true.

Who would have thought when shortly before one o'clock the crowd rose to Greg Chappell in salute of his superb innings of 131 that by evening his performance would have to take second place? If figures in cricket did not hold such a compulsive fascination, he and Massie would indeed be seen on twin pinnacles of equal stature, for one achievement depended on the other, and was complementary to it.

But for Chappell's admirable effort of concentration and the unwavering judgment with which he brought his fine, upstanding stroke-making into play over a stretch of six and a quarter hours, Massie could not have exercised the dominance he did over the England batting in the afternoon.

It is time, before saying a word about how Massie wreaked his havoc, to applaud the two other men who had so important a hand in the course of events, Lillee and Marsh. Lillee has taken only four wickets in the match, but they are exclusively among batsmen one to three, who have made 38 runs among them in the two innings.

It is Lillee's extra brand of speed that has been at the root of England's discomfort, just as it was at Old Trafford, where his eight wickets might well have been the key to victory if Massie had been available at the other end.

The fourth Australian to come into the story was Marsh, whose virile 50 in an hour and a quarter assured Australia of the lead that was essential to them, and who has emphasised in both these Tests how greatly he has improved as a keeper. Eleven catches he has made so far in the series, and I have a note of only one put down.

He may not have been the best in Australia when he got the job, but it will not be long before he is numbered in the company of great Australian keepers, in worthy succession to Tallon, Langley and Grout. As to Marsh's batting, uninhibited and adventurous as it was, it was a long way from unscientific slogging. The foot is generally near the ball, the head behind it and the top hand in command. Like much else in the cricket, it was an illustration of old-fashioned principles.

Now how did Massie on so true a pitch, with his brisk, but not in any way unusual pace, induce such a state of mind that from the moment of Boycott's unlucky dismissal one could scarcely see where the next run was coming from?

The key lay in the variation he made in the direction of attack by switching between over the wicket and round, a tactic well rehearsed in the Australian camp and practised by Massie for long periods – so Richie Benaud, that arch-plotter, assures me – in the Old Trafford nets while the first Test was going on.

If the right-arm bowler keeps close to the stumps when firing from round the wicket the angle is fairly akin to that of the left-armers, such as Alan Davidson, who used his line and late swing to create such hatefully difficult problems. Massie succeeded by keeping a full length and demanding a stroke made tentative by the possibility of late swings in either direction. He is also a master of pace-change, so that the batsman cannot 'play the arm'.

This is not the moment to censure the England batsmen. No one blames them more than they will be blaming themselves. If Boycott, allowing the ball to hit his thigh, but apparently losing it for the vital second when it jumped and then actually dropped between his legs back on to the stumps, had not met such an unusual end the innings might well have taken a different course.

There was, however, one obvious technical counter to Massie's coming round the wicket, and it seemed looking through the glasses, that only Smith, in his two and a half hours of staunch defiance (the only innings deserving of the name), adopted it.

His guard looked to be about middle or even middle-and-off, and he seemed to be opening his stance a bit to compensate for the difference in direction. The others, apparently, took leg stump as usual, giving the bowler a bigger target to aim at, and tending thereby to be playing across the line of the ball, always giving hope to Marsh and the Chappells, who caught in the slips almost as well as they batted.

A last word, not exactly of hope, but possibly to uplift English spirits a shade: Gifford and Price are in residence. Could they – somehow – conjure another 25 or so? Strange things can happen when fast bowlers are faced with the seeming inevitable. Many will recall Lord's '61, when Australia, needing only 69 to win, were 19 for four against Truman and Statham. Thereupon Burge, who ultimately settled things, was missed off Statham off the last ball before lunch. If that catch had been held...

Meanwhile, the selectors have done the right and timely thing by appointing Illingworth for the rest of the series. This is no time for a new face on the bridge.

The captain has brought England to supremacy over Australia. Now he faces adversity, and this will be the acid test of his leadership. He is the last man to think that one lost Test match is the end of the world.

MCC, by the way, announce that no 'exhibition' will be staged at the game's conclusion: what more flattening anti-climax could there be than that? Her Majesty is due at three-o'clock today and it is a great disappointment that she could not have been present at Saturday's full house.

An artificial knockabout would, however, be no dish to set before the Queen.

----

27 DECEMBER 1972

LEWIS ROUNDS OFF HIS FIRST TEST WITH FINE CAPTAIN'S FLOURISH

E. W. Swanton

Delhi

England won the first Test against India by six wickets with more than three hours to spare.

England's six-wicket victory, gained shortly after lunch on Christmas Day, came at the end of a thrilling match by virtue of an unfinished stand of 101 between Tony Lewis, the captain, and Tony Greig, who thus scored 108 runs in his two innings without being out.

Greig, with two wickets and five catches in addition, no doubt made the outstanding English contribution, with Arnold's nine wickets scarcely behind. But the most significant achievement belonged to Lewis, who in his first Test and with a duck in the first innings, and no previous form to fortify him, took out his bat for 70 made in less than three hours without a vestige of a chance.

It is the measure of his achievement that in MCC's three previous post-war visits to India England had won only one Test out of 15 and lost three. It was the first defeat for India since Wadekar assumed the captaincy, and narrowly won two rubbers last year against the West Indies and England. For Lewis to have thus succeeded within a month of flying from London, and after only three matches, argues special qualities of leadership and management, and the cheers should be echoing from Lord's to Cardiff and back.

When readers were left in suspense before the holiday England were in the process of succumbing in their first innings to Chandrasekhar, who on Saturday morning gobbled up the last four wickets to give him 8 for 79. With a bare lead of 27 England by persistent pressure had the first five Indian wickets (with absolutely no help from a placid pitch) for 103 with 50 minutes off the third day to go.

The stand between Solkar and Engineer would have been stifled almost at birth if a straightforward return catch had been taken by Pocock. As it was, these two stayed until after lunch on the fourth day to add 103 before Knott darted round in front of Engineer to take a characteristic diving catch off bat and pad.

To the general surprise, India's last five wickets subsided for only 27 runs, the left-handed Solkar being last out caught in the deep field by Roope, substituting for Cottam, who had bruised a foot. England therefore needed 207, with all the time in the world, but facing the moral ascendancy established by Chandra and also by Bedi.

A start of 20 for two was, of course, deplorable, but Denness and Wood then added 56 at a run a minute, 35 of them to Denness, whose ease and polish first held out hope of the target being within range. Lewis held on with the sturdy Wood for the last 40 minutes of the fourth day, but the latter was out fourth ball next morning.

At 107 for four, with only Knott of the reputable batting remaining, Greig joined his captain and in the coolest and most judicious way these two settled the issue.

----

7 AUGUST 1973

RAIN AT BRAMALL LANE END

Michael Melford

Sheffield

It had stopped raining at Bramall Lane yesterday morning, but the night's deluge had left puddles on the square, and soon after 11.30 play was abandoned for the day.

Only one more day's play remains, not just for this Roses match, but for cricket at Bramall Lane, where it was first played in 1855, eight years before the formation of the Yorkshire County Cricket Club itself. Soon, a new stand for Sheffield United Football Club will be rising over the cricket square, and next year Yorkshire will play two matches in another part of Sheffield, at Abbeydale Park, pending a decision on a new home.

Born just before the industrial revolution and the steel industry changed its environs from green fields to chimneys and terraced houses, Bramall Lane has long had a grim attraction for many cricket lovers, not least because of the native wit with which the crowd used to lend character to the cricket.

Each of those who came to watch cricket here – and there were 8,000 on Saturday, when apparently a combination of untypical pitch and inglorious batting caused the fall of 17 wickets for 173 – will have his own memories.

Arthur Fagg, umpiring this last match, will recall the day in 1936 when he was the only Kent batsman not out to Hedley Verity, who took nine for 12, and indeed caught Fagg off another bowler. Bill Bowes's memories must surely be happy ones, for he took 151 championship wickets on the ground. Here, a venerable Fred Trueman led Yorkshire to an innings victory over the Australians in 1968, and here Geoffrey Boycott made his maiden hundred in 1963. Here, further back, Lord Hawke shared in a last-wicket stand of 148, which is still the Yorkshire record, and here, in 1919, Holmes and Sutcliffe first opened together.

Not all the triumphs at Bramall Lane have belonged to Yorkshire, though out of 163 championship matches here they have won 71 and lost only 18. In 1930, Grimmett took all 10 wickets here, and in 1935 Jock Cameron, the South African wicket-keeper, hit Verity for his famous 30 in an over. The first match of all, in 1855, was lost to Sussex by an innings. In 1902, Australia won the only Test match played here by 143 runs. J.M. Kilburn, in his farewell to Bramall Lane in *The Cricketer*, writes of disappointing gate receipts and murky industrial haze as the reasons why Test cricket never returned, and the climatic disadvantages of Sheffield, in its bowl, figure among my own memories. On a day in the 1950s, when the rest of the country sweltered under cloudless skies, play in a match against Surrey at Bramall Lane was stopped at half-past two by bad light, and never resumed.

Today, if the sun and wind of yesterday afternoon continue their good work, there will be one last day's play. But this evening, the record books will close on 118 years of cricket at Bramall Lane.

---

29 SEPTEMBER 1974

RICHER REWARDS BUT MORE TRAVEL FOR PLAYERS

E. W. Swanton

At the end of another season, with the weather shedding unprecedented floods of tears at its decease, the unending question poses itself: Whither cricket? To which the short answer is that it depends from which angle one examines the subject.

Suppose we get the worst over first, and consider the picture of first-class cricket and the lot of the English county cricketer of the '70s. He is beginning to earn rewards more commensurate with his skill than in times past. But to chase the money made available to the game by sponsorship, he spends the summer hunting up and down the motorways and the byways. The current player scores half as many first-class runs as his predecessors, takes half as many wickets, but covers two or three times as many miles (one county estimates its car mileage at 10,000 a season, and that might be a conservative figure). He never gets a Sunday to himself, at weekends he finds himself playing two matches at once, under different regulations and conditions. The various forms of the game draw from him different but largely conventional responses. Each form has its own pattern, none of them particularly encouraging the individuality that has always been one of the precious charms of cricket.

Batting is more uniform in quality than of yore, the best players lacking the genius of the old masters, those down the order a good deal harder to get out, by bowling which in its turn has fewer contrasts in pace and method. Spin is woefully scarce (hence the resurrection of Fred Titmus).

The brightest aspect of the county game is the fielding which, in teams almost wholly composed of men in their physical prime, touches new collective heights – though this excellence, by a tiresome perversity of circumstances (aided by selectors who are apt to pay insufficient regard to its importance) stops short of the England eleven.

So far not so good. The TCCB must be given much credit for encouraging and channelling the sponsorship, which has given county balance sheets an altogether healthier look. It is inevitable that this infusion of money has been achieved at some cost. Yet one can visualise a more convenient seasonal pattern emerging which would benefit all concerned – and which, above all, would help a raising of the standard of play, reflected in due course in the quality of the England eleven.

In the long run, that is all-important. Neither commercial patronage nor public support would survive a descent of the Test side to the status of a second-rate power. I would like to see less travelling, greater flexibility in the fixtures, allowing more Championship matches, the artificial element in one-day cricket decreased by an abolition of any overs limit on a bowler's activity, and, consequent on this, the upgrading of all 60-over matches to first-class status.

It is illogical that matches with the widest appeal (even 'The World Cup') should be deemed of inferior degree. It does not need the publication of the final batting and bowling averages – with the West Indies' new captain heading the one and their new young fast bowler the other – to remind anyone of the predominance of overseas cricketers. Yet the young English names are slightly more plentiful than of late.

Note that of Botham, a youngster full of cricket, of whom I am glad to hear from Brian Close that he's keen to learn. After a session in the field, he comes to the captain and says: 'And what did I do wrong today, then?'

In Essex, they are keen on Gooch, a Leyton boy whose taste for the game was sharpened when he visited the West Indies with the England Young Cricketers. Tavarè, of Kent, and Hignell, of Gloucestershire, are names which will soon be better known especially since they go up next month, respectively, to Oxford and Cambridge.

There are signs with some University colleges of a more liberal admissions policy, which would have considerable importance for cricket since the flow of talent from Fenner's and The Parks has grown thin. No need to underline what such men as May, Cowdrey and Dexter have meant to English cricket – or, for that matter, the contribution being made to the counties today by Gilliat and Brearley, two of the best captains.

Doug Insole, a Corinthian himself, who as chairman of the TCCB Cricket Sub-Committee, surveys the game with a shrewd, perceptive eye, points to the loss to county cricket also, because of ever-lengthening seasons, of the football element. Shortly after the war there were some 40 pro footballers playing; there are now about three.

So new avenues of recruitment are crucial, and they are being built and widened under the broad umbrella of the increasingly active National Cricket Association. The Young Cricketer tours are of obvious value at the top of the scale, fed by the English Schools CA, the independent schools and the National Association of Young Cricketers.

We shall never have here a uniformly graduated system as in Australia. But the ambitious cricketer today, thanks very much to the NCA, is having the way ahead signposted in a way unknown in the past. But are the boys in State schools generally getting a chance to play? I had a depressing letter the other day from a reader whose garden overlooks the very fine GLC playing fields at Roehampton, set in the midst of a large population of schoolchildren. All summer the only cricket played on this expanse has been two or three games of the little Church Primary School. This is a shocking waste of facilities, caused presumably by the lack of interested staff.

---

5 DECEMBER 1974

THOMSON AND LILLEE TOO GOOD FOR BRITTLE ENGLAND

AUSTRALIA BEAT ENGLAND BY 166 RUNS

E.W. Swanton

Brisbane

Australia's fast bowlers were too much for England's brittle batting on the last day, sweeping away the final defences with an hour and 20 minutes to spare. England got precisely half-way to the impossible target, losing by the amount of their score of 166.

There have been 17 Tests in Australia involving England since 1958–9, and this is only the third Australian victory. But it was certainly decisive enough. The extra speed and fire of Thomson and Lillee, in that order, were the vital factors.

Thomson had the lion's share of the wickets, and such was his lift off the pitch, that no one was comfortable against him. He was truly fast as was Lillee, in phases England had no respite all day from either one or the other. It would be agreeable to say that England had nothing with which to reproach themselves, but that would be stretching the truth. The fact is that only Amiss got a ball against which there was scarcely a defence.

Knott stayed for two hours in mid-afternoon and nearly everyone contributed a little. But too many imprudent strokes were offered by seasoned cricketers, and a strong self-discipline is sure to be required over these next two months if the Ashes are to be still in suspense when Melbourne is reached for the sixth and final Test.

I can imagine followers at home wondering whether the fast bowling offended the law in persistent shortness. The answer is that Lillee was warned for intimidation when bowling at the tail-enders, and I would say that both he and Thomson were near the knuckle. They were tempted by the unusual bounce to be had at the city end of the pitch. Batting was certainly no bed of roses.

Australia had to wait only until the fifth over of the day for their first success. Luckhurst, his body too far from the line of the ball, steered a shortish one comfortably to first slip. No stroke had been called for. Edrich, fortified by a pain-killing injection, came in after all in his usual place, taking his bruised top hand off the bat after playing each stroke. For three-quarters of an hour he batted according to habit, but was then beaten by a ball that may have swung into him a little: not a very fast one.

Denness was greeted, not unpredictably, by a nasty short ball that hit him on the side or upper arm and, like another Scots captain in Australia, by name D.R. Jardine, forbore to rub the affected spot. Denness started well, but after a quarter of an hour, he saw Amiss caught at third slip off a wicked flier that there was little chance of avoiding. Then Fletcher and his captain lasted until lunch. Chappell had used speed from the pavilion end all morning, Lillee and Thomson taking turns towards the end which gave the biggest bounce – and also the widest variety of bounce since a few scooted through very low.

Denness had shown his strokes from the start, but soon after lunch he failed to get on top of a square-cut and Walters took another fast catch at third slip. Calamity piled on top of calamity as Fletcher was caught in the gully off a leg-break from Jenner that really went, and Greig succumbed to a fast one from Thomson that yorked the leg stump. Greig, whose habit is to hold the bat on high as the bowler comes up, was late on getting it down.

So, in two and a half hours all told, the cream of the English batting was dispersed: Everyone, that is to say, except Knott, now joined by Lever with three more bowlers to follow and three and a half hours of the game remaining. Lever was frankly nonplussed by the situation, yet managed to survive for 40 minutes before fending a ball on his pads rather feverishly to short-leg.

Underwood, bearing his growing repute as a batsman, stayed for more than an hour until after tea, and so long as Kent in these two survived, the game was not over. Underwood, however, fell somewhat from grace when he tried to hit Jenner over his head and lobbed a catch to mid-on. When Knott played Thomson on to his stumps to be ninth out, the end was at hand. The game has been watched on this greatly improved arena by 62,000 people, the biggest Test crowd here for 15 years.

Denness, after the game, thought that the pitch could not be described as satisfactory because of the unevenness of the bounce, but had no complaints and, in congratulating Australia, vowed that England would come again. He was particularly emphatic in his appreciation of the umpires, whose performance he described as 'highly commendable'. This, at least, was good to hear.

---

10 JANUARY 1975

EDITORIAL

WE WASN'T ROBBED

Off to Australia go the Ashes, and that in all justice is where they should be. Forget about bad umpiring decisions: they usually even out in the end. And what sane man would be an umpire these days, when slow-motion replays on the telly may immediately cast doubt on your honest but fallible decision? Forget about the partisan crowds too. They were not so partisan as to deny Cowdrey an affectionate welcome or loud applause to those heroes of our second innings rearguard action who earned it. Let us only be sorry we didn't give them more to applaud. Filthy manners on the field can be neither forgotten nor forgiven. Captains and umpires must be firmer about these; meanwhile let us not forget that some of our own cricketers have in the past set a shocking example.

There remains the sore point of intimidatory bowling. Let us bear in mind that much bowling so-called is just bad bowling, meat and drink to top-class batsmen; that no decent batsman has anything to moan about if he is hit below the belt by a ball of good length; and that we took a battery of five fast bowlers to Australia, who were presumably meant to frighten the Aussies but did not. Some of these factors deserve another look from cricket's mandarins. But none of them taken singly or together can upset the fact that we lost to a younger, fitter, better balanced and better equipped side. We need a side of this sort. We must wonder whether our cricketing arrangements, with so many fixtures, so many one-day games and so much imported talent, are well fitted to produce one.

---

2 MARCH 1975

DEFYING DEATH – ODDS SHORTEN

Tony Lewis

The last time death was cheated on a first-class cricket field as Ewan Chatfield thankfully managed this week I was there, just a few yards away, standing at gully.

In the summer of 1971 my Glamorgan team-mate Roger Davis was hit on the side of the head just behind the ear by a ball which Neil Abberley of Warwickshire had whipped off his toes right off the meat of the bat. Before we realised what had happened his body was in violent convulsions; by the time I reached him his face was deep dark blue and contorted; when two doctors arrived he was motionless and within seconds declared lifeless.

The next few seconds as mouth to mouth resuscitation brought him back to life remain indescribable. In New Zealand this week Peter Lever cried. That tells enough. When Roger Davis fell everyone in the game all over the world who fielded close to the bat on the leg-side fell with him for a moment in imagination. So it was with Ewan Chatfield.

Reverberations raced around the world to everyone who picks up a bat in first-class cricket. 'That could have been me. There but for the grace of God ...' Instinctively, too, one's mind turns to the great fortune of the MCC side in that no one was killed by Thomson or Lillie in Australia. History at the moment gives long odds against that happening on the cricket field, but the odds are shortening because these days many more bouncers are bowled at home as well as abroad.

Only once was I hit in the face while batting in a career which extended from 1955 to last summer. I tried to duck under an intended bouncer in a Test match against Pakistan at Hyderabad. As soon as the ball was thumped into the ground I decided to duck under it. However, I took my eye off the ball. The bowler did not get the bounce he was looking for and the ball cracked me on the jawbone just below the ear. I cursed myself for not obeying the laws of survival. If the ball is going to hit you, watch it hit you, then instinct will ensure your escape.

Against Peter Lever who is not genuinely fast in the Thomson-Tyson sense this can be reliably put into action. Exceptional speed, however, can bring involuntary reactions: fear can freeze a batsman for that vital split second and leave him fending off danger in a bad position.

How high will it bounce? I must watch it. How late can I duck? I must be on the back foot, ready. Which way shall I duck? Or shall I hook? If these thoughts scurry through a top-class batsman's head how much more confusing and dangerous it must be for a tail-ender who does not possess the skills and reactions.

As Peter Lever immediately lost his appetite for cricket, so the Glamorgan bowlers, after their horrible experience, did not wish to bowl with anyone standing at short square-leg. They said their hands perspired at the thought and sometimes they struggled to grip the ball firmly. The fear passed, as Lever's will, but that is twice in five years that a cricketer has died and lived again on the pitch. I have no fancy remedies.

Captains should not play fielders too close to the bat. Umpires should caution a bowler and stop him bowling if necessary in accordance with Law 46 for 'persistent intimidation'. Physical courage is very much a part of cricket especially at top level, and Test Match cricket must be uncompromisingly played for the highest stakes.

For some reason, tail-enders are better players these days – better blockers at least. Styles have changed from the days when Fred

Trueman was able to proclaim about the bowler with a bat in his hand, 'one in t' block 'ole and one round t' earhole and it's good day my son.'

---

25 MAY 1975

MY LORD'S, LADIES AND ...

Tony Lewis *watching for Test match clues ... and prams at the Nursery end*

Unchain yourself, Rachael Heyhoe Flint from the Grace gates – 'the strife is o'er, the battle won.' Lord's has fallen; hitch up your skirts, ladies, Mecca cannot be withheld from you any longer. Prepare to take guard against Australia on 4 August at cricket's headquarters.

So, John Frederick Sackville, the third Duke of Dorset, had it right long ago when he wrote in that *Ladies and Gentlemen's Magazine* of 1777: 'What is life but a game of cricket? And, if so, why should not ladies play it as well as we. Mind not, my dear ladies, the impertinent interrogatories of silly cockcombs or dreadful apprehensions of demi-men; let your sex go on and assert their right to every pursuit that does not debase the mind.'

Whew! Quite a lad! He would have seen beauty in the discovery of round-arm bowling by Christina Willes, not the awkwardness of a girl compelled by her voluminous skirts to adopt a new style of bowling which her brother introduced to the national game. It was wholly accepted 20 years later. Many members of MCC then and now would say that Christina's rightful place was cutting the sandwiches for the pavilion tea.

Yet, what about Lord's itself? Will this ancient preserve of all things masculine be able to cope with petticoat cricketers on the day? No doubt chief coach, Len Muncer, will be able to accommodate the prams at the Nursery and the older offspring will probably have the run of the Ladbroke's crèche.

Would an advance tour around the Pavilion help you ladies? Just to avoid embarrassment. You see, it was all right David Steele going down one flight of stairs too many on his way to the crease against Australia last summer, but I must warn you that the men's basement loo is not the quickest and certainly not the most attractive way to the middle.

Up the wide, silent, rubber stairs, three flights to the changing rooms. The furniture is as you would expect: hand-me-downs from Thomas

Lord, reupholstered by Sir Pelham Warner in the '30s. Arthur Negus would go wild about the contraption which once held together Compton's knee. You can see it on top of his old locker. You will see dents in the wall where furious English batsmen have thrown their bats and an item less attractive is the faded left-over jock-strap of Peter Parfitt, which even the bomb disposal squad refused to handle. Yes, the feeling of participating in history will be important to you.

I wonder, as you descend to the middle across the Long Room, whether the scent of Estée Lauder will turn crusted heads on the ancient high stools? 'That's old Bakewell's girl isn't it? H'm. Well made, good sort, I remember her mother, y'know. Old Buns Bakewell taking a hundred before lunch at Gunnersbury in '34. Damned attractive player.'

More likely the old brigade will turn and stare, perhaps disbelieving, even now, though the first ladies' match on record was in 1745, that our women cricketers understand anything of the game's technique. To them, Netta Rheinberg is the name of a dry, white wine. Women cricketers have been viewed with suspicion for so long because four days before the present Lord's ground was opened in 1814, the landlady of the public house at the fields was handling some gunpowder. A spark from the fire caught it and it went off with a huge bang seriously injuring the landlady, her sister, and the four little girls. Since then budding suffragettes have been excluded.

Until now, that is, and at this famous moment, every MCC stalwart fidgets but takes it like a man. I confess to Rachael just as Betjeman's subaltern did to Joan Hunter Dunn, the graceful sporting girl who beat him at tennis … 'how mad I am, sad I am, glad that you won.'

---

23 JUNE 1975

LLOYD SEIZES THE WORLD CROWN

Tony Lewis *reports from Lord's*

All honour and the glory to West Indies! This sunny extravaganza of world cricket culminated in Prince Philip presenting the Prudential Cup to Clive Lloyd as West Indian songs and dances rang out over Lord's.

Requiring 292 to beat West Indies, Australia lost by 17, though much of the damage was done by their own careless running between the wickets. The most mercenary-minded cricket administrator, viewing from a distance, may have been sharpening a claw or two in his armchair at home, ready to dig a finger into the Prudential pie which is going to be worth well over £200,000 in gate money accrued from an overall attendance of 158,000.

However, no one with any sensitivity for a sporting occasion will care a jot for the cash — just at the moment. Similarly, the thousands of uncommitted spectators who filled the enclosures at Lord's cared nothing for the outcome, because they sensed that before them was an unprecedented cricket extravaganza — a very special, indeed unique, sporting battle for the Prudential World Cup.

Aptly, almost miraculously, the glorious sunshine of the past fortnight appeared again as if on cue. Ian Chappell won the toss for Australia and made a challenging decision to field first.

There was nothing in the air that remotely sniffed of Headingley. It was a plain, sky-blue calm day. Chappell had in mind, more likely, the habit of the West Indies captain Clive Lloyd for 'inserting' opponents. It had been their success formula throughout and without a ball bowled, Chappell had snatched away their elixir.

The location of the strongest West Indian encampments was immediately evident, Gilmour, the scourge of England, was no-balled three times in the first over, the bells rang and the flags waved. The excitement subsided as Greenidge and Fredericks prepared to take on Lillee and Thomson in the early overs of concentration.

The first moment of drama was a trick to the eye. Fredericks swung a Lillee bouncer for a six over the head of long leg. Yet he slipped as he completed the shot, foot-faulted and dislodged the bails. Kallicharan, twice voted Man of the Match last week, sailed in to a confident start, but when the score was just 27, he played an over-ambitious shot outside the off stump and was caught by Marsh behind the wicket. It was a flicked shot aimed square on the off-side, but Gilmour got some bounce and Kanhai and Greenidge were thrown onto the defensive.

There was an obvious uneasiness in the bounce which was accentuated by the height of Walker. Frequently he hit Kanhai's bat near the splice and runs came slowly and with great difficulty.

Greenidge departed to a fine low catch by Marsh off Thomson's slower ball. Kanhai got well and truly stuck in a defensive rut, and it was Lloyd who gave the West Indies' innings real momentum. In easy, but most destructive, style he hooked Lillee for a huge six, then, off the back foot, coaxed Walker through the extra cover field. To this point Ian Chappell had persevered with two slips and a gulley, but this was the signal for defensive patterns to take shape and quickly deep men were out on the mid-wicket and square-cover boundary.

Poor Kanhai spent 11 overs without scoring a run as Lloyd plundered on. Still, experience told him to persevere. The partnership eventually realised 149 in 36 overs, Lloyd's 100 coming in an innings of 24.3 overs.

Gilmour came back with a spell of tight bowling which got rid of Kanhai, Lloyd and Richards and at 209 for 6 in the 46th over Australia appeared to have a chance of controlling the game. Yet Boyce added a typically erratic contribution, blasting his way to 34 and once again throwing Ian Chappell back on the defensive.

Australia's innings began serenely enough, though McCosker and Turner had no style to excite the aesthetes. McCosker, particularly, got himself turned around awkwardly to work anything arriving on the line of middle and leg stump through mid-wicket. This, of course, makes him vulnerable to the ball that moves away to off, and when the score was 25 Boyce found the edge of his bat and Kallicharran held a fine catch, low down at second slip.

Two run-outs suddenly placed Australia's cause in peril. First Turner, when the score was 81, was involved in a misunderstanding with his captain and was run out by an underhand throw from Richards. Only a direct hit would have succeeded, as indeed it did with Greg Chappell.

Brother Ian ran the ball out square on the off-side, Greenidge and Richards could not agree as to who was going to field it. Greenidge relaxed, Richards turned and recovered the ball, then on the pivot threw down the only stump he could possibly see.

The third run-out was beyond all comprehension, especially as it saw the departure of the captain himself. Richards again was the destroyer. He first mis-fielded, Chappell hesitated and then set off, Richards recovered and once more spun around to throw the ball just above the bails for Lloyd to break the wicket at the bowler's end.

The innings collapsed with worthy but vain intentions from all Australian batsmen. Lillee and Thomson putting on a bold 41 for the last wicket. The West Indians' fielding never lapsed, some of their throwing-in was quite breathtaking and no one would complain about their worthiness to wear the Prudential Crown at the first time of asking. Nor could there be any argument about naming Lloyd as Man of the Match.

---

6 JUNE 1976

STAINLESS STEELE

Tony Lewis

Trent Bridge

For England a day of slow pleasure, but then happiness earned the hard way, is all the sweeter. This Test match is not exactly a bundle of joy because a game without flight and spin can be dull watching. So how else could England proceed, but painstakingly, against a battery of fast and fast-medium bowling?

There was a hero and that, at least, gave us romance. Every gesture and stroke made by David Steele personifies determination and, to the delight of everyone, he managed the century which eluded him at Headingley last summer as England reached 221 for 3 by the close. His transformation from the solid, unspectacular player for Northamptonshire to the Test match hero is the matter of which great stories are made. The long, drawn-out trials of the Test match game probe the temperament, illuminate the strengths and lay bare the weaknesses.

Steele has the fighting heart of a great trouper and the solid technique which can drive bowlers to tears. His forward defensive stroke will surely be written into cricket's folk lore along side W.G.'s brown boots with which he used to trap the yorkers. He batted for all but four balls of the day's play and England, in search of a total of 295, which would avoid a possible follow-on, must have been glad to see him on their side. Bob Woolmer, too, showed the appropriate spirit. Let us say good words of Tony Greig at a time when some of his judgment is open to criticism. He preferred players with stout hearts and he has been proved absolutely correct. Nor is it too late for Closey to contribute.

England began the day with all their wickets intact, requiring 295 to avoid a possible follow-on. Once again it was backs to the wall and it was easy to imagine a cool, calm day at Trent Bridge hotting up as soon as the West Indians unleashed their fast men.

It was an exciting confrontation, the old hands, recalled specially for their sangfroid, chewing defiantly behind the splice of the bat as Roberts and Daniel snorted in their bouncers. It did not turn out that way and when one considers the panic which thrust the selectors and the captain into defensive thinking, one can loudly reiterate the unwritten law of the game: 'Don't cross your Trent Bridges until you come to them.'

Many factors were in England's favour. The absence of Michael Holding was one. The presence of Wayne Daniel was another because umpire Bird issued final warnings to him running through on the wicket as early as his third over. He looked to be landing somewhere about middle and leg stump. A repeated offence and he could be banned from bowling again in the innings. Neither he nor his captain viewed his bowling with any confidence after that.

Furthermore, the pitch was dry and slow. Roy Fredericks was twirling his chinamen and googlies in the 26th over. Viv Richards joined him at the 31st. The outfield, which had been wet enough to hold up many of Richards's thunderous shots, was now running faster. John Edrich leaned into a forward defensive stroke off Julien and the ball sped to the square cover boundary. However, before this a major upset hit the English camp.

Mike Brearley was caught after a juggle and a sprawl at third slip by Richards off Julien. It was only the fourth ball of the morning – a sad departure for a man in his first Test. The first three balls were inswingers and this one was the perfect variation, running away to slip and bouncing just above waist-high.

Back at Middlesex, I suppose, the news was not good. Three of their representatives – Gomes, Brearley and Daniel – had mustered four runs between them, Daniel getting all of them. David Steele entered to patriotic cheers. On each forearm he wore a white sweat band. He clearly expected to be out there a long time.

Clive Lloyd placed nine fielders close to the bat in catching positions. Steele mishooked Roberts and the catch just cleared the close ring on the leg side. Edrich was dropped at slip by Kallicharran. It brought him a single and an important milestone was passed. He became only the 13th batsman to score 5,000 runs in Test cricket.

Yet these two dug in and the fightback was securely under way. The West Indians buzzed around the bat, but their lack of a top-class spinner became another England advantage. So often the Saturday of a Test match is a slow and bitter war of attrition. England were prepared to graft; West Indies were happy to wait.

For a while, before lunch, Lloyd toyed with the wrist spin of Fredericks, remembering no doubt that Steele had been somewhat bamboozled and bowled by a googly at Arundel. It all but worked, but against Edrich, who came close to being caught and bowled.

After lunch, Lloyd was in no doubt about his plans. Roberts opened up at the pavilion end followed by Daniel and Julien succeeded Fredericks from the Radcliffe Road end. Roberts was hostile, Julien steady and teasing on or around off stump, but Daniel was positively inspired.

There is a lot of Charlie Griffiths in his run up. Although he stretched out unevenly for the crease in the final strides, he got plenty of body into the action. Yet the strength of strongly built West Indians is often in the power of a whiplash arm action. The Caribbean abounds with wild-eyed fast bowlers with 'rubber' arms.

Edrich's bat jarred as a thick edge flew off to Murray; safely held. Brian Close came in. His bald head gleamed in the sunlight, his jaw jutted; he approached yet another comeback innings with familiar, even tread. The large West Indian contingent loved him. 'Behold you live, Grandad. Grandad live for ever more!'

Yes, the tension he knew, but not quite the speed this time. He was dropped by Greenidge at second slip off the first ball – a fast but straight-forward chance. Daniel was not disappointed long, because a couple of runs later, Close was gone.

It was just a touch to the keeper, but a touch is enough. 105 for three, but Steele still in residence. He stuck out that notorious front foot and planted the middle of his bat in the way of the ball. He scored runs from glancing shots to fine leg and from occasional flourishes off the back foot on the off-side. He looked uncomfortable against bouncers, but undisturbed by them. He looked likely to offer a catch and the West Indians in the rhythm section of the crowd, banging hands and tea chests, knew it.

'Cum'on, Steele, hook 'im; cum'on Andy, cook 'im' – a pleasing war song put to music. His almost inevitable 50 came up, which extended his remarkable run for England – five fifties in seven innings.

Steele and Woolmer cooled the West Indian aggression, but carelessly left themselves open to a run-out chance. Fredericks threw down the wicket leaving Woolmer stranded. He looked yards out, but umpire Spencer ruled otherwise. Next ball Steele edged Holder low and wide to Murray's right hand. It was a difficult, diving chance which just did not stick. Woolmer and Steele put on 116 runs of immense value. Steele arrived at the golden three-figure target with a series of hooks and hair-raising runs.

It meant a lot to him. It meant a lot to England, too. It is still a long road out of the briars, but Stainless Steele, as he is known by friends in the game, is still wading out of them with scarcely a scratch.

---

4 JULY 1976

THE PERFECT PUPIL

Kent hung on tenaciously in the face of a large, destructive century by Barry Richards in a Hampshire total of 315. Both sides took four points and if the weather remains dry the spinners, already well worked, may decide the outcome.

The legendary Kent and England all-rounder Frank Woolley, looking fit and alert in the Band of Brothers enclosure, approved of the innings of 179 he saw played by Richards yesterday. It was full of free-flowing shots, orthodox as well as improvised. Mr Woolley is on holiday in his native county and will soon return to Chester, Nova Scotia, his Canadian home. He was the scorer of 135 centuries, including nine double hundreds. Twenty-eight times he took 10 wickets in a match.

'Play safe until that one comes down outside the off stump,' he said. 'Then drive it.' It might have been taken as a naive over-simplification by those listening had not Richards been doing exactly that at the time.

The Mote Ground is up on a small plateau above the low-lying centre of Maidstone. The grass was scorched, the sun again showed no mercy and everything was hazy except for the statuesque Richards. They say he has been ill with food poisoning. A return to his favourite diet, the Kent attack, was obviously what was needed. His team-mates had joked that for the only time since joining Hampshire his name was not in the national averages as published in the morning. He answered them in the only way and middled the ball from start to finish without appearing to move his feet very much.

Shepherd bowled intelligently, getting some late drift either way in the air from a full length, but Richards leaned on the ball and swung the bat through the orthodox arcs. It all seemed so simple and probably is if you can commit yourself as late as he can. He lost Lewis when the score was 4, Turner at 71 and Jesty at 86. He looked as unmoved by those accidents as he was by the gestures of attack which Mike Denness made around his pads when Underwood bowled. The pitch was dry, turned a little and will obviously turn more.

Kent were sensibly intent on biding their time. Five of them sat on a long perch in the covers. Gilliat was more flamboyant and looked in good form before he struck Woolmer, the short square-leg, on the arm with a full-blooded sweep off Underwood. Woolmer left the field, but carried on after lunch when Gilliat played the ball straight to Woolmer once again, who this time was standing back at square-leg to take the catch. Enter Sainsbury and Kent moved in to close quarters again.

As long as Richards batted Kent were not in charge of their destiny. He developed a taste for the sweep; stepped outside leg to hit Johnson to the off; lifted both spinners over the top; and he struck Elms for three fours in one over. Sainsbury and Richards put on 100 in 22 overs, Sainsbury's offering being 15. Richards eventually chipped a ball from Shepherd to mid-wicket and padded peacefully back to the shade in his plimsolls. If his timing had been less than perfect it was because he had set himself small challenges along the line, sometimes nominating the shot before the bowler had licked his fingers. Yet it enhanced the virtuosity and the crowd loved it.

When he was out the ball started turning again! Underwood persevered, pushing the ball quite quickly. Rice played across one, Stephenson edged one to Knott and, all in all, his figures were a handsome reward for his usual plucky effort.

———————

11 JULY 1976

POOR GREIG HAS TO GROVEL

Tony Lewis

The West Indians, notably Greenidge and Richards, took runs almost as they pleased, though not without care and reverence for the balls that turned and lifted, at Old Trafford yesterday. They made centuries of unassailable style and, although there were curious moments of deceleration towards the end of the innings, Lloyd was still able to set England a forbidding 552 runs to win the third Test in 13 hours 20 minutes.

A more aggressive attitude from the West Indies could have left England a longer vigil at the crease before the end. As it was Edrich and Close batted through 80 minutes of fast bowling on an uneven surface. There are few others I would have backed to survive until Monday.

For England this was a day of few options. It did not matter what roller the West Indians used on the wicket; whether England bowled seam or spin; whether those entrusted with the ball attacked leg or off. The West Indians were in the masterful position of being 303 on with nine second innings wickets standing and Greenidge and Richards at the crease.

Perhaps there were a few English prayers for rain, the only possible saviour though it would have taken a great worshipper of cumulus nimbus formations like Geoff 'Noddy' Pullar, the former Lancashire and England opener, to have spotted a distant depression on such a sunny morning.

Lancashire lads always said that the prospect of a day's fielding was enough to send 'Noddy' to his prayer mat or, rather, rushing to his window at the back of the players' shower room at Old Trafford. 'Noddy's window' is now part of the folklore. 'Ay, there's a drop cummin' up,' he would enthuse. 'Wi' luck we'll be back in by half-three.'

Clearly nothing was going to stop Greenidge and Richards from setting up the assault. Greenidge became only the second man in England West Indies Test history to score two centuries in one match. George Headley did it twice, at Georgetown in 1929–30 and at Lord's in 1939. No England player has done it.

Hendrick and Selvey opened up with two slips; soon there was only one. The batsmen matched each other for strokes of beauty and power.

Richards flashed Hendrick through square cover for 4. Had no one told him that square-cutting is a risk on wickets of uneven bounce? Greenidge leaned far on to the front foot to square drive Underwood; he thundered a cover-drive of pure Caribbean pedigree off a Hendrick half-volley, weight massively on the back foot. Richards square-cut Underwood one ball, then late-cut the next of good length with instinctive touch. The ball flew off to the fine third-man boundary over the hard, dry earth.

What a triumph for Greenidge! His studied defence has sometimes made him look vulnerable and, indeed, he had a lean spell of lbw decisions last year. The sheer style of his innings both at Lord's and here at Manchester will be recalled by many in years to come as the perfect West Indian blend of physical power and art. His century was acclaimed by all. He played the next ball on to his wicket: the score 224 for 2.

Richards, by this time, was in full command, combining watchful dead bats against Underwood and Pocock with wristy drives through mid-wicket or vicious cuts. Greig laboured under the taunts of the West Indian crowd, 'We want Greig — we want Greig.' I had the feeling that they meant it. Having taken the verbal battle to the opposition, as he did demonstrably against Australia, he may find that this time he has built his own funeral pyre now that he cannot get runs or wickets. He pretended he was going to bowl at one point.

It is an unnecessary pressure for an England captain, but there truly does come a time when the fighting talk has to stop and the fighting action begin. I hope the captain's fortunes change.

Clive Lloyd's problem was scarcely arithmetical. It was simply a question of when to halt the destruction of the English bowling and unleash his demons. As long as he was striking Pocock for 6 over the sightscreen and Richards was feathering late-cuts past Close, or scorching straight drives past Pocock to the accompaniment of West Indian choruses, 'We shall not be moved,' it seemed a shame to end the Caribbean orgy. Lloyd hoisted Selvey into the safe hands of Underwood at wide mid-on — 129 minutes at the crease for 43 — but expectations of a declaration before 3.45 which would have split up the remainder of the day's play into two sessions, disappeared as Kallicharran arrived in the middle.

As it was, the West Indian innings meandered on pointlessly. It was surely in Lloyd's interest to accelerate — not slow down — and get English wickets while the weather remained fine. Ball by ball, over after over, the West Indians gave England the hope that a rainy two days on Monday and Tuesday would salvage a treacherous situation.

Should Greig have set more attacking fields? Certainly Underwood would have got among the wickets and the run-getting would have been less comfortable for the Tourists. The argument is mainly academic because Lloyd was able to declare at five o'clock.

Roberts and Daniel steamed in. Close drew back because the tantrums of the crowd were disturbing him. Lloyd, a few overs later, went to request a reasonable quiet from the musical section. Dust rose from the wicket and the change in pace was obvious. Edrich watched one ball scream over his right shoulder and another creep low past the off stump. Batting was now a different game; there was no respite from fast bowling.

Only the brave, the technically sound and the extremely lucky all rolled into one were going to survive. The senior citizens were all of these. Close chested off a rising ball from Holding. Roberts was rested after three overs, but Daniel looked even more dangerous. Possibly the three of them pressed too hard. Close was hit again, this time by Holding. Close's first move is towards off stump and they appeared to be able to catch him in that line with sharply rising balls. His legs crumbled for a moment. Another bouncer later and umpire Bill Alley warned Holding for excessive use of intimidation. The crowd were incensed, the tom toms beat louder and a small fight broke out.

The tension was only broken when a lad ran on to the field and offered Edrich a joke bat which was a foot and a half wide! There were laughs all round and Padmore was brought on bowling to just two slips with 15 minutes to go.

---

5 SEPTEMBER 1976

MUSHTAQ MEN CUT IT FINE

Tony Lewis

Lord's

Northamptonshire carried off the Gillette Cup, the first major success in the history of the club. Lancashire's 195 for 7 after Mushtaq had put them in, never appeared adequate, yet balancing Lancashire's vast experience in these competitions against the jitters of the novice, left the result wide open.

Twenty-five thousand spectators paying a record £82,500 earned the suspense if not the brilliance. Indeed, it was a dark and sinister start for Lancashire who had won the Cup four out of the last six times.

Northants took the initiative. Apart from forcing Lancashire to bat first they took two of their wickets for 17 runs. Engineer succumbed to the magnetism which always draws his body to the off and his bat to the leg, expensive stuff if he connects, but on this important occasion he did not and lost his leg stump to Dye. Nought for one wicket.

Harry Pilling is a little man to send to a crisis but he is war-proof as his records will vouch. Wood played at being immaculate for a while, but the bounce extracted by Sarfraz and Dye was surprising. Mushtaq did not miss a trick. He brought up Cook to square-leg and within a couple of overs Pilling had popped the ball into his hands. Then, another unlucky blow to Lancashire. A lifting ball from 'Doc' Dye struck Wood on the hand. He was in agony as he had been in the Test match at Lord's back in mid-June. Not even the freezing spray could cool the pain and he retired to hospital for X-ray and played no further part in the match.

Lancashire lost his bowling as well as his batting and in their cups last night I am sure Northants will have acknowledged their fortune. Just when Hayes looked likely to force Mushtaq back on the defensive he hooked at a short ball from Hodgson who had replaced Sarfraz at the pavilion end and lobbed up a simple catch to the bowler to make it 45 for 3. Abrahams could be expected to be young and vulnerable. He was correct and straight and prospered as his captain, Lloyd, found the timing to hit boundaries.

Larkins had bowled well enough, swinging the ball into these left-handers' leg stumps. They wafted the bat at balls outside the off-stump, but it was not until Lloyd cracked a cover-drive, square off the back foot, that the Northants attack appeared to be fizzling out. There was still Bishen Singh Bedi to call on. In more than one way he played an important part in this first innings. To begin with he bowled beautifully (an adjective which takes in the aesthetic as well as the technical appeal of his bowling).

He bowled Lloyd off his pads, though the shot through mid-wicket was hardly out of the text book. Abrahams was tempted by flight to cut, and suddenly found the ball too far up and turning enough to tip his off stump.

Mushtaq had handled his bowling faultlessly. There were overs from Sarfraz and Dye up his sleeve. His attack had soldiered through the danger of the partnership of Lloyd and Abrahams – 95 in 91 minutes – but the sting has often been in the Lancashire tail, especially in the bat of David Hughes. Hughes was cautious until the final over. Simmons and Ratcliffe had gone; the Northants fielding was unflagging.

I tried hard to excuse Mushtaq, whose captaincy had been exemplary, but I could not. I was led on by Bedi's figures of 3 for 26 off 10 overs. Should he give the left-arm spinner the final over or turn to Dye? The argument should have resulted in Dye's recall, but Bedi was chosen. Hughes, as he did to John Mortimore at Old Trafford some years ago, whacked him to all parts of the field. The last over was 4, 6, 2, 2, 6, 6. Bedi, in panic, pushed the ball through too quickly, and applauded the shots too quickly. Northants were struggling. Very few batsmen can slap Dye about in this sort of cricket and the 26 runs which came were a dangerous loan to the opposition.

Yet 195 for 7 was a modest total and Virgin and Willey went after it confidently. Under low cloud and poor light batting suddenly became a more controlled exercise. It was no fault of Peter Lever or 'Leapy' Lee. Roy Virgin and Peter Willey just looked as if they knew better what to leave alone. Then, when the period of settling in was complete, they opened out.

For such infants in the 'big time' Northants performed with creditable cool. After 28 overs they had scored 79 and were well in the game, if not quite as advanced as they would have liked. Yet, what should have been a steady exercise became a mission of nerves and trepidation. Mushtaq tried to hustle it along but skied a simple catch. Steele played with the utmost sense in proper tempo until even he was shaken by the reality of a shiny cup coming nearer to Northampton. Larkins was out aiming across the line, and in the last 13 overs 50 runs were required. With ten overs to go a rate of 3.5 an over would suffice.

Ratcliffe, down on the long-leg boundary, dropped a hard flat chance offered by Steele off Hughes with the score at 165. Pilling threw down the stumps from mid-on and Cook did well to make his ground after the fastest single. There was no hint of submission by the holders. Lever brought a ball back off the wicket and Cook jabbed down the bat to get an inside edge down to fine leg. Arms went up. In reality the pressure on Northants was subsiding on the score-book but it rarely does in the mind when the prize is that great.

Horror of horrors, David Steele got out in the 56th over. Andrew Kennedy, fielding at straight mid-wicket as sub for Barry Wood, caught his misdrive off Hughes. Sarfraz heaped panic on the situation by sweeping his first ball high in the air down to long leg. It bounced short of Ratcliffe. The situation bore the hallmark of disaster. By now the Northants players were walking round the Rose Garden, locked in the lavatory, or peeping through their wrought-iron balcony.

Three overs, 8 to win and by coincidence or planning, Hughes, Lancashire's slow left-armer, was bowling at the death as Bedi had been for Northants. Sharp settled it with a commonsense straight forward full face of the bat.

---

23 JANUARY 1977

SUGAR, SPICE AND ...

Tony Lewis *on Greig's change of fortune and Lever's secret weapon*

'Nothing brings a Prince more prestige than great campaigns and striking demonstrations of his personal abilities.' I think Tony Greig would say: 'Hear, here,' and slap old Machiavelli on the back.

Until this series (in India) the England captain has carried all the scars without being able to record a victory. At this very moment the blond colossus is probably being borne by rickshaw down from the faded Ritz Hotel, which sits sadly on a hill in Hyderabad, through a jumble of existences which make up the road-side civilisation of Southern India.

I always felt sorry for the thin, poor man pulling the rickshaw. I was told not to. If he did not do that he would be out of work and rupeeless. Down through the rough huts, 15 oxen to a third of an acre; then past the fine houses, walled and guarded, on to the Secunderabad Club perhaps, for long cool drinks on the terrace, a haven where the Indians have inherited British tastes and added their own enviable calm.

Greigy will be followed like the Pied Piper, touched by any who can get that close; his appearance will stop the carts, Vespa-taxis, cars and buses, and the old man ogling from his trading hole in the wall will run out and offer sugar cane to the conquering hero.

India and cricket are like that, as the England captain would already know, and from the start he has treated the country as a stage. He is not the first. There have been many English cricketers who have caught the affection of the millions by their humour demonstrated on the field. Kenny Barrington was one. It is the proper way out there and earns applause at home too ... if you win.

It is impossible to read a Test series from this distance, however familiar one is with the country, yet observations can be made which are factual. I did not laugh at Madras in 1973 when Pataudi and Duranni, who got away with incredible leg-before appeals, then scored runs, but could not field. After supplying medical proof which was impossible to dispute, two youngsters came on to do their fielding. I did laugh this time when Dennis Amiss took a double hundred revenge in the first Test at Delhi, retired to his bed and was replaced by the bouncing Derek Randall.

I have enjoyed odd tales of Greig holding up bowlers who want to wheel away the overs at a hypnotising pace, even if he has to go down on his knees to the crowd before he gets off the mark. That takes some doing. Most incredible of all has been the news that the Test wickets have turned. India's skill, as I recall it, was to turn the ball on wickets where our spinners could scarcely divert it off the straight. Did they play into our hands?

Still, more than anything it is the experience which has counted, given intelligence and stature to the leader and taught perseverance with the faster bowlers. The main runs have come from those batsmen who were out there in 1973 and the fast men have taken most wickets. I remember Alan Knott expressing the opinion last time that we should play four fast bowlers with Derek Underwood. He cannot have been too far out with that comment.

It was nine and a half years between MCC tours last time. No one had been there before. This reasonably prompt return has been the inner strength of Greig's effort.

This is the first time that Tests in India have been played with Indian balls. Mind you, the talk about Vaseline and shining the ball illegally is a mystery to all who have soldiered out there before. Ask Butch White, Alan Brown, Barry Knight, Jeff Jones, John Price or David Larter how they used to keep the shine on, and they would look at you with some disbelief. Shine? If you coated it every six overs with gloss paint, the ball would still feel like a rough coconut in your hand.

John Lever obviously has reversed all the known laws of swing. Perhaps he shines the seam and picks the panels? His inswinger is not such a devastating ball in Essex. Is Bishen Bedi, a Northern Indian, whose head is very much on the block down South, clutching at a straw? Right or wrong, the Indian captain has to face up to the fact that swing bowling is not necessarily a lethal weapon. The ball swings every day of the week in Britain and if the Indian batsmen cannot cope, then their skills cannot be too mature.

By the failure of the class batsmen, Gavaskar, Viswanath and Patel, to make many runs, the ordinary players have not been raised. Whether the famed Indian spinners are in decline, too, is another question one would like answering by the team when it returns home.

Whatever the reasons for success, it would be wrong to attach everything to the few. I have received letters to say that the team spirit is magnificent, the out-cricket some of the best ever seen, and the leadership dazzling.

Bravo, Greigy! You deserve it after enduring the blitzes against Australia and West Indies. And if familiarity with the conditions helped in India, might not the same work in the Centenary Test in Melbourne?

Better the devil you know — a consolation, now I come to think of it, for all English batsmen at home who await the return of John Lever with his secret weapon. Normally fast bowlers set off for India with engines ticking smoothly and power in hand, only to return like dusty old bangers. J.K. Lever appears to have been traded in for a new model.

---

16 MARCH 1977

ENGLAND LOSE, BUT RANDALL MAKES A FIGHT OF IT

Ray Robinson

Melbourne

England were beaten, as expected, in the Centenary Test in Melbourne yesterday. What was not expected, however, was the slender margin of

Australia's victory, and Tony Greig, the touring captain, was right to point out that the loss of this one match was outweighed by England's recovery of batting stature.

A thrilling last-day recovery, inspired by Derek Randall's 174 – the Nottinghamshire right-hander's first Test century – swept England to a total of 417 – 11 runs beyond the highest winning fourth innings in any Test. Alas for Randall, Greig and England, it was still 45 runs short of the asking total. So Australia triumphed, as they had in the first-ever Test between the countries, and by an identical margin.

Yet, for seven and a half hours, England had threatened the impossible, clinging to the lifebuoy offered by Randall. England's latest Test hero is slightly built – 5ft 8½ in tall and 11 stone; yet his strokes skimmed over the Melbourne outfield as smoothly as the Queen's Rolls-Royce. Randall, forever restlessly fiddling with his cap maintained his aggressively watchful vigil for the equivalent of a day and a quarter, enabling England to average 3¾ runs an over. Most of Randall's 4s were placed through the off field; his cover-drives were unexcelled on either side. He went through a difficult time after a Lillee bouncer had struck his cap, felling him. Amiss his batting partner, walked anxiously towards him; but Randall moved a dozen yards to leg, then returned to shape up again.

However, he hung his bat out riskily at Lillee's outswinger and Chappell's outcutter several times, to Amiss's obvious concern. Soon, however, he had recovered his poise, and he and Amiss carried their third-wicket stand to 166 in three and a half hours. Amiss, except for brief uneasiness against the new ball, coped far better with Lillee than in the first innings. But he was surprised by an incutter from Chappell after reaching 64 off 185 balls in 233 minutes, and Marsh soon snapped up Fletcher, off Lillee.

Randall ploughed on, his serene progress interrupted by two untoward incidents. In Lillee's 23rd over, one delivery reared past the Englishman's raised bat and right shoulder, hitting something en route. Randall pointed to his shoulder; Lillee, appealing, pointed to the bat and spoke to Randall, who again fingered his shoulder.

Randall's end seemed to have come when, after making 161, he was given out by umpire Brooks, to a catch by Marsh off Chappell. Randall, resigned to his fate, began to walk, when Marsh sportingly indicated that he had not caught the ball before it hit the ground. Brooks conferred with Chappell, and Randall was recalled to continue his punishment of the long-suffering Australia attack. But he was soon to go. His fifth-wicket partnership with Greig had produced 56, when Randall, pushing forward to O'Keeffe's leg-break fell to Cosier's bat-pad catch.

Randall swished his bat disappointedly at the grass as the noise of the crowd's applause followed him off. His sterling innings earned him the 1,600 dollars award as Man of the Match. Two overs late O'Keeffe drew Greig into another short leg catch by Cosier. It was 369 for 6 and the Australians sensed victory. O'Keeffe dismissed Lever lbw, and a smart catch by Chappell helped Lillee send back Old. Underwood soon followed.

Knott, meanwhile, had been vigorously run-hunting since his captain's departure; but after hitting five fours in 42, he tried to drag a straight ball off his stumps and became Lillee's fifth victim for 139. Lillee finished with a match analysis of 11 for 165. His jubilant team-mates carried him off; it was the least he deserved.

---

14 MAY 1977

GREIG SACKED AS ENGLAND CAPTAIN

Daily Telegraph reporter

Tony Greig was stripped of the England captaincy yesterday at the emergency committee meeting of the Cricket Council, the game's ruling body in England.

The committee spent four hours discussing Greig's activities in connection with the cricket 'circus' being organised by Mr Kerry Packer, the Australian impresario who has television and newspaper interests. They decided that Greig had admitted involvement in the scheme and, without informing Lord's, took part in 'recruitment' of players for an organisation which has been set up in conflict with a scheduled series of Test matches. 'His action inevitably impaired the trust which existed between the cricket authorities and the captain of the England side.'

The committee concluded that 'as far as the captaincy of England is concerned the Cricket Council will be instructing the chairman of selectors, Alec Bedser, that Tony Greig is not to be considered for this position for the forthcoming Test series against Australia.' No action is to be taken against Greig and two of his recruits, Derek Underwood and Alan Knott, both of Kent, as players until an emergency meeting of the International Cricket Conference, the world's ruling body, can be arranged.

Alec Bedser, chairman of the selectors said: 'It is very sad. We shall, of course, consider Greig as a player when the time comes.'

---

21 AUGUST 1977

PACKER: HIS SIDE OF THE STORY

A CUP OF TEA ... WITH NO SUGAR

Alan Lee

Kerry Packer is a palpably weary man. His legs ached, his shoes were off and he yawned regularly as we talked. But the iron resolve remains, blended with a determination to keep every channel of compromise open to the last.

I was the last port in his latest stormy visit to these shores. Within hours, he was stepping back on to the jet he uses as most others use the Tube. Yet he was willing, even eager, to talk of his plans. As he eased his legs on to a sofa, he confided: 'You know, when I'm tired at the end of a busy day, I sometimes ask myself why the hell I got involved in all this.'

That confession was human enough. But the heavyweight Australian, who is moonlighting the richest crop of cricket talent to a promised land and stopping off for an exchange of views with the establishment rulers, soon sounded the war cry.

'There is absolutely no chance of us quitting; no way that this series will cease in less than three years. It is 95 per cent certain that it will then continue on a permanent basis,' he declared. His rider was even more significant: 'I am prepared to go back and talk to the ICC at any time they feel ready to compromise — despite all that has happened. There is still time.'

So why, I asked, did he walk out of the meeting with that International Cricket Committee? 'I didn't — I have never walked out of a meeting in my life.' And with that, Packer's side of the story unfolded.

'The ICC sent me a telegram an hour after I had left England, saying they were willing to see me. I flew back four days later, but as soon as I arrived at the meeting, it was obvious they were not interested in making a deal.

'They put a number of points to me, including the transfer of control over my series to the ICC. I didn't object. But after their third point, I reminded them that there were things I would want as well – that is what compromise is all about.

'There was a dead silence. Then they read their fourth point – another ultimatum. Eventually, I got through and told them first I would insist on no victimisation of my players, and second that I wanted to buy the Australian TV rights when ABC's current contract expired. They could name the price.

'I suggested it would be better if I withdrew while they discussed it. They offered me a cup of tea and I walked around Lord's for forty minutes. When I went back in, they just came out with another ultimatum, saying the ICC could not sell rights in advance in this way. I then asked if we could set up a working committee to find a formula. No answer – they just read the ultimatum again.

'In desperation, I asked if there was anything else I could do. Not unless I was prepared to accept their terms, they said. I then asked if I should leave and they said yes ... and that was my walk-out.'

Packer is wholeheartedly committed to the success of his venture, but he is not in principle against its being controlled by the recognised authorities. He believes that the ICC never really wanted a compromise, but he hopes that some talks, even independent of the hierarchy, can take place.

England captain, Mike Brearley, is fervently seeking a solution that would preserve his team, and the idea of discussions between Brearley, Tony Greig and two establishment figures is surely not unreasonable. Packer, I am sure, would approve.

What he does not approve is the almost savage vindictiveness he has suffered from some quarters. So I collected together the bullets most commonly fired at him, and tried again. His reactions were revealing. Why did he say he would call the whole thing off if he won the TV rights?

'I never said that. The whole thing was distorted beyond belief. My point was that if a compromise had been reached and the ICC took control of the series, I would slide into the background. 'There was never any question of me not paying the players. The whole idea of this scheme is that the top cricketers should earn more money.'

Why did he pick Tony Greig as captain of the World team? 'There have been World elevens in the past who have not performed to their potential. Mine was not going to fail, so I wanted a good captain and a strong and dedicated man. Tony Greig fits the bill.

'I think he has been unfairly victimised for his part, although I wasn't surprised when he was sacked as England captain. I think we have formed a good working relationship. I like Tony as a fellow and I like the way he works. Above all, I like his grit.'

Is he worried about the Australians' failure this summer? 'Why should I be? I've got Ian Chappell, Dennis Lillee, Gary Gilmour and others to come in. Anyway, these boys were young, it was a first tour for many of them and they were playing in conditions very strange to them.'

Is he really concerned about the welfare of his players? (At this point Packer swung his legs off the sofa and launched an offensive that would have done justice to his father; a one-time amateur heavyweight champion of Australia.) 'People say I'm not – well, why do they think I'm fighting in the courts to keep my players in county and Test cricket? It will cost me £250,000 and the result won't affect me at all. If the players are loyal to me, I will be loyal to them – it's a two-way street.

'I would suggest that it is the ICC who don't give a damn about the players. The curious thing is, the only way county cricket will be harmed is if I lose this case and they lose their top players. Who will want to watch then?

'My scheme has already increased the financial incentives available. There are incentives to become a champ – and that's how it should be. If you don't win, you don't get the same rewards. It's the same in all walks of life. Cricket has never had an "A" stream before. I'm providing it – a "Super A" if you like.'

Packer finished on a note that was thoughtful, slightly bitter. 'It hasn't been easy. The amount of work involved has been horrifying. I always knew there would be a furore, but I have been disturbed by some of the one-eyed views expressed. I would call it a lack of professional integrity.

'Nobody likes being pillorised,' he added, with a hint of a smile. 'But I'll survive.'

26 NOVEMBER 1977

PACKER ELECTRONIC SCORER RUNS WILD

Tony Lewis

Melbourne

The second day in Packerland was much like the first. The concrete cage of a stadium is so immense and the spectators so few – under 1,000 at the start – that play was silent and remote.

My favourite toy, the electronic moving message on the scoreboard, told us that the WSC Australians had declared at 276 for 8, news which was appetising enough to cast a spell of anticipation over a capacity 77,000 had they been there because Dennis Lillee was about to roar in on his come-back and the men facing him were Barry Richards and Majid Khan.

Yet nothing stirred save perhaps the shuffle of one of the many barmen who manned long smart bars without drinkers or the waiters in the restaurants who nodded with penguin politeness to invisible diners. Every facility on the ground is open.

Wayne Prior bowled at the other end and the pitch bounced more unevenly than on the first day. Cracks appeared by the close but that is quite the custom in this climate. Prior found the edges of both opener's bats, then persuaded Mushtaq to perform a contorted scoop shot to mid-on. By mid-afternoon the mood had changed. The crowd had swelled, the temperature was now more than 100 degrees and that good old Australian abuse was picking out the Pommies more accurately and loudly enjoying the demise of the world side. Collis King profited from Ian Chappell's close fields by picking up some scorching boundaries square on the off-side with slashing cuts.

The left-arm slow bowler Bright, not known for imparting great spin on the ball, got one to turn enough to secure a Procter edge to slip. The poor electronic scorer then went berserk. Five capital letter Ts appeared and guessing Mr Packer now to be capable of anything, it was suggested that the indication was that the last five balls had turned. With two days to go the WSC Australians are 208 ahead.

Today the much publicised nine television cameras arrive. The microphones concealed near the stumps will certainly add a dimension to armchair viewing. So the crescendo of thundering hooves from your television may no longer be the Lone Ranger approaching, but Dennis Lillee in full flight. Transmission will begin at the first 'Super-Test' next week.

Television may, of course, be the beginning and the end of Kerry Packer's true interest. Already the players have invited John Newcombe, the president of the Association of Tennis Professionals, to outline the workings of a world-wide association of players.

Tony Greig envisages a similar body of cricketers taking an active part in the running of the game: 'The control of the game must go back to the boards. It would mean nudging Mr Packer into a corner, leaving him with his television coverage, then joining the two games together again so that we are all one and far better off for this great fight.'

For the moment I believe the players will be happy to see the television cameras arrive. They have been made into saleable superstars by them and until someone thinks Packer players worth seeing in the flesh they will need to be sustained by them.

---

23 JANUARY 1978

SUTCLIFFE, THE MASTER OPENER, DIES AT 83

E. W. Swanton

Herbert Sutcliffe, the Yorkshire and England batsman, and opening partner for county and country to Percy Holmes and Sir Jack Hobbs respectively, has died aged 83.

Sutcliffe's career from the moment of his entry into the Yorkshire eleven in 1919 was a success story almost without the suspicion of a break. He scored 1,839 runs in his first year, headed the county averages, and forthwith established himself with Holmes in a first-wicket partnership which in the following 15 years broke all records.

In his first Test (in 1924 against South Africa) Sutcliffe helped Hobbs, the greatest batsman of the day, in an opening stand of 136. In his next — and his first at Lord's — he made the first of his 16 hundreds for England. The following winter in Australia with MCC he had the best figures on either side, averaging 80 in the Tests. At Melbourne in one of the classic stands of history he and Hobbs batted all day for 283.

When England at last regained the Ashes at the Oval in 1926 it was an even more remarkable partnership of 172 with Hobbs on a most difficult wicket that settled the issue. Of all his innings, Sutcliffe was proudest of his 161 on that momentous day. He was twice after that on the winning side with MCC in Australia. Between 1928 and 1932 he three times topped 3,000 runs. Against Essex at Leyton he made the highest score of his life, 313, in the partnership with Holmes that broke all records – 555 for the first wicket.

His 50,135 runs average 52, is the most ever made in a career by a Yorkshireman. Only six batsmen in the world have totalled more runs. He twice hit two centuries in a single Test match.

What a monument of achievement! Yet when contemporaries and critics discuss Herbert Sutcliffe in the context of the other great names of history they do so generally on a note of qualification. The fact is he was the perfect second string, the subsidiary in a technical sense not only to Hobbs, 'the perfect batsman', who died in 1963, aged 81, but also to the more brilliant and likewise more mercurial Holmes.

Sutcliffe was a good cutter and a brave, if upward hooker. Gripping the bat with the face unusually open he habitually played the off-side ball square of the direction expected. You could not say that he was a master of all the strokes, but he used what he had to the maximum purpose.

He was a master of the short push for one, and there have never been two such judges of a single as Hobbs and Sutcliffe. Their understanding was so complete that they seldom even needed to hurry. The foundation of Sutcliffe's cricket was a wealth of determination and concentration, and an unruffable calm. His black hair gleaming in the sun, legs crossed in an aloof, superbly-confident manner when at the non-striker's end, he epitomised self-confidence and good sense.

So it was in his personal life. One of the long string of Yorkshire cricketers deriving from Pudsey he was about to blossom on the county scene at the outbreak of the 1914–18 war, during which he rose from the ranks, finishing as a captain in the Yorkshire Regiment.

Playing in an age in which professional captaincy was almost non-existent he once declined with the height of dignity the leadership of Yorkshire. On his retirement at the age of 44 he became a successful man of business. He served many years on the Yorkshire committee, became, rather late in life, a Test selector, and was president of the Forty Club.

The high repute of the professional cricketers of his day as sportsmen and gentlemen in the truest sense owed much to the example of such men as he. Sutcliffe's wife, Emily, died in 1974, aged 75. In recent times he had lived at the nursing home at Keighley, Yorks, where he died.

---

1 JUNE 1978

HEADING FOR STATE OF FACELESS MEN

Tony Lewis

Without the television captions I would not have been sure who actually batted for Derbyshire against Middlesex last week. Did Jim Laker and Richie Benaud get it right? If I told them that Hill – incognito in his shiny white helmet and barred visor – had batted twice, would they believe me?

Derbyshire's young batsmen came on to the field looking like men from another planet – 'one small step for man' – and out to the middle. Hill it was ... I think ... who scored half-a-century and more, but when he left terra firma for the dressing rooms he acknowledged the crowd's ovation with a robot's raising of the bat. He did not touch his helmet or even raise the visor. The faceless man passed on.

When cricket entered the age of the navy blue cap, I thought we had reached the height of anonymity, but while helmets concealing the identity look like the trappings of the supreme sub-epsilon state is that the way we want to go?

Watching the helmeted Derbyshire men play the spin of Emburey and Edmonds was straight off another planet. I suppose you are allowed to ask an umpire to hold the headgear until the bouncers return, but who wants to see David Constant and his colleagues with a cranium under the arm walking the Bloody Tower?

It also makes nonsense of it to see a batsman at one end girded up against the fatal blow while his partner looks to be playing a different game bareheaded at the other. I want to make it clear that I am not appalled by the decision of cricketers to wear head protection, but just by the sight of it. Mike Brearley was one of the first to take cover. You only have to look at the style of helmet he uses. He looks to have a couple of chapattis tucked away under his cap in case he needs a snack. However, Brearley and the opening batsmen need this most valuable piece of equipment in the current game. The truth is that too many bouncers are being bowled.

When Bob Willis went around the wicket to angle a bouncer in at Iqbal Qasim he bowled a fast, short-pitched delivery to a non-recognised batsman. This was simply outside the letter of the playing conditions. Within half-an-hour of that injury to the Pakistani I had moved from the Press box, where the reaction had been generally one of objection and anger, to a group of former players up the other end of the ground.

The players' verdict was that Willis was justified. They agreed in advance with the TCCB's creed issued later in the week that night watchmen if sent in to protect a recognised batsman should themselves be equipped to face all sorts of bowling. Why should Willis have some of his teeth drawn for the first 40 minutes of a morning's play when he would be hoping to blast in at the top batsmen with a new ball.

Consider the gamesmanship that can be employed. If a side has lost quick wickets to fast hostile bowling the captain could immediately send in a non-recognised batsman. If that man can defend as well as an Iqbal Qasim or an Underwood and bowling cannot be short-pitched, then a useful respite will have been gained.

The number of bouncers bowled in first-class cricket has increased. Colin Cowdrey, at the end of his long career, believed that they had trebled. Nowadays there are certainly more generally fast bowlers at large, most of them imported.

When Mike Denness's England went to Australia in 1974–5 they let the bouncers fly, but found that short balls from Old and Arnold were hooked or comfortably avoided because they were not fast enough. Those of Thomson and Lillee were fast and nearly unplayable and a threat to life itself. From then on international cricket became more and more a battle of bouncers. Tony Greig recently wrote that he thought America might take to watching cricket, but they would need to see a lot of exciting bouncers – a sort of roller-ball cricket.

Sadly, the trend is threatening some of the art of both batting and bowling. Alec Bedser, chief scrutineer of bowlers in the county game, will tell you how very few have the ability to swing the ball. In the effort to bang in regular bouncers the bowling action can be distorted. Ian Botham is an example of a lively fast-medium bowler who can tear off the odd very quick delivery. However, he does not possess a genuine fast bowler's action. The extra speed is generated by strength of arm and not by rhythm of body.

Most batsmen play real fast bowling on the back foot. The tendency always was to move back and across just before the ball was bowled. Reg Simpson is always quoted as a great player of the quickies and he worked it out that way.

However, the modern profusion of bouncers has got many batsmen into a groove of shifting across the crease before even a medium-fast bowler sends down the ball – Randall and Gooch must number among the fringe Test players this summer, but there are hosts of others. The art of standing still at the crease, head steady and balanced is the disappearing art I referred to.

The answer may be to restrict bouncers even further to a maximum of one per over and to inform not only the fielding captain of his duty when a non-recognised batsman comes in, but also the batting captain of the fine distinction which separates a night watchman from a batsman proper and how he is likely to get his man hurt if he proves capable of holding of a Test attack for 40 minutes or so as Iqbal Qasim did.

---

19 OCTOBER 1978

OBITUARY

FRANK WOOLLEY: MASTER BATSMAN

E. W. Swanton

Frank Edward Woolley, who has died aged 91, at Halifax, Nova Scotia, was one of the great cricketers of history and, in particular, the pride of Kent. He was as graceful a batsman as ever played.

The beauty of his play was in spite of a quite apparent stiffness of limb and gait. As with Denis Compton, one tends not to notice a certain awkwardness of movement in the joyous contemplation of the stroke. Familiarity and affection breed a blindness to such a detail. And if

Woolley, coldly analysed, was hardly a graceful figure, he was a supremely rhythmic, stylish, debonair striker of a cricket ball.

Charm is a difficult virtue to dissect. The late R.C. Robertson-Glasgow began his *Print of Frank Woolley*, in that delightful series of his, by saying that 'he was easy to watch, difficult to bowl to, and impossible to write about'. The key to his play, as with all the very greatest, was an extraordinary refinement of timing, and that, again, seemed to derive from the severe simplicity and correctness of his method.

Here was this extremely tall, slim figure, swinging his bat in the fullest and truest pendulum through the line of the ball. There were no kinks or ornamentations – no one surely was ever so free from mannerism? Here comes the ball, there goes the foot, down she comes and through. Naturally enough, Woolley was a glorious driver, while to the slower straight one he played a perpendicular back stroke with a power which could be generated from the easiest laziest swing.

But of the more delicate strokes, he was equally the master, and here was to be seen his amazing keenness of eye. He was a glorious cutter, and no one turned the ball more finely and prettily off his legs. Such is a brief technical appraisal of his batsmanship, but what endeared him to the ringside, and at the same time made him so devastating an opponent, was his whole approach to batsmanship.

The modest, self-effacing companion of the dressing-room quickly became an utterly disdainful, aloof antagonist at the wicket. Mr Robertson-Glasgow, in his article, went on to say that Frank Woolley was never known to express a particular liking or distaste for any bowler. He seemed superbly indifferent to who was bowling, or how they were bowling. The bowler, you might say, was an anonymous privileged contributor to his art.

He sometimes got out, I believe, because he had refused to recognise a particular trap set for him. He certainly paid the penalty, now and then, for taking to himself a bowler whom a comrade did not relish, seeking to knock him off. The thing he never seemed to contemplate, let alone to fear, was getting out himself. He was the antithesis of the calculating, bread-and-butter run collector. He played the ball on its merits, and he played for his side.

In the nineties he batted precisely as he would bat after the century was reached – which perhaps is why he was comparatively often got out just those few runs short of what to most cricketers is the important goal. Perhaps the more astute of his opponents tempted him to risks at this time.

He was a Kentish cricketer of the county's golden age. In his first year, as a lad of seventeen in 1906, he played with K.L. Hutchings, J.R. Mason, C.J. Burnup, and R.N.R. Blaker in the team that first brought the championship to Kent.

'We were never allowed to play for averages in the Kent side,' he wrote in *Wisden* on his retirement, and went on to say that it was ever the policy that the pitch must be occupied all day after winning the toss. Such was his early environment, the influence of which so firmly shaped his attitude throughout his cricket life.

I trust to have given a faint picture of Woolley as a batsman to those who never watched him play. Those who saw him even in the closing years of his life on the Kentish grounds, white-haired but spare and upright, looking like a retired bishop, will not easily forget his natural dignity and handsome appearance.

As to his bowling, I have not attempted a description, for his serious efforts ended in the early '20s, and I have only the memory of an occasional over, of the easy slanting run, left hand behind the back, and the poise of the high action.

But it is as well to remind the young that before the 1914–18 war he was not only the best all-rounder in England, but very nearly the best slow left-arm bowler; likewise, too, and right up until middle age, one of the finest slip fieldsmen.

He took 1,017 catches, more than any man. He cared little for figures yet only Hobbs narrowly bettered his aggregate of 58,969 runs (including 145 centuries). Only 25 bowlers have taken more than the 2,088 wickets.

The innings one has seen from him come readily to mind in swift kaleidoscope. Two brief but perfect gems at Lord's, both oddly enough, scoring 41 runs, one against Australia in the Second Test of Bradman's first tour, the other his farewell in Gentlemen and Players at the age of 51; several prolonged and severe chastisements of the Champion County bowlers at the Oval – he averaged 100 in this annual fixture; a lovely piece of play that enriched a cold Trial Match at Old Trafford; and, for Kent, a century before lunch against Nottinghamshire at Canterbury after rain, on a nasty flying pitch.

Alas! that one knows so many of the greatest only at second hand, the classic 95 and 93 at Lord's against Armstrong's Australians, in his own view the best innings he has ever played.

He was quite active into his late 80s and in January 1971 flew to Australia to watch the last two Tests. Nine months later, in Canada, he married for a second time, his first wife having died 10 years earlier. His second bride was Mrs Martha Morse, an American widow.

---

10 DECEMBER 1978

BOYCOTT, A SEVERED HEAD?

Tony Lewis

'What did you do in the Great War, Daddy?'

'I fought for the committee, son, but messy business you know, Civil War. Always takes a victim's head, one way or t'other.'

Geoffrey Boycott's head may only be rolling in depression in his room on the other side of the world in the Sherrington-Perth Hotel, but 'tis as good as severed. He had married himself to Yorkshire cricket for life. He may have fallen because of his own myopia but no one can imagine how he can live without the game and the White Rose banner. No one in cricket would have wanted his demise to have been so public and so final … except him.

In the end, his critics outnumbered his supporters but it all amounted to fratricide, Yorkshiremen v Yorkshiremen, and therefore the victory cannot be so sweet for Mr Connell's General Committee or the Cricket cabal which eventually took away Boycott's captaincy.

They have destroyed one of their own and to what good? Geoffrey Boycott can look at himself in the mirror for the rest of his life, soul search and cry 'mutiny', but he himself will never change. I doubt if he can ever bring himself to play for Yorkshire again and why should he? If cricket is still his passion, far better he attaches his batting skills to another cause earning the regard of all and sundry again as the finest batsman in the country.

It is natural to sympathise with him but he will not be impressed nor will he find it possible to forgive any of those who have plotted against him, written or even talked treason. His chief target, the Yorkshire committee, must ask themselves not if they have been too hard but too soft. Should they not have rejected the idea of making Boycott captain in the first place? Is it not their continued ambivalence on the subject which has led their best player, not along the road to authority as senior man in their side, but to the block as a leader of mistaken idealism?

So many times in recent years at the close of a Yorkshire season have Yorkshire members been treated to the sight of their players hustling committee men into corners, gossiping behind pillars and gradually undermining everyone's confidence in the club. The committee must now lay clear plans and work to recruit and train the sort of cricketers which will give their captains a far better chance of success than Boycott had.

What of John Hampshire's taste for public dissent? Once he refused to support Tony Greig when in an England side at Headingley, saying that he was not able to try his best for a South African captain despite the fact that he was wearing the England Lions on his chest.

Then again, there was the notorious blocking demonstration against Northamptonshire last summer – his anti-Boycott demo. Both mutinous acts were carried out to the detriment of the team and very publicly. He will find that it has been much easier to lead a revolt and take the Yorkshire side to the odd win than it is to establish trust all round in his new captaincy.

I believe Hampshire can do it, but he, too, should be examining his conscience in the mirror. It was almost his head gone, not Boycott's. Finally it should not be thought that Yorkshire's problems are unique. The captaincy problems of many counties are chronic, though by the divine right of their history Yorkshiremen take themselves more seriously than most on the subject of cricket.

It is time for every county to see the sense in grooming captains, taking the responsibilities, the judgment and the basic unselfishness second nature for those who eventually take over a professional team. Cricket is desperately short of leadership by personality. Mutiny followed by the worker's choice of captain is not going to be the long-term answer for which Yorks must now set about looking.

GOOD BUYS IN THE MARKET

Tony Lewis *asks: could Packer's style work here?*

The big, black panthers in strawberry-mousse clothing closed in, patient but lethal, around the Australians. This lone figure in wattle yellow fidgeted, though he stood bravely upright. For him there could be no easy escape. He was stuck out there in the middle, trapped in the floodlights, relying on his skill and reflexes – no one else's – to repel a flashing white ball.

'Come on, Aussie, come on,' blared the public address speakers and 45,000 of his fellow-countrymen joined the act. The sheer loneliness of a batsman was never so well illustrated when friend and foe alike dressed in white.

Again the panthers crouched, coiling the vertebral spring, ready to pounce on to the catch or leap into a loud appeal. Nobody doubted the loneliness of the umpire, either. The decision was torn out of him with yelling and jumping, arms raised to the sky. If he turned them down they kicked the dust, snarled and prowled. The lonely arbiter made off to square-leg.

Yes, the cricket at Sydney last week was vivid entertainment and so it should be because World Series Cricket is a brilliant marketing exercise of which the guiding principle is the public's pleasure. Give the people what they want, or, as I more often heard it put: 'It's bums on seats that count.'

Long-legged girls woo the crowd with promotional literature, including scorecards which carry the photographs of all the Packer players. No one passes incognito in this set-up, though Kerry Packer himself is working hard at his personal retreat into the shadows. Drinks go out to the players by buggy and the public address system does even more addressing.

The yellow Australian hit a four. The finger went on the button and out came that war cry again, 'Come on Aussie, come on.' Incredibly, this World Series jingle is now in the Top Ten of the Sydney charts and last week climbed 22 places to number 33 in the national ratings.

You've been training all the winter,
And there's not a team that's fitter,
And that's the way it's going to be;
'Cos you're up against the best, you know,
This is super tests, you know.
You're up against the best the world has seen.
Come on, Aussie, come on,
Come on, Aussie, come on.

Lillee's pounding down like a machine,
Pascoe's making divots in the green,
Marsh is taking wickets,
Hooksie's clearing pickets,
And the Chappells' eyes have got that killer gleam.
Come on, Aussie, come on, come on,
Come on, Aussie, come on.

Packer has given the public free parking at Sydney, free transport out to the Waverley ground in Melbourne, he plays his cricket when they have the time to watch it – at night – and with a white ball which they can see better.

Rain rarely stops play, ground conditions are always playable and there is not light bad enough to bring the sides off the field. Most of all, by relentless television exposure, all his players are individual star personalities. You cannot eat a McDonald hamburger without thinking of Wayne Daniel's television commercial.

A night at a World Series cricket match is more like a trip to the Catford dogs than a day at Lord's. Kerry Packer plays the abbreviated game of monopoly best, the short game, sharing out the properties first and surging into the quick climax.

The only difference between him and anyone else in the limited-over cricket business is that he only deals in Mayfairs and Park Lanes. The Old Kent Roads are playing for Australia in the Tests. What can the English learn from the World Series adventure? In one-day cricket should not England poach Packer's marketing treatment as he once poached their best players?

In England, the John Player, the Benson & Hedges and Gillette matches are already well attended. Whatever the cost of installing floodlights or whatever the possibilities of adapting football grounds to cricket in the summer months, the resultant increase in income from this one-day cricket would hardly warrant the huge expenditure. More importantly, the game itself would be distorted. Football pitches are too narrow and the British evenings are simply too cold. Who wants to reduce the game to a frozen pageant for Humpty Dumpty players wearing four sweaters.

The white ball is very popular, day or night, with Australian specta-tors. Balanced against the merits is the bowlers' opinion that it does not swing enough. Batsmen like it until it becomes dull and dirty after 20 overs or so. The World Series cricketers frequently change the white ball after 25 overs nowadays. No doubt manufacturers could perfect it. Would it solve the problems of bad light in this country? As I have said, Packer tries anything, refusing to keep the entertainment off the stage. 'Light meters,' said a devoted World Series follower, 'what use are they? You can't play with them.'

Can the Test and County Cricket Board and its member counties do more? The Board has a Committee which thinks only of the public. It cannot match Packer's power because it does not own a national televi-sion channel or a national newspaper. However, it should be fairly observed that there exists liaison with British Rail for excursions with a match ticket to Tests away from London.

As for spectator comfort, Edgbaston has led the way with its execu-tive suite, the ultimate, but also one should note the new bucket-back seating at Headingley and the Oval – splinters are on the way out! It's as well to remember, too, that such seats costs £10 to £14 each and installing 2,000 of those is enough to make the Exchequer cough and splutter. Mr Packer, on the other hand, appears to have limitless funds.

Perhaps at County level the marketing message has not been fully developed, for example, to the shop on the corner where Mr Packer hands out tickets free of charge. However, the reason most cricket lovers do not go out to the County Grounds on a day off from work is as much to do with the discomfort and catering as the play itself.

It must be conceded at this end that Kerry Packer's methods are entirely his own, suiting his unique circumstances. His cricket is not the leading principle in his marketing policy but rather the elevation of individual players to TV stardom. His show-biz presentation is strictly Palladium style, and the old image of cricket is disappearing.

Both MCC and TCCB have always legislated 'in the interests of cricket and cricketers' and so they may decide not to try to emulate World Series cricket at all, but to sell the quality of life and sportsmanship inherent in the traditional game. Fair dinkum cricket, as they say, in Australia.

But there is an area of Packer strategy which stands out as appropriate to the British game, and that is the education of the fringe sports lover who knows nothing of this particular game. Cricket probably does not sell itself hard enough to the non-committed in this country. Just think how many millions of people have had no cricket background in school or at home and therefore have no understanding of the basic joys of the game. To them cricket is a mystique, the slowest and most boring game in the world.

The game needs popularising as well as just televising ball by ball and the starting point, as Kerry Packer has indicated, may be in the personalities involved especially in the short game, even indoors and certainly on Sunday afternoons.

There is nothing like competition in the market to sharpen up the ideas and the Australian tycoon has surely persuaded by now the diehards that County cricket is now a lively business as well as a gentle tradition.

---

26 AUGUST 1979

THE DAY THE CIRCUS HIT TOWN

Tony Lewis *on the long-awaited champions*

History is defied. Essex, friendly, quixotic Essex, have won the County Championship.

From skipper H.G. Owen and all who pioneered from 1895, to Keith Fletcher's boys in 1979, over a century's cricketers have toiled, seamed and spun in the land of the three scimitars before the title finally came their way. It was almost in Essex's character never to win it at all. They have always been a delightful roadshow whose charm was one day their brilliance, the next their vulnerability.

They were a 'natural' to be taken for 721 in a day by the 1948 Australians at Southend, but then in 1957, with almighty Surrey on the rampage, who else could scramble past the follow-on, bowl out Surrey for 119, and then proceed to smash off the 256 runs to win in under four hours against Bedser, Loader, Lock and Laker to win by two wickets. Only Essex.

They played mostly at Leyton, which was rural in the early part of the century, but when London's eastern suburbs spread, engulfing the County ground, the Essex circus set out around the county to play their cricket on eight of nine grounds every season: Leyton, Southend, Westcliff, Romford, Brentwood, Ilford, Colchester, Clacton and Chelmsford.

On the road went every piece of equipment, hundreds of yards of seven-foot screening with poles, stands, chairs and benches, scoreboard printing machinery, boundary boards, a heavy roller, marquees and a portable office. And later went the famous double-decker buses which housed the scoreboard and the ladies' loo.

The modern Essex, set calmly into action by Tom Pearce after the Second World War, resumed the have-bat-will-travel spirit. From 1949 Trevor Bailey became first assistant secretary and later secretary: 'It was wonderfully impromptu stuff. I recall a game at Romford when there was a huge crowd and I had to ask the opposing captain if I could leave the field to put on my secretary's hat and attend to the latecomers. I did. I went off and helped shift some tables and found room for the extra people to sit on them right in front of the sightscreen. We were always impoverished. No one ever got turned away.'

Unfortunately, as far as Championship hopes were concerned, the travelling circus act always hampered Essex. They had many fine sides playing well under the leadership of Pearce, Insole, Bailey and Taylor, but they were effectively playing all their matches away from home.

In 1965, Chelmsford went up for sale. Trevor Bailey attended a dinner to celebrate Worcestershire's Championship and told Warwickshire representatives, whom he met there, that Essex would like to buy the ground. Essex were short of cash, but Warwickshire came up with an interest-free loan. So at Chelmsford this weekend a quiet glass should be raised in the direction of Edgbaston because the home base has been a important fact in the advance to the top.

Keith Fletcher was groomed for captaincy. He used to stand at first slip, advising his old captain Brian Taylor. Mind you there was a time when I thought there was only one conversation. 'What d'y think, Fletch?' 'Slip 'm Boycey from the other end, Tonker.' Fairly simple tactics, often effectively repeated.

Now Essex have their most talented team of all time and they are splendidly led by a thoughtful, modest man, whose shy prep-school walk out to bat belies a competitive spirit. His achievement is that he has managed to bring out the best cricket from his side without depressing their own personalities and their love of fun. Essex are entertainers.

Consider the most extrovert, Ray East. When he bowls his Pinocchio legs and windmill arms conceal his skill. His love of comic mime sets everyone laughing. Yet the pathos of this particular clown is that his serious intent is often lost amid laughter. However, Ray East is good enough to play for England; most professionals will tell you that.

The batting has been speedy and talented with the classical McEwan, Gooch in full flow, lusty Pont, wisdom from Denness, Hardie and Fletcher himself. There is promise from Lilley, consistency with gloves and bat from Smith. With the ball, Lever has been a sheer sensation, backed by inspired effort from Phillip and Turner, as well as by the two patient mature artists Acfield and East.

In 1979, Essex have gloriously proved in days of increasing financial reward that money need not be the incentive. They have played at cricket, not manipulated it for cash, and have transmitted their own obvious enjoyment to their patient and loyal supporters; the prize all the more delightful because of the ... well, er ... brief 103-year wait.

---

30 DECEMBER 1979

BEYOND THE LAW

HOW IS IT POSSIBLE FOR JUSTICE TO BE MISCARRIED SO FAR?

Tony Lewis *deplores a cowardly act*

Did Dennis Lillee not hold up a Test Match for nine minutes by refusing to exchange his aluminium bat for a wooden one? Was that not Lillee I saw bustling off to the Perth pavilion and returning defiantly with the selfsame aluminium blade? Who was it who threw the bat many a yard as the Australian captain Greg Chappell walked silently, but authoritatively, to the square with a suitable replacement?

If that was not Lillee then it was the most amazing illusion performed since woman was first sawn in half. He should be admitted instantly to the Magic Circle, or else, if witnesses are to be believed, including thousands at the ground and millions watching television, Dennis Lillee should be suspended from the game of cricket as run by the Australian Board of Control.

However, the Board claim to have seen nothing. In that infamous nine minutes, laughter stirred up by the clang of bat hitting ball changed to hatred even among Lillee's home crowd. Here was an individual putting himself above the game. He was bigger than cricket itself; the umpire's judgment was being trampled on; this was Lillee's law in action and the world of cricket was stuck with it.

In trying to work out how the Australian Board reached their decision simply to reprimand him severely and not to ban him altogether, one has to conclude that Lillee was not defiant but was only involved in discussions with the umpires, that he was justified in arguing the legality of his aluminium bat and that his only offence was of choosing the wrong time and place to express his opinion.

There is nothing in cricket's laws forbidding an aluminium blade. Indeed, Lillee had used it in the previous West Indies Test Match at Brisbane ... but without making contact with the ball.

In this case Mike Brearley could be accused of complaining too soon after one outside edge and a clonk for three through mid-off. The metal had been rigorously tested in the factory. I was told it was softer than willow and it was rather like hitting a soggy Christmas pudding with a loosely-strung tennis racket.

Therefore the umpires may have been unfair and precipitate in calling on Law 46 – Fair And Unfair Play – to dismiss from the game, in the full view of millions, a bat which had been specifically designed to be an asset to the game as a whole and, of course, in which Dennis Lillee had a serious business interest.

A top-class bat now costs £50 or thereabouts. Lillee's much cheaper bat might well have become the salvation of many young boys, but now,

having been sent off the Test Match field, it can only be advertised –
'aluminium bat as used by ... no one'.

We hear that the umpires made no specific report on Lillee's behaviour. That too can be justified. Greg Chappell solved the problem before
the ultimate action of reporting was necessary. So we had reached a
situation in which the manufacturer of a product had found himself
ejected from the market for no reason tenable in the laws of playing
conditions of cricket save the issue of 'fair and unfair play' which was
decided upon after only two balls.

Is it time to wheel in the lawyers again? The Board may suspend
Lillee, but can they outlaw his bat? Professional cricket is now big business, but that does not necessarily mean a lowering in the standards of
behaviour. There are many who conduct their business affairs on the
highest moral plain.

Sadly, Lillee, an outstanding cricketer, is getting it all wrong as an
entertainer and as a businessman and the Australian Board look to be
straining to help him commit a very public suicide. In short, the Board
is getting the behaviour it deserves.

––––––––––

CHAPTER 5
THE 1980s

INTRODUCTION

Under the editorship of W.F. 'Bill' Deedes the *Daily Telegraph* enjoyed a circulation of a touch under 1.5 million by the start of the 1980s. Its place at the forefront of British quality journalism was secure and its coverage of sport reflected its position in the market place. The number of column inches dedicated to sport grew during the course of the 1980s and cricket played its part.

Largely owing to the brilliant summer of 1981, cricket was able to regain some of the attention lost during the years of conflict and controversy in the 1970s. Thanks to that summer of '81 cricket had its first genuine superstar of the post-war years in the formidable shape of Ian Botham.

The paper's leader writers had only been concerned with the darker sides of cricket during the Packer and D'Oliveira years. Now they could celebrate cricket for the right reasons. 'As for Ian Botham, he is the Boy's Own hero,' was the paper's verdict at the height of the 1981 Ashes.

The three Ashes victories of the 1980s were celebrated and enjoyed but it was of course the duels with the West Indies that were deemed the real test of England's standing in the world game. In 1984 Michael Carey, by now the *Daily Telegraph* cricket correspondent following the retirement of Michael Melford, was on hand to report on the 5–0 'Blackwash'. Fast bowlers were the kings of the game and England's lack of a Marshall, Holding or Garner led to a nationwide search for talent. The *Daily Telegraph* had little trouble with its own search for talent. The author Sebastian Faulks was sent to interview Dexter and cast his eye over the hopefuls, who included one H. Larwood from Nottingham.

Away from the international game, county cricket was enjoying a revival. The deeds of Viv Richards and Joel Garner at Somerset were matched by the skills of Richard Hadlee and Clive Rice at Notts. The biggest names in world cricket were on show at county grounds as international calendars allowed time for stints in county cricket. But of course conflict was never far away. Yorkshire cricket was split into factions over the sacking of Geoffrey Boycott, and here we have a seat in Sheffield Town Hall in 1984 as hundreds attended a meeting designed to end the internecine conflict.

The civil unrest spilled to other parts of the county game. In 1986 Somerset cricket was split by the decision to sack Viv Richards and Joel Garner, and the scenes at Sheffield Town Hall were replicated at Shepton Mallet's Bath and West Showground.

Change was also in the air at the *Telegraph*. In 1985 Conrad Black acquired control of the newspaper and within a year Max Hastings had been appointed editor. By 1987 Fleet Street had been left behind as the newspaper followed an industry trend by moving east to the Isle of Dogs.

Towards the end of the decade the position of cricket correspondent was again vacant and was unfilled by the time Mike Gatting led his team on the Ashes tour of 1986–7. The BBC's Peter West filled in and the newspaper employed the former England fast bowler, and by now Sydney resident, Frank Tyson to provide the expert cricketing commentary. Tyson was so successful that he was invited to cover the visit of Pakistan the following summer.

---

16 MARCH 1981

ENGLAND CRICKETERS MOURN THE 'COLONEL'

KEN BARRINGTON WAS A MENTOR WHO HAD DONE IT ALL HIMSELF

Michael Melford

Bridgetown

The death of Ken Barrington in Bridgetown at the weekend robbed world cricket of one of its most friendly and helpful officials. He was devoted to his job of passing on the benefit of his experience to the present young England side.

Dubbed the 'Colonel' by the players, he was not just an assistant manager and coach, but a loveable, utterly loyal member of the team who was never unkind. From the undoubted talent of the younger players, Barrington had hoped to develop one of the strongest England teams for some time. He would talk for hours on what was needed and on the progress already made to this end.

He was immensely hardworking and had one great advantage in acting as mentor to the young players: he had done it all himself. In particular, he had done it in West Indies in 1959–60 against the fast bowlers led by Wesley Hall. He had been through something similar to what today's batsmen are being subjected, and he had triumphed. The 1959–60 tour was one of the highlights of a career in which courage and determination played a major part and which he ended after suffering a heart attack while playing in a double-wicket tournament in Melbourne in 1968.

Born into an Army family, he came from Reading on to the Surrey staff in 1948. By 1953 he was in the Championship-winning side and he played his first two Tests, against South Africa, in 1955. He made 31,741 first-class runs and 76 centuries, 20 in Test matches. Of the latter, many were dogged fights against adversity, but his 115 in Melbourne in 19656 had all the fluency of his younger days.

His craggy features were emblematic of his determination as a fighting batsman of rare qualities. He achieved the distinction of making 1,000 runs in a season on 12 occasions. Having made what seemed a full recovery from his heart attack, he led an active life, running his garage, playing golf to a handicap of five and taking enormous pleasure from the cricketing progress of his son, Guy, now 12, and from any other cricketing activity.

Only last Thursday, he was re-elected to England's Test selection panel for 1981. Alec Bedser, chairman of the Test Selection Committee on which Barrington had served since 1972, spoke for many throughout the world, yesterday:

'You couldn't have a better companion. He was a most conscientious person, not just at cricket, absolutely reliable. A wonderful chap to have around.'

22 JULY 1981

WILLIS ACHIEVES UNBELIEVABLE WITH 8 FOR 43

Michael Melford

Headingley

Just occasionally in life the unbelievevable does happen. It happened on the last day of the third Cornhill Test at Headingley yesterday when England, who had seemingly been within a few minutes of defeat on Monday afternoon with Ladbrokes offering 500–1 against them, bowled out Australia for 111 to win by 18 runs.

Ian Botham hauled them up from the depths on Monday and, having made 149 not out, took the first wicket when Australia batted yesterday. But the 130 which Australia needed was very little on a pitch still producing the unpredictable ball but no more often than when they were making 401 in the first innings. At 56 for one indeed Australia seemed to be cruising home.

Then Bob Willis, having switched to the Kirkstall Lane end, began to bowl as straight and as fast as at any time in the long career which has been miraculously extended after injury. He has only once produced better figures than 8 for 43, but that was not in a Test match. His inspired spell began 20 minutes before lunch when he took the first of three wickets in 11 balls. It ended 70 minutes after lunch when he knocked out Bright's middle stump and England incredibly had levelled the series.

The inspiration was not confined to Willis, for England threw themselves frantically about the field and, until the last few seconds, held all their catches, the best of them one by Botham and two by the agile Gatting while Brearley conducted operations with the unflappability which has coped successfully with numerous tight limited-over finishes in the past.

Twenty-four hours earlier England were 135 for 7, still needing 92 to avoid an innings defeat, and a few prescient clients were subscribing £52 to Ladbrokes. They have won between them £26,000.

Only once in more than 100 years of Test matches has a side following on been victorious: England won by 10 runs in Sydney in 18945. That makes this an extraordinary feat, but it is more extraordinary still to win from the sort of situation in which England found themselves before Botham and Dilley took over.

England's innings lasted another 20 minutes yesterday morning before Willis was well caught at second slip by Border in Alderman's second over with the new ball. Botham had driven Alderman handsomely past cover in his first over and five runs had been added. The last-wicket stand had made 37 in 31 minutes during which Willis received nine balls. The last three wickets had added 221 and, as at Trent Bridge, Alderman, who had not played in a Test before this series, had taken nine wickets in the match.

The only conceivable reasons then that one could find why Australia should not make 130 were conditions in which the ball might swing, a bad start which might lead to panic – or, a brilliant piece of bowling. Yet, on a lovely fresh sunny morning, the new ball swung little and the Australians set off as if the task was trifling, Wood hitting Botham's first two balls for four. In Botham's second over Wood drove and apparently hit ground and ball at the same time, Taylor taking the catch. The score then advanced uneventfully to 56 before Willis, in the second over after changing ends, made a ball lift and lob up from the handle of Chappell's bat.

Hughes played a form of steer towards third man fairly profitably in the first innings but now he met a ball from Willis which lifted more than expected and Botham dived at third slip to catch him two-handed to the left. Three balls after, Yallop fended off a ball towards Gatting at close short-leg. Gatting instinctively was back on his heels but recovered to scoop the ball up near his toes.

At that, they went in for lunch with the score 58 for four and an England win suddenly in sight if the inspiration could be sustained afterwards. Willis, running in downhill, tended to overstep and the fear was that his rhythm might be upset by concern about giving away a dozen runs in no-balls. He brushed this aside to such an extent that in 32 balls he took six wickets for eight runs.

The first wicket after lunch was the valuable one of Border. Old brought a ball back to knock out his leg stump off the inside edge. In Willis's next over Dyson, hooking, was caught at the wicket. In his next Marsh hooked off the top edge and Dilley, backing downhill just inside the long leg boundary, had an unenviable catch, but everything was coming off now and he held it safely chest high. In Willis's following over Lawson touched a wide one to Taylor and Australia were 75 for eight.

Hereabouts it looked as if Australia had decided that the way to play was to hit straight and often as Botham had done. In Bright and Lillee they had two experienced cricketers to put this into effect and the match was slipping away again when Lillee miscued a stroke off his legs. Gatting at mid-on had to move fast to reach a ball never very high but he hurled himself forward and caught it.

For Bright, Brearley now chose a field with two slips and the rest spread round the boundary. Botham had replaced Old and, after a leg-bye, had Alderman twice dropped in three balls by Old at third slip, the first chance sharp but straight, the second low and left-handed. Mercifully it did not matter. For his next ball Willis produced a yorker. Bright drove over it and a never to be forgotten Test match was won and lost.

---

22 JULY 1981

EDITORIAL

HOW IS THAT?

Certain of England's cricket players are said to be cross with the Press. They need not be angry with us. Through many matches lost and drawn we have held our editorial peace. One day things would come right; and so at last they have. England's extraordinary victory against Australia by 18 runs is only the second by a Test side made to follow on. The first was in Sydney in December 1894 when England – in what a dog-eared *Wisden* describes as 'possibly the most sensational match ever played either in England or Australia' – beat the old enemy by 10 runs.

There were two heroes in the 1981 repeat. Bob Willis, no longer in the first flush of youth, bowled as a man possessed. His eight wickets for 43 runs were prodigious, and his no-balls were as chaff. As for Ian Botham, he is the Boy's Own hero who, disgraced and mocked, threw the bat as though he were playing in the nets against a bunch of one-armed schoolgirls. This, mark, on a wicket which might have been prepared by grave-diggers rather than groundsmen. Relieved of his captaincy he was his old self. The role of the new captain, Mike Brearley, must be to draw out his genius, to be Boswell to his Johnson, Watson to his Holmes, Marshall to his Snelgrove.

But these three gentlemen should not bother to upbraid the Press. In victory be magnanimous; deeds speak louder than words. They should glory in the moment and not think of the past or future. Why wonder whether we shall have to wait ten long summers for another English victory or pretend that the present Australian or English sides rank among the really great? What matters is that this was a perfect Test Match which England won against odds that were at one stage quoted at 500–1. Perhaps, reflecting on this apparent impossibility in Ottawa, Mrs Thatcher may sleep a little easier.

---

3 AUGUST 1981

BOTHAM PUTS ENGLAND ONE UP IN SERIES

Michael Melford

Edgbaston

It happened again yesterday, amid even more hysterical excitement than at Headingley, for there was a much bigger crowd. When all seemed lost, England snatched back the fourth Cornhill Test at Edgbaston, bowled out Australia for 121, and won by 29 runs.

The margin was slightly larger than before, the final swing came much more suddenly, but the match-winner was the same, Ian Botham, this time with the ball. He took over when Australia, needing 151 to win, were 114 for 5. Mike Brearley, the captain, said later that Botham came on with some diffidence because he thought others were bowling better. Anyhow, he took the last five wickets for one run in 28 balls.

At 10 minutes to four, Australia, with Kent and Marsh together and only 37 needed, were starting what looked like a final assault against bowlers who were entitled to be wilting a little on a hot, tense day. Forty minutes and eight overs later, it was all over. Australia, who a fortnight ago seemed about to go two up in the series, were 2–1 down in it. There was another parallel with Headingley in that the 52 runs which John Emburey coaxed from the last two England wickets on Saturday evening, and the end of an innings in which England had scarcely distinguished themselves, proved all-important. There is a huge difference between having to make 100 and having to make 150.

Of England's early batting on Saturday, all that needs to be said at the moment of a glorious but very lucky victory is that in cutting out the rather light-hearted approach of the first innings, they went too far to the other extreme with a strokelessness which could only keep the bowlers on top.

In a way, yesterday's was a more remarkable win for the England bowlers than that at Headingley, for they had a slower, less bouncy pitch. Because it was so sluggish, the occasional eccentricity was less likely to be fatal, the error could often be corrected, the bat removed in time. Yet in any close match like this on an unpredictable and, for Edgbaston, utterly untypical pitch, luck plays a big part. Yesterday England had some astonishing pieces of luck. As they occurred, England seemed to be strengthened by the thought that they really could do it again, while Australia felt the shadow of Headingley draw ever nearer.

For much of the day, after Australia at 29 for three had made a bad start, it seemed as if they could recover. Allan Border batted for three and a half hours and Australia were at one time 87 for 3 and again 105 for 4. But every time Australia had victory within sight, a wicket fell and England were back again. Border's wicket was lost to the biggest slice of luck of all, when a ball from Emburey stood straight up as he played forward and gave him no chance.

The luck had turned against Australia early on a cloudless morning when Dyson and Border resumed at 9 for 1 as if the task was not one to cause great difficulty if approached with reasonable care. There was nothing then to suggest that at lunch Border would have added only 11 runs and would then have batted two-and-a-half hours in all for 13. After 20 minutes Willis, who as at Headingley found new fire and accuracy in the second innings, brought a ball back sharply to have Dyson lbw, so sharply that the batsman clearly thought it would have missed the leg stump. After another 20 minutes Hughes hooked Willis, slightly off-balance but with a fine ringing sound from the bat. The ball might have gone anywhere but flew straight to Emburey at deep backward square-leg near the boundary and was safely taken.

Willis's next ball must have been within a whisker of bowling Yallop but a slow recovery was on the way. Apart from an awkward low chance which Border gave to Brearley at first slip off Willis when he was 9 and the score 40, there were no further Australian mishaps before lunch when the pressure seemed to be easing on the batsmen. Emburey turned the occasional ball but could not at first create the same apprehension in the batsmen as had Bright, left arm over the wicket with the rough to aim at. Botham tried a spell well wide of the off stump but without encouraging the two left-handers to err or even to play very often.

After lunch Border and Yallop gathered confidence and when Willis, who had bowled his heart nearly out for 90 minutes before lunch, came on again, Yallop played him for two 4s behind square-leg. In Emburey's next over, however, as the match was slipping away from England, Yallop nicked a ball on to his boot whence it popped up to Botham at silly point. Yallop and Border had added 58. By now the bowlers had inevitably lost their freshness and Border, in his fourth hour, seemed to have worked out what was needed. But at 105 he could do nothing about the ball from Emburey which lobbed from high up the bat to short-leg.

At 114 for 5 Australia still seemed to have matters under control, but after Marsh had hit Emburey off the back foot for 4 he pulled across a yorker in the second over of Botham's spell which was being bowled very accurately on a full length. The next ball came back rather low to have Bright lbw. The removal of two seasoned, capable batsmen in two balls was a devastating blow for Australia. England by contrast had come a long and heartening way from the nadir of mid-afternoon on Saturday, when, with six wickets down, they were only 46 runs on.

Lillee stayed for 20 minutes amid a rare din for a Test match in England and then drove at a wide ball from Botham leaving him. Taylor dived a long way, and, having got there, was lucky to hold the catch at the second attempt. Kent, looking reasonably authoritative amid the hubbub, began refusing singles to keep the strike from Hogg and had just spurned one when he drove across an inswinger from Botham and was bowled. It took Botham three balls to produce an inswinging yorker to bowl Alderman and, only 12 days after Headingley, history had repeated itself.

8 AUGUST 1981

PROFESSIONAL GURU BY ANY OTHER NAME

Tony Lewis

Mike Brearley returns. Immediately England, the habitual losers, become the winners. What is more, they win matches they should certainly lose. What does this man have? A mystique has settled over him. He no longer wears whites and carries a bat; he plays in a cloak and waves a wand.

However, there are intangibles. One is his effect on the team. There was bound to be loyalty because these are mainly the players who came together under his captaincy. They enjoyed success, they made more money than anyone had ever dreamed of making from cricket and, above all, they found that they could rely on his inquiring mind to untie the problems, apply reason to a profession which was fogged by tradition and, when on the field, he was clear-sighted and positive.

Following Ian Botham's rather groping reign – and that is understandable too because Botham is 25 and Brearley 39 – the England players badly needed someone to follow. When the captaincy is uncertain, the group fragments into camps of mini-leaders. When Brearley came back at Headingley, England played badly, but they were at least all striving in the same direction.

Also intangible is the effect he has had on two of the cricketers who have exploded back to their best, Bob Willis and Ian Botham. Willis now runs in as if he has a rocket tied to his tail and Botham's vast energy has snorted out in the Australians' faces, whereas before, when he was in charge, the true Botham was painfully contained and repressed in the mould of the selfless man he thought he ought to be.

Brearley's return has briefly solved the captaincy dilemma, but the selectors must learn one lesson. If they are to give it to a young man again, then it will take him time, David Gower, like Ian Botham, might find, given the responsibility, that his playing standard too would dip.

Every captaincy is different because it reflects the mind and the personality of the leader. On the field it is easier to dissect. This is where Brearley puts down his wand and proves his understanding of the game and of the players on his own side and those against him.

Defending those small totals in the last innings at Leeds and Birmingham were meticulous demonstrations of who to bowl, when, at whom and to what field-settings. Balancing the ring of close fielders for Emburey with those protecting the boundary was delicately done. Most of all, he had to create a false situation in the minds of the Australians, and the hustle around the crease transfixed them, even though the ball only turned a little.

It was clever captaincy, but Mike Brearley would admit that he is not in possession of super-knowledge. The image of the grey-haired guru, or the academic head awash with Cambridge degrees is false. Mike Brearley is a thorough professional, and proud of it. In many ways he has led the profession of cricketer into the '80s. He plays the game hard and for money. He has made a particular point of not allowing the various media to make their livings off his back without getting his recompense. He has rationalised the profession. No longer do agency photographers snap the England side and sell their prints for profit – not without first paying the players.

Maybe it is the combination of his roles – managing director off the field and captain on it – which has sealed his support and has given his players the confidence in themselves to attack Australia and hound them mercilessly into two astonishing defeats.

His example should silence forever those who argue that captaincy is not all that important and that, in Australian style, 11 men should be chosen and the best captain from their number.

---

6 SEPTEMBER 1981

CASHING IN ON THE LAST BALL

Tony Lewis *at Lord's on the first NatWest final*

Derbyshire beat Northants off the last ball of the match, an exciting end to the first one-day competition sponsored by NatWest. The scores were even, 235, but Derbyshire won because they had lost fewer wickets.

Northants will curse themselves for not putting the game safe with their batting after a splendid start by their openers. Derbyshire settled comfortably into the rhythm of chasing runs at under four an over but perhaps they relaxed too much and found themselves thrown on the bravado of Barnet, Tunnicliffe and Miller to pick up the tempo over the last overs to snatch the victory off the final ball.

It was a lovely day for the first NatWest final and all the more so for the presence of Derbyshire and Northants, two clubs whose rare visits to the big time brought the romantic lustre of anti-heroes. The flags were limp on the pavilion poles. In front of the Tavern the partisans congregated, Northants, rather chic and French in their maroon and white flat caps, the Tudor Rose pinned on; Derbyshire much more the British day trippers in porkpie sunhats, chocolate, amber and pale blue with the rose and crown imprinted, so this, too, was a battle of the roses.

The ground was dry, and the pitch firm. Wood won the toss for Derbyshire and chose to field first. The louder their followers chanted 'Darbyshur, Darbyshur', the farther Larkins and Cook hit the ball. Indeed every time the ball was stroked for four the rallying songs burst out with blinder loyalty. They were like boxers on the canvas leaping up spontaneously at the count of two.

Larkins and Cook provided a flow of delightful runs, though they were restricted by the combination of Wood and wicket-keeper Taylor, standing up to the stumps. Larkins lifted Wood for six over square-leg and whipped Newman off his toes to the same area. Cook was slower but correct and steady. It took him longer to risk the shuffle down the pitch to drive Steele over his head and next ball, through the covers for 4.

The batsmen played in blue helmets which were obviously heavy, hot, and blatantly of the wrong colour. Larkins called for his maroon cap, I was happier with that. He was not. Two balls later he holed out at square-leg. Lightheaded, maybe? Ninety-nine for one in the 29th over.

Derbyshire fielded well in spite of the lightning fast outfield. Newman, the young fast bowler, looked quick enough, but, for a while, laboured a little on his extra long run. However, he came back strongly and found greater profit once his line had moved from the leg stump to off.

Cook completed a splendid century off 142 balls with a crisp boundary through mid-wicket off Hendrick. But his side lost their way once he had gone. Run-outs, mostly initiated by Wood's agile fielding, ripped open the batting order and turned a powerful innings of huge potential into a modest self-sacrifice.

Lamb and Willey especially were far too valuable a pair of wickets to throw away. Wood's fielders retreated to the boundary lines with three overs to go. They found themselves in surprising control; 204 for 4 had become 235 for 9 at the end of the 60 overs and Derbyshire had given themselves a real chance of winning a limited over contest for the very first time.

If there was a surge of confidence in the Derbyshire dressing room between innings, they may not have imagined how the opening bowlers Sarfraz and Griffiths would swing the new ball. Wright and Hill were pushy and tentative. Control of the tempo was intriguingly back with Northamptonshire.

Hill collected 14 runs in 14 overs before mistiming a pull shot. Wright towered correctly over the pitch of every ball but he and his normally prolific partner Kirsten could not match the earlier fluency of Larkins and Cook.

Wright and Kirsten then became the spoilsports of the whole season. Used as we all were to a collapse around every corner, here to foreigners, New Zealand and South Africa, combined, saw a good pitch, played straight and collected a couple of half-centuries. It was stark efficiency for a long time before eventually Wright revealed the virtuoso touches, down the wicket to Sarfraz, or back on the stumps, thumping the ball through extra cover or mid-wicket. Kirsten matched him; Northants were now under pressure.

Relief arrived in the form of Mallender, bowling from the Nursery end. Twice in an over he struck the pad and got the verdict from umpire Constant. Wright and Kirsten were gone. Could this be the way back into the contest for Northants? Sixty runs were needed off 10 overs. Northants had exhausted their ideas of slow bowling after Willey's immaculate contribution and a poor imitation by Williams. It was back to Sarfraz.

Wood paraded with a cheerful of confidence but Sarfraz had the answer to him with a ball that was slanted into his off stump, moving off the seam. So it was seven overs in which to score 47 and Barnett playing with the full flourish every ball. Steele was castled but still the Derbyshire chorus had retained enough voice at the Tavern to yell through a few military marches adapted to simple lyrics such as Darbyshur, Darbyshur.

Out flowed the heroics — brilliant fielding of Sarfraz off his own bowling, tight running between the wickets by Barnett and Miller. The light chilled. The Dickie Bird light metre would have had them off the field.

Thirty four off four – the field bar two goes back to the fence, the fielders themselves have trouble in sighting the ball off the bat. They did not need to see Miller's 6 to square-leg off Sarfraz. Twenty off three, five wickets in hand. Barnett was run out. Well, that's how it happens at this stage. Northants were winning – no they weren't. Tunnicliffe whacked fours, square and straight. Twelve came off Sarfraz's last over.

Seven required off the last over. Two off the first ball by Miller; then a single. Four off four balls then 4 off three. A single. Three runs needed off two. It was dark. Darbyshur, Darbyshur where were Northants? Two runs off the last ball – ah! but one run would do, a tie would make Derbyshire the winners, because they had lost fewer wickets.

The final ball was bowled to Tunnicliffe. Miller backing up, appeared to overtake in flight. It hit Tunnicliffe's pad. Miller arrived like the cow in the china-shop and no Northants' player could turn to throw to the bowler's end. It was over. Derbyshire had won and it was worth singing for.

---

17 MARCH 1982

ANGRY PROCTER QUESTIONS RIGHT TO BAN REBELS

John Mason

Durban

Mike Procter, captain of South Africa and, until this year, a figure of heroic proportions for more than a decade on Gloucestershire's behalf, believes that the cricket authorities in England are about to be very foolish.

'If it is truly thought in England that Graham Gooch has to be rapped for coming to South Africa, and the punishment is to be removal from the Test team, I find that extraordinary.' Procter, who previously has politely declined to discuss the rights and wrongs of the tour by Graham Gooch and 15 English cricketers, underwritten by South African Breweries, broke a self-imposed silence reluctantly.

'I'm a professional cricketer, like the others, that's all,' he told me. 'After years of playing in England, I suppose my views must be pretty well known. I know that those who want to play multi-racial cricket in South Africa can do so. The administrators and cricketers have worked hard to bring this about.

'So I get angry, very angry, when someone such as Gooch – name me a better batsman in England, someone who over a period would score more consistently? – is criticised for coming here. What's he done wrong?

'He's not broken a contract. He's available to his county when required. How on earth it can be thought that the punishment for coming to South Africa to play multi-racial cricket should be to leave a man out of the Test reckoning is quite beyond me.

'Let's assume that India and Pakistan do play in England in the summer. I have played with and against the leading players of both countries, especially the Pakistanis. I know them well. Now what's going to happen at Bristol or Taunton or Chelmsford when the tour matches are played? Are the visitors going to look down the team list and say: "Right, we'll play against him – but not him. Goochie and J.K. no go, Fletch OK, Humpage no, Unders no. Now let's see – we had better speak to Mrs Gandhi to see if we can play against Clive Rice."'

Having warmed up with a few shots all round the wicket, Procter tucked handsomely into his verbal task in his next blast. 'Are you telling me,' he demanded, his face creased with pained surprise, 'that India and Pakistan can play against Allan Lamb, South African born and bred, in a Test match but not against Graham Gooch.

'Or anyone else who has come to South Africa on this trip, players who come to play in a multi-racial set-up as a result of an offer made to them as professional cricketers, a business arrangement that they have the freedom to accept, or decline as they wish.

'It's not an offence to come to South Africa from Britain. No law is being broken. Allan Lamb – or Tony Greig, come to that – can live here, grow up here, return here and that's all right, as it should be, of course. But Goochie comes here, takes two hundreds off our bowlers in a week, is paid a fee for his services and, so they tell me, finds himself unlikely to be chosen for England in the near future as a result.

'Well, I'm no legal man, as the world knows but I would question the right of any authority to deny someone the opportunity of playing for his country. Anyone of the proven skills, no matter who he is can play cricket for South Africa.'

With that Procter slowed to a canter, presented that cool stare that used to make batsmen quake (or bowlers tremble, depending upon his role at the time) and suggested that, though he will be absent from the English county scene, for the first full summer since 1968, he would not greatly miss it.

'Please don't get me wrong. The friends and the places, I shall miss very much – but not the cricket. It's been a long haul and I don't want that commitment any longer now that I'm in my mid-30s. I'll be back for about six weeks in July and there is the little matter of a single-wicket meeting with Ian Botham. I'm looking forward to that. I've got one or two things I want to discuss with him anyway.'

---

31 MAY 1983

ESSEX v. SURREY

Rex Alston

Chelmsford

Surrey were bowled out for 14 when they replied to Essex's total of 287 in the Schweppes County Championship match at Chelmsford yesterday. Keith Fletcher, the Essex captain, had made 110.

Surrey's total was only two runs better than the lowest in first-class cricket – 12 by Northamptonshire at Gloucester in 1907, and by Oxford University, batting a man short, against MCC and Ground at Oxford in 1877. Yesterday's innings lasted 14.3 overs. Norbert Phillip took 6 wickets for 4 in 7.3 overs and Neil Foster, 21, 4 for 10 in seven overs. Foster had a serious back operation a year ago and made his first appearance in the senior side since then only because John Lever has a hairline fracture of his right foot.

The heavy roller had been on the pitch between innings, but this could not account for Surrey's disastrously feeble batting. Butcher began the procession when he was well caught at the wicket, and the next six batsmen to depart were out for nought. Most of them played back to Phillip, who kept the new ball well pitched up. Foster disposed of Needham, and Phillip was surprised and delighted to have the dangerous Knight and Lynch lbw.

Clinton, top scorer with 6, watched these disasters from the other end before swinging on the leg side and giving David East a good catch. When Clarke joined Monkhouse at 8 for 8 it looked as though Surrey would set a new world record, but a wild slog by Clarke just reached the square-leg boundary for the only 4 of the innings and Monkhouse edged a 2 before giving Phillip his third lbw.

---

29 JULY 1983

HUMPAGE SAILS IN AND RUINS KENT HOPES

Derek Hodgson

Edgbaston

An interesting tactical exercise for aspiring captains might read: 'Contrive a means of dismissing or otherwise containing G.W. Humpage (Warwicks). Explain and discuss. N.B. Facetious answers such as "put Larwood on" will not be tolerated.'

Christopher Cowdrey is still working on his thesis. For an hour around lunch yesterday it seemed he might make Warwickshire follow on. Humpage, with another very professional century in a deceptively amateur spirit, mocked such hopes. Lloyd, driving Ellison fiercely through the clearer air and across a faster outfield, had raised 41 out of 80 when Underwood appeared to make the odd ball grip sufficiently to cause alarm.

He held one back slightly to deceive Lloyd and then bowled Smith at 93. Had Benson been able to hold a running catch at long-on, off Kallicharran, Underwood's figures would then have read 11–7–6–3. The West Indian was in no mood to be shackled and fell in the second over after lunch, in wild pursuit of Jarvis, outside his off stump. Warwickshire were then 82 short of the follow-on figure with their first three gone.

Amiss, as usual, enjoyed his first whiff of crisis. Humpage, whose bat, any bowler will tell you, is broader than the regulation width and springloaded for extra propulsion, brought a holiday air to the other end. In the next 98 minutes, 100 runs were added, 67 of them by Humpage in a cheerful barrage of cuts and drives, through and over the field that nonplussed even Underwood. His fellow-spinner, Johnson, was despatched over long-on for 6 off successive balls.

Humpage, missed at deep square-leg by Benson when 60, was eventually caught by the same man at mid-off. His 150-minute innings also contained 13 fours and his impetus carried Warwickshire to a fourth batting point when Paul Smith and Ferreira added 77 before the declaration.

Hogg might have had not one but two wickets in his second over but the likelihood is another declaration because both teams need to win. But how does one declare against Humpage?

---

5 MARCH 1984

NEWLY CROWNED BOYCOTT REFUSES TO GRANT ROYAL PARDON

Graham Jones

One moment of acrimony set the seal on what was supposed to be Yorkshire Cricket Club's 'peace rally' in Sheffield this weekend. At the end of a sometimes stormy annual meeting, the man at the centre of six months of division and rancour, former captain and now committee strong man Geoffrey Boycott, publicly snubbed the new club treasurer, Mr David Welch.

Encouraged by other new committee men to shake hands, put differences aside, and look to the future, Boycott refused. Then he launched into a tirade against his assumed 'foe', whom he accused of failing to support him when the old committee sacked him in October.

That, in a nutshell, was the Boycott affair: A man so dedicated to winning, he was not content with his supporters' landslide win with 19 of the 23 vacant seats on the Yorkshire committee. He wanted every single non-Boycott man purged. There is an insecurity about Boycott, the master batsman who has risen to top status in his profession, but who takes criticism so heavily; harbours grudges so badly.

This is why Boycott became an issue with other Yorkshire players and the old committee. After the election results leaked out on Friday, the leader of the dissident 'members 1984' group, Mr Sidney Fielden, talked of being 'magnanimous to those defeated'.

But even without Boycott's petulant display afterwards there was little magnanimity at Sheffield City Hall on Saturday, as 1,000 members picked their way laboriously through a patchwork agenda. The meeting started off well, with all the air of a coronation. Dressed in a maroon suit with matching snakeskin shoes, which in the dim light of the great oval hall appeared a regal purple, Boycott arrived smiling half an hour early and strutted round imperially in the lobby seeking out his campaign organisers.

He shook hands like a victorious American primary candidate, and talked of 'enjoying his day'. The crown prince then took up his appointed and hard-won position in the front row, just below centre-stage.

Even when caretaker chairman Mr Norman Shuttleworth held aloft the gilded John Player Trophy (to aficionados, merely tinsel, the county championship last won 15 years ago is the real prize), most eyes were on another, more revered, Yorkshire idol. Mr Shuttleworth appealed for an end to 'suicidal tendencies'.

'Let us try to look forward to what we hope will be a very successful future,' he said. There was hearty applause for that. But the heady atmosphere started to shatter with some prickly questioning for the caretaker treasurer Mr Welch, 42, of Rotherham, about the cost of the special general meeting at Harrogate called by the old committee and proving its undoing. This turned out to be £28,000, of which no less than £13,306 had gone in legal fees.

'This shows that the only people to win are the lawyers,' said Mr Shuttleworth, instinctively finding an enemy to unite pro- and anti-Boycott factions (later he tried Lancashire with equally successful results). When one lawyer did jump into the fray he was howled down.

Mr Matthew Caswell, legal adviser to the 'members 1984' group, tried to block the permanent election of Mr Welch, with the backing of the Boycott conclave. But Mr Caswell's hog-the-cameras style and verbiage was too much for more down-to-earth Yorkshire folk. He failed miserably. While the mood in the Boycott camp was still occasionally vengeful, the feeling in the hall was clearly more inclined towards unity, and the handful of votes against Mr Welch looked hopelessly out of touch.

Certainly among ordinary members there was a feeling of relief that their hero Boycott was back, and that out were what dissidents' group secretary Mr Tony Vann called 'the gin and tonic brigade who ran the club like a closed shop'.

'We have done it now,' said Mr Jonathan Plews, 35, a company secretary from Sheffield. 'Now it is all about improving performances on the field.' Mr Raymond Wolstenholme, 78, a Yorkshire member for 60 years, said: 'It is time to get down to it and stop the bickering.'

So had peace at last broken out in Yorkshire cricket?

One clue was that people were, rather like the Labour party, talking about 'degrees' of brotherhood. Mr Reg Kirk, of Hull, a dissident leader and the man most likely to be the club's new chairman, said: 'A lot of people are espousing the cause of unity. But what we want is unity with democracy. There are 10,000 members of Yorkshire. The committee must not be selfish, it must listen to their wishes and then we might start to have a happy and successful club.'

Conspicuously absent at Sheffield were the old guard. Missing were former president Norman Yardley, former chairman Mr Michael Crawford, and the two prize 'scalps' of last week's postal vote. They were Fred Trueman ('I think I will just sit back and watch the party because it ain't half going to be a fiasco'), and cricket sub-committee chairman Mr Ronnie Burnet ('Not one of the new members of the committee knows anything about cricket.').

Clearly, morale and leadership are the key to the future, and in Sheffield yesterday a fascinating 'play within a play' of three former Yorkshire and England captains was acted out.

Centre-stage was Boycott, the prince who clearly did not enjoy his investiture, still cursing under his breath when a member of the old guard spoke, and sauntering off afterwards refusing interviews and talking of 'things to do'.

Stage-left, was team manager Ray Illingworth, agonised, perplexed; the axe lingering over his head and now lingering some more until the first meeting of the new committee on Thursday.

Stage-right and stealing in and out almost unnoticed, was Brian Close, the prodigal hardman returned to the feast, his eyes twinkling mischievously as he contemplated what is likely to be a significant role in the reshaped county.

'The team is not big enough for two captains,' was the cry of all those wanting to get rid of Illingworth. With David Bairstow intact, leading the team on the field and supported by pro- and anti-Boycott factions alike, the county now finds itself not with two captains, but four.

Peace and reconciliation? The play goes on.

---

7 JUNE 1984

BILL VOCE, PRINCE OF BOWLERS, DIES AT 74

E.W. Swanton

The name of Bill Voce, one of the best of all left-arm fast bowlers, who died in Nottingham yesterday aged 74, will be associated for ever in history with that of his great partner for Notts and England, Harold Larwood.

Together they had the chief part in winning the County Championship of 1929: together, under the stern instruction of their captain, D.R. Jardine, they perfected in the 1932–3 Test series in Australia the fast leg-theory attack which came to be known as Bodyline.

Larwood so injured his left foot on that tour that he could never again recapture anything approaching his phenomenal speed, though he soldiered on for several more seasons of county cricket at fast-medium pace in company with Voce, his junior by five years.

Both before and after the Bodyline tour the Notts bowling, on the orders of the captain, A.W. Carr, sometimes overstepped the margin of fair play, and it was not until Notts put the leadership into more acceptable hands that relations with several of the counties were repaired.

Happily, too, though Larwood's Test days were past, the breach with Lord's that had prevented Voce's selection for England for four of his prime years was healed, and he sailed for Australia again with G.O. Allen's team for the 1936–7 tour. With 26 wickets at 21 runs each he headed England's Test bowling averages, and such was the paucity of talent after the Second World War that in his 38th year, he made a third tour to Australia in 1946–7.

The spirit still was as willing as ever but of the fire and elasticity of that bounding run and classical delivery only spasmodic vestiges remained. Circumstances, then, prevented Voce from building up over a long but interrupted career the sort of figures his excellence as a cricketer deserved. However, in first-class cricket he had 1,558 wickets at 23 runs each. His dangerous batting brought him four hundreds and an average just short of 20. In 27 Tests he took 98 wickets at 27 a time. He was an admirable fielder with a formidable throw.

Voce as a tall, slim lad walked from the colliery town of Hucknall to Trent Bridge in the late '20s in search of a trial. There his natural talent was at once recognised. He had a long loose arm and a natural flowing action, with the ability, bowling over the wicket, to swing the ball either way in the air. After the shine had gone, now round the wicket, he straightened the ball still at lively speed, unless the conditions suggested slow-medium spin. He was indeed an artist and an athlete quite out of the ordinary.

Bill, after his retirement, was in much demand as a coach, and at the age of 70 was still wheeling away at Lord's at the MCC Indoor School and enthusing the boys with his humour and friendliness.

---

4 JULY 1984

GREENIDGE GIVES ENGLAND THRASHING

Michael Carey

Lord's

Gordon Greenidge made an unforgettable and unbeaten 214 at Lord's yesterday to take the West Indies to victory over England by nine wickets in the second Cornhill Test, giving them a 2–0 lead in the series.

With a grandeur that produced a splendid climax to a splendid match the West Indies in five memorable hours made 344 from 66 overs, a fourth-innings target only bettered in England by Bradman's Australians who made 404 for three at Headingley in 1948. It was only the 10th time that a side had exceeded 300 in the fourth innings of a Test match to win.

Greenidge and Larry Gomes, whose unbeaten 92 was the product of another composed innings, added 287 for the second wicket and England's only success was a run out on a day when their bowling limitations were exposed by the combination of a mild pitch and the devastating quality of the opposition. Greenidge's innings, his 10th three-figure score in Tests, was the ninth double century at Lord's and has been surpassed only by Bradman's 234 in 1930 and Hammond's 240 in 1938 – further proof, if required, of its excellence and place in history.

Even then, it was not enough to earn him the Man of the Match award exclusively. The adjudicator, Godfrey Evans, decided to share it between Greenidge and Ian Botham, an unprecedented decision in Cornhill Tests and one which will be much discussed despite Botham's fine all-round performance.

On the basis that such awards should be linked to match-winning performances when possible, Greenidge can feel denied, not least as Botham's magic deserted him when England most needed it. Indeed, he and Willis, Saturday's heroes, were relegated to the role of yesterday's men when the mighty onslaught began, though this was not until some time after Gower's declaration, which asked the West Indies to score at around 62 an hour.

This came after England had batted on for 20 minutes and added 13 runs for the loss of Lamb and Pringle, the 12th lbw victim of the match, and at first, there was no hint that an historic day lay ahead. Greenidge, indeed, had to jab out a boot to avoid playing on in Willis's first over before he had scored. It probably passed almost unnoticed, yet how often are such moments a fleeting indication that it is going to be someone's day.

For Greenidge, it was the cue to play the innings of his life, yet the bat was passed more than once while the ball was moving about and at 29 he clipped a no-ball from Willis into Lamb's hands at square-leg, continuing this remarkable sequence in this series.

At that point, England bowled encouragingly well, conceding only 10 runs from eight overs, as indeed they had to on this pitch against opponents who in their previous eight Tests had not lost a wicket in their second innings.

England's solitary, deceptive success came when Haynes started for a single, slipped when sent back by his partner, who had also set off, and was beaten by Lamb's direct hit with an under-arm throw running in from square-leg. By now, Greenidge was starting to bang the bowling about with formidable power, especially off the back foot, and would not have complained when England regularly bowled to his strength around his off stump, in the hope of inducing an error.

At lunch, the signs were already ominous with runs coming at four an over despite the modest start, which meant that a predictably moderate over rate was not going to make all that much difference. Alas, when Gomes had made only five, he perpetrated his solitary error, offering a slip catch in Foster's first over which Pringle comfortably dropped, possibly because he had not stayed down long enough.

Foster was not at his best, but at the same time went as close as anyone to dismissing Greenidge, who first lifted him just wide of mid-wicket and then saw Lamb, at cover, make a valiant attempt to hold an improbable catch off another powerful stroke.

Greenidge had then made 80. He soon moved to three figures, out of 149 in only 34 overs, and hereabouts the West Indies were helped by Botham's inability to bowl to a predominantly off-side field, which provoked several pointed discussions between him and his captain.

Perhaps this was dominating Botham's thoughts when at 110 Greenidge edged Willis to him at a catchable height at slip, but for once his lightning reactions deserted him and down went England's last real chance.

Gomes, meanwhile, had started to cream the bowling around with great comfort, especially against Miller who, operating from the Nursery end, could not summon up enough accuracy to check the flow. Even with Miller, England managed only 25 overs during the two-hour afternoon session, but 132 runs came from them and by tea Gomes had reached 50 from 73 balls and the heads were noticeably starting to drop in the field.

Soon afterwards, Greenidge lifted Botham for six into the Grandstand and by now England found it impossible to bowl at him, not least Botham, who found control elusive in three overs costing 29 runs. Greenidge then went to 200 with a remarkable stroke, a top-edged hook which carried for six over long leg.

He had long since left behind the previous highest by a West Indian at Lord's, Haynes's 184 in 1980, and when the partnership reached 250 it bettered West Indies' second-wicket record against England by Kallicharran and Rowe in Barbados in 1974.

At the end, Greenidge had faced only 242 balls, hitting 29 fours and two sixes, batting riches which were matched by gate receipts of more than £500,000 for the first time at a Test in this country.

---

21 OCTOBER 1984

SEARCH FOR CRICKET SAVIOUR

Sebastian Faulks *on Ted Dexter's bid to find a 'proper' fast bowler*

Ted Dexter describes himself as a 'keen amateur golfer' (he won the President's Putter a couple of years ago), and to gain access to his West London house you have to skirt round two mighty bags of clubs. He was also in his time a fairly useful cricketer, though there is little sign of it. Even the sitting-room bears only one photograph of his lordship at the crease: forcing the ball through the covers off the back foot.

Dexter, however, has not lost interest in the game itself, and one ambition remains: to find a proper fast bowler for England. With the help of Webster's bitter, two tins of which sit on the sideboard of the brown Victorian sitting-room, he is searching the country for a likely young man.

He is looking not for a bowler as such, but for an athlete who can chuck the thing down at a tremendous pace and then be taught the skill of bowling. 'Obviously you couldn't create a batsman or a wicket-keeper or even a slow bowler out of someone with no experience, but with a fast bowler I think it can be done.'

He cites Frank Tyson and Jeff Thomson as two bowlers who took wickets, at first anyway, on pace alone. 'Tyson won a series for England and some of his wickets came from full tosses.' The winning candidate could, Dexter thinks, play for England next year.

One wonders what a craftsman like Brian Statham would have thought of that. 'Well, in 1959 Alan Moss, the Middlesex seamer, took 50 wickets in May. We went to the West Indies in November and he didn't take another wicket until February. Out there the pitches are hard rolled mud. The ball doesn't move off the seam, and unless you can really bang it in, you don't get people out. That's why they bowl so fast.'

Young men were invited to enter through forms distributed in pubs. Six were selected at Edgbaston recently; they included a boxer, a footballer, a javelin thrower and a 6ft 4in twenty-year-old from Coventry called David Dismore, who can run 60 yards in under seven seconds and bowl a ball nine yards off a couple of paces. 'If he can get it that far,' grins Dexter, 'the muzzle velocity must be tremendous.'

Dexter has secured the cooperation of all the first-class counties for his quixotic scheme. Whether this shows their kindness or their desperation is unclear. But the final six chosen (from a total of 3,559) will be coached during the winter by their local county clubs.

The budding Lillees will also be laden with advice from the politburo of English fast bowling at a weekend seminar at Edgbaston. John Snow and Bob Willis will help on the technical side; Alec Bedser will tell them how to please the selectors (there must be a few current players who would like to be in on this session and BBC commentator Ron Pickering will be adding own touch of verbal magic).

Even if a genuine fast bowler is found, he may not, Dexter admits, find a place in his county team. With so much one-day cricket, they would sooner have a medium-pacer who can spear it in at the leg stump and keep the runs down. The one-day game is another factor in England's failure to produce fast bowlers. 'I went to the finals of the Under-15 competition the other day and it was a 20-over match!'

The fastest bowler he faced was Wes Hall. 'He was a step-up in pace from Trueman and Statham.' He reckons that Holding at his fastest, Tyson, and 'possibly Marshall, though it's hard to tell,' are a step up again. England's current bowlers lack pace *and* grace. 'Agnew is a stringbean. Ellison's a decent bowler, but he's not really an athlete. Allott's a bloody good bowler, the best we've got, but he plods in like a policeman in his size 13s.'

At a recent trial, the Oval was a dangerous place to be, as yellow balls rained down out of a damp sky, one of them shattering Ted Dexter's megaphone. The England hopefuls were a nervous and scruffy bunch in a mixture of tee-shirts and training suits; but their enthusiasm – if not always well-directed – was immense.

Alec Bedser and Ted Dexter discussed the importance of a big bottom. 'That lad there, you see, he's got it.' 'Yes,' added one of the playing staff, 'that girl candidate at Edgbaston, she had it, too.'

Many of the candidates looked rather frail as they wobbled around under catches propelled from a machine by former England bowler Geoff Arnold. They were put through a variety of running and throwing exercises, most important of which was a simple measurement of how far they could bowl the ball before it bounced. Anything over 70 yards was good.

Bob Willis, whose retirement is partly responsible for the whole project, looked on in a blue track-suit. He thought he could bowl it no further than 70 yards himself. 'But, remember, these lads are young and fit, and I am old and tired.' Yesterday's bunch contained an interesting prospect of a Mr D. Lillie. Earlier, there had been an exciting entry form from a Mr Larwood of Nottingham. When approached by the organisers, he turned out to be 38, to know nothing of the project and never to have taken exercise in his life.

'If you're really fast,' says Willis, 'you will always get picked. If I was fit, I was always in the England team.' Alec Bedser recalls Bill Copson, the Derby miner who first played cricket on top of a slag heap at the age of 19 and, within three years, had taken the wicket of Jack Hobbs at the Oval.

So, is there life after Willis? Certainly there is no lack of effort. The young pretenders go through contortions. I saw one of them, in his eagerness, release the ball too soon and watch it roll backwards: a total of minus five yards.

Bedser and Mickey Steward of Surrey talk of the lack of moral fibre in the way we live now. Boys don't chop enough wood and their parents drive them to school; but Dexter remains confident that one of the 200 young men in the Oval trials will play for England one day. One only hopes for the sake of the commentators that it is not A. Czarnobaj of Ely.

---

16 JANUARY 1985

GATTING 207 AND FOWLER 201 IN RECORD MOOD

ENGLAND PILE UP MASSIVE 611 FOR 5 IN MADRAS

Michael Carey

Madras

Graeme Fowler and Mike Gatting each scored their maiden Test double century in Madras yesterday, leaving England in an unassailable position in the fourth Test with a lead of 339, five wickets in hand and two days' play remaining after today's rest day.

A total of 611 for five, made from 170 overs, not only reflected the way that England had pursued their objective of grinding India's bowlers into the dust, despite considerable attempts to slow the game down which produced two warnings from the umpires, but also rewrote a chunk of the record books.

In the 108 years since Test cricket began, England had never before had two double century-makers in the same innings. Consider some of the great names who have figured in their 610 Tests and this morning the toast therefore, gentlemen, is Messrs Fowler and Gatting. It was England's highest total on the sub-continent and before yesterday's events no English batsman had scored more in India than Dennis Amiss's 179 in Delhi eight years ago.

The whole magical day was played out to a carefully planned scenario. After Fowler and Gatting had ensured no early breakthrough would allow India even a glimmer of hope, the strokes followed. Even bowling aimed at the leg stump to defensive fields was only partially successful late in the day as England made 141 from 30 overs in the final session which, with the need to complete 80 overs, ended some 33 minutes after schedule.

By the time India obtained their first breakthrough, Fowler had gone on to the second double hundred of his career and had established a second-wicket record against India of 241 with Gatting, who then surpassed his unbeaten 136 at Bombay in admirably controlled style and added another 144 in 33 overs for the third wicket with Lamb.

India's captain, Sunil Gavaskar, was absent from the post-lunch carnage because of what he described as an allergy on his hands. But in adversity he was magnanimous about Gatting's innings which he described as 'most magnificent – he batted with a confidence which I did not think this English side possessed.'

Only in the final half-hour or so, when England felt the need for not one but two lower-order batsmen to try to slog their way past 600 did they lose credibility. How sad that Gower, short of runs though he may be, could not relish the chance of walking to the middle with the scoreboard reading memorably 563 for three.

By the time he appeared (and ironically was obliged to play out the last over surrounded by close fielders) the task had been achieved. Now, whether they opt to bat on a little longer tomorrow, England will be able to bowl to claustrophobic fields, no matter how the pitch plays. If anything, it had lost a little bounce yesterday and Fowler and Gatting achieved their aim of negotiating the pre-lunch session with only one alarm when Fowler, at 160, slashed Sivarama hard just wide of first slip.

They discovered that they could maintain a rate of three runs an over without anything lavish. Indeed, when Fowler prospected outside the off stump Gatting, as ever, was quick to offer advice and it was Fowler who began the assault with two perfectly struck sixes in one over from Yadav.

Gatting went sturdily on, cutting, forcing or sweeping with scarcely an error, until he reached three figures and Fowler reached 200 in just over nine hours when he was a shade late to a ball from Kapil which he touched to Kirmani and walked before umpire Ramaswamy could give him out – if in fact he was going to.

Lamb's start coincided with a good spell by Kapil and with Sivarama also bowling well at this stage, there was a period of reconnaissance in which Lamb, hesitating in his response to Gatting's call for a single to long-on, would have been run out at 22 if Vengsarkar's throw to the wicket-keeper had been anything like accurate.

Gatting, meanwhile, at 125 had seen Sivarama perhaps get his finger-tips to a half-driven low return chance, but otherwise little happened to suggest England's highly clinical approach would be disturbed, and Gatting was soon striking the ball to all parts with glorious certainty and timing. Both he and Lamb found that Chetan Sharma could be hooked regularly. Once the running between the wickets had settled down, they also picked up the ones and 2s and a massive leg-side 6 by Gatting off Shastri sent the total past 500 in the 145th over.

By now umpire Ramaswamy had spoken first to Gavaskar and then to Amarnath, leading the side in his absence, about India's dilatory tactics which led to only 50 overs in the first four hours. Eventually Gatting moved so effortlessly through the 190s that he produced two reverse sweeps off Shastri, who was attacking leg stump to a predominantly leg-side field, and Amarnath led the handshakes when a typical stroke through the covers off the back foot took him to 200 in just over eight hours.

Lamb then went, aiming to hit Amarnath through mid-wicket and with Gatting perishing on the long-on boundary, it was odd that with two recognised batsmen to come and India on their knees, mentally at least, England ended the day the way they did.

17 JUNE 1985

E. W. Swanton

Percy George Herbert Fender, the Surrey and England cricketer, who has died aged 92, was one of the best-known personalities of the inter-war years, a figure of glamour on the field and, occasionally, of mild controversy off it.

As a St Paul's schoolboy he played first at 17 for Sussex in 1910, changing his allegiance in 1914 to Surrey and helping them, not a little by his all-round cricket, to win the championship of that year, shortened as it was by the declaration of war.

Afterwards his reputation quickly grew as an unorthodox, dangerous hitter, a guileful leg-break bowler, and brilliant slip-catcher. In 1920 at Northampton he reached a hundred in 35 minutes – a time which to this day has not been bettered, though in a farcical travesty of the game it was equalled by Steven O'Shaughnessy two years ago for Lancashire against Leicestershire.

He went with J.W.H.T. Douglas's MCC side to Australia in 1920–21 and pulled his weight on a tour in which, so soon after the war, England laboured at a crippling disadvantage. He also toured South Africa in 1922–23, and played 13 times in all for England, with a respectable degree of success.

His great deeds, however, were for Surrey, both as player and over a span of 11 summers (1921–31) as captain. To his leadership he brought much the same characteristics as he showed in his own cricket. In a more formal age he was an experimenter, always looking for a gamble and not infrequently bringing it off.

Despite the perfection of the Oval wickets, and with generally slender bowling to discount great batting strength, he often came near to winning the Championship without ever quite doing so. Often in the '20s he was tipped as captain of England, but other men were preferred, some scarcely his equal either as captains or cricketers. He was said not to be in favour 'at Lord's', partly because of his outspokenness, and the fact of his periodic ventures into cricket journalism. He also wrote in the idiom of the day four books on Anglo-Australian Test series; reference works which have their value still.

With his tall slim figure, dark crinkly hair, horn-rimmed spectacles, receding chin, silk neckerchief and unusually long sweaters he was the cartoonist's dream. No one, surely, of the older generation who saw him play will forget him. At his best he was a highly effective, as well as a spectacular cricketer.

In the wake of the BBC 'Bodyline' programmes it should be added that the portrayal of Fender was a caricature ridiculous to all who knew him.

In his career Fender made 19,034 runs, including 21 hundreds, at an average of 26, and took 1,894 wickets at 25 a time. But like some other amateur all-rounders of his day – R.W.V. Robins springs immediately to mind – he was not a man to be assessed on the basis of figures.

---

1 AUGUST 1985

IMRAN'S BRIGHT 89 LIFTS SUSSEX

Michael Austin

Eastbourne

Imran Khan enlivened an uninspiring day with a cultured three-hour innings of 89 as Sussex meandered towards 227 for 6 off 86 overs against Kent at The Saffrons yesterday.

Baptiste, working assiduously on a pitch which was no one's friend, returned 3 for 86 after Benson, Kent's captain in the absence of Cowdrey who has a recurring side strain, had lost the toss. Perseverance ruled, but Imran's inspiration thankfully intervened in mid-afternoon, following the initial loss of 90 minutes' play through the effects of the previous day's rain. The Pakistani, blending timing and power, forced the ball off the square after lesser mortals had laboured to escape the strict confines of Kent's bowling, together with the temptation to play premature strokes.

Underwood, a remorseless taker of Sussex wickets over the years, provided a rare instance in recent years of a slow bowler being granted the new ball at the start of a championship game. But a damp patch, the size of a dinner plate, offered him modest assistance.

In contrast to the day's gentility, Baptiste and Jarvis tore out the off-stumps of Mendis and Green and, later, Lenham, 19, playing his second championship game, edged an intended drive to reward Penn.

A groundsman's hut doubles inadequately as a press box at The Saffron's, but viewed from these Spartan surroundings Imran's innings added even more lustre to a day barely offering a launching pad for Kent's further elevation from fourth in the table.

His collection of drives helped to yield 17 4s but his most delicate and intrepid stroke on this pitch was a sweep off Underwood, who eventually removed him with an admirable, two-handed, low catch off his own bowling.

---

23 JUNE 1986

JIM LAKER – FINEST OFF-SPIN BOWLER

Michael Melford

James Charles Laker, who died yesterday aged 64, was one of the finest off-spin bowlers in the history of cricket, perhaps the finest. Certainly he holds a record never likely to be equalled.

His 19 wickets against Australia in the Old Trafford Test of 1956, for which he will always be remembered, are two more than has ever been taken by anybody else in a first-class match, let alone in a Test match.

Jim Laker's career coincided with an era of uncovered, slow-turning pitches but no one else brought to them the same unrelenting accuracy, allied to considerable powers of spin. A quiet, reserved thinker on the game with a somewhat flatfooted walk, he did not give the impression of great vitality on the field, but caught many good catches, usually in the gully; he was also a hard-hitting batsman at number eight, good enough to make 63 at Trent Bridge against the 1948 Australians.

His origins will seem strange to present-day cricketers. A Yorkshireman who played in the Bradford League for Saltaire before joining the Army in 1941, he began to make his name later in the war in good-class cricket in the Middle East.

He had been more of a batsman in the League but now began to concentrate on off-break bowling, and while awaiting demobilisation in London in 1946, joined the Catford club. From there it was a short step to the Oval and Surrey – with Yorkshire's permission.

At the end of the 1947 season in which he played his first championship matches, he was picked for the tour of West Indies under G. Allen and was the most successful bowler despite his lack of experience. He was one of those bowlers who suffered while Australia made their 404 for 3 to win at Headingley in 1948, but in May 1950 he upset a Test trial at Bradford by taking eight wickets for two runs. In August 1953, his partnership with Tony Lock had much to do with England's recovery of the Ashes at the Oval.

Just over a year later, he was surprisingly left out of Len Hutton's team which retained the Ashes in Australia but he remained an important part of the strong England bowling side of the 1950s until he retired in 1959 when still a very good bowler. The publication of Laker's autobiography, including criticisms which he much regretted subsequently, led to the withdrawal of his MCC honorary membership.

However, in another publication he put the record straight and returned after two years to play for Essex for three seasons. The MCC membership was restored and he moved on eventually to a new and successful career as a television commentator on cricket.

Though he had not always been in good health in the last few years, his sadly premature death will be a particular shock to viewers who may not remember him when he was a great bowler but who have been long accustomed to his sound, unflappable interpretations of televised matches.

---

9 NOVEMBER 1986

SHOWDOWN AT SHEPTON MALLET

Nigel Dudley

'Taunton does not look like a place seething with revolution,' said Peter Roebuck, captain of Somerset County Cricket Club, as he walked down the main street. But Taunton's calm is misleading. Along with every other town, village and hamlet in Somerset, it is deeply split over the county's decision to sack its West Indian stars: Viv Richards and Joel Garner.

It is without doubt the worst crisis in the county's history. The turmoil it has caused within the club is matched in recent years only by the split in Yorkshire over Geoffrey Boycott. The anger and passion which have been simmering for two months since the club announced that New Zealander Martin Crowe would replace the West Indians will be displayed in full today as the club debates a motion of no confidence in the committee.

'I think it will be a very hot debate and that emotions will rule the day,' says Roebuck. By six o'clock this evening the members, who are meeting at Shepton Mallet's Bath and West Showground, will have decided whether or not to throw out the committee. Should the committee lose, it will mean further elections, the reinstatement of Richards and Garner, and Roebuck rushing up to put in his resignation before he is sacked. A victory for the committee will mean the departure of Ian Botham.

'The choice for members is between a club in which the battles continue and one in which we can achieve a strength and a unity by careful, slow changes,' says Roebuck. The origins of the dispute lie deep in Somerset's history. Until the 1970s it had little success and was more accustomed to being nearer the bottom than the top of any championship.

The arrival of the West Indians and the home-grown talent of Ian Botham changed all that. Richards, Garner and Botham became heroes and superstars. But, in recent years their appetite for the grind of county cricket seems to have faded. The county which, with three of the best players in the world, should have challenged for the highest honours, was once more nearer bottom than top.

In 1984, the three stars were all on test duty and a young New Zealander, Martin Crowe, joined the county. More than just a talented young cricketer, Crowe seemed to represent new hope. Unlike the aloof superstars who, like their critics allege, performed only when it suited them the smart, well-dressed Crowe appeared to have a refreshing zest for the game. Cricket rules allow counties to have only one overseas player – Richards and Garner can both play as they started before 1979 – so Somerset could not play all its overseas stars.

Consequently this summer, the club had to make a rapid choice when Crowe was approached by Essex. It was, for Somerset, a choice between the club's future and past glories. 'We consider it to be the wrong decision,' says Richard Weston, a 42-year-old Taunton solicitor, who acts as the rebels' spokesman. The reasons the club has given do not stand up to close analysis. They do not stand up on cricketing, financial or discipline grounds.

The rebel members set out to overturn the committee and, before most people knew what was happening, friendships were destroyed and charge and countercharge were swapped with a vigour and spleen quite the equal of 'Dallas'. It is far from easy to cut through the passion and emotion to find the key issues. But these are more important than the personal scars which may last. They concern the relations between club and players, between star players and the rank and file, and between the club and its members.

There seems little doubt that the presence of the star players had become disruptive. Players have described the 1984 season when the stars were away as being like 'Hungary before the Russian tanks rolled in'. It took two more years to face up to the need for action because, 'we were like people with a toothache who did not want to go to the dentist,' says Roebuck.

On the other hand, it is now generally accepted that the club did not carry out the decision not to renew Richards's and Garner's contracts with much sensitivity. 'At no time does it appear that Joel and Viv were told what was going on (the discussions with Crowe),' says Richard Weston. 'Viv had been told in June that his future was with the club and that they were both going to stay. They must have had every justification in believing they would be offered new contracts.'

The club's version is that they started last season with the intention of keeping them on but that experience led them to conclude it was impossible. 'We ought to have consulted them more,' says Roebuck. 'But I don't know if it would have done any good. I believe that however we might have done it this battle would have happened.'

Both sides remain confident of victory, though most estimates expect the rebels to be defeated. Whatever the result Somerset cricket will never be the same again. Even if the club wins, it accepted that major changes must be made in the way it operates. The constitution will have to be changed and Roebuck believes there will have to be 'a sense of unity between the committee and players: we must have a closer relationship between the cricket committee and the cricketers.'

For Roebuck, it has been a traumatic time. He wishes that he could have been in Australia rather than playing in a drama that seems like an episode from 'Dallas'. Maybe on Sunday he will wake up to realise that, like Pamela Ewing, he has just had a very bad dream.

---

14 DECEMBER 1986

THE BLISSFUL STATE OF ONE-UP

Tony Lewis

Australia

HAVING A LOVELY TIME ... SO FAR

England are still living blissfully in the State of One-Up, where there is no dissension, only daily ease. Wives are welcome, nets are good, room service immaculate, the Press are part of the family and even if the gloomy weather is rubbing out the sun-tan, there is little that a dozen oysters 'natural' and a bottle of McWilliams dry white will not cure.

The State of One-Down seems a long way away, though there are some who have been there to see an England squad fragmenting. Indeed, many have also been to Two-Down, where players' wives began to criticise the captain; Three-Down, where the sniffer dogs leap along the hotel corridors, and Four-Down; where unrecognised 'cricket writers' arrive with photographers who hang upside down from trees outside Ian Botham's bedroom window. Five-Down is where the captain gets hanged in public, but not until he gets home.

So this is a happy state, with a cheerful captain and a pleasant manager who has a friendly assistant, where a relaxed team moves sweetly from place to place, complaining only that the in-house movies are the same in every five-star hotel in Australia. There is a limit to how often you can watch Pretty in Pink followed by Poltergeist Two.

Players mostly retreat to their rooms; they are rarely spotted at the ground level of a hotel. Both England and Australia are billeted together in Adelaide but they are mere tracksuits which pass in the night.

There is only one minor disappointment to record and that is the public reprimand given to Mike Gatting for oversleeping and missing the start of the Victoria game. It was a totally unnecessary and embarrassing own-goal by the management who were wrong to blight the career of Gatting in this way.

You cannot frog-march the leader into the market square and pillory him. All the situation required was an apology from Gatting to the Victorian Cricket Association and to his own team and for the manager to inform the Press that it had happened. Then he might have pulled a ring off a tinny with the skipper and underlined his broader responsibilities.

Gatting is doing well enough. He promoted himself boldly in the Test batting order and succeeded, giving Gower the chance to find his touch at number five. When England were forced to contemplate taking the field for the current Test without Ian Botham, it was Gatting who worked hard at his bowling in the game against Victoria in Melbourne, toiling for more than 20 overs an innings to be in reasonable form for the Test.

When Botham became a spectator, who went to the key position of first slip? Gatting. He is leading by example, the only way he knows, because, like Allan Border, his opposite number, he is not yet an outstanding cricket thinker when the game is on the move.

Perhaps leading Middlesex, a successful side with many talented bowling options at his disposal, has not given him the experience to look after a young man like DeFreitas when he is struggling against Test batsmen ... not enough adversity perhaps. Yet he is learning.

In the first two Tests he tended to put on Emburey and Edmonds and allow them to carry on in their set-piece way with their cage of close fielders. Here at Adelaide there was an excellent last session on the first day when Gatting and the spinners worked out a defensive arrangement of deeper fields which frustrated the centurion Boon and 'strangled' his wicket. It was an element of flexibility which comes with the confidence of seeing it work well.

Another healthy sign of living in the State of One-Up is that the senior players are still supporting the captain. Here Gatting is fortunate indeed to have the devotion to duty of Botham, Gower and Lamb in the middle-order batting and of Edmonds and Emburey, the pillars of the whole bowling. Only Lamb is still to make an impact on the Tests, but, unless he has been robbed of his talent by an unknown force, his runs will come.

Citing only the old hands is not to underestimate the contribution of the others, but the point is that when the Tests are lost the nasties come to the surface and senior players gather small flocks of discontent around them.

Perhaps more than anything the contentment of Ian Botham, now with wife and family around him, has allowed Mike Gatting room to grow and establish his own chirpy front. How lasting this happy order will be will only be judged when England are losing and that cannot happen … at least until Tuesday.

---

29 DECEMBER 1986

A SIGHT RARER THAN HALLEY'S COMET

Frank Tyson

Melbourne

In my time I have had unusual experiences: I have seen Halley's Comet and two Centenary Tests. But yesterday in Melbourne I witnessed one of the rarest sights of all: Australia losing a home Test against England in less than three days.

The viewing of the Comet was predictable and the Centenary games pre-planned. But Australia's defeat by an innings and 14 runs in Melbourne's Fourth Test was the unexpected and supine capitulation of a reputedly international team on a fair cricketing wicket.

England's thumping triumph was earned by sheer unadulterated professionalism. There was a chalk and cheese difference between the two teams. Australia in the field bungled several chances. Chris Broad hit a masterly 112, but he should have been caught when he was 75.

When England stepped on to the field on the third day with a morale-boosting lead of 208 there was a sense of purpose in each and every player's step. Their bowlers knew their targets. The eventual Man of The Match, Gladstone Small, fired his fast broadsides at the outside edge of David Boon's bat with gratifying results. The Tasmanian opener did not have one opportunity to deploy his favourite on-drive.

DeFreitas, newly equipped with immaculate line and length, frustrated Jones into cutting at a ball that was far too close to his body. Even Australia's front-running batsman, Allan Border, was enticed into repeating the slashing edge outside the off stump which led to his first-innings downfall.

But it was in the fielding department that England won the test. Gatting and Emburey caught like angels at slip, while the rank and file of the side chased and returned every ball as though their lives depended upon it.

Gatting's captaincy never faltered. The morning's session saw him ring the bowling changes with an unsettling effect. He stationed his fieldsmen with the acumen of his Middlesex and England mentor, Mike Brearley. He never permitted his bowlers to stray from their appointed task of line and length.

Australia's defeat in Melbourne leaves them in a quandary. They placed their trust in bits-and-pieces bowlers, one of whom, Greg Matthews, was never even given an opportunity to display his skills.

Captain Allan Border now admits that this was a mistake in policy. But when the crunch came, it was the batting department that let the home side down. Moreover, the defection of the rebel tourists to South Africa has left Australian cricket with little reserve strength of Test match calibre.

---

15 JANUARY 1987

FIFTH TEST – FINAL DAY

JOHN BULL'S CHARGE FAILS — BUT IT WAS MAGNIFICENT

Peter West *reports from Sydney on a thrilling climax to one of the best Test matches he ever hopes to see*

After a day when the fortunes of both sides ebbed and flowed in compelling fashion, Australia won the Fifth Test here in Sydney with one over remaining.

What chance could England possibly have of making 320 to win, when on either side of the lunch interval, they lost, first, the wickets of Gower and Athey, who had built a promising platform, and then those of Lamb and Botham for a pittance? Yet we then admired a century partnership between Gatting and Richards which, by the time the last mandatory 20 overs began, left England to make another 90.

At that juncture I was hoping to report that the captain should be the toast of all England as he led a likely victory charge, with the best innings he has played for his country. 'I thought we should be positive,' he said afterwards, when Allan Border affirmed that he had not liked the situation at all. 'I thought we had probably had it,' the Australian captain admitted.

Then, the picture changed again. Gatting, four runs short of a magnificent hundred, richly deserved, was caught and bowled by Waugh in the second of the last 20 overs. John Bull had led from the front for three and a half hours, hitting a 6 and ten 4s. The regularity of Australian appeals, he said, reminded him of being in India.

It was soon apparent, save for several brave shots from Emburey, limping slightly between wickets with his groin strain, that the shutters had to be raised.

A draw was in prospect when Sleep, in two balls, had all Australians, on the ground or off it, in a ferment of expectation.

Richards, pushing forward, was bowled by a wrong 'un. Edmonds, doing likewise, but playing no stroke, was lbw. Nine more overs remained, and Australia had two more wickets to prise out. Small survived six of these, against the spinners, but in the 18th Reid was recalled and took a tumbling catch at slip off the fourth delivery.

The last man, Dilley, arrived with 14 balls left. He scored a couple off the first, and kept out the next. Now Sleep to Emburey, the atmosphere supercharged. He blocked the first five balls but perished on the back foot, bowled by one that kept low.

It was right that so splendid a contest should have a positive result; and no one should begrudge Australia their joy. After all, England have won the series by two matches to one.

Gatting was asked whether he thought the tour had been somewhat tarnished by this defeat. 'Not at all,' he replied. 'We've had a great game, and it could have gone either way. And we've still got the Ashes.'

England restarted their innings on a sunny morning at 39 for 1, and Border began with Taylor and Reid. It was a lively, accurate spell from Reid, five overs for 11 runs. Shrieks for a catch behind, off Athey's boot, and another, off Gower's hip, illustrated how tautly Australian nerves were stretched. In the first hour England advanced by another 32 runs off 16 overs.

Border, slow left-arm, now gave himself a bowl, and he achieved the breakthrough. Gower was advancing profitably against Sleep with several fours lofted over the infield. But he could not fend down a ball from Border that turned and bounced higher, and he was caught at backward short-leg.

Then, to the first ball of the next over, Athey aimed a sweep at Sleep's leg-break and was bowled behind his legs. It was so different now. Border clustered the bat against two batsmen, Lamb and Gatting, not yet established. The first interval arrived with England at 101 for three. Border, 8–5–9–1, had taken his first Test wicket for four years.

England would have lunched with even less appetite had they foreseen what occurred in the first over afterwards. Off Taylor's third ball, Lamb was caught at silly point. To the next, Botham spooned a catch to the diving Wellham.

What price England now? Yet an hour later, Gatting had made 40 out of a 50 partnership with Richards, and moved to his own half-century with three thumping 4s off three long hops from Sleep.

As the tea interval approached, Border turned to Hughes for the first time since Wednesday. In his first over Zoehrer got both hands to a low edge from Gatting, then 70, but the ball spilled out of his gloves.

When Gatting was dismissed, the sixth-wicket stand of 133 was an England Test record on this ground. Taylor's two further wickets, allied to his previous six as well as to two endurate innings, won him the Benson & Hedges Man of the Match award, which is no bad way to start a Test career. Broad, having made three hundreds, won himself four gold goblets and a gold tray as Man of the Series.

---

9 JUNE 1987

EDITORIAL

MEN IN WHITE COATS

Should *Wisden* ever include in its records section a table of the most acrimonious Test matches, the one between England and Pakistan that ends today at Old Trafford would be a candidate for consideration. It sounds unwholesomely partisan to blame the visitors, but justice requires that it should. Pakistan went into the Test under strength. Captain Imran Khan was unable to bowl and fiendish leg-spinner Abdul Qadir is still in Pakistan nursing his sick wife. None of the team's four bowlers seemed on top form, and they bowled at a painfully slow rate. Substitutes ran on and off the field not so much to cover for genuinely injured players as to allow those in retreat a rest from the cricket and from the foul Manchester weather. Javed Miandad, acting as captain during one of Imran's absences, kept up non-stop conversations with his colleagues and opponents, much to the batsmen's annoyance.

The innocent observer may be forgiven for wondering what the umpires' role in this has been. Their job of enforcing the laws does not include eradicating gamesmanship. So, if fieldsmen (and the acting captain to boot) distract batsmen, bowl ten-minute overs, swear or decide to leave the field, there is little the umpires can do without provoking an international incident. The Old Trafford Test has signalled very clearly the need for cricket to have an international panel of umpires, like most other major sports. Our own umpires are the best in the world. But when hard, pseudo-political questions of interpretation have to be settled on the field, it is best to have the law laid down by those who cannot — however unfairly — be accused of prejudice.

---

31 JULY 1987

OPPOSING VIEWS

Sir — From Geoffrey Wheatcroft's TV column, page 8, 29 July: '... even as adagio a test match as the one which petered out yesterday ...'

From Peter Deeley's Test match report, page 28, same issue: 'one of those games that left everyone privileged to watch the final hours emotionally drained, players and spectators alike'. From Frank Tyson's Test match comment, same page, same issue: 'the exhilarating vagaries of Test cricket were flaunted at Edgbaston yesterday ... a grand climax'. 'Petered out' as opposed to 'emotionally drained', 'exhilarating vagaries', 'grand climax'.

I know Mr Wheatcroft writes for the same paper as Mr Deeley and Mr Tyson. Was he watching the same Test match?

Bill Grundy
Stockport, Cheshire

---

24 AUGUST 1987

GAVASKAR AND IMRAN LEAVE FOND MEMORIES

Peter Deeley

MCC's bicentenary, which has been so far an ode to all that is best in the game, was tinged with some sadness on Saturday as cricket's most notable retirees, Gavaskar of India and Imran of Pakistan, reminded us of what will be lost with their going.

Beyond the pleasure of seeing great players doing what comes naturally, this Lord's gala has offered the hidden bonus of sport's ability — when so minded — to override the boundaries of race and nationalism.

The eye had already been caught by the brick red patka of India's Maninder and the green cap of Imran patrolling the same boundary rope as if partition had never happened. Then on Saturday there was the blessed sight of Bombay's Gavaskar caressing the ball to all corners while Lahore's Imran was firing sixes off Emburey like an Exocet missile.

No doubt there will be many attempts to get these two to change their mind but at this level of talent one can understand the wish to go out at the top rather than on the slide. With Lord's suffering the drenching that seems inseparable from the Saturday of a big game, the captains are now envisaging declarations in order to set up a run chase for the Rest of the World on the last day.

As Mike Gatting said, 'we don't want a boring draw,' a comment amplified by Allan Border, 'with the quality of batting on this wicket, it might otherwise end up that way.' After a final flurry of runs in the evening gloom from the West Indians Harper and Walsh — who covered the distance between creases in such giant strides that one felt there should be a handicap system (the three-legged or sack race comes to mind) — Rest of the World declared at 421 for 7, 34 behind MCC's 455 for 5.

With neither Miandad nor Qadir able to bat, Gavaskar had begun cautiously though there was also the X-factor of Marshall who is proving that he is without peer among pacemen. He had Dujon caught in the first over to add to the scalp of his countryman Haynes, bringing the wry comment that West Indian batsmen 'don't like it up 'em' more than any others.

While the wily Gavaskar faced just five balls from Marshall in his first session, Imran was left to survive as best he could, that glacial composure unruffled by inside edges and snicks that fell frustratingly short of the slips. The fiery period survived, Gavaskar moved serenely to his first Lord's century while Imran raked the pavilion. With 95 runs scored before lunch, the lost opening half-hour seemed almost irrelevant.

The pair had added 180 in 136 minutes before Imran, 82, was bowled by Shastri trying, if anything, to increase the pace. Then, against the back-cloth of distant thunder and lightning, Gavaskar took his personal tally beyond that of Gatting 24 hours earlier and on to 188 before Shastri – the reward for another lovely spell of bowling – had him caught and bowled.

The crowd rose as did the fielders as Gavaskar, his headband his halo, eventually disappeared from sight and into history. Will we see his like again?

Emburey got his first wicket at international level this season since the one-day Pakistan matches when Kapil was caught in the deep. But then the weather took over. To pass the time, the crowd turned to the Mexican Wave and – horror of horrors – were joined by an MCC member from the top row of the pavilion. Would that Bateman the cartoonist had been there to record the scene.

Miandad, who has a back spasm triggered off by his short bowling spell in MCC's innings, is expected to be fit to bat on Tuesday. As his captain, Border, said: 'He shouldn't have bowled but didn't tell me about this problem.' (An illustration of the pitfalls that face a captain trying to weld 11 talents into one unit.)

Qadir, the bowler Miandad was standing in for, also expects to have his bruised spinning finger healed in time for today. With the wicket showing signs of response to the spinners, we may well see the slow bowlers assuming the ascendancy today or tomorrow.

But whatever the pattern of the last days, the players have already given the match just the degree of seriousness it deserves. Mike Gatting says: 'It has been a very good feeling having a lot of great players around from all the different countries. It's a marvellous spectacle and a privilege to have played in it.'

---

12 OCTOBER 1987

ARMY TAKING BITE OUT OF TERROR

In Pakistan, if you want something done, even in cricket, you turn to the army. When Donald Carr, a member of the World Cup organising committee, visited the old Rawalpindi club ground four months ago, it hardly looked equipped for the task of staging an international game, writes Peter Deeley.

So the Sappers moved in. They relaid the outfield, renovated and extended the pavilion and began building an infrastructure of stands for the public and gantries to house the television and radio teams.

To do so, they had to close off a main road but when the army issues an order, no one argues, certainly not the politicians. The work cost, in all £100,000, and the ground capacity was extended from 7,000 to 17,000. What is more it was all finished on time.

Military men are as thick on the ground here as MCC ties at Lord's. Pakistan's President, General Zia-ul-Haq, personally ordered the army into the job. A lieutenant general is President of the Board of Control for cricket, locally a major general was appointed i/c the organising committee and a brigadier heads the Rawalpindi ground committee.

To add to all that, army commandos are bolstering security today 'to control any terrorist activities' at the stadium where President Zia and Princess Alexandra were expected.

Dogs and scanning devices will be on standby at the ground in case of any security alarms. On the list of items banned from the ground are food, cameras, binoculars, vacuum flasks and transistor radios. That would effectively get most journalists turned back if they were not VIPs. There is also a VVIP category: the army chiefs of course and other incidental actors, such as the players.

There have been several bomb blasts in Rawalpindi, near the national capital Islamabad, and with the cricket ground close to the army general headquarters, the commandos moved in to take over security 48 hours before the match.

About 200 people have died this year in bomb attacks which Pakistan blames on the Soviet-backed government in neighbouring Afghanistan. Five people were killed by a bomb blast at a Rawalpindi bus station last month, and four people were injured by one in Islamabad's main vegetable market on Monday.

---

9 NOVEMBER 1987

WORLD CUP FINAL

ENGLAND'S RUN-CHASE IS DOOMED BY HISTORY

Peter Deeley *sees England fail to break a pattern as Australia turn the screw in the Calcutta heat*

The psychological disadvantage of having to chase a set total was once more demonstrated by Australia's seven-run win over England in the World Cup final at Eden Gardens, Calcutta yesterday.

As in the previous three World Cup finals the benefit of batting first has been fully exploited by the winners. After the game Allan Border, Australia's captain, said his side had batted when conditions were at their best, and Mike Gatting said the wicket had become slower and harder for batting when England were at the wicket.

But Gatting emphasised that his comments about the pitch should not decry Australia's fighting effort in the field. Australia's bowling was the tighter and apart from one short spell in the middle of the England innings when seven runs were given away inside two overs from mis-handling, they fielded like men possessed of the chance to show that Australian cricket had finally emerged from its doldrums.

The setting for the game before a 80,000 crowd, almost the number that Lord's might expect for a five-day Test, was as colourful and exciting as only this frenetic Indian city of 12 million could provide.

As for the cricket from an outsider's point of view, there was relief that the occasion was not after all to be a re-run of past Indo-Pakistan conflicts. The well-behaved crowd, however, may have felt cheated. Instead of the flamboyance of the East they were given heavier Western fare — technique, not pyrotechnics. Boon and Marsh gave Australia their fifth major opening partnership in this series they were helped by the inaccuracy of Small and the occasional bad ball from DeFreitas, but then Foster came on, dropped straight on a length and bowled Marsh.

Jones swept the first ball of Hemmings's second spell for six, but soon popped up a catch to Gatting at mid-wicket and, with the scoring rate dropping like a stone as Foster, Emburey and Gooch applied the brake, McDermott was sent in up the order.

He swiped for eight balls, saw Gooch put down a caught and bowled chance, then was bowled for 14 by the England opening batsman. One over more and Boon's fine knock of 75, which won him £900 as man of the final, was over. He swept at Hemmings but skied the ball to Downton.

Gooch had been instrumental in tying down the batsmen, but it seemed that Gatting entrusted him with one over too many, his eighth going for 10. At this stage, though, it was difficult to contain the Australians, Veletta walking impudently down the wicket to Foster for instance, 22 coming off his last two overs. The final five overs went for 47 runs, which Gatting acknowledged later was about 20 too many, and Australia finished on 253 for 5, a total beyond the grasp of almost all sides batting second in the tournament.

Those who had argued for Broad's return were reinforced by the setback which befell England, Robinson falling lbw first ball to McDermott off the fourth ball of the innings. Micky Stewart, England's team manager, defended the selection on the grounds that it would not have been easy for Broad to pick up his rhythm after missing four games. The 10-over analyses of Reid and McDermott, each giving away only 17 runs, illustrated the difference between the two opening attacks.

Gooch might be termed a partial failure. When O'Donnell had him lbw for 35, the bowler went whooping down the wicket at this prize, a tribute to his victim's reputation. Waugh had an eventful time in the field, stepping back over the line to catch a Gatting hit for 6 off May when he could have taken the ball on the field. Then he fired in a return which ran out the gallant Athey for 58.

That was a considerable blow to England's hopes; the earlier mortal stab to the heart was probably Gatting's attempt on 41 to do a reverse sweep off the first ball Border bowled. Coming off the bat it hit the batsman's shoulder — as Gatting confirmed after the match — and popped up to Dyer.

Gatting will no doubt come in for criticism for playing the shot. He himself would not agree afterwards that it was injudicious, though he conceded it might have been wiser to have seen more of Border's bowling first.

Only Lamb offered much resistance after that with 45 in 55 balls, but like all the later batsmen he was being asked to accomplish the implausible. England needed 75 off the last 10 overs, then 46 off five. DeFreitas kindled a tiny flame with 4, 6, 4 off three deliveries from McDermott, but in the end the margin was just beyond them. Gallant fighters, but not champions.

---

9 DECEMBER 1987

UMPIRE ACCUSES GATTING

Michael Austin *reports from Faisalabad on the war of words which scarred yesterday's play in the Second Test*

Shakoor Rana, the umpire, last night threatened to pull out of the Second Test in Faisalabad unless he received an apology from Mike Gatting, the England captain, following a war of words just before the end of yesterday's play.

Mr Rana, 54, said after the close of play: 'I am reporting Gatting to the Test and County Cricket Board, the tour manager Peter Lush and the Pakistan Board for using foul and abusive language. No captain has spoken to me like that before.' Later Mr Rana said he would not take the field today unless Gatting showed contrition, prompting fears that the whole tour could be in jeopardy.

A productive day in cricket terms for England was especially prosperous for Emburey, who took 3 for 26 as Pakistan struggled to 106 for 5 in reply to 292, Broad making 116 in seven hours and Qasim returning 5 for 83.

In other respects, a more unsavoury saga would be difficult to imagine. It ended with Gatting and Mr Rana exchanging words almost eyeball to eyeball during the final over and being separated by Athey who ushered away his captain. Sadly Gatting, having urged his tour party to keep their heads in controversial circumstances, lost his during a finger-wagging, heated argument with Mr Rana who had earlier given two dubious decisions against England.

The triviality of the cause and the violent verbal aftermath sums up the powder-keg on which this three-match series sits. A five-match programme would probably not last the course. Mr Rana, umpiring at square-leg, intervened when Hemmings was running in to bowl because he believed that Gatting was changing his field behind the back of Salim Malik, the batsman.

Gatting, who was fielding at backward short-leg, said: 'I had already informed Salim that I was bringing in Capel, the deep square-leg fielder, and when Hemmings was running in I indicted to Capel with my hand that he had come in far enough.

'All I was trying to do was to get in another over, but obviously the umpire thought I was cheating. A few words passed between us but I am not saying what because I don't want a slanging match. I just felt that it was not his job at square-leg to inform the batsman what I was doing. I did nothing for which I need to apologise,' he added.

The play had followed the now familiar pattern of an armed truce between England and the umpires. Mr Rana had given out French, stumped, though his back foot seemed anchored in the crease and he rejected a confident appeal against Ijaz for a catch at short-leg. Athey, fielding at silly mid-off, directed a lengthy lecture to Ijaz, who had been given not out, stood his ground and then asked Mr Rana to intervene.

England's tour management of Mr Lush and Micky Stewart said they had not seen any Test series marred with incidents such as these. 'They should not occur,' asserted Mr Lush who said that no member of England's party would be disciplined as a result.

---

7 MAY 1988

HICK TOUCHES GREATNESS WITH UNDEFEATED 405

David Green

Taunton

Graeme Hick, Worcestershire's 21-year-old Zimbabwean batting prodigy, made further claim to be included among the great names of cricket with a monumental innings of 405 not out against Somerset at Taunton yesterday.

Worcestershire, who shortly after lunch on Thursday had been tottering at 132 for 5, declared at tea yesterday at a highly prosperous 628 for 7 and by the close had Somerset struggling at 103 for 4.

Hick's innings occupied nine and a quarter hours and included 35 fours and 11 sixes. It is the second-highest County Championship score, exceeded only by Archie MacLaren's 424 for Lancashire on the same ground in 1895. Other records were established along the way, Hick's sixth-wicket stand of 265 with Rhodes, who made 56, and his unbroken eighth-wicket partnership of 177 with Richard Illingworth, 31 not out, both eclipsing the previous best for the county.

Hick's runs were scored out of 550 made while he was at the wicket, a startling proportion, particularly as Somerset captain Peter Roebuck frequently had five men on the fence when Hick was facing, while setting attacking fields for his partners. His first-class run tally for the season is now 815 and with a possible seven innings remaining he should be the first player to reach 1,000 runs before the end of May since New Zealand's Glenn Turner, another Worcestershire player, did so in 1973.

Hick said: 'I started getting tired towards the end of each session but I enjoyed a bit of luck after getting 300 and I took it as it came.' A feature of Hick's play, which throughout was masterful, powerful and strictly orthodox, was the almost metronomic rate of his scoring until a tremendous late surge of strokes brought him his last 105 runs in only 71 minutes.

When Hick, on 179, and Rhodes on 40, resumed their innings yesterday morning Worcestershire were well placed at 312 for 5. The pitch, though placid, seemed likely to take spin increasingly so Worcestershire were naturally looking for a massive total. The batsmen proceeded with care against steady medium fast-bowling from Jones, Mallender and Rose. Mark's tidy spin-off was also treated with respect and the dogged Rhodes took 100 minutes to advance to his half-century.

After five and a half hours' resistance Rhodes struck a long hop from Dredge straight to mid-wicket. Lunch came with Hick on 257 and one was slightly surprised that his measured play had produced as many as 78 runs during the morning.

Newport lent valuable assistance as Hick, now confronted entirely by fields designed to prevent boundaries, picked up ones and 2s steadily.

When Marks bowled Newport with one that turned considerably Somerset were certainly more concerned than their opponents. Hick now began to cut loose, reaching his 300 with two 6s in three balls from Rose, one straight and one over mid-off. From that point Somerset's weary bowlers had no chance of stopping his gallop.

Hick's fourth hundred, which came off only 58 balls, contained eight 6s and six 4s. He reached the target with his final 6, over mid-wicket off the hapless Dredge, who was playing in his first championship game since 1986.

Neale's declaration at tea was designed to give Worcestershire sufficient time to dismiss their opponents twice. He was not, apparently, aware of the proximity of MacLaren's record score which certainly saved him much agonising.

Roebuck found that misfortunes seldom come singly as, bent with care, he fell leg before to Radford's second ball. Then Hick, whose energy throughout his innings had been astonishing, came on to bowl off-spin, with almost immediate success. Felton, who had shaped confidently, soon drove him into short extra's hands. Radford had Hardy caught behind, Hick trapped Harden leg before and Somerset still need 376 to avoid following on.

---

10 JUNE 1989

WAUGH'S CENTURY SHOULD BREAK OPEN THE FLOODGATES

AUSTRALIAN VIEWPOINT

Mark Ray

Why has it taken Steve Waugh 42 innings and 27 matches to make a Test century?

Waugh came into the Australian team when aged 20 with much expected from him. Plus he had the dual responsibilities of an all-rounder, especially in one-day matches with much of Australia's game now built around his talents and his capacity to handle pressure. That he survived all that pressure as well as criticism from some commentators, who thought their State side had a better all-rounder, is evidence of his great talents.

Last season, against a fearsome West Indies attack on fast Australian pitches, Waugh made two great 90s in the first two Tests, taking the game back to the bowlers by rocking on to the back foot and playing that square drive-cut that even brought admiring cries of 'sweet, sweet' from the West Indians.

Waugh is as competitive as he is gifted and arguably his best moment in that series was when Viv Richards sauntered out to bat in his 100th Test, the first of the series. Waugh was bowling and he gave Richards three bouncers in a row. A battle between two proud, gifted cricketers continued during the series and finished with honours about even.

At Worcester a month ago Waugh greeted Ian Botham the same way. That we have to wait a while for that battle is quite disappointing. As a man, Waugh is quiet. He gives little away except the impression that he has great reserves of character as well as ability. He is quick-witted in a dry self-effacing way, more like an Australian of the 1920s or 1930s than one of the brash, superficially nationalistic '80s.

All the Australians revere that baggy green cap but none more than Waugh. He usually bowls in it in the nets, especially in Australia. Shades of Clarrie Grimmett. After only one Test hundred from 42 innings, Waugh is hardly a great player yet. But he will be.

---

14 JUNE 1989

ENGLAND SUFFER AGAINST VINTAGE ALDERMAN

AUSTRALIA BEAT ENGLAND BY 210 RUNS

Peter Deeley

Headingley

This was one Australian soap opera which should have been X-rated for domestic audiences. England lost six of her leading batsman in the middle session at Leeds yesterday in a dismal collapse whose roots were as much psychological as physical.

From a passably comfortable lunchtime anchorage of 66 for 1, the home side reached a nadir, two hours later, of 154 for 7. The end came after tea in a sultry stickiness that must have seemed like a Brisbane home-from-home to Allan Border. In all, England had been dismissed in 238 minutes and Australia still had in hand 7.4 overs plus the extra hour.

It was hard to recognise batsmen who only days before had seemed able to dominate a moderate attack. In particular, we were shocked by the manner of David Gower's dismissal for 34, chasing a leg-side ball from Lawson. England's captain had lost his wicket that way in the first innings. This time he had just played a rather uncontrolled shot, almost one-handed, which brought a boundary and the Australians had called up a leg-slip.

Lawson asked the question again, Gower went for it and Healy held the chance. It was not the example we looked for from an England captain. A jubilant Border put his finger on the main cause of England's demise when he said: 'I was surprised how rapidly they went down in the afternoon. But they were batting under a bit of pressure.'

Border had batted on for 43 minutes in the morning, leaving England a target of 402 which, to win, had to be achieved at a rate of 4.8 an over. His biggest problem seemed to be the breakdowns of the computerised scoreboard, which was perhaps striking in sympathy with England's plight.

Chris Broad's early departure, leg-before to Alderman to a ball only just above ankle height, thankfully turned out not to be typical of this last-day wicket. While Gooch and Barnett were together there was a smidgen of a chance of an England run chase. But Alderman's fifth ball after lunch trapped Barnett and Taylor took a good low catch at slip. Lamb, who seems a one-innings man, again went bat-pad to the Boon–Alderman partnership and it was up to the resolute Gooch, together with Gower, to seize on Alderman's departure from the attack to build a face-saving stand.

They had reckoned without Lawson, who claimed the wickets of Gower and then Smith – only three balls at the wicket – in four deliveries. Hughes has worked hard in this game to show that behind the clown image lies a good, honest fast bowler and he blew away the corner-stone of England's resistance, Gooch, leg-before for 68, though it might have been passing leg stump.

But the man-of-the-match award deservedly went to Terry Alderman, 10 for 151 in the game. Like good wine he seems to be maturing with age. In 1981 here he took 42 wickets in a six-Test series. We shall need a computer (preferably not Headingley's) to measure his progression this time if he continues to improve.

Gower enters hospital this weekend for an exploratory operation on an old injury in his right shoulder whose mobility, he said, had 'markedly deteriorated' in the past 10 days. But at this stage he emphasised there was no suggestion of missing the second Test at Lord's. Whether the shoulder was hurting him more than the defeat, it is no exaggeration to say Gower seemed almost choked with emotion.

With the Australian team's pop music system blaring out in celebration over his head, Gower conceded that the mood upstairs in the England dressing-room was 'hardly euphoric'.

He refused to go into a point-by-point analysis of the team's failures. 'All I really want to say is that we were out-performed in all departments. But there are five more Tests and whatever disappointments we have had here won't stop us coming back with a vengeance at Lord's.'

---

29 AUGUST 1989

ENGLAND EXPECTS ... AN AWFUL LOT OF A CRICKET CAPTAIN

Michael Calvin *looks at the many qualities needed to survive unscarred the harsh demands of leading a failing national team*

WANTED: England cricket captain. Experience preferred, playing ability optional. Clean character, sense of humour and faith in human nature essential.

Happily married teetotallers with degrees in African politics and economics should apply immediately to E.R. Dexter, c/o Lord's cricket ground, London NW8. Such an advertisement would not deter those children, of all ages, who hammer tennis balls against the garden fence in the belief they are an undiscovered Boycott.

But, in the real world, natural enthusiasm has its limits. Just ask David Gower. Or have a brief word with Mike Gatting, Ian Botham, Christopher Cowdrey, Graham Gooch, John Emburey and Bob Willis.

Occasionally the improbable does happen – after all, at the Fosters Oval yesterday they temporarily ran out of lager and England saved the follow-on against Australia in the sixth Test. But the prospect of a man emerging unscathed from the England captaincy, one of the most punishing jobs in British sport, is highly unlikely.

Gower's demeanour today, at the end of an Ashes series which has established him as the butt of more jokes than Les Dawson's mother-in-law, will be revealing. He deserves forgiveness if he acts like a prisoner who has heard the cell door slam behind him for the last time. For he would not be human if, beneath the veneer of easy humour, there are gaping psychological wounds.

In this wretched summer, Gower has reached too often for the flip comment to be entirely convincing. His attitude has smacked of a man attempting to laugh instead of succumbing to the temptation to cry. Therein lies the harshness of his job: a rational, immensely likeable individual finding himself the scapegoat of a deeply flawed system that embitters its principal characters.

One suspects that Gatting is quietly enjoying the consternation at suggestions, denied yesterday, that secret efforts have been made by the authorities to persuade him his future lies as England captain in the West Indies rather than as a leader of a rebel tour to South Africa.

There is an honourable school of thought that, by so publicly challenging the authority of an umpire and admitting involvement with a barmaid, he did not deserve the honour and attendant responsibility of captaining his country. But he has clearly been alienated by the inept handling of his departure from the post, and is not the first to feel he has been denied a fair trial by an unholy alliance of weak administrators and hysterical journalists.

Like it or not, the England captain is a sitting target for the tabloids. The level of public scorn — English cricketers have plumbed depths previously occupied by British tennis players — can be irritating; the intrusion into one's private life infuriating.

Even Willis, who enjoyed a fair measure of success, ended his career a sour, self-defensive man. He objected to the intensity of attention, and became so sensitive to criticism he bred an unhealthy insularity within the team.

It is inevitable that personality defects, which would have been disguised in previous generations, are magnified by the microscope of today's publicity. The unsuitable character of Botham, for instance, was taken apart, piece by piece.

Gooch and Emburey did not hold the job long enough to feel the full force of the prurient interest in their lives. But the example of Cowdrey, shamefully discarded after one Test last summer, emphasises that one does not need a long run in charge to be scarred by the experience.

It seems clear that the job specification of an England manager requires revision. There are, however, some compensations for the indignities suffered this summer. There was another demonstration of genuine sympathy for Gower when he was out yesterday, and the saving of the follow-on was accorded a standing ovation.

Making a virtue out of mediocrity may not be the ideal inheritance for a new man like Peter Roebuck. But, then again, Gower has had plenty of practice. Wouldn't it be wonderfully ironic if an application for the extension of his contract was in the post? ...

CHAPTER 6
THE 1990s

INTRODUCTION

The appointment of Christopher Martin-Jenkins in 1991 as cricket correspondent was a move that continued the *Telegraph* trend of employing a
familiar voice to lead its cricket coverage. Martin-Jenkins followed
Howard Marshall and E.W. Swanton, who both combined the role of
cricket correspondent with broadcasting jobs with the BBC.

One of the first pieces penned by 'C.M.J.' was a touching tribute to his
former BBC colleague John Arlott, who died in December 1991. Arlott's
voice defined an era of cricket coverage on the radio and the *Telegraph*
was in the lucky position of having one of his fellow commentators on
the staff. Indeed, Arlott's final words on Test Match Special were, 'After a
few words from Trevor Bailey, it will be Christopher Martin-Jenkins.'

It was during the '90s that we begin to see the names that would
become familiar to millions of Telegraph readers. Martin-Jenkins was
joined by Mark Nicholas, Simon Hughes and Martin Johnson, who
joined the *Telegraph* from the *Independent*.

The age of the sports columnist was upon us and the *Telegraph* secured
the services of Michael Parkinson and Sir Tim Rice. Parkinson relished
his return to sports writing and his columns quickly gained a large
following. His reminiscences of Yorkshire cricket in particular were
poignant and perceptive. By 1995, Parkinson's writing was recognised
with the Sports Feature Writer of the Year Award from the Sports
Journalism Association. He wrote on a wide range of sports but it was
cricket that was his first love. Here we see him recall his days with
Barnsley Cricket Club and fond memories of Harold Larwood.

The growth of sport within the newspaper led to the inevitable
launch of an independent, stand-alone sports section in 1991. Initially the
section was confined to a Monday but soon spread to the Saturday news-

paper and within a decade would be published daily. Cricket was given room to breathe and the comprehensive coverage of Test matches that marks the newspaper's approach today was born during the early '90s.

Another first for the *Telegraph* was the launch on 1 November 1994 of the newspaper's website. The Electronic Telegraph was the first national newspaper website and cricket reports quickly became an integral part of its early identity.

Not to be left behind, the *Sunday Telegraph*, following the appointment of Scyld Berry as cricket correspondent, added the England captain Mike Atherton to its stable. Atherton penned his own pieces and grew in stature as a writer during the late '90s. In August 1998 he wrote in graphic detail of the fearsome prospect of facing Allan Donald at his peak. Reading his piece, it is easy to imagine peering through the grille of his helmet as Donald cranked up the pace.

The use of ghosted columns became more widespread but they are not included in this book. Only pieces where the authorship can be identified have been considered.

---

8 APRIL 1991

HICK PLAYS IT STRAIGHT TO THE TOP

Christopher Martin-Jenkins

The language of Vincent Crummles, the theatrical impresario, was, you may remember, not powerful enough to describe the 'infant phenomenon'. At times language has hardly been able to do justice to the talents of Graeme Hick, now officially qualified by residence to play for England.

The days of hair-splitting about how long that qualification should have been are over. The time may well come when Zimbabwe, the land of his birth, achieve Test status, and ironically they would be much more likely to do so if Hick were still available to play for them.

But the tobacco farmer's son from Trelawney with a host of Yorkshire-born ancestors in both his maternal and paternal bloodlines has been publicly committed since 1986 to playing for England and is officially deemed to have started his qualification period from 1984. The die is cast.

Hick is about to become a wider hero than he is already and one should frankly rejoice that he is likely to be a credit to himself and both his countries when the Test centuries arrive, as arrive they surely will. He is clean-shaven, clean-living, open, modest and well-mannered. He is good-looking enough to attract the girls, though shy enough to arouse their motherly, rather than their predatory, instincts.

He strides to the crease the moment the first wicket falls, his colleagues saying that he can hardly wait to get to the middle. Once there, he plays beautifully straight and with a quite unmistakeable appearance of class. One might wish for more delicacy of touch at times, a more varied artistry, but hardly for more power. There is more in his style of the Botham than the Gower, the Dexter than the Cowdrey, the Hammond than the Hutton.

The prospect of his walking out to bat against the West Indies this summer is exciting, however much some may regret the distinctive African-Colonial twang which will be evident in the television and radio interviews.

It is partly a reflection of our 'multi-ethnic' society and partly of recent history in southern Africa that Hick's will not be the only colonial strains emanating from the England dressing-room this season. Moreover, they will be balanced by a Caribbean lilt here and there.

If they care deeply enough for their adopted country's cause, no one can reasonably object. Although recently reduced from 10 years to seven, mainly, it seemed, to accommodate Hick, the qualification rules for England are more stringent than elsewhere – enough to keep out mere mercenaries. One must hope that the welcome Hick receives from everyone will itself be wholly unqualified.

Some, however, will be bound to resent Hick's presence in the side, which, barring an uncharacteristically bad start to the season, can safely be predicted for the first one-day international at Edgbaston on 23 May. By coincidence, this is the date of his 25th birthday. Having celebrated appropriately, no doubt, his first Test cap should follow on 6 June at Headingley, the day after the Derby, although I doubt if Hick will be having a bet.

From an early age, after all, he has set his sights on the top of the cricketing tree. A century maker by the age of six, for Banket Junior School against Mangula (105 not out, 96 of them in boundaries), this thin, asthmatic child made six more hundreds for the school and took 115 wickets at a rate of one an over and at an average of 3.01.

Moving to Prince Edward Boys High School in what was then Salisbury, he scored more than 1,000 runs in his first year in only 14 matches at an average of 270. A bout of meningitis set him back in 1980 but only temporarily interrupted a succession of equally prodigious performances.

Like Miss Ninetta Crummles, he clearly had to be seen to be believed. His progress since he began playing with and against adults is more widely documented. He has had his setbacks. He came to the World Cup with the Zimbabwe side in 1983, but did not play. He took time to start playing big innings in international matches and when Worcestershire took him on to play for their 2nd eleven in 1984, it was primarily because of his ability as an off-spin bowler.

But his performances told the truth: for Worcestershire 2nd eleven he scored 964 runs in 10 matches at 64 and took a mere 23 wickets at 33. The balance has been much the same since, relatively speaking, and I think it is fanciful to believe, as an England selector does, that he may be a force as an off-spinner at Test level. A useful contributor at times, a la Border, would be more realistic an expectation.

So the story of modestly accepted success has continued, most famously with his 1,000 runs before the end of May in 1988, a rare achievement made possible by the phenomenal 405 against Somerset, and culminating in a century against the West Indians at Worcester. That triumph has been balanced by failures in three one-day finals at Lord's and a worryingly slow start to his recent season for Queensland.

His career average stands at present as the fifth best of all time. He scored his 50th hundred in his 249th first-class innings. Only Bradman — 50 in 175 — has been more prolific in this respect.

He will surely make a success of his Test career, although his pleasingly simple batting method, lacking suppleness, will be ferociously tested by the best of the West Indian fast bowlers. Graeme Hick is no more another Bradman than he was a second Miss Crummles. In his own right, however, he should adorn the England side, this season and beyond.

---

18 NOVEMBER 1991

FUTURE ON A STICKY WICKET – BARNSLEY HAVE GROUNDS FOR QUESTIONING THE TRUE MEANING OF CHARITY

Michael Parkinson

NEWS ITEM: 'Barnsley Cricket Club, who number Geoffrey Boycott, Dickie Bird and Martyn Moxon among their former players, may be forced to leave their ground midway through next season. The lease under which they have paid a peppercorn rent for over 50 years expires on 1 August and the owners of the ground, a local charitable trust, have offered a new three-year lease at £22,750 a year. A spokesman for the Trust said: 'We have sympathy with the club but we have been advised by the Charity Commission that we have to obtain the best possible income for the charity for the nine acres of land near the centre of Barnsley.'

SOUNDS OMINOUS. Nine acres near the middle of Barnsley. Make a lovely car park, or a hypermarket, or a car park for a hypermarket. Whatever happens, you can bet any money that it won't be what it has been these past 50 years or more: a proper cricket ground. It wasn't some odd patch of grass on which cricket was played or an acre or two of grazing pasture with a wicket on it.

It was, and is, a real cricket ground with a scoreboard, a substantial pavilion and the truest wicket I ever batted on. It is no coincidence that the three best-known cricketers it produced – Boycott, Moxon and Bird – were all opening bats. They learned on the perfect surface.

I joined the club 40 years ago. In those days you auditioned and waited for the call. The decision was sometimes one of life or death because the wickets we played on in the local leagues around Barnsley were death traps. We would have had a better chance of survival playing on the main line between Doncaster and Kings Cross.

My local club, where I grew up watching my father and later playing with him, was located in a farmer's backyard with cornfields on the boundary and daisies and buttercups in the outfield. The pavilion was made of wood and we had a huge teapot, enamelled and bottomless.

Then we moved two fields away on to a brand-new sports complex and for a while the pitch was a nightmare. Before the opening we instructed our groundsman, Old Cheyney, to produce a surface good enough to last for the official ceremony.

After that we would have to take our chance. His remedy was a strip concocted of marl and horse manure. 'Oss muck. There's nowt like it,' he'd say. He rolled it flat and let it set and although it looked an odd colour it certainly made a presentable batting surface.

On the day of the opening it rained and Cheyney's masterpiece became an evil smelling quagmire which necessitated the police evacuating people from their nearby homes. What is more, in receiving the ceremonial first ball to declare our new ground officially open, our captain played forward to a delivery of no great menace and lost his teeth.

This was not quite as dramatic as it sounds because the ball didn't hit him in the mouth but just below the heart. In fact, exactly on the breast pocket of his shirt which is where he stored his teeth while batting. Some time later we entertained the Barnsley 2nd eleven. This was important. This was us against the Folks Who Lived On The Hill. More importantly, this was my audition piece.

Our opening bowler at the time was a big lad called Terry MacDonald who was a pro boxer, and a good one. He was also quick and on our wicket unplayable and lethal. The Barnsley batsmen, coached to move into line with the head behind the ball, soon realised that such a technique would guarantee them a bed in the local infirmary. They were chopped down but they didn't argue. For one thing Terry was too big but they also knew we had to play them on their patch. 'Let us see how good you are on a proper wicket,' is what they said.

I can remember to this day what it was like arriving at the ground. There was a man on the gate taking money. The scoreboard was like you saw at county grounds with an operator and individual as well as team scores so you needn't keep count in your head. I always did just in case the scorers missed a run. So did Geoffrey Boycott. But he auditioned later.

The dressing room had enough pegs for all of us and hot and cold running water. And when you walked down the steps in front of the pavilion you passed through a little gate on the way to the wicket. And what a wicket.

Subsequently I played on all of Yorkshire's county grounds and later on most of our Test grounds and can honestly say that the wicket at

Shaw Lane was as good as any. If you could play straight you could hang around for a long time with a walking stick. I did a lot of hanging around in the next few seasons. I wasn't much of a stroke player but I could certainly loiter.

This characteristic was noted during my audition performance by a man sitting by the sightscreen. Having observed me for about half an hour he shouted: 'I don't know thi' name lad but I have to tell thi' tha's got about as much life as a bloody tombstone.' I got to know him well over the coming season. He always sat in the same place and never changed his opinion of me.

As I walked to the wicket he would say in a loud voice: 'Oh God, not 'im again.' He was merciless but not particular. Anyone and everyone who played for Barnsley at that time suffered. He had a running feud with our skipper and pro, a nuggety little man called Ernie Steele. At the time the Barnsley Club, with commendable courage, had decided to blood young players in the first team. It was a brave decision because the Yorkshire League is one of the strongest and most competitive leagues in the land. It was also at a time when people used to watch league cricket, so we had our supporters to think of.

What it really meant was that Ernie Steele had a thankless task which he performed with great skill and forbearance. But there were times when the situation got the better of him. I remember playing once at Castleford, I think it was, against a young and fearsome quick bowler called Broughton who later played county cricket for Leicestershire.

I opened and didn't get too many in my half of the wicket from Mr Broughton, the majority of his deliveries bouncing way above my head. It wasn't that dangerous, but, on the other hand, it made scoring difficult. At the fall of a wicket Ernie Steele made his way to the middle carrying a pair of step ladders. It was a fair point to make but it wasn't very subtle. And it did much to improve Mr Broughton's aim.

During this period when we didn't win many games Ernie took some terrible stick from our regular barracker. I remember one match when we were getting a pasting in the field and every time the opposition hit a boundary our barracker would shout: 'Put a man theer Ernie.'

After this had been going on for some time Ernie lost his temper and rounding on his critic bellowed from the centre of the field: 'And how many bloody fielders does tha' reckon I've got?' There was a pause and his critic shouted back: 'Not bloody sufficient.'

This wasn't the idyllic image of English club cricket. This wasn't about the smell of the cut grass and the gentle sound of leather on willow. This was altogether more rugged. This was the whiff of cordite and the sound of men at war.

The rules were simple. Show no mercy, expect none in return; take no prisoners. I was a battle-scarred veteran aged 20 when I was joined at the wicket one afternoon by a 15-year-old wearing national health spectacles and a school cap. The fast bowler shouted to the stumper: 'What's this then does tha' reckon?' 'Looks like he's lost his mam,' said the keeper.

All this by way of introducing the lad to the joys of playing with the men. The bowler winked at his colleague, marched back to the end of his run-up quite convinced that this was a doddle. His first ball was just short and outside of the off stump whereupon he played the most beautiful back-foot shot between the bowler and mid-off. It was classic in execution, the left elbow as high and pointed as a church steeple.

The ball whistled past the bowler and rattled the sightscreen. The bowler gave me a wry smile. 'What's his name?' he asked. 'Boycott. Geoffrey Boycott,' I replied.

I don't even have to close my eye to see the young Boycott now, nor the unrazored Dickie Bird, nervous as a grasshopper, or the awesome Hubert Padgett, the best striker of a ball I ever saw at club level, or Graham Pearce, splay-footed, tireless, forever moaning but a marvellous bowler with the new ball. I remember fielding in the leg trap as Ellis Robinson bowled his off-spin and watching in awe as George Barnett at cover-point swooped and threw his flat whistling throw to the top of the stumps.

I remember the wind coming over the hill and the noise from Oakwell when the season overlapped. I remember learning the most beautiful of games in the best possible manner: on a decent wicket playing with men who knew.

If the time comes when there will no longer be a cricket pitch at Shaw Lane it will be a tragedy for the community and for Yorkshire cricket.

The Charity Commission says that the Shawlands Trust, which owns the ground, should get the best possible income for the charity. Is it not also the purpose of a local charity to be concerned about how best it can serve the people of the local community?

Anyone who has even the beginning of an idea about changing the use of the ground from anything other than a place where cricket is played should be aware that they are contemplating sacrilege. They should also know that the place is guarded by ghosts and that they are in danger of suffering the Curse of Parkinson.

They should tread softly. They are on hallowed ground.

---

16 DECEMBER 1991

JOHN ARLOTT: POET WITH A POLICEMAN'S EYE

Christopher Martin-Jenkins

Stephen Hearst, the Austrian-born Controller of BBC Radio 3 during the 1970s, used to say that cricket commentary had become 'an art form'. If true, it is John Arlott who made it so. It may be said without fear of contradiction that he was the best cricket commentator there has ever been.

He not only had every necessary attribute, but others which lifted him into a class of his own. His voice was attractive and distinctive. He spoke with effortless authority on cricket because, though he never played it to any high standard, he had immersed himself in its history, laws, customs and characters. He could instantly place any event or incident he was describing into its proper perspective. Above all, he saw the game with a poet's emotions and a policeman's observant eye, and he described all he saw by thoughts and words which seemed always measured, never hurried. His vocabulary was that of an immensely well-read mind and his sentiments and judgments were tempered by a rare wisdom and humanity.

The apt, colourful, picturesque, witty phrase seemed to come naturally to him, not least when the unexpected occurred. Examples pour back to the mind from BBC archives or personal memory: when Tufty Mann, of South Africa, dismissed George Mann of England, it was 'Mann's inhumanity to Mann'; when Bill Edrich bowled he was 'convinced one day he will burst on his way to the crease — as it is, he merely explodes when he gets there.'

He could make the unmemorable memorable — such as an inspection of the pitch after rain or umpires choosing a new ball when the first had gone out of shape – but if one remembers one particular day when his mastery was at its most compelling it was the June Saturday in 1975 when Clive Lloyd was dominating the Australian attack in the first World Cup final at Lord's.

Arlott, too, was in his high-summer prime: 'And they've scored off the last 15 balls: it's now difficult not only to bowl a maiden over but apparently to bowl a maiden ball ... Gilmour comes in, bowls, and Lloyd hits him high over hill and dale and mid-wicket, the stroke of a man knocking a thistle top off with a walking stick. No trouble at all, and it takes Lloyd to 99.

'Lloyd 99 and 189 for three. Umpire Bird's having a wonderful time, signalling everything in the world, including stop to traffic coming on from behind. But he lets Gilmour in now and he comes in, bowls, and Lloyd hits him into the covers – only half-fielded there on the cover boundary, and the century's up and the whole ground seething with West Indian delight.'

That same year, the first streaker, one Michael Angelo, invaded the field during the Lord's Test and Arlott took the novel event in his stride: 'Oh and a freaker, we've got a freaker down the wicket now. Not very shapely, and it's masculine, and I would think it's seen the last of its cricket for the day ... Many of course have done this on cold rugby grounds, but this chap has done it before 25,000 people, on a day when he doesn't even feel cold.

'And he's now being marched down in the final exhibition, past at least 8,000 people in the Mound Stand, some of whom, perhaps, have never seen anything quite like this before.'

... Arlott used to quote the C.L.R. James dictum 'what do they know of cricket who only cricket know?' It was greatly to his advantage that he knew much else besides, particularly about literature and wine. I remember feeling inadequate one day at lunch at his home in Alresford – he lived there, until his retirement, in a handsome old coaching inn, the Old Sun – when he mentioned in passing that *Tristram Shandy* was the finest novel in the English language.

I had not even read it. Nor had I any knowledge of the vintage red Burgundy he was consuming on that occasion with such voracious pleasure and in quantities which amazed me but which, far from fuzzing the mind or slurring the speech, merely seemed to make his brain more fertile and his tongue more agile.

He could, however, get quite earthy, even crude at a hotel dinner table late at night. There would be passion in his views on all sorts of matters, including politicians, old cricketers and the cricketing establishment, for whom, generally, he did not have much time. Happily, the feeling was not mutual: MCC, for example, made him an honorary life member.

They recognised, no doubt, that not only was his influence on cricket broadcasting great – he was to that medium what Sir Neville Cardus was to cricket writing, an artist rising above artisans – but so also was his influence on the game. Without ever needing to gild the lily, he was the vessel through which thousands of new devotees were first attracted to cricket. The Hampshire burr became the sound of summer, as Howard Marshall's sonorous tones had been before the Second World War and Brian Johnston's irrepressible good cheer has become in the years since. Arlott retired to Alderney in the Channel Islands at the end of the 1980 season. He died there on Saturday morning with his devoted third wife Pat and his two surviving sons by his side. A third son was killed driving a car his father had given him for his 21st birthday present and John never forgot him or forgave himself: he wore a black tie ever after. It was a true indication of his resolution and compassion.

He was also a prolific, skilful and civilised writer, as cricket correspondent of the *Guardian*, regular magazine contributor and the author, co-author or editor of some 80 books and booklets dating from 1943.

Three-quarters of them were about cricket. His poems reveal his great sensitivity. He wrote hymns too, though when once he went to a school to hear the first rendition of one of them, he complained afterwards to a friend that they had altered a line and 'ruined the sodding scansion'. Thus, characteristically, did he mix the spiritual and the vulgar.

Such extraordinary output helped to make him wealthy and allowed him to build up a priceless collection of first-edition books and vintage wines.

Born in Basingstoke in 1914 and educated there, he worked in local government, including a job as clerk in a mental hospital, before becoming a policeman, first as a copper on the beat then as a detective sergeant. In 1945 he joined the BBC as a producer in the literary department of External Services, succeeding George Orwell. There, in 1946, he found his forte, describing, at first only to overseas listeners, the matches of the Indian touring team. That Hampshire accent offended some, no doubt, but not the head of Outside Broadcasts, the pioneering Seymour de

Lotbiniere, who spotted the genius in the young poetry producer. 'For me,' said Arlott, 'it was a sort of seventh heaven to be watching cricket and talking about it and being paid for it.'

Of all the plaudits which came his way, including an OBE, he deemed the presidency of the Cricketers Association, the players' body, his greatest honour.

Two of his own lines, written to Andrew Young after reading his poems, might sum up his wonderful gift for illuminating description: So clear you see these timeless things That, like a bird, the vision sings.

---

25 APRIL 1992

Scyld Berry

At 11 o'clock on Thursday morning English cricket enters a new era. The Victorian period will be declared over. Ever since counties began to play one another in the mid-nineteenth century, enabled to do so by the railway's invention, their matches have almost invariably been scheduled for three days. Not any more.

Some will lament, others rejoice, as they do when other changes to England's historical legacy are mooted and made. The debate between proponents of three- and four-day cricket has been heated, like that between monarchists and republicans, or C of E traditionalists and the supporters of women priests.

In cricket, however, there is one basic agreement: that three-day championship games on covered pitches no longer work. Just as rugby and football grounds have become smaller, in the sense that players have grown fitter and faster, so is the temporal space of a three-day game now insufficient.

We bat first on a slow, bland pudding to score 340 for 5; you declare at 300 for 4; we make 260 for 4, thanks perhaps to some friendly bowling if time is short; you chase 300 in the last four hours, as if in a limited-overs match. Good riddance to contrived rubbish.

So there were two possibilities. Either the three-day format had to change, or the covering of pitches – and here we come to a generation gap among the debaters.

Those of longer memory can recall great games on pitches damaged by rain, not just on the 'stickies' of Brisbane, but the Hobbs–Sutcliffe partnership at a wet Oval in 1926 to regain the Ashes, one of the most heroic traditions – perhaps the most illustrious of all – in the history of English cricket. It would be wonderful to glimpse such cricket again; but I do not think the clock can be turned back.

The simple reason is that the faster the speed of a laterally moving ball, the more dangerous it is to a batsman. On that Oval 'sticky' the Australians used the leg-spin of Grimmett and Mailey and the off-spin of Richardson, which were both ineffective; opposed by great batsmanship, no doubt, but still ineffective. On a wet wicket the faster leg-cutter has to be more useful than the leg-break, the in-seaming ball more useful than the off-break.

All right then, say the traditionalists: let run-ups be exposed to rain as well so that seamers slip over and leave the bowling to spinners. But I have seen Malcolm Marshall, off a shorter run-up than that of Fred Titmus, bowl rockets up a batsman's nose; and Wasim Akram, say, could do the same, or Allan Donald.

If pitches and run-ups are uncovered, I fear injuries will rise above their present level, already close to unacceptably high: both to batsmen struck by unpredictable lifters and to pace bowlers risking their footholds in the name of professionalism.

Besides, English cricket in the late 1980s was often played on surfaces which were effectively uncovered. Sick of the declaration game, counties ordered pitches that were wet through human application of the hose as opposed to natural rain. The only player to prosper was the hack, seam-up medium-pacer, and the consequences to England's Test team in 1988 and 1989 were disastrous.

Batsmen were out of touch when they came to the truer surfaces of Test cricket, pace bowlers were used to seeing the ball move of its own accord, not making it do so by their own hand.

There was one alternative: creative groundsmanship. During the mid-'70s, at Grace Road in Leicester, Ray Illingworth had his groundsman produce the perfect pitch for three-day cricket. The middle was green and grassy for seamers, while each end was bare and dry on a spinner's length. In 1975, when Leicestershire won their sole championship, four of their spinners took 40 wickets or more in some brilliant, well-balanced cricket. Then the TCCB decreed that pitches thereafter should be evenly cut. They must have been half-cut themselves.

So four-day cricket it is, as a three-year experiment. Let us give it a chance because, on the evidence to date, more four-day games produce a definite result than three-day games – 65 per cent to 47 per cent over the last three seasons – and they are more likely to do so without declarations and 'joke' bowling.

The whole tone of our first-class game should become healthier too for the reduced amount of cricket. When last did a county eleven run down the pavilion steps and throw the ball about in sheer animal pleasure at being outdoors in the summer's air? Not beyond May, I would wager, for thereafter the aim is individual survival, perhaps a one-day trophy, and never mind the championship, unless you are Essex.

For too long – since one-day cricket took over – the essential attribute of the modern English cricketer has been stamina. Recently I asked Andy Moles and Tim Munton of Warwickshire, two of our keenest professionals, how many days a week they would ideally like to play. Both said five, as will be the average case from now on, not seven, as it often used to be, interspersed with late-night driving.

We should not try to ape the Australian game. England's domestic cricket must always have its tranquillity, its history and nostalgia, its echoes of pastoral (in England it is still a field, in Australia a ground). But our county cricket should become more vigorous and visibly enjoyed, more intent on excellence. To this end a four-day championship might just be as lucky as a four-leaf clover.

---

27 APRIL 1992

LOST FOR WORDS AS SUN SETS ON CRICKET OUTPOST

Tim Rice

I fear that I am better known these days for my love of cricket than for the odd words I have scribbled down in the tea interval for various musical extravaganzas.

Taxi-drivers ask me for my opinion of Ted Dexter rather than of Andrew Lloyd Webber, which is probably good news for both gentlemen (only joking, Andrew), and if my plane ever goes down I suspect I would get more lines in *The Cricketer* than in *The Stage*. I hope so, anyway.

It is thus ironic that a lyric-writing commitment prevented me from visiting Australia and/or New Zealand for the recent World Cup. Worse, my contract necessitated my being in Los Angeles, California, for the duration of the entire tournament.

Out there, even being D.R. Pringle's benefit chairman cuts little ice. I had never missed a World Cup before — the first three in England, the fourth in India and Pakistan — and I had made elaborate plans to be Down Under for the fifth by early 1988.

Unfortunately, the executives of Walt Disney Studios failed to consult the ICC or the ACB before planning, for March 1992, a series of crucial meetings concerning two animated feature films which required my services. As all sensitive, creative people will know, one has to follow the call of one's art when it is heard, particularly if you are being paid for it.

However, as news of the England team's triumphant progress filtered through to the cricketing desert of Sunset Boulevard and environs, and as their appearance in the final looked more and more likely, I could no longer remain content with news gathered via the previous day's *Daily Telegraph*.

I began a search for a couple of English pubs in the Santa Monica district who were alleged to have the relevant equipment but these transpired to be rather seedy joints permanently tuned into football, run by rather unsavoury characters whose demeanour did not encourage requests for channel-hopping.

I enlisted the assistance of P.H.L'E. (Hugh) Wilson, formerly of Somerset and Surrey, currently resident in Los Angeles. He had his ear to whatever ground there was as far as minority sports were concerned and eventually discovered that a group of enterprising cricket fans at the University of Southern California had booked a TV link-up with Melbourne for the final and were selling seats in the campus cinema for $15.

The timing for live viewing was much better than it would have been in England as LA is six hours ahead of Melbourne (although a whole day behind). We would therefore be watching from 8 p.m. onwards, a civilised kick-off time, with the prospect of an England win by about 4 a.m.

What we did not realise until the last minute was that the group of enterprising cricket lovers were Pakistani and, as we settled into our seats in front of a 15ft Graham Gooch, we were outnumbered 198 to two.

A backstage curry in the interval was included in our ticket price, but no drinks, even soft ones, allowed. The noise from the toss onwards was staggering. I was taken back to days in the Shed at Stamford Bridge in the early '60s, though even those vociferous louts would have struggled to have kept going at full tilt for the best part of eight hours.

The Southern California chapter of the Imran Khan fan club were not in the slightest bit loutish, but they were more than a match for Bill Lawry and Tony Greig with the TV sound at maximum volume.

The comments and chanting were primarily in Urdu but as any Urdu cricket commentary will reveal, English cricketing terms and expressions have been absorbed straight into the language without alteration. Consequently, the non-Urdu speaker hears 10 incomprehensible words followed by a phrase in perfect English such as 'over-rate' or 'slashing outside the off stump'. One easily got the gist of the Pakistani supporters' mood when words such as 'Alec Stewart' were followed a few moments later by 'outside edge' and what sounded like 'on your bike', but I might not have heard everything perfectly.

In between overs the satellite beamed us a strange variety of messages from the ether, clearly at random and beyond the control of any broadcaster. Sometimes we were treated to adverts for restaurants in Karachi, sometimes to snatches of a disembodied Henry Blofeld, sometimes to pastoral views of the Australian countryside. Sometimes just interference.

All the time one experienced that enjoyable sensation of straddling the globe, of moving great events to one's own patch, of bringing the mountain to Mohammed.

I had never watched any of the previous World Cup finals with such intent, or without a beer, barely missing a ball and certainly missing no incident.

I fear that in Melbourne the social aspects of the night might have distracted from the sporting and I am already making inquiries about tickets at USC for 1995.

30 APRIL 1992

LEICESTERSHIRE (342 AND 142—3) BEAT DURHAM (164 AND 318) BY SEVEN WICKETS

Christopher Martin-Jenkins

To the sound of mellow bells from the eleventh-century cathedral, Durham's first championship match finished at the University ground yesterday evening in a worthy and extremely hard-fought seven-wicket win by Leicestershire.

By then the point had been proved again that four-day matches on covered pitches, whatever their shortcomings, enabled county sides to achieve genuine results without artifice. The game took its toll: David Graveney has already gone in the hip – Paul Parker will lead them today at Worcester – and Ben Smith's twisted ankle is now in plaster.

Both sides, however, can derive some satisfaction from a match greatly enjoyed by the locals, not least the students who were able to watch free from a steep bank yesterday while Ian Botham worked off his irritation at having his new sponsored Mercedes broken into overnight by hammering potentially match-saving sixes into their midst.

Leicestershire were left with 141 to win after Parker and Botham had put on 178 in an admirable partnership which broke a record for Durham's fifth wicket which had stood since the First World War.

Happily it was a young(ish) English fast bowler who got Leicestershire back into the game, David Millns taking 5 for 12 in seven overs with the second new ball. Equally happily, Nigel Briers, their dedicated captain, took them to within 27 runs of victory.

Durham's second innings owed almost everything to Parker and Botham and it was the leonine all-rounder who led the way again in the morning, moving with irresistible strength to a century – only, incidentally, his 37th in first-class cricket – off a total of 98 balls.

Having given Parker more than three hours' start, he got to his hundred first, but Parker's contribution was in its wholly different way equally valuable. Parker made his first appearance for Cambridge two years after Botham first played for Somerset and he now has 43 hundreds, few more earnestly grafted for than this one.

Botham hit five 6s and seven 4s and the nearest poor Hepworth came to dismissing him with his off-breaks was when a spectator in a white raincoat held an excellent catch 20 yards beyond the square-leg boundary.

A stiff-armed straight drive off Mullally was a still more remarkable stroke. But the moment when he drilled his 105th ball to mid-off was the one in which Durham effectively lost. Durham, although beaten here, have the talent and must cling to the pioneering spirit.

---

21 MARCH 1993

ENGLAND IN SRI LANKA

Scyld Berry

After the rest day in the Test against England, Colombo's afternoon newspaper, *The Observer*, had for its back-page headline: '"Murali" and "Warnay" should deliver the goods'. It was a spot-on prediction in that Sri Lanka's two off-break bowlers certainly threw up something extraordinary in the course of their historic victory over England.

Perhaps dear reader is tired of hearing excuses about English defeats in Asia: it has been throat and tummy, the toss and slow turners, all winter long. But on this occasion I swear, by all the tea in Sri Lanka, that there was an extenuating circumstance. England lost because the home side's two main spinners made the ball turn and bounce by illicit means.

Try standing chest-on to an imaginary batsman, point your leading left foot to third man, grip the ball for an off-break and – minding the ceiling – bowl it from high above your head, above your left ear in fact. It will be an anatomical miracle if you can do it without bending your elbow.

This was the method of Muralidaran, a slender little Tamil boy from Kandy, the only Tamil in the team. While to the naked eye his action was just a whirl, on a slow-motion replay you could see his arm was no straighter than his bat was during that match-winning stand for the ninth wicket, when England's pace bowlers so relished the sight of him backing away that they forgot the existence of stumps.

After taping the action of the other spinner, Jayananda Warnaweera, who captains Galle on the south coast, England's players swore blind that he threw every one of his off-cutters. But an elbow which stays bent is not a throw, and it would be safer to say that it was his quicker off-cutter which broke the law: a spitting cobra of a ball which turned and reared at the midriff, as Spofforth and Trumble, J.T. Hearne and Macaulay must have done on old-time sticky-dogs.

Yet Muralidaran toured England in 1991 without being no-balled, and Warnaweera has been on several tours, according to a history of Galle not written by Caesar. And the longer they go on without being no-balled, the more difficult it will be for an umpire one day to stick his neck and arm out.

The answer must be that if having an ICC Match Referee is to be of any use whatsoever – a point as yet unproven – he must make it part of his brief to film, analyse and judge upon suspect bowling actions.

During the long gap which can be anticipated before the ICC does anything, the TCCB can tell the Sri Lankan Board behind the scenes that a three-Test series will not be granted until the throwing has been straightened out. So far England have been ungenerous in their dealings with Sri Lanka: don't give a country Test status if you are not ready to play regularly and help raise its standards. But now the TCCB should use a Test series as a bargaining counter.

---

14 JUNE 1993

ALL AUSTRALIA HAILS THE BALL FROM THE BOWLING BRADMAN

Peter Fitzsimons

It's been 10 days now. Ten days and here in Australia we still haven't come to the end of hearing about The Ball. You know the ball I mean. I'm talking, of course, about the first ball of Shane Warne's first over in the first Test of the Ashes at Old Trafford.

I'm talking about the one where, after that absurdly understated run-up by the fascinating blond bombshell, the ball left his wondrously talented arm to land with a telling bite of dust in front of the umpire at square leg before spinning fiercely to the left to rise up and buzz around Mike Gatting's head a couple of times, all the while singing Advance Australia Fair to further confuse him, before dropping right on to the stumps and knocking the bails back to their rightful position during any English innings – right on the ground at the base of the stumps. Howzat?

Not only out but something rather more than that. Let the Ashes series continue for another 1,000 years and men and women will still say that this, this, was the finest ball bowled – the Ball of the Millennium. To some, this was the ball that conclusively demonstrated beyond all measure that though Australia has laboured long, she has at last given birth to the bowling equivalent of Sir Donald Bradman.

Or something like that. Actually, it did seem a rather goodish sort of delivery. And it really was interesting the way Warne did it. Got the ball to spin, apparently, by dextrous use of his fingers and that is why it turned to the left like that to hit Gatting's wicket. Amazing.

More interestingly, though, has been the all but instant deification of Warne in Australia's popular imagination. In the time since he bowled it, his name and image has become apparent everywhere we look – on the television, in the newspapers, on T-shirts, on pages of magazines we see floating down the gutter. All of us now know more about That Ball and Shane Warne's life than Switzerland knows about snow. When I turn on my radio – 'and in more news from the Australian team in England, Shane Warne ...' – he's there too.

You get the drift. The question is why? Why such an immediate and overwhelming reaction? Part of it is surely that, just as nature abhors a vacuum, so too does a sporting nation like Australia hate to be without a real sporting hero on which to fasten its immense affection. Fact is, the country has been a bit light on international sports heroes of late.

Marathon runner Robert de Castella has retired, golfer Greg Norman seems lately more American than Australian, America's Cup supremo Alan Bond has gone bankrupt and our tennis players seem only briefly to thrash around on the court in Grand Slam events before being ushered to the exit without so much as a 'thanks for coming'.

Enter, stage left, Shane Warne. All hail the conquering hero in a sports contest that is, after all, the one we hold dearest to our hearts. Warne's sudden elevation may be further explained by the fact that he has achieved great things in an old and mystical area of cricketing skill which we all thought had gone down with Atlantis. Many of us have heard about 'googlies', 'wrong-uns' and 'slippers' all our lives without ever quite knowing what they were – quite simply because no one was doing them any more.

Now, praise the Lord and pass the binoculars, an ancient art has been revived – an art which makes all other cricketing skills appear crass by comparison. As one local writer put it, rather poetically, 'leg-spinners are the game's magicians, the fly fisherman in a world where others get their catch by tossing a stick of dynamite into a stocked dam.'

And to think we used to worship at the altar of such unsubtle fast-bowling barbarians as Dennis Lillee and Jeff Thomson makes us all wonder what on earth we were thinking of.

Now, in Warne, we finally have a worthy heir to the three Australian spin greats of the past, the ones our fathers and grandfathers have often raved about – Bill O'Reilly, Clarrie Grimmett and Richie Benaud. Of course, after That Ball, there can be no doubting that Warne is far and away the greatest of them all and that's one in the eye for our fathers, but as a minor matter of interest each of those three past greats also used to hurl down their own Ball of the Century.

As a case in point, the Australian cricket writer, Phillip Verriman, last week dug up the account of a ball delivered by O'Reilly during the 1938 Test series in England which turned the Test match on its own.

The account was by the British writer, Ralph Barker, and he detailed how Joe Hardstaff, the England batsman, had been unwise enough to belt O'Reilly to the boundary for two fours in a row – the second off a no-ball – and how O'Reilly had apparently been so angry he could barely raise spit.

'With dramatic emphasis,' Barker wrote, 'O'Reilly paced out his run again, gesticulated fiercely, as though the call of a no-ball constituted a personal outrage, and thundered up to the wicket to bowl the next ball. Like the girl in the novelette, O'Reilly was never more thrilling to watch than when he was angry. This time, he was livid with rage.

'No one on the ground had seen a ball like it. It was the greatest ball O'Reilly ever bowled. It was not only fast, really fast, it was a vicious leg-break. Hardstaff sparred at it in bewildered fashion, and the ball just took the top of the off-bail.'

Sounds just a touch like Warne's ball doesn't it? OK, so it didn't manage to sing the Australian national anthem as it hit, but still it wasn't bad.

2 AUGUST 1993

Michael Parkinson

Prologue tapes, secretly recorded by a group of MCC members known as the Archangel Gower Group, have been made available to the *Daily Telegraph*. They throw new light on the selection of Michael Atherton as captain of England.

The meeting lasted two and a half hours, which is the time it takes to boil 50 three-minute eggs, or, looking at it another way, about 15 minutes less than required by the Australian team to bowl out England.

CAST

DEXTER: Edward Dexter, chairman of selectors, nicknamed Lord Ted (no one can remember why). Renaissance Man: racehorse owner, whippet breeder, Hell's Angel, expert on pollution on Indian sub-continent and the effect of astrology on Test matches. Is not like other men. One observer close to the TCCB once said: 'He looks like the sort of man who keeps a pet haddock in the bath.'

WHEATLEY: Ossie Wheatley, chairman of the TCCB Cricket Committee. Called 'Ossie' as an abbreviation of his christian name 'Ossified'. Little is known about Wheatley except that he objects to England captains fraternising with barmaids. He played for Glamorgan and is generally thought to be the reason why the England selectors stopped going down there in search of talent.

SMITH: A.C. Smith, chief executive of the TCCB. His achievements include handing over the England team to a brewery, coloured clothing on Sundays, painted logos on our cricket grounds, appointing Keith Fletcher, retaining Dexter. Capped six times, a fact thought by many to be the first manifestation of the England selectors losing their grip.

FLETCHER: Keith Fletcher, England manager. Essex man much loved in all parts of the North Country, particularly Leeds. Doesn't say much but when he does we are generally thankful for his reticence. His record as a leader of men is only equalled by a few Italian generals in Second World War. His appointment means that the one member of the current Essex squad not recognised by England is the physiotherapist.

STEWART: Micky Stewart, former manager of the England team now in charge of cricket coaching. Father of Alec Stewart, vice-captain of England and candidate for the captaincy. His relationship with his son is well known to all except Dexter, as will soon become apparent. Alec Stewart starts the meeting by leading the committee through a 20-minute session of squat-thrusts and push-ups.

THE ACTION

DEXTER: Gentlemen, your nominations for the next captain of Tetley's, er ... sorry, I mean England.

FLETCHER: Righto guv. What abart Pringle, Foster, Childs, Such, Hussain, Stephenson, Prichard, Topley, Ilott, Garnham, Salim Malik and Agatha Backcracker?

DEXTER: Who?

FLETCHER: She's our physiotherapist.

STEWART: My nominations are Alec Stewart, Rod Stewart, James Stewart, Jackie Stewart or Stewart Grainger.

DEXTER: I've seen them all play except Alec Stewart. Who's he?

STEWART (a trifle angrily): He's our wicket-keeper, one of our best batsmen and my son.

DEXTER (in a huff): Your son? We can't have that. The Press will accuse us of necrophilia. Leave the room immediately.

At this point the tape becomes somewhat confusing as voices clash. Stewart can be heard protesting his innocence as he is led away by two brewery bouncers provided by the sponsors to guard Dexter's pet haddock while he is on England duty.

DEXTER: Let's press on gentlemen, as I hope to get to the evening meeting at Fontwell.

WHEATLEY: Steady on. We can't be seen to be rushing things. If we get this matter over in 10 minutes people will be wondering why it takes five of us to pick an England captain. My nomination for the next captain of England is Graham Gooch.

DEXTER: But he's just resigned.

WHEATLEY: From what?

DEXTER: The England job.

WHEATLEY: How long has he had that?

DEXTER: About three years. I'm amazed you didn't know.

WHEATLEY: It takes a long time for news to reach Glamorgan.

SMITH: Personally, I think the next England captain should be good looking, charming, tactically astute, popular with the public, comfortable with the media and a Test player of proven quality. Someone like David Gower. I nominate the chairman of Tetley's.

DEXTER: For God's sake, don't mention the name Gower. Before you know where you are they'll have hired the Albert Hall for a protest meeting.

To sum up, gentlemen, let me nominate who I take to be the main contenders from the list of names before us. As I see it, the choice is between Agatha Backcracker, Salim Malik, Stewart Grainger and the chairman of Tetley's.

However, my own nomination and the man I think most suitable for the job is young Ethelred.

CHORUS: Who?

DEXTER: You know, the tall lad from Lancashire who opens for us.

CHORUS: Atherton.

DEXTER: That's the bloke. So it's unanimous. Well done. Get him on the phone and tell him that all he has to do to make the job his own is thrash the Aussies in the next two Tests and then beat the Windies.

WHEATLEY: What's he like this Atherton?

DEXTER: Don't know. Never spoken to him.

SMITH: Speaking on behalf of the TCCB, does he like Tetley's?

WHEATLEY: I hope he doesn't fancy barmaids.

FLETCHER: Cor, swipe me wiv a jellied eel. I don't like Lancashire. It's too far away from darn sarf and they speak funny up there.

WHEATLEY: Now we have a new captain, can I ask if you have thought about what you might do, Ted?

DEXTER: Well, there's Newmarket coming up, a whippet breeders' convention in Solihull I must go to, a motorcycle scramble in Nuneaton and a rally of Hell's Angels at Stonehenge. Then there's the annual meeting of the Flat Earth Society and, of course, the Ryder Cup.

WHEATLEY: I was thinking about cricket.

DEXTER: Oh that. Well, there's a trip to the West Indies coming up. I think I'll find a nice hotel with a golf course and watch it on telly.

FLETCHER: So you are not going to resign, guv?

DEXTER: Why should I?

FLETCHER: Some blokes fink there are others who might do the job better.

DEXTER: Like who?

FLETCHER: Well, one who got a mention was Geoffrey Boycott.

At this point there is the sound of bodies crashing to the floor as if in a swoon. Eyewitnesses later confirmed to the *Daily Telegraph* that at the mention of Boycott's name Dexter, Wheatley and Smith swooned away with a savage attack of the vapours.

They were revived by a team of paramedics skilled in treating Boycott Syndrome, which is the name given to the trauma afflicting members of the TCCB when they hear his name.

At this point Stewart re-enters the room having escaped his minders, who are taking Dexter's pet haddock for a walk.

STEWART: I've got some new names for the captain. How about Payne Stewart, Andy Stewart, Donald Ogden Stewart, Paul Stewart, Dave Stewart, Stewart of the Glens, Stewart of Arabia ...

He goes on to list many more members of the Stewart family before reading the complete list of Stewarts in the London telephone directory. The first tape runs out with Stewart reciting: 'Yancey Stewart, Yozza Stewart, Zacharias Stewart, Zebedee Stewart ...'

NEXT WEEK: Part two of the Dextergate Tapes. More sensational revelations as Dexter's top lip moves for the first time, Fletcher is persuaded to cross the Severn Bridge, Wheatley bans barmaids at Lord's, Stewart nominates all the Stewarts listed in the Glasgow telephone directory, Smith is voted Landlord of the Year by the Brewers' Federation of Great Britain, and Dexter's haddock is made an honorary member of the MCC, the first time a fish has been granted the honour. PLUS: Was an England selector the 'Headless Man' in the Duchess of Argyll case?

---

19 NOVEMBER 1993

Mark Nicholas

The telephone rang last Friday and immediately I knew the voice. My heart missed a beat. His voice is distinctive but often rambling and vague: here it was clear and quite certain. 'To be honest,' he summarised, 'I've had enough.'

And that was that, the end of David Gower's amazing career, a career in which he had never compromised, had always been himself: no posing, no con and few tantrums. Such ordinariness confused people who searched for more, but he did not pay homage to the ideals of others.

Throughout, he conducted himself in a quiet, ambassadorial manner and spiced it with a dry, sardonic wit. When they wanted histrionics, he was flip; when they wanted grand speeches he chose wry observations. And now it has all gone, given away when there was plenty left – only no one that mattered knew how to find it.

As a batsman he was an artist and an author, a poet and a musician. He brought creativity and showbiz to his game and attracted actors, writers and rock stars who, knowing the demands of the great stage, were dazzled by his elegance and ease. Not since Greg Chappell and Majid Khan, Barry Richards and Tom Graveney, has the old game been so comfy on the eye. Rarely has there been such uncommon, near-miraculous timing.

The greatest tribute to his play came from Sir Richard Hadlee, who knew a thing or two, and said: 'He was a key destructive player ... a very tough competitor and bloody difficult to get out.' Gower will have enjoyed that, what with the endless accusations of indifference. After all, he would muse when criticised, where did those 8,231 Test runs come from? So, why on earth was he so trampled on when he trampled on so few? When he first lost the England captaincy the chairman of selectors, Peter May, mumbled only: 'It's time for a change. Aren't all decisions difficult?' and left it at that. After Ted Dexter sacked him news leaked that he had not been the first choice anyway.

In recent years nobody in a position of power has found it easy to cope with the Gower Thing. So dignified is his response to retribution that guilt overcomes the executioner.

Yet he has frustrated, too, and annoyed with his cussedness. By the end of last season he could barely bring himself to turn up for Hampshire's Sunday league matches, so great was his loathing of them. He should have been able to live with them knowing their importance to the county's following. He should not have played that ridiculous stroke before lunch in Adelaide knowing Graham Gooch's insistence on pragmatism. He should not have been caught at cover when, in the last championship game before the selectors chose the touring party to India, Gooch bowled a gentle, wide half-volley to a ring of six defending fielders on the off-side. It was bait and the fish bit.

Here, I think, is David Gower's greatest flaw: an inability to under-stand when he has disappointed other people. It comes from a complete lack of ego, which is at once his most endearing trait and his most infuriating. If Gower scored a delicious two-hour hundred and you glow in appreciation, he would probably register surprise that you had watched it at all (in his four summers at Hampshire I missed no more than five minutes of his batting, so thrilling was its potential).

Once, in a pre-season match, he was fielding on the mid-wicket fence and he did not bother to save a boundary for he was busy chatting with a friend.

Later he did not bother to bat for long, having a thoughtless swipe at a straightish ball. On both occasions the silence of his colleagues told the story. Later we hauled him in, questioning his motives and telling him that he was playing cricket with young men who aspired to all he had achieved, that he was in a true sense their hero. He was quite taken aback by such an idea and by the thought that anyone cared for a practice match at all. There was no malice in his reply, nor is there in any of his excesses.

He took the criticism gamely and vowed to do better, but found it difficult to do so, until the occasion warranted it. Gooch, who was leading England well, wanted a fuller, more apparent commitment (Gower's least favourite word – 'How have I survived in 117 Tests without this wretched commitment?'), a nine-to-five approach and Gower, disappointingly, would not give it.

THIS is why he did not tour India, this and the dodgy argument about the over-35s. England had toured successfully without Gower the previous winter, beating New Zealand and reaching the final of the World Cup, and the selectors probably felt that his eccentricities were easier to handle at home.

A year ago, before the tour was underway, I had dinner with two former England cricketers and three enthusiastic amateurs – friends of Gower who knew their cricket. The amateurs were incensed at his omission and would vote for the rebel group. Strangely the cricketers were not so sure, thinking that Gower might have been (a) a talent on the wane and (b) a pea out of its pod.

The real crime was not selecting him last summer when Shane Warne was taking wickets with his trickery and Merv Hughes with his personality. Gower did not take much interest in the melodramatics of a bowler and had comfortably repelled Hughes before. He also knew something of leg-spin, having countered Abdul Qadir in his pomp. Did the selectors know, I wonder, that the three most successful West

Indian batsmen against the Australians last winter were the left-handers Lara, Arthurton and Adams? When Hampshire played Australia, Border did not select Warne saying: 'I don't want Smithy to see too much of him, or for that matter David, who even your selectors are bound to pick soon.'

But still he was left forlorn, unable to sense a mending of the ways and a further opportunity. He could take no more of the humdrum and he did not want his mates wondering, as he frequently did, why he bothered. He is a good fellow to be around, with his brainy banter and barmy bonhomie, and he was special at team meetings, where his communications skills were exercised. Phil Edmonds said that when Gower was captain of England he gave the smartest team talks of all.

The wild rumour, suggested by Edmonds in this paper, that Gower was cornered into retirement by Hampshire's insistence that he needed pre-season preparation, is untrue. There was no negotiation on the topic: he simply had to decide whether he would play for England again and, if not, whether he would do justice to his county contract. It took him a fortnight to decide on the name Alexandra for his daughter, so little wonder it took some time to make this other important decision. It will not be long before Alexandra looks to mother him – he is that sort – and we have all tried to do so in our different ways.

Hampshire have accommodated his whims and distractions, and he has appreciated their patience. Our players will miss him dearly, for he brought sanity and wisdom to the strange, closeted world of the county dressing room.

For my own part, I was overjoyed to sign him, but at times I have torn at my hair through his insouciance. I will, I know, cry out for his batting, which was littered with genius, and for his company at the dinner table when an away trip holds no charms.

His first boss, Mike Turner, best summed it all up: 'A free spirit has been frozen out and the game is the loser.' Cricket needs the style and expression of David Gower. It will be much less rich without him.

----

18 APRIL 1994

PARALLELS OF PERFECTION

Simon Hughes

It is two weeks since the publication of the 1994 *Wisden Cricketers' Almanac*, and already its premier record table is out of date. The name at the top of the list of highest individual Test match innings should read B.C. Lara and not G. St A. Sobers. There are several parallels between the two innings.

Both were made by young left-handers with an immense career ahead of them. Both spanned three days' play in the blistering heat of the West Indies where weary bowlers finish up running in as if they are wading through mud.

Gary Sobers set the record for the highest individual Test innings at the age of 21 when he made 365 against Pakistan in Kingston, Jamaica, in 1958. He never thought that feat would be broken, even saying so recently in the pavilion named after him at the Bridgetown Oval.

'The modern era of limited-overs cricket produces batsmen who don't really have the ability to bat a long time,' he pointed out. Sobers batted 10 hours for his 365 not out, Lara in fact was at the wicket for just over 12 for his 375 though he only faced 535 balls. What took the time was his first 10 runs (more than an hour) and his last 20 (50 minutes). In between, incredibly, he scored at nearly a run a ball.

During his innings 36 years ago, Sobers was not concerned about records, believing that he could just carry on batting until the West Indies captain of the day, Gerry Alexander, decided to declare. Lara clearly felt the same, never curtailing his relentless assault until within sniffing distance of his target. He slept fitfully overnight, which was only to be expected, so did Sobers – 228 not out on the third evening.

It did not affect either of them, though. They were so high on adrenalin and did not notice their tiredness, nor the passage of time. Graeme Hick remembers being in a similar state during his 405 not out at Taunton in 1988. 'Milestones didn't really dawn on me, neither did the length of time I'd batted. I just found the whole innings so exciting there was no chance to feel tired.'

Wasn't it tempting to hare down the wicket and have a big swing just once in the 300s? 'Not at all. There were so many gaps and I was seeing the ball so big I didn't need to take chances. Run making was easy at that time.' Those were the days.

Sobers passed Hanif Mohammad's 337 with a push to leg, and Hanif, who was fielding at cover came up to shake his hand. Later, when Sobers had reached 363, the Pakistan captain asked Hanif to bowl. Later that year Hanif was run out going for his 500th run – still a first-class record.

Hanif wanted to bowl left-handed. 'You can bowl with both hands if you like,' Sobers remembers saying. And duly passed Len Hutton's 364. Like he has been at many of Lara's innings, Sobers was in the West Indies dressing room yesterday to share the moment, and came on to the field immediately afterwards, to embrace him, accompanied by a stampede of supporters, and 30 or so helpless police.

'I think Brian Lara was the only person playing who could have broken my record.' he said. 'If you watch him play you never see him use his pad, he hits the ball with the bat, and that's the way the game should be played.' All the England fielders also converged on Lara to congratulate him – it was the closest many of them had been to him for at least two days of play.

So what is it about left-handers? Their union boasts the two highest Test innings of all time and the most Test runs by one player (Allan Border). Well, the truth is, unless the ball swings, or spins extravagantly, they are much harder to bowl at.

Most deliveries projected from right arm over the wicket have to pitch outside the leg stump to hit the wicket, anything pitching on off-stump gives them width to work with because of the natural angle of the bowler's trajectory.

Added to that, left-handers are not as common (except in the current West Indies middle order) so the whole discipline of containing them is less familiar. Ironically, Chris Lewis chose the position of 570 for four to demonstrate the art of restricting left-handers, finding pace, swing, and lift to obstruct Lara's passage.

The crowd gasped as twice his inside edge was passed but somehow the ball missed the wicket, almost as if it was not there. Clearly this was meant to be, and evoked memories, of a time when John Emburey captained Middlesex during a particularly high-scoring match at Headingley. At a tactical talk in the lunch interval he advised us to 'bowl for run-outs'.

Australia obviously received the same message when they prised out Lara this way for a mere 277 in Sydney, but no one else has cottoned on. So England's loss is Warwickshire's gain. Good luck county bowlers this summer – I'm glad I'm not among you.

---

7 JUNE 1994

GENIUS AT WORK IN PHENOMENAL FEAT

Christopher Martin-Jenkins

Word had seeped through the Trent Bridge press box long before England had completed their innings victory against New Zealand. Brian Lara was breaking records again and this time it might be something really special.

In the time that it took me to get from Nottingham to Birmingham Lara's score moved from 315 to 429. On the way, Radio Five Live was transmitting, movingly, the events commemorating D-Day from the beaches of Normandy. They put the significance of what was happening at Edgbaston into perspective, but 6 June, nonetheless, will be a never-to-be-forgotten date in cricket's history, too.

It was not as hot as it had been in Antigua, seven weeks before, when Lara passed Sir Gary Sobers's Test record; nor were the circumstances as demanding – the game was destined to be drawn from the moment he resumed this innings at 111 not out – as they had been in the early stages of the fifth Test against England when he had begun by rescuing the West Indies from a start of 12 for 2. Nevertheless, this was phenomenal batting by an imperishable genius.

I was in time to see him go past Bill Ponsford (437), B.B. Nimbalkar (443) and Don Bradman, whose 452 not out, along with Len Hutton's 364 were the best-known records of my schooldays.

By now the premier Durham bowlers had retired to the shadows of the outfield, though the fielding remained, surprisingly, admirably keen. They must all have been tired, but none more so, surely than Lara. Yet when he was 459, a drive to extra cover off Phil Bainbridge failed for once to reach the extra-cover boundary and Lara ran four instead. His fitness these amazing last few weeks has been as remarkable as his appetite for runs.

Finally, at half-past five, a ball after he had been hit on the head, changing his mind about hooking at a 'bouncer' from John Morris, he crashed his 62nd four, between mid-off and extra cover, to claim the record that has pride of place as the first in *Wisden*. One of the first to pay tribute was Hanif Mohammad, whose world record he broke: 'He's very short and many other short Test players have scored lots of runs, like me, Sir Don Bradman and Sir Len Hutton.'

Denis Compton said: 'I don't know how he does it. He's obviously a very great young player who is going to keep on breaking records. But why talk about records? He's quite simply a great player, one of the best ever. He's got things that us boys never had.'

---

22 FEBRUARY 1995

INDIA IS RAPIDLY LOSING ITS ABILITY TO FRUSTRATE

Simon Hughes

In the Mary Whitehouse League of complaints, some of England's cricket teams touring India must be in the top division. At various times in the last 20 years they have blamed the heat, the dust, the food, the hotels, the pollution and, of course, the umpires for their poor performances.

With the 1996 World Cup in India, Pakistan and Sri Lanka just around the corner, it is heartening to report that visiting India today is not a harrowing experience. The country is still riddled with petty bureaucracy (which we taught them) and getting through official channels can take an age. Haggling is still the norm for everything from taxi fares to telephone charges, and auto rickshaw rides are like grand prix arcade games.

In Dhaka, Bangladesh's capital, where England A play their second one-day international today, the rickshaw occupied by Richard Stemp and Keith Piper was jolted off the road by an errant bus.

There have been improvements for touring cricketers. Within India, the players' mountain of luggage used to be hauled by road, often affecting major matches. In 1984 Australia's luggage lorry had an accident en route to Jamshedpur and 30,000 people in the ground were told the start was delayed because of damp. When the lorry eventually turned up, the heavens opened and the match was abandoned.

By the time Graham Gooch's tour arrived in 1992–3, improvements had been made, and the baggage was transported mostly by air. The best Indian hotels are spectacular. The England A team have been surprised by the palatial marble foyers, the health clubs, the multi-cuisine restaurants and the satellite TV stations showing live Five Nations rugby. The players' hotels on the county circuit are tacky in comparison.

Water in most hotels is drinkable, their ice for drinks made with sterilised water. Bottled water is still advisable elsewhere. The lunch-spread at grounds – pasta, curries, soups, barbecued chicken and nan bread cooked at the table – satisfied even the faddiest of eaters. England A's emergency supplies of tinned tuna and Marks & Spencers flapjacks have remained unopened.

When it comes to drinking, the high glycerine content in Indian beer means it is better shaken up and showered over your successful teammates than drunk, but European beer is freely available at various American-style bars in Bangalore and Bombay.

A large rat scuttled across the dressing room in Delhi and someone shouted 'quick, jump on it,' but an official reassured everyone saying: 'Don't worry, it's one of our members.' It was an isolated incident, though. Flying cockroaches, humming about like miniature Messerschmitts, seem to have been virtually exterminated, and electric insect 'zappers' are installed in most bedrooms and restaurants.

Best of all, you are less likely to be given out for a rash shot than you once were. Since 1990, better incentives have prompted 28 former first-class players to join the Indian umpires list, and 10 former Test players recently sat the registration exams and practical. Six, including Bishen Bedi, failed.

The umpires are taking a hard line against players – Sanjay Manjrekar was sent to an imaginary sin-bin for showing dissent last month – and suffer less from an irresistible urge to raise their index finger when the clamour round the bat reaches fever pitch.

… We'll have to find another country to complain about.

13 MAY 1995

SECOND DAY OF FOUR: GLOUCS 388 FOR 3 V. NOTTS

Christopher Martin-Jenkins

Bristol

The groundsman's dog was leaping for joy and stolid Gloucestershire folk were blinking at the scoreboard in amazement. 100 for no wicket, it read at lunchtime; 230 for none at tea; 388 for 3 at the close.

In the cosy tea-room, the members were chatting away merrily. Those who arrived at the ground after work must have thought, resigned as recently they have become to disappointment, that it was Nottinghamshire batting. Emphatically, however, it was not. Nottinghamshire, sans Chris Lewis and with Chris Cairns unable to bowl, were actually bowling rather ordinarily and fielding without a suspicion of fervour, none more downbeat than their captain and overseas player.

The latter could barely bring himself to take his hands out of his pockets all day. It is not as if it is exactly tropical in Dunedin or Wellington. When your bowling is depleted and the pitch is as good as this one – true and not without life – it is actually the time to fling yourself at everything, as Derek Randall, for one, would certainly have done. Hang-dog body language seldom deceives, and the catches duly went down.

Let me, however, take no credit away from Dean Hodgson and Tony Wright, whose felicitous and attractive partnership of 361 is a record for the county's first wicket. It may not lead to victory in what, after the first day washout, is likely to become an old-fashioned declaration match, but it was symptomatic of the fact that the season at Bristol has opened in a more optimistic atmosphere than any for a long time.

There have been four wins out of four in the Benson and Hedges, and though they lost their opening Britannic match, it was after making Surrey follow on, which was a trifle freakish. No more so, perhaps, than this splendid opening partnership, which became the highest by a Gloucestershire opening pair in the championship when it reached 316.

It surpassed the one scored against Sussex at Hove in 1968 by Arthur Milton and one David Green, a regular inhabitant of these columns.

One half expected him to walk out to the middle with a pint for both heroes.

Green made 233 on that occasion on his way to 2,137 runs in the season and such was the splendour with which 'Billy' Wright struck his pulls and straight drives after reaching his 14th first-class hundred in just under four hours, it is possible to envisage this becoming his best season, too.

He surpassed his previous highest score, 184 here against Leicestershire last season, and when finally he clipped Andy Pick off his toes to deep square-leg, he had plundered 17 4s and four 6s.

The stand had ended three overs earlier, after six hours, when Hodgson was finally caught at long-off after 365 minutes. He had hit 15 fours and his driving, especially, had been pleasing to the eye, and admirably straight, which was true of the bowling only in fits and starts.

---

24 JULY 1995

HAROLD LARWOOD: THE MASTER PAID A HEAVY PRICE FOR HIS GREATNESS

Michael Parkinson

Long before I ever met him I knew him well. My father told me he was the greatest fast bowler that ever drew breath and paid him the ultimate compliment of hero worship by copying his run to the wicket. Jack Fingleton, who also knew what he was talking about, said he was the best fast bowler he ever faced. He was, said Fingo, 'the master'.

Harold Larwood was a giant in my imagination, a legendary figure whose bowling frightened the greatest batsman there has ever been (and a few more besides) and in doing so created a political brouhaha of such resonance it echoes still, 60 years on.

When I first saw him standing outside a Sydney restaurant in 1979, he looked like one of the miners who would loiter around the pub on Sunday mornings waiting for the doors to open at mid-day.

He seemed uncomfortable in his suit as if it was his Sunday best, his trilby hat was at a jaunty angle and he was smoking a cigarette which he cupped in the palm of his hand as if shielding it from a wind.

He was medium height with good shoulders and the strong, square hands of someone who had done some shovelling in his life as well as bowling. My father, in heaven at the time, would have been delighted with my impression that he and his great hero were peas from the same pod.

On the other hand, I had expected something altogether more substantial, someone more in keeping with the image I had of a man who terrorised opponents and whose fearsome reputation was such that at one moment in time governments were in thrall as he ran in to bowl.

In all of sport there never was a story to match the Bodyline saga. At its heart was the ultimate sporting challenge: a contest between the two greatest players in the world. In 1932–3, Donald Bradman was in his prime, the finest batsman of his generation, or any other before or since. Harold Larwood was also in his pomp, the fastest bowler in the world and about to prove himself the most lethal and unerring there has ever been.

The impresario of this world title contest was Douglas Jardine, the captain of England, patrician, implacable and a terrible snob who treated Australians with a contempt he never bothered to conceal. The story that unfolded around these three characters had everything except sex and a happy ending.

I was tempted to say it would have made a marvellous soap for television, except one was produced and a right mess they made of it. The controversy stirred by bodyline pursued Harold Larwood all his days. It changed him from a cricketer into a hunted man who hid away in a sweet shop in Blackpool before being persuaded by Jack Fingleton to seek a new life in Australia, where he ended his days surrounded by his large family in suburban Sydney amid the accents that once denounced him as the devil.

It was Jack Fingleton and Keith Miller who arranged my meeting with Harold; Bill O'Reilly was there too; and Arthur Norris and Ray Lindwall, so you could say I was in the best of company. There were so many questions I wanted to ask but dare not unless I turned what was a friendly lunch into a press conference. In any case, in that company I was superfluous to requirements except as a witness to what happened.

We sat at a round table on a spring day in Sydney. We all drank wine except Harold who said he was a beer man. 'Always had a pint when I was bowling,' he said. 'We used to sneak it on with the soft drinks. A pint for me and one for Bill Voce. You must put back what you sweat out,' he said.

'I hope you weren't drunk when you bowled at me,' said Jack Fingleton. 'I didn't need any inspiration to get you out,' Harold Larwood replied. Jack said of all the bowlers he faced Larwood was the fastest and had the best control. 'He was a very great bowler. Used to skid the bouncer. Throat ball,' said Jack.

Larwood took the compliment and said: 'You might not have been the best batsman I bowled against but you were certainly the bravest. I could hit you all right but you wouldn't go down. You weren't frightened, not like one or two I could mention but won't,' he said.

Tiger O'Reilly said he was once sent out to bat against Harold when the ball was flying about, having been instructed by his skipper to stay at the crease at all costs. He was endeavouring to follow these instructions and was halfway through his back-lift when Larwood bowled him a ball he sensed but did not see. 'I felt the draught as it went by and heard it hit Duckworth's gloves,' said Tiger. Being a sensible fellow he decided on a new method which, as he described it, involved his standing alongside the square leg umpire with his bat stretched towards the stumps.

'It was from this position', said Tiger, 'I was perfectly placed to observe a most extraordinary occurrence. Larwood bowled me a ball of such pace and ferocity that it struck the off bail and reduced it to a small pile of sawdust.' When I first told this story a reader wrote to say that what O'Reilly claimed was clearly impossible. I wrote back informing the reader that O'Reilly was Irish and heard nothing more on the matter.

Jack Fingleton told Harold Larwood: 'You didn't need to bowl Bodyline. You were a good enough bowler to get anyone out by normal methods.' It was the first time during our luncheon that anyone had mentioned 'Bodyline'. Until then, the word had ticked away in a corner of the room like an unexploded bomb. Harold smiled. 'I was merely following the instructions of my captain,' he said. He produced from his jacket pocket a yellow duster and unfolded it to reveal a silver ash tray. The inscription said: 'To a great bowler from a grateful captain. D.R. Jardine'. The lettering was faint from nearly 50 years of spit and polish.

Jardine was the Field Marshal of bodyline, Larwood his secret weapon. Jardine was the strategist, Jardine the assassin. I think it wrong to portray Larwood as the unwitting accomplice as some have done. It underestimates his strength of character, denies his intelligence and, most of all, does not take into account his determination to show Bradman and the rest of the Aussies who the boss really was.

But whereas Jardine fully understood the consequences of what he planned, Larwood was never likely to begin to fathom the undercurrents of intrigue created by his captain's strategy. They did for him in the end.

At our lunch, Harold recalled the day in 1933 when an Australian supporter accosted him and said: 'I hope you never play cricket again.' Harold Larwood replied: 'How dare you say that when cricket is my life, my job, my livelihood.' It wasn't too long before his critic's wish was granted and Harold Larwood, who thought he had been playing cricket for a living, wondered if he might have been mistaken.

After Jardine's team had thrashed the Australians, Harold Larwood, who was injured, went home ahead of the main party. He told me he realised he was to be made the scapegoat when he arrived in London to be confronted by a mob of journalists without any help from the MCC, who left him to his own devices.

Before reaching London, after his ship had docked in France, Larwood had been joined by his Nottinghamshire captain, A.W. Carr, who he took to be his official escort. Carr quizzed him about events in Australia which Larwood answered candidly as he would to his skipper. It was only when they arrived in London and Harold found himself on his own that he realised Carr had been working for a newspaper.

Harold said he arrived in Nottingham by train in angry mood in the early hours of the morning, to be greeted with brass band and a hero's welcome. Ordinary cricket lovers had no time for the political arguments taking place between the governments of Great Britain and Australia. All they cared about was England bringing home the Ashes and, as far as they were concerned, the man who did the job was Harold Larwood.

He enjoyed his celebrity for a while and capitalised on it. There was talk of making a movie and he went to Gamages store in London for a week to demonstrate bodyline bowling to an admiring public. For the week of personal appearances he earned five times more than he was paid for the entire tour of Australia.

He told us that the worst moment came when he was asked to apologise for the way he had bowled. He refused. 'I had nothing to be ashamed about,' he said. He never played for England again and he had only a few more seasons with Notts. Disenchanted, he bought a shop in

Blackpool and didn't even put his name above the door in case it attracted rubber-neckers.

It was here that Jack Fingleton found him in 1948 and persuaded him to emigrate. Jack, who also worked as a parliamentary reporter and knew his way around the corridors of power, pulled a few strings and arranged that the prime minister of Australia, Ben Chifley, be on hand to greet Harold when he arrived.

Mr Chifley was a dinki-di Aussie with an ocker accent. After introducing the two men, Jack left them to have a natter. Ten minutes later, he was joined by the prime minister. 'He's a nice bloke but I can't understand a word he's saying,' he said to Jack. Ten minutes later, Larwood appeared. 'It was nice of the prime minister to see me, but I wish I knew what he was on about,' said Harold. So Jack Fingleton sometimes interpreted for two men who both thought they were speaking English.

Harold laughed as Jack told the tale. 'And I still haven't lost my accent,' he said. And he hadn't. 'Coming to Australia was the best thing that happened to me. I've been very happy here. I was signing in at a golf club some time ago and came to the bit where they ask you where you come from and my friend suggested I put Nottingham down in the book. I told him my home was in Sydney and pointed out I had lived in Australia longer than their best fast bowler, Dennis Lillee.'

We lunched together twice more before he became housebound because of his blindness. I called to congratulate him on being awarded the MBE in 1993. I didn't tell him it was 60 years overdue. Like elephants, the establishment have long memories and small brains. With Harold gone, only Bradman remains of the key protagonists in the Bodyline story. Neither man has told the whole truth, choosing to keep to themselves what they really thought about each other.

In that sense, the story has no ending and both men will be remembered for what we don't know about them as they will for their deeds on the field of play. Between them, the Boy from Bowral and the Lad from Nuncargate played out a story that will forever interest lovers of cricket and social historians looking for clues about the attitudes and mores of that time.

I was lucky to meet Harold Larwood and treasure the memory. I never saw him bowl, but my father did and Jack Fingleton, too. I think Jack should have the last word. 'One could tell his art by his run to the wicket. It was a poem of athletic grace, as each muscle gave over to the other with perfect balance and the utmost power. I will never see a greater fast bowler than Larwood, I am sure of that. He was the master.'

---

10 SEPTEMBER 1995

Scyld Berry

Edgbaston

It was a typical Warwickshire performance, and recovery. At 125 for 5 wickets, their main batting having not come off, they were losing their grip on Derbyshire and the championship. Two and a half hours later – the time Trevor Penney and Dermot Reeve took to add 168 – they were in the lead and back in control again.

Warwickshire should, of course, be stronger than a depleted Derbyshire in any event. Yet their revival was still a fine example of how they succeed. Most sides set out to play cricket; Warwickshire set out to win at cricket.

Supposing both counties were at full strength, Warwickshire could not be called vastly more talented. What they have, and Derbyshire do not have, is the magic formula, by which one or two players always come good, even if the rest get out of bed the wrong side.

Yesterday Wasim Khan, out in the first over, was another specialist batsman to fail – and on a pitch fresh enough to have something for seamers. When Roger Twose was caught behind, in his last home championship game (at least as an England-qualified player), the bull's horns were there for the taking.

First it was Dominic Ostler who exemplified, in modern Australian terms, 'game toughness'. It was his turn to come good – helped by Allan Warner dropping his hook when 31 – as Ostler had not made a championship 50 since 7 July, or of any kind since 9 July.

Secondly, and more so, it was Reeve who turned the game round, while Penney played himself in. Until Reeve's entry, Derbyshire's bowling was at times competent, at times ordinary. Under Reeve's influence it soon became extraordinary in its incompetence.

Time and again Reeve helped himself to singles by turning the medium-pace to deep fine-leg. Then Reeve found himself glancing

Simon Base to short fine-leg and gaining no single. His response was to sweep the next two balls high past the fielder for two and four.

This was Base's first championship game of the summer, to fill the gaps left by Devon Malcolm and Phillip DeFreitas. But he showed no signs of rustiness whatever. Soon he was no-balling as if he had never been away.

After Kim Barnett had tried his leg-breaks, Base demonstrated that he too could bowl long-hops outside leg stump. The culmination was an over that cost Base considerable irritation and 23 runs, including the customary no-ball, as he pitched short on both sides of the wicket, in a corridor of utter certainty.

Although Reeve steered an off-side bouncer to slip, the last ball before tea, Penney carried on to his fourth century of the season by lofting that legendary off-spinner, Tim Tweats, straight for his 16th four. He also became the first Warwickshire player to reach a thousand runs for the season, which suggests their batsmen score sufficient runs, not too many.

Derbyshire's morale in the field – apart from some ragged bowling, they missed two catchable chances from Penney in one over – may not make them formidable opponents in their second innings. If this is the case, and Warwickshire win, the champions will secure their second title of the year if their rivals cannot also win their games in this round.

It would be unfair though to complain that Warwickshire have thrived again thanks only to their lively pitches at Edgbaston. The fact is that they have won six out of eight home matches, excluding this one; while away from home they have won six out of seven so far.

Playing two games at Uxbridge has not done much for Middlesex; they have won five out of eight at home, before this round, against six wins out of seven away. It is Northamptonshire who have principally benefited from home advantage, winning six out of seven at home to date, five out of eight away.

Ever more invigorated by Derbyshire's bowling, Penney and partners carried their county's lead past 100. Allan Donald will have plenty to bowl at in his last home game, as this seems certain to be.

———

3 MARCH 1996

Scyld Berry

It always happens in Pakistan and India when England are losing, and has done ever since the tour of 1976–7 when Tony Greig, the showman, had everyone eating out of his hand. Many, but unreported, have the press conferences been when the England captain has said in an unsubtle aside, or in a contemptuous glance: 'somebody remove this buffoon.'

What is more, it will continue to happen, being a symptom of underlying malaise. The attitude of this England party is wrong, not just that of their captain towards the local press. They try as hard as they can in the matches, but deep down many would rather go home, which is not unnatural as they have been abroad for 11 months of the last 26, with two long domestic seasons in between. They have simply had enough, and in such comments it shows.

One of Holland's county cricketers, on meeting up with England in Peshawar, was moved to opine: 'They're so haughty, and they have very little to be haughty about.' Their mood is like that of students going into exams without having done their revision. They can answer the easy questions (Holland, UAE), but when something harder trips them up, and knowing they are responsible, they take their grumpiness out on others.

Attitudes could have been different if England had been given the right amount of rest and some preparation. They were allowed a couple of weekends at home in October, another in January. At the end of March they will have another before the counties drag them away on pre-season tours so as to keep their sponsors and members happy.

England's cricketers are made to serve two masters, and the proverb still holds good. Once they are Test players, Australians play seldom if ever in the Sheffield Shield, Pakistanis in the Quaid-e-Azam, or South Africans in the Castle Cup.

England's cricketers used to serve two masters, but not every year. If Graham Thorpe is chosen next winter, at the age of 27 he will have been on as many tours, full and 'A', as Alec Bedser and Fred Trueman combined in their careers. It wasn't a level playing field in their day either, as England's professionals faced Test teams largely composed of weekend club-playing amateurs.

Only the West Indian Board has driven its players harder, following up each county season with several tours each winter. They have aged their players prematurely, and helped to reduce world champions to pitiable laughing-stock in Pune.

England had no preparation of the right sort either, and this is not just a matter of nets. If Dennis Silk had been given his way by the county chairmen, and Shenleigh Park had been purchased as a centre of excellence, England's players could have been tutored in a few words of Urdu and Punjabi; shown a few slides of 4,000-year-old Indus Valley civilizations like Mohenjadaro and Harappa, to dispel any notions of cultural superiority; told how to handle the press, by thinking up a few comments in advance, and offering them almost irrespective of the question, coherent or not.

English cricketers need preparing for Pakistan more than for anywhere else. After all the public apologies they have had to make here, the players should know that Pakistan, unlike India, tends to confront. If your gratuity is insufficient, a Pakistani will tell you so, not bow a servile knee.

Ask an official here the simplest question and he may not know the answer or even understand, because martial law governments feared nothing so much as literacy and education. And the region which is now Pakistan used to elect 'panchayats' at village level; it was the Raj which installed remote, unaccountable administrators, a system ideal for corruption when Pakistan inherited it.

The sadness is that Mike Atherton more than anyone else is prepared to have a sympathetic interest in his surroundings, but not when denied any time and space for himself. The TCCB could appoint the sunniest extrovert as captain, and within three years reduce him to a grumpy wreck, as every long-term incumbent post-Packer has at some time become.

Were the TCCB based in Nairobi, they would no doubt draw up a schedule that would take the keenness out of Kenya. This is a body which gave Keith Fletcher a five-year contract, and did not offer Bob Woolmer even an 'A' tour. Perhaps most unforgivably of all, the counties and TCCB combined have taken much of the joy out of cricket for England's players.

At least in the last few days a puff of wind has come to stir England's sails, suggesting they are due for the one decent phase they have on every tour, however abject. But would it not be better in the long run if they were knocked out in the quarter-finals, otherwise nothing will be done? Should they reach the semi-finals, we will hear the refrain that England are great at fighting back, when even a worm will turn when its place is at stake.

But whatever the result of today's match against Pakistan, and of England's quarter-final tie, they have – though not for the first time – touched rock bottom this winter. And it is not principally the fault of the players.

---

27 APRIL 1997

DENIS COMPTON: MY MEMORIES

Tony Lewis

Denis Compton came into my life as a cigarette card: dark-haired, handsome, three blue seaxes and a smile: He was part of the John Player and Sons 1938 series. My cricketers were not gummed into albums. They were working cricketers, scratched and scarred.

Their daily work was in the schoolyard in Neath. In the late 1940s they were my currency in high-risk games called 'blows' or 'flicks'. To enter a blowing game you had to place a card on the pile, facing downwards, and then took your turn to blow what was left of the pile off the flat stone ledge at the Senior Boys' entrance. You pocketed those which fell face upwards. Flicking was simply a matter of toeing the line and flicking the card further than anyone else from a relaxed grip between the first and second finger.

In fact I only had one Denis Compton, which has been reinforced during the past week of mourning. There was only one Denis Compton. His job in my home was much more crucial. Denis Compton was the best player in my eleven, on rainy days in front-room cricket which we played on our knees. The bowler sent down a fast or spinning marble to a batsman who was kneeling defending his five-inch stumps with a miniature wooden bat.

Compton bowled under-arm spinners left-handed, fielded at slip to the bowling of Farnes, Verity, Robins, Goddard and Voce and when batting swept everything from anywhere. The cards were carefully placed around the field, Barnett at cover, Yardley stayed near the bowler. They got dog-eared.

And then I saw him play. I really did. At St Helen's in Swansea, Glamorgan versus Middlesex. Last week I was trying to put a date on it. I rang Glamorgan's amiable secretary, Mike Fatkin, and told him I was 10 at the time but I thought Compton made 67. It was 1949 and I went to see Stan Trick, the left-arm spinner who played for my home town, Neath. I was sitting on the boundary line just beneath the rugby stand. I still see one stroke. Trick bowled, Compton swept the ball with a straightish bat, fine, for four. Not out 67, with a lot of cutting and sweeping.

Back in the early 1950s, when Don Bradman's book *Farewell to Cricket* came out, I searched for tributes to Denis Compton, and found: 'Often have I seen our bowlers astonished when they sent down a specially good ball only to see it countered by his splendid defence.' Many have since endorsed Bradman's view – not at all underlined during the past week – that Compton was one of the game's best defensive players.

For several seasons in the press box when I started writing he gave me a warm, sort-of-know-who-you-are greeting. He never got round to my name; such detail was not for him. Then one day he opened the school exercise book of lined paper on which he penned his *Sunday Express* column, looked up and said: 'How are you Tony, old boy?' I am still thrilled that I was one of Compo's 'named' friends.

I remember he had his likes and dislikes. He liked a fun game not drudgery, liked watching Gower not Boycott, abhorred helmets and arm-shields, liked gin and champagne not halves of bitter, liked ladies, loved Lord's, liked appointments, but not keeping them.

My wife and I walked into the Denham golf clubhouse one sunny Sunday lunchtime to see Denis order a bottle of champagne. He looked around and saw us.

'Hello darling' was his safe greeting of wives and lovers. 'I can't think of a better couple to help me celebrate.' He called for two more glasses. 'To celebrate what, Denis?'

'Here's to Mr Gower. Yesterday at Manchester he beat Mr Boycott's Test aggregate. Bloody good news, old boy. Good luck darling.'

To Denis Compton, blessed were the stroke-makers and party-goers, but blessed also was he himself with the genius to make his name so special in the eyes of young boys. He made county cricket a dazzling possibility for so many and Brylcreem was the precursor of much that would make a professional cricketer's life profitable.

He will always live in my home, still housed with those torn companions in a rectangular tin box which has a coronation portrait of Queen Elizabeth on the lid, which once contained toffees 'Made in England by Edward Sharp and Sons Ltd., of Maidstone, Kent'. And to die on St George's Day. You could not get more English than that.

---

23 MAY 1997

Martin Johnson

Headingley

English cricket has been arguing for years about how to catch up with the Australians. Cut down the county programme, uncover the pitches, set up an academy ... and all the time the answer was staring us in the face. Ban floppy hats and issue everyone with an electric razor.

In direct contravention of the England and Wales Cricket Board's new sartorial guidelines, the first Texaco Trophy contest wasn't even a close shave. Whether England can keep this up for the Ashes is another matter, as the last time the urn resided here, not even Old Father Time had much of a beard.

It is not, however, how smart the players look in their tailored blazers, but how smart they are between the ears. It was here at Headingley, in the first Test of 1989, that Australia first demonstrated how far England had been left behind in the areas of preparation and tactical planning, since when the worm has taken longer to turn than the QE2.

The main difference between these two sides since then has been the degree of ruthlessness. When England lost the last Test of their winning 1986–7 tour, it was suggested to Mike Gatting that it had worked out well for everyone. England had retained the Ashes, while Australia had partially managed to woo back a public rapidly deserting to one-day cricket.

'Are you potty? These buggers wouldn't give us anything, and neither should we,' was the gist of Gatting's riposte, and his point has been thoroughly proved since then. Whenever England have been on the canvas, there has been no helping hand, just a boot in the ribs.

The optimism which usually accompanies the start of a new international summer rarely survives much beyond the end of May, but yesterday there was a vibrancy about England which suggests that better times may lie ahead. They also managed to get themselves out of a nasty hole, which is not something they often do, despite many years of practice.

The first part of the job yesterday was not to give the Australians any free runs in helpful bowling conditions, and this, thanks largely to Darren Gough and Robert Croft, they managed to do. They are the kind of sparky characters that a dressing room needs, and were just about the only two England players to rise above the team's poor attitude in Zimbabwe.

There was a determination not to enjoy Zimbabwe that had to be seen to be believed, not least because the locals were so hospitable. Or at least they would have been had the players bothered to get out and meet them a bit more. And what happened when they flew on to New Zealand? They further insulted the Zimbabweans by saying that it was nice to be in a 'civilised' country.

No wonder the ECB are busy arranging courses in public relations. When England toured India in 1993, the players complained of being misrepresented by unflattering photographs, and in some instances they had a point. They were pictured, for example, shortly after disembarking from the overnight sleeper from Bubaneshwar to Calcutta, which is the kind of journey not even the local rodent population undertakes with much enthusiasm.

However, they also managed to turn up for the post-match presentations in Madras in an assortment of shorts, T-shirts and grubby hats, and the ECB are quite right in making the judgment that a team have less chance of playing the part if they fail to look it.

The selectors have also managed to embrace the concept that players can be blooded at international level on the basis of talent rather than whether they are old enough to receive an official ECB shaving mug. At 26, Adam Hollioake can scarcely be described as a youth but, by English standards, it was a bold selection.

This type of cricket does not necessarily unearth a Test player, but it is a good barometer of temperament, and Hollioake is clearly not short of that commodity, given the way he responded to England's precarious predicament of 40 for 4 when he came in. After coming through the required period of teeth-gritting, Hollioake and Graham Thorpe won the game in a canter.

Michael Atherton did not survive long enough to disprove or otherwise Geoffrey Boycott's assertion that the captain was a 'slowcoach', which is not unlike Ronald Biggs complaining to British Rail that his train was late. If it's PR they want, England should look no further than Boycs.

---

25 JUNE 1997

Tim Rice

A few more weeks like the one just gone and I shall have to think seriously about writing musicals again – it would be considerably less taxing. For nine days solid I and many like me have been subjected to the most unyielding pressure thanks to our unstinting devotion to the summer game ... Sunday, 15 June: Grudge fixture against William Heath's Gentlemen. Long drive to deepest Wiltshire for 11 a.m. start. Take two wickets for 39 in 4 overs – encouragingly economical with satisfactory strike rate. Out second ball but showing considerable improvement in getting caught attempting sophisticated leg glance. Gripping finish in the gloom at 8.15 p.m. – defeat by three runs. Home by midnight to fax from opposition saying this was cricket at its very best – everyone was a winner. Draft rude reply.

Monday, 16 June: Tom Graveney's 70th birthday. Long drive to deepest Gloucestershire for 7 p.m. start. Superb celebration of the great man's three-score-and-10 with moving tribute from Arthur Milton the highlight. Basil D'Oliveira and Peg Lindwall among many on top form. The latter reveals that she is responsible for cricketers rubbing the ball on their trousers rather than their shirts. Apparently the Aussies used to have their flannels dry-cleaned at their board's expense whereas shirts were the wives' responsibility – once the immortal Ray had been persuaded to change where he rubbed, the whole world followed. Home by 2.30 a.m.

Tuesday, 17 June: Mike Atherton benefit dinner. Long drive to London Hilton. Write grace in taxi on way to dinner. Huge turn-out and all present in buoyant mood, anticipating great things at Lord's. Consequently my grace goes down a storm, though such was the mood of bonhomie, selections from Martin Guerre would have received a standing ovation. David Lloyd and Rory Bremner on top form. Jeffrey Archer as auctioneer cracks good gag about Conservative election campaign. Athers makes a well-deserved bundle and we all retire hurt at 2.30 a.m.

Wednesday, 18 June: Lord's Taverners Eve Of Test Dinner. Long drive to London Hilton. Huge array of stars turn out with the newly ennobled Lord Cowdrey, Taverners' president, controlling festivities with the sure touch first displayed at Melbourne in 1954. Tom Graveney OBE and Sir Alec Bedser guests of honour. Seventy-five per cent of the diners there for the second consecutive night, 45 per cent having simply stayed put since Tuesday. Tony Greig makes brilliant speech about the trials of facing Lillee and Thomson, gets huge laugh with 'grovel' reference and is received as warmly as could be. Jeffrey Archer as auctioneer cracks good gag about Conservative election campaign. Home by 2.30 a.m.

Thursday, 19 June: The big day. Thousands converge on Lord's in the rain. Not a ball is bowled. Lunch lasts four hours during which Bill Brown, still spritely well into his eighties, is pressured into recalling his unbeaten 206 here in 1938. Paul Sheahan remembers the freak storm at the Oval in 1968 when the crowd was dragooned into helping the ground staff in drying the playing area. Fortunately the occupants of Roger Knight's box are not called upon for that purpose today.

Friday, 20 June: Day off. Recover from Thursday by driving 250 miles to sing with rock band for three hours non-stop. Keep in touch with what play there is via radio, and note, not for the first time, how Test Match Special is cruelly treated by Radio 4 programmers. How can the BBC in 1997 fail to provide a true every-ball-bowled service, which they accomplished with ease in 1957? Even the odd five minutes missed is a stab in the heart. Home by 4 a.m.

Saturday, 21 June: Back at Lord's refreshed after relaxing Friday. An in-and-out day spent loitering within tent and Allen Stand in the company of Aussie team relatives. England slump to 77 and then have a nightmare in the field making hosting the Australian side's loved ones an easy task. Mrs Matthew Elliott has a particularly good day. Bev Waugh, athletic and sparky mother of Mark and Steve, signs me up for tennis and swimming coaching next time I'm in New South Wales. I leave next Thursday. Home by 8 p.m., asleep by 9.30.

Sunday, 22 June: Almost zero prospect of play does not prevent 100 per cent turn-out of friends and gate-crashers in box for free lunch. When play finally begins, almost at the end of the day, the hour and a half is as fascinating as one could hope for. Australia playing with one-day fervour for fast runs, England at one point taking three wickets for nothing. Reflect that had the day's play begun on time, the approach of both sides would have been completely different. In which other sport would rain do anything other than delay play? Give Richie Benaud a lift back to his hotel. Rewarded with Richie's incisive personal summary of the match to date. Do not therefore have to watch highlights and have much-needed early night.

Monday, 23 June: At last a full day's play, and a fine one too. England restore honour and all are delighted to see Mark Butcher break through. An England victory was never remotely a possibility after Saturday which quietly pleased super-patriot Jonathan Wyatt, whose father, R.E.S., will now go down in history as the only England captain to beat Australia at Lord's in the twentieth century. Despite the vile weather, this has actually been a gripping match with much to admire and enjoy. Attempt non-cricket evening by going to see Everly Brothers at the Albert Hall, who open their act with Bowling Green. No escape.

---

19 JANUARY 1998

Michael Parkinson

We haven't had many wicket-keepers in Yorkshire, only seven or eight in a hundred years or more. David Bairstow was one of them. He understood he was part of a great tradition but wasn't overawed by it. In fact, not much fazed David Bairstow. Or so we thought.

I remember when he came as a schoolboy into the Yorkshire team, which in those days was not so much a cricket team, more an academy of cricketing knowledge run by Brian Close and Raymond Illingworth where it was accepted sprogs kept their opinions to themselves until they had earned the right to address such illustrious company.

I was in the dressing room when Brian Close returned in foul humour having been given out lbw. As the captain addressed his players on the subject of blind umpires they pretended to busy themselves with other tasks to avoid catching his eye and being drawn inevitably into the tirade. All save the young Bairstow, who gazed in wonder at his captain in full spate.

As he paused for breath Close looked at Bairstow and said: 'And what does tha' think, young 'un?' Bairstow said: 'I think tha' goes on a bit.' He didn't muck about with niceties either as a player or a man. If the ball was up he smacked it, if he didn't like you he told you so. A true son of the soil that shaped him. Built like a muckstack and indestructible. So we thought.

When he finished playing county cricket he came down to Maidenhead and Bray now and again and helped us out. It was enlightening to see him with our players; encouraging, cajoling and sometimes bollocking them to better things. He played every game like a Test match. It was the only way he knew.

He was the best of company, intelligent and perceptive in everything he did and said except when it came to business ventures and dealing with Yorkshire County Cricket Club.

He felt snubbed by Yorkshire and no amount of persuasion and arguing by his friends could convince him otherwise. It was sad to see such a dedicated Yorkshireman at odds with the institution he loved and admired beyond all else apart from the family.

In the past couple of years I detected a sadness in him, an uncertainty about what the future might hold. The eternal predicament of athletes is not that they retire too soon but that they retire at all.

Yet David had been working as a commentator for the BBC and was doing well. It wasn't a fortune but it kept him in touch with the game he loved.

I saw him during the last cricket season. He had put on weight but seemed as vigorous and robust as ever. When I was told he had committed suicide, I said: 'Don't be daft. Not Bluey.' Not that strong, fearless laughing mate I knew. Now all I can think is why, old lad, why?

---

31 JANUARY 1998

Martin Johnson

Away from the four-star hotels, Kingston is not quite the palm-treed paradise the tourist brochures would have you believe, and while most of the local industry revolves around making coffee, there's also a bob or two to be earned from making coffins. However, if picking a rum-fuelled argument in a downtown bar remains the simplest method of attempting suicide in Jamaica's capital (albeit only by a short head from attempting to cross the road during rush-hour) then batting against Courtney Walsh and Curtly Ambrose on Thursday morning was a more than a viable alternative.

Batting against the West Indies over the past couple of decades has always attracted a hang-glider's insurance premium, and rarely more so than here at Sabina Park. In 1986 the next man in had to take guard while they were busy retrieving a piece of Mike Gatting's nose from the ball, and on the same ground 10 years earlier, Bishen Bedi opted to declare India's second innings closed rather than become the cricketing equivalent of Field Marshal Haig. Keith Fletcher once said that when the West Indians were bowling, he even watched the TV highlights from behind the sofa, and if the scheduled first Test of 1998 had not been called off, it's doubtful whether Sky would have been allowed to continue their coverage before the 9 p.m. watershed.

After the toss there was the traditional press box sweepstake inviting tenders as to the teatime score, and one or two were in the region of 15/20 for no wicket. This was not so much because they thought that England's batsmen would be scoring particularly slowly, as the belief that the West Indies would by then be batting. Whether or not the match would have been called off so abruptly had Walsh not been replaced as captain is a moot point. It is more or less accepted practice for tail-enders to make rapid strides towards the square-leg umpire rather than risk decapitation, but Brian Lara would have been expected to stand and earn his VC, posthumous or otherwise.

As far as the crowd were concerned, it's mildly surprising that there wasn't more in the way of protest. There were more than 1,000 England supporters in the ground, and they were not in Jamaica simply for the sun and rum. If that had been the case, they'd have gone to Montego Bay, not Kingston. However, just like the home supporters, they wandered around with the kind of blank, dazed expressions not seen since England were bowled out for 46 in Trinidad four years ago.

Many of them made a beeline for the pitch, which in days gone by used to be like no other in Test cricket – as black and shiny as a tap dancer's shoes. Then they dug it up because of lack of pace, leaving it with the appearance of a battered straw hat. While the old surface was flat, this one was not dissimilar to one of Kingston's B roads, and one female spectator from England felt the need to fill a handkerchief with soil samples to take home as a souvenir. She didn't need a trowel, as it came away like a rhubarb crumble topping.

Others made for the pavilion enclosure, where an interesting, if somewhat one-sided, conversation took place between two rival supporters. One of them was sporting the familiar uniform of the English supporter overseas — cream long-sleeved shirt, MCC tie, calf-length shorts, black socks, and red face. 'Do you know what they should do?' he spluttered, but we never did find out, largely because his West Indian opponent had a sizeable advantage in the decibel department, and appeared to have made an earlier start on the rum punch.

'How did you ever get an empire, man?' he demanded to know, tossing in names like Raleigh and Drake, and maintaining an unshakeable theme that the English had all the vertebracy of an amoeba. 'You don't like it, battin', why you not declare? Where you Winston Churchills? Fightin' on the beaches!'

Some of us fought back the urge to point out that, while the pitch did indeed resemble a beach, the 57 minutes of play we had just witnessed did not represent the Sabina Park groundsman's finest hour, and that both sides — not just England — had agreed to up stumps and leave town. One of the advertising boards inquired: 'Are You Man Enough To Have A Vasectomy?', but England were merely drawing the line at having the operation performed by Ambrose and Walsh.

Meantime, the carnival-like atmosphere on the Red Stripe Mound continued, cricket or no cricket. The band played on, just as it did when the *Titanic* (currently showing at the Kingston Roxy) went down, broken only by a loudspeaker announcement. 'Apologies to Mr Andrews, the vodka is on the way.' Just the sort of thing you'd hear over the Tannoy at Lord's, really. Part of the new enclosure, developed in an attempt to match Barbados and Antigua for Test match atmosphere, contains an artificial beach, complete with sun-loungers, umbrellas and swimming pool, and a good many of its patrons did not seem to either care, or notice, that there wasn't actually any cricket taking place.

Another West Indian supporter, in front of the pavilion, was busy informing anyone with a pink complexion, a Gullivers' Travel bag and a Sunday League shirt, that English batsmanship had become totally spineless since the days of Geoffrey Boycott. His natural modesty would doubtless have prompted Geoffrey to disagree with him, but England's batting barnacle-turned-media pundit was not around. Or if he was, he was keeping an unusually low profile.

Boycott had flown into Kingston on Sunday night, amid rumours that his assault conviction in France had had his various employers shifting uneasily in their seats, and, sure enough, as the week went on, it transpired that of his original contracts to work on this Test for TWI (the TV conglomerate supplying, among others, Sky), BBC Radio 5, a local radio station and the *Sun*, only the *Sun* had survived.

Early fears about the pitch, plus the business in France, may have made various employers fearful of any mischievous on-air badinage along the lines of: 'How long do you think it might take the bruising to go down then, Geoffrey?' But it at least solved the usual Sky problem of how to keep Boycott and Ian Botham at a safe distance from one another. Bosom buddies they are not, particularly after Boycott appeared, complete with sponsored shirt, for Imran Khan in the ball-tampering libel case.

The week began with the West Indian newspapers taking more of an interest in the Super Bowl than the cricket, and, with Caribbean youngsters now growing up on a diet of satellite sport from the USA, cricket is now under real threat as the major sport in this part of the world. West Indian cricket badly needs a shot in the arm, especially after the three-Test annihilation in Pakistan, and the kind of debacle we have witnessed here is not exactly calculated to provide it.

---

2 AUGUST 1998

DONALD, ME AND THE BATTLE OF TRENT BRIDGE

Mike Atherton

'Change of bowling. Right arm over the wicket.' What umpire Steve Dunne doesn't say is that it's going to be quick. Very quick. It's Sunday evening, third session, and South Africa's great fast bowler Allan Donald is back for the crucial spell of the game. A cacophony of encouragement from slips and the effervescent Jonty Rhodes. 'Get us one now A.D.' Got to see this through. Do it yourself. Don't leave it to anybody else.

Now he is charging in. He looks pumped up. Head still, stand tall, play straight. It's a loosener, short and wide, cash in. Don't really connect but the pace of the ball sends it past Gary Kirsten at gully and Rhodes at point. Four runs. Feeling good. Survived the over.

'Coming around the wicket,' and again this bland, rather anodyne statement from umpire Dunne signals a new challenge. Plenty of short balls on the way. Be brave. Careful, too, of the ball angling across the stumps. Play for your off stump. It's short and at the hip, tuck it away for a single. Let Nasser Hussain take some heat – as Geoffrey Boycott said, the best way to play fast bowling is 'from t'other end'. Trouble is they've got one at the other end.

Next over and the barrage begins. It's short, quick and at me. I've got in an almighty tangle. Big, big appeal. Not out. He looks upset, they all look upset. He says something (in English if they want you to hear, in Afrikaans if not). It's in English. The crowd's too noisy, can't hear.

Just keep staring, the bowler's got to turn away first. Compose yourself. It's short again: another tangle and this time the ball drops short of the fielder. Got to take some blows here. Short again, clips left shoulder, quickest ball yet. A quick look at the speedometer shows 90 mph! Somebody's turned the radiator up – it's hot out here! End of the over. Survived. Abuse from the fielders as they walk in between overs. To be expected. This is Test cricket. Give some back.

'Gerry, short leg. Paul, leg gully.' Hansie Cronje in Jardinesque mode signals the beginning of another over. Doesn't take a genius to know what he's going to bowl. Memories of Sabina Park here. Don't let him bombard you now. No fielders out, half a bat on it and it's runs. It's short, hook, top edge, but it's safely over Paul Adams for two. Experience is helping me here. Been through it before. Adams now drops back to deep square. Huge gap behind short leg. Clip off the hip for one, get down the other end and get Nasser on strike! It's full and across him. Snick. Mark Boucher's dropped it! Big let-off for Nasser and us. End of the over and all the South Africans commiserate with Boucher – good teamwork. They are a tough and united team, and not beaten yet, not by a long chalk. Donald runs from fine leg to Boucher – touching moment.

Talked to Nasser in the middle. 'Work hard now, Nass. Forget the last ball.' The next over and it's possibly Donald's last. Keep concentrating now. No mistakes now. No risks. Man back so don't hook. Sway and duck and play for your off stump. Adams is loosening up. Survived the over. 'Change of bowling, left arm over and through.' Survived the spell. Don't relax now though, keep concentrating ...

But in the end that battle was only a small part, albeit an important part, of what was a magnificent Test match in which an assortment of characters and cricketers held the stage. Much has been written of my joust with Donald: some negative things, of umpiring decisions, of batsmen not walking, and sledging. Every person, however, that I've spoken to has seen it in a positive light and said it was some of the most compelling cricket they have seen. Enough said. I have an enormous amount of respect for Allan Donald. 'Great' is a much overused word but I'm sure he fits comfortably into that category – all pace, fire and heart. I learnt very early on in Test cricket from the Australians to leave behind what happens on the field and, at the end of it all, we shook hands, said well played and shared a beer. As indeed have both teams this summer.

The next day could never have matched the intensity of the previous evening and so it proved as we eased to our victory target. We still had to do the hard yards but the sting had been drawn the night before. Of course it would have been nice to have completed a hundred, but Alec Stewart had been sent out with instructions from Angus Fraser to thwart it, so as to keep his man-of- the-match award safe. The jealousy of a trundler!

Driving to Trent Bridge before the match I remembered a conversation I had had with Boycott after the drawn match in Johannesburg three years ago. 'You'll win the next match in Durban, you know!' When I asked why, he said: 'History has a habit of punishing those that don't take their chances.'

As it happened rain ruined that finely poised Test match in Durban, but it was those same thoughts that filled my mind going to Nottingham and at the moment of victory. I felt the pace of South Africa's batting on the second day at Old Trafford and their failure to finish us off had really given us a life from which we breathed new life into the Test series at Trent Bridge.

Certainly now the summer has taken a turn for the better. After the disillusionment that was the third Test, cricket is all the rage again. Even those thrifty Tykes have been moved to buy tickets in their droves.

It is good also to be back in the runs and to repay the faith that two people in particular have shown in me. David Lloyd who, in his own way, said: 'You've got to get through the turnstiles early to see you play!' after another early season failure. And Graham Gooch who sent me, in many ways, a moving letter during those dog days saying I had worn the three lions with distinction before and would surely do so again.

And now finally the team stands on the brink of some success. Players of my era, the Stewarts, Frasers and Hicks for example, have played much cricket for England with little success against the 'big boys'. This week's match will be a massive Test match for us.

And there's 'Freddie' Flintoff, pitching up for the first time, straight in at first slip, trundling a few seamers and having a merry swish at Allan Donald, as though he was playing for St Anne's in the Northern League. I can only hope winning becomes more of a habit for him than it was for me at the start of an England career. It is important that it does.

---

4 JANUARY 1999

WARNE'S MAJOR MOMENT IS RAPTUROUSLY ACCLAIMED

Mark Nicholas

All he did was take off his cap, and immediately the crowd erupted. He was standing at short extra-cover for the bowling of Stuart MacGill when Mark Taylor gave him the nod that it was time. Nine months had passed since Shane Warne had bowled a leg-break for Australia. During that time the most talked about shoulder in cricket has been rebuilt. Its owner was in a sling for six weeks. The physiotherapy, the massage and the daily exercising seemed never to end.

For the most revered son of Australian sport, for the surfer of a decade ago turned spinner of the age, this was the biggest over of his life. Bigger than the over which turned the World Cup semi-final against the West Indies in India, bigger than the World Cup final itself in Lahore, bigger even than the first over that he bowled for Australia on this very ground exactly nine years ago.

Warne was roundly booed when he walked in to bat on Saturday, but he was booed in an amiable way as if he were a boy exposed for cribbing in the classroom.

The boos gave in to applause yesterday as he went to his captain, who stood by the stumps at the Randwick end of the splendid Sydney

Cricket Ground. The sponsored shades were carefully folded, and, with the beloved 'baggy green', handed to umpire Hair.

He had put on weight, we all agreed, and looked more wrestler than wrist-spinner, but what could you expect from all those pizzas and no more cigarettes, we agreed further. His lips were painted in suncream. His bleached locks were cut short for the occasion, and the ever-present Nike ear stud sparkled in the strong sun.

Mark Butcher was on strike, a left-hander with the fast bowler's footmarks to fret over and no history of success against spin. Here Butcher was up against the master of spin and not for a moment would you have bet against this bloke with 313 Test match wickets to his name.

Warne settled at the end of his approach in that deliberate, imposing way of his. The huge, capacity crowd fell silent. Then, perhaps the greatest slow bowler of them all took a deep breath, wrapped his famous fingers around the ball and set off on his journey.

The first one was perfect, an 'as I was saying before I was so rudely interrupted' ball that Butcher blocked. Warne breathed out. The second was similar, but Butcher chose to make his defiant point and slogged it over mid-wicket for four.

Warne squinted and licked his lips. The third one was on the spot again and Butcher, unsure of the direction of the spin, propped forward. Warne, sensing the uncertainty in his opponent, turned crisply for his mark.

The fourth ball was the one. The inevitable moment that only the most confident and most gifted sportsman can contrive, the performance when the world is watching. Butcher played back to a leg-break which ripped into his pants; back he played when he should have been forward. He was plum lbw to many people, no issue.

As Daryll Hair began to raise his finger, Warne ran at Ian Healy, his old accomplice, and at Mark Taylor, his general. The others came too, to acclaim the living legend who was back among them. The 40,000 people in the SCG stood to worship, the noise they made in his honour was unbelievable.

Warne might have got it wrong in Sri Lanka four years ago, when he dealt dirty by accepting money from an Indian bookmaker for pitch and team information, but Australia loves him all the same. He thrills the people with his style, his smile and his resounding successes. He is an entertainer, a bon viveur in a world of sporting stereotypes, and, Lord knows, cricket has few enough of those to seduce its audience.

His final figures were barely worth a second glance — he was MacGilled yesterday, as were five of the England batsmen — but the loop and the dip and the threat were there; if not quite the fizz, the zip or the side-spin of old. The leg-break worked nicely, and there was plenty of over-spin to savour, thus the extra bounce and the hurried batsman.

A couple of flippers and a googly or two completed the set on a most satisfactory day for Australia when Shane Warne took his 314th Test wicket.

It all suggested that there were plenty of revolutions left in his shoulder yet.

---

21 JANUARY 1999

Simon Hughes

They say having kids changes your life and it's true. Getting up in the dark to give the boy child his milk does have its plus points if Australia v. England is live on television. But now the little blighter has worked out how to switch channels to watch Teletubbies.

If I try to switch it back to the cricket there is a performance rivalling any Dominic Cork appeal for lbw, and I'm stuck with Dipsy prancing about instead of Gough strutting his stuff or Warne spinning his web.

And yet, the closer you look, the more similar the programmes are. Teletubby-land is a green swathe with herbacious borders like the Adelaide Oval (one of TV's commentators, Allan Border, used to be known as Herbie). Their colours mirror the pyjamas worn in one-day series and Teletubby house is a modern take on a cricket pavilion with lookouts and automatic doors making gatemen redundant.

Inside are all the things you're familiar with in a modern English cricket pavilion. Beds, a toaster, large amounts of custard (chief sampler G.A. Gooch) and a machine that hoovers up all the leftovers (Robert Croft?). And, of course, no trophy cabinet. No point in having one with bare shelves is there?

That's not all. The rabbits running about everywhere are symbolic of anyone who bats in the lower half of the England order. And whereas the announcement 'Time for Tubby bye-byes' might two years ago have been dreamt up to headline an article on Mark Taylor's poor batting form, it is now the equivalent of the man on the Tannoy at the SCG saying, with England's eighth-wicket pair together, 'And now, from the Randwick End, Glenn McGrath'.

The sight of a third umpire's monitor built into Tinky Winky, Lala, Po and Dipsy's stomachs is final proof to me that Teletubbies is the focus of the ECB's crafty plan to bypass school cricket and promote the game to the under-threes. Its practically indoctrination, to which Darren Gough and Dean Headley have fully subscribed with their frank admission that Tellytubbies is their favourite TV programme (fact). Hey, Dipsy even looks a bit like Goughy, and Lala was certainly modelled on Shane Warne. He even tosses a ball from hand to hand.

Gough and Headley have definitely been two of the major plusses Down Under and long may that continue. Here are two guys who have hostility, heart and humour. One of the minuses was the continued inability of English players to conquer good spin bowling.

Check *Wisden* 25 years ago, reporting England's 1972–3 tour to India and Pakistan. 'Amiss, Wood and Roope are all gifted and often devastating players in England. But in India, against bowlers like Chandrasekhar or Bedi, they seemed to be handicapped by the sort of cricket that produced them. Years of stereotyped cricket against seam bowling produces only good players of seam bowling. That is how limited English cricket has become.' Sound familiar?

So what to do? I've said it before and I'll say it again. Get the British-born Asians involved more. It is in these communities where England's spinning strength lies. There could be more than 500 ethnic minority cricket clubs in Britain, though no one knows for sure, as most play in unaffiliated competitions outside the league system. There is undoubted spinning talent there. I've seen it.

The plight of 19-year-old leg spinner Imran Zafar, who was twice promised an invitation to the Yorkshire nets but none materialised, is typical. An ethnic minority select eleven has applied for matches against some county second elevens, but has so far heard nothing. The more the counties can encourage these people, the better our playing of spin will become. Perhaps the ECB's best step is to encourage the makers of Teletubbies to introduce an Asian one. Perhaps they could call him Abra-cadabra.

17 MAY 1999

Michael Parkinson

The opening ceremony of the Cricket World Cup was a feeble overture for a major event. They have had better do's in Cleckheaton, and VE Day in our street left it standing. In fact, the entire lead-up to the event has been feeble and amateurish.

I have seen little or no advertising. Where were the poster and the television campaigns heralding a great sporting event?

I know we are besotted by football to the exclusion of all else, but even more reason to make the nation aware of the alternative. It is no good tippy-toeing about. Cricket has got to get stuck into the opposition if it is to survive and prosper.

A concert planned for the Albert Hall was cancelled because of lack of interest, and/or artists being unavailable. Given the length of time this World Cup has been in the planning I find that unbelievable. The World Cup song will not be released until the end of May. What on earth is the good of a theme song being published halfway through proceedings? Again, the organisation looks sloppy and disorganised.

But the most disappointing and pitiful sight of all was the pavilion at Lord's barely half full on the opening day. Those MCC members who boycotted the opening day because they had been asked to pay for tickets did cricket a great disservice.

They showed the world the smug, selfish face of privilege. They demonstrated the stupidity of allowing a private members' club to have such a powerful and malignant influence on the game. Just when cricket is trying to broaden its appeal, MCC gargoyles scare people off. They should be told by the sensible men at MCC – and there are a few – that Lord's does not belong to them. It belongs to the world of cricket. If that is not acceptable, cricket must find another home. Then MCC members will have the place to themselves and nothing to bellyache about.

Please God.

19 JUNE 1999

Martin Johnson

It's the eyes — barely visible through two narrow slits, and as cold and unblinking as anything you'll see on a fishmonger's slab — that let the bowler know exactly what he's up against. If they'd belonged to a baddie at the OK Corral, Wyatt Earp would not so much have reached for his six-gun as the lavatory paper.

When the heat becomes unbearable, as South Africa found out in two epic back-to-back World Cup encounters, Steve Waugh is the last man out of the kitchen. In selecting a man to bat for your life, you'd eliminate Geoff Boycott on the grounds that watching him would render life not worth living, and plump, every time, for the man who is the biggest single reason — Shane Warne included — for England having lost every Ashes series since 1986.

His features, as cracked and leathery as a dried up billabong, give another clue to the fact that this is a man devoid of frippery, a man with so much steel that a crisis sends ballbearings rather than corpuscles coursing through his veins. If they cast the Waugh twins in a remake of *Zulu*, it's not hard to picture which one would play the Michael Caine role, idly swishing flies from his saddle, and which one Stanley Baker, up to his neck in sweat and sandbags.

The contrast between Mark and Steve is all the more remarkable for their having emerged from the same womb, roughly 90 seconds apart. Mark, all style and class, is the gambler, who occasionally gives the impression that his mind wanders off to the card table, or the 3.45 at Randwick. Games of chance, however, have no such appeal for Steve, despite a deadpan expression would make him a hell of a poker player. His brother uses a rapier, but Steve goes to work with a chisel.

Another clue lies in the hairstyles. Mark's locks look as though they've had more than a passing acquaintance with the hairdryer, while Steve's coiffeur might have been the result of five minutes in the shed with an Australian sheep shearer. Content, rather than artistic impression, is what makes Steve the competitor he is, and in a perverse sort of way, Australia will be happier if they're 10 for 3 when he walks out to bat tomorrow.

In terms of style, Waugh is as poetic as the verse on his fan club's website. 'Our Stevie, Who Isn't Yet In Heaven, Thy Kingdom Come, Thou Shalt Get A Ton.' Ye Gods. In terms of substance, however, Waugh epitomises the single biggest difference between Australian and English cricket teams of the past decade. He does it not for himself, but for his country.

If the rules allowed a Chinaman to play for England on the basis that he had a great-great grandmother who once visited Stoke Poges, they'd pick him, and the consequence of expediency has been a succession of teams whose individual talent has been in direct contrast to collective bottle. Waugh himself has some sage advice on the latest English Cricket Board manoeuvrings in this direction, namely to appoint, if needs be, a coach from Mars or Pluto if he has a bit of success on his CV.

'Appoint an Englishman,' says Waugh. 'Australia has got its own team song, and I can't imagine someone from England singing that song with us after we'd won a Test match. When it comes to crunch time, desperation time, if you're not born with that inner passion, you can't make it up.'

England's abject run of failure against the oldest enemy goes back so far that it is something of a surprise to realise that the last Australian survivor of a losing Ashes series is not only still alive, but captaining the current team. His cricketing character may well, in fact, have been moulded by his early experience of the international game. 'I was a loser for quite a few years,' says Waugh, 'and I didn't much care for it.'

When Australia arrived in England in 1989, they had been humbled on their own soil by Mike Gatting's team two years earlier, and competed with an intensity which made David Gower's side look as though they were playing a cucumber sandwich match on the Duchess of Arundel's back lawn. And Waugh played a gargantuan role in launching what has now become a serial drubbing.

When Angus Fraser bowled him in the third Test at Edgbaston, the scene of that extraordinary semi-final on Thursday, Waugh had been batting for 13 hours and five minutes in the series without losing his wicket. Fraser finally defeated him with the 568th ball he had faced, during which time he had racked up 393 runs.

If Waugh had a perceived weakness, it was, as Corporal Jones would have said, that he didn't like it up him. Michael Atherton caused something of a media stir before the 1994 tour of Australia by suggesting that Waugh might have benefited from wearing incontinence pads under his flannels when the artillery was up around his nostrils, but it didn't bother

Waugh. Plain speaking is his own kind of language, and in any case he was already taking steps to eradicate this one area of vulnerability.

He gave up hooking and pulling, not because it frightened him, but because it got him out too often. In his own words he is 'a bit more conservative than I used to be. It's not so much a matter of cutting certain shots out, but I pick and choose which deliveries to attack much better than I used to.'

He has, unlike Mark, learnt to play to his own expectations rather than that of others. The young, wet-behind-the-ears Steve Waugh was labelled a stroke-player, and played not to let other people down. Now he plays not to let himself down. He has a simple plan for an essentially simple game. Concentrate, watch the ball, and either play it or leave it.

Waugh's philosophy is also mirrored in the way he produces hard-back tour diaries for the Australian book market. He never uses a ghost writer, and every word is his own. As it is when he is at the crease, if a job's worth doing, he does it himself.

It's hard to believe now that Waugh was under pressure as captain at the start of this World Cup, with a number of respected Australian commentators expressing the view that Shane Warne, with his more aggressive and innovative cricketing brain, would have been a better choice as successor to Mark Taylor. You can have an argument both ways. The Richie Benaud style of leadership, or the Ian Chappell. What England wouldn't give for such a choice.

Nothing said more about Waugh than when Paul Reiffel turned a match-winning catch into what might have been a match-losing six at Edgbaston on Thursday. Ten Australians hung their heads in horror, while the captain's expression betrayed not a flicker of what must have been a similar internal emotion.

Off the field, however, Waugh is a long way from being the taciturn, poker-faced individual he is on it, and one of the better examples of his sense of humour accompanied a moment of deep personal disappointment. Shortly before the fourth Test of the 1990–1 Ashes series, Mark, expecting to be named 12th man, was approached on the outfield of the Adelaide Oval by his elder brother: 'Congratulations, you're making your debut.' Mark said: 'Great. But who's been left out?' Steve replied: 'Me, you bastard.'

23 AUGUST 1999

ENGLAND v. WEST INDIES

Martin Johnson

The Oval

When Nasser Hussain announced before this Test that he had total faith in his batsmen, it marked him out as a) new to the job and b) the sort of chap whose beliefs might also extend to the tooth fairy and Father Christmas. And yesterday, he became the first England captain to stand on a balcony and announce that he was 'very proud' of the lads at the same time as the crowd below were launching into a rousing chorus of 'We've got the worst team in the world'.

No one expected Hussain to say what he really thought of his players, at least not in public, but 'very proud'? As defences go, it was like Ronald Biggs's barrister informing the jury that his client had merely boarded the mail train to rummage around for a letter that had got lost in the post.

On the not unreasonable assumption that the England and Wales Cricket Board are slightly less proud of the lads than Hussain, English cricket will now enter its annual cycle of soul-searching, and decide that the way forward is to appoint a working party. This often leads to epoch-making decisions, such as appointing another working party to examine the recommendations of the original one.

Bringing in new players is an obvious path to head down, but then again, the list of players invited to represent England in recent years adds up to only a marginally slimmer volume than the London telephone directory. And in any event, all the evidence points to the fact that when the selectors trawl their net through county cricket, it is the equivalent of attempting to locate a Michelin chef in a transport cafe.

New Zealand were understandably delighted at winning the series, and may even knock the All Blacks off their back pages for 24 hours, but elsewhere in the cricketing world, series victories against England now command roughly the same type size as the greyhound results. The days have long gone when beating England represented the taking of a scalp. Nowadays, it's the equivalent of stealing a blind man's wig.

One of the surprises of the summer has been the way New Zealand have added a spikiness to their cricket, largely, one suspects, thanks to the influence of an Australian coach. Not so long ago, the Kiwis were so anonymous that Scotland Yard's search for Lord Lucan was largely concentrated around the New Zealand middle order, but the aggression they've been showing all through the series surfaced yet again yesterday when Dion Nash and Ronnie Irani became embroiled in such a frank exchange of views that the umpires felt obliged to ask the New Zealand captain to calm his bowler down.

One other aspect of this series has been, from both sides, the singularly inept batting. This is something of a universal trend, in that Test matches uninterrupted by the weather rarely end in a draw any more, and the days when you could confidently expect a side winning the toss to have trouble deciding whether to declare on the second evening or the third morning have long gone.

In the first summer of the 1990s, a three-Test series between England and India produced a total of 4,640 runs for 81 wickets, which works out at around 58 runs per wicket. By contrast, in the final summer of the 1990s, four Tests yielded 3,092 for 125, which works out to about 25 runs per wicket. A bowler used to be able to leave the field at the end of an innings and soak his aching bones in a Radox bath. Nowadays, he's barely had time to turn on the tap before someone's telling him to start strapping on the pads.

Only once in this series has a batsman put you in mind of Colin Cowdrey, and that was on Saturday when Adam Parore pulled off a brilliant replica of one of Cowdrey's trademarks – the elegant shouldered-arms leave. The one difference was that Cowdrey chose to leave deliveries outside his off stump, rather than those heading for the middle one.

England's highest individual total of the summer came from a bowler who went in as a nightwatchman and who is currently broken down. Andrew Caddick has been the one bonus, although the final irony yesterday was that the man named as England's player of the series is a New Zealander. It almost goes without saying that New Zealand's least productive player of the series, Roger Twose, is an Englishman.

6 NOVEMBER 1999

MALCOLM MARSHALL: A MAGIC FAST BOWLER FOR ALL SEASONS

Mark Nicholas

Moments before midnight on Thursday, Robin Smith telephoned with the numbing news we had feared for most of the week. Malcolm Marshall had died.

Cancer of the colon got him during the early summer and, in a remorseless pursuit, nailed him before the autumn leaves finished their fall. He was 41 years old.

Marshall's last Test match in England was at the Oval in 1991. Smith recalled how he ground out for nearly five hours against typically accurate fast bowling that allowed him no quarter. He remembered vividly how stuck he became with his score at 98 and how Marshall, sensing the unease, altered his field to place another slip and leave just two men on the leg side. Three balls later he bowled a soft half-volley at leg stump which Smith pushed comfortably into the vast open space at mid-wicket. Smith is certain Marshall gave him that hundred. Marshall, to the end, would not have a bit of it.

A remarkable cricketer and a very special person has gone. As Colin Ingleby-McKenzie, Hampshire's cavalier captain in the '60s, said yesterday morning: 'We must assume that the great Maestro in the sky was short of a class all-rounder.'

If there was an element of ruthlessness about Marshall's bowling, there was not a hint of anything but warmth and generosity in his personality. He was a sportsman driven by self-belief, ambition and hope, but always he remained a players' man – forever lifting spirits, experimenting and educating both friend and foe in the nets, suggesting this and demanding that.

His high standards set the tone for teams in which he played and coached. It was not always possible for lesser talents to climb the mountains that 'Macko' managed but it was fun trying and more fun still to watch at first hand his own astonishing deeds.

He was a cricketer of indomitable spirit, immense will, utter dedication and supreme skill. He took 376 Test match wickets and 1,651 in all first-class cricket – 823 of those for Hampshire in a county career which began at the snow-covered racecourse ground in Derby in 1979 and finished when the knackering diet of a four-day County Championship and three one-day competitions became too much for him in 1993.

Briefly, he then played for Natal in South Africa, leading them to the Castle Cup at the first attempt. No one is more upset today than the South African bowler Shaun Pollock, who attributes many of his qualities as a cricketer to Malcolm's guidance.

In Barbados, where the magical island is today in shock, trophy after trophy, honour after honour came his way. His closest friends, Desmond Haynes and Joel Garner, who were with him through the glory years, were with him in his final moments, as, of course, was Connie, his wife. She said he went peacefully, without pain. His own father had died in a motorcycle accident before the boy got out of the cot. It was his grandfather, Oscar Welch, who introduced him to the game and played with him day and night.

The young Marshall preferred batting – always did, actually, and he could play a bit, too – but learnt in the playground at school that you didn't get a knock unless you bowled out the bloke who was on strike. So he skipped in 15 yards, hit a few fellas on the head and castled the rest.

By heaven, he could bowl quickly when he chose – Bobby Parks, our wicketkeeper, was 31 paces back one day at Portsmouth – and the skidding, screaming bouncer was the most chilling part of his armoury. Yet his real talent was in understanding his opponents, conditions and pitches and in being able to adapt. He was a natural outswinger of the ball and by the late '80s, when he had mastered the inswinger, he at times appeared almost unplayable.

In 1992 Hampshire were bowled out cheaply by Essex in a crucial Benson and Hedges match. Marshall, who was desperate for a day at Lord's with his beloved adopted county, won the match in minutes by trapping Graham Gooch, John Stephenson and Mark Waugh lbw to leave Essex on the ropes at 5 for 3. He finished with 4 for 20, the man-of-the-match award and, two months later, with the cup itself.

Gooch thought him the finest bowler he played against. Viv Richards calls him the greatest of all fast bowlers – 'the man with the biggest heart and the smartest brain'. For my part, I shall remember the laughter, the dancing eyes, and the incessant, always enthusiastic, chatter. If much of Malcolm characterised the calypso cricketer, much, too, epito-mised the model professional. From Sydney to Southampton, in Barbados, Bournemouth and Bangalore, Malcolm Marshall was a man for all seasons.

---

14 NOVEMBER 1999

SHAPING UP IS PROVING A HARD TASK FOR FLINTOFF

Scyld Berry

Endowed by nature with fine talent, but without the mental strength and systematic approach to make the most of it, and preferring a comfortable existence to the rigorous pursuit of excellence: nobody personifies the present state of English cricket more than Andrew Flintoff.

If anyone was born to lead an England revival, if not quite be a second Botham, it is Flintoff. There has never been a specialist batsman of massive build, 6ft 4in as the Lancashire lad is, who has consistently succeeded at Test level: he would be too big a target for the fast bowlers and his centre of gravity too high for the yorkers. But if Flintoff can bowl, and therefore hold on to his place through the lean times, and bat like an all-rounder as Botham did, he should be capable of 5,000 Test runs.

The problem – the biggest problem of England's tour so far indeed – is that Flintoff cannot bowl, which means that England cannot field a balanced side for the first Test at Johannesburg. Darren Gough, Andy Caddick, Alan Mullally and Phil Tufnell, backed up by Flintoff, batting at no. 7 with judicious panache, as he did in his first innings here in Bloemfontein, against an old ball, and banging it into these hard pitches at pace: nothing much wrong with that.

But if Flintoff cannot bowl (he is currently given two to three weeks before being fit), and there is no all-rounder in the side apart from Alec Stewart, England are all square pegs and round holes. Four seamers with Michael Vaughan's off-spin is insufficiently varied; and three seamers with Tufnell is too light on pace for The Wanderers, especially if Gough can only be used in short bursts. Flintoff's failure to be fit to bowl is the crux.

It also threatens the psychological welfare of this England party, fragile in confidence as they already are after their defeat by New Zealand. In recent days, after a dressing-down early on the tour, Flintoff has been doing his fitness work, and the decision to keep him on tour was taken partly so that England's fitness trainers could keep an eye on him, not let him balloon at home. But if there is any shirking here, the presence of a highly-paid passenger not pulling his weight will fester and infect.

And this has been known to happen before. Probably the most severe criticism ever levelled publicly at an England cricketer by officialdom was that directed by Lord MacLaurin in his recent autobiography *Tiger by the Tail*. According to the chairman of the ECB, Flintoff was almost thrown off England's A tour of Zimbabwe and South Africa last winter, 'the trouble being that his approach doesn't always measure up to his talents'.

Before that A tour, every member of the party passed a medical check except Flintoff. After a warning, according to MacLaurin, Flintoff at a second check was found to be in even worse condition, 'not that he seemed to care'. On hearing the news, MacLaurin says he scoffed at the implications, saying: 'OK, what are you going to do about it – give me a couple of hundred lines?'

Part of the responsibility for breeding such a complacent attitude lies with the England selectors. On the urging of the England coach David Lloyd, who since his Lancashire days has seen Flintoff as his prodigy, they selected him for the last two Tests of the 1998 series against South Africa. Never mind that Flintoff has a batting average below six from three Test innings, and a bowling average of 112: he can now boast 'of England' on his sponsored car, just like Ben Hollioake and Chris Read. At the age of 20 they have all found themselves at the summit, prematurely pushed there rather than through their own drive.

Just as significantly, Flintoff's agent has been able to use the 'of England' tag to drive up his wages. After protracted negotiations this autumn, a one-year deal was agreed which did not break the county's existing wage structure (his salary is understood to be £70,000 before bonuses). His contract, however, has a three-year option attached to it, with the implication being that if Lancashire do not break their wage cap and increase his salary to almost six figures from next year, Flintoff will find another county.

Here we come to the source of the disease of cross-subsidising which harms English cricket. The bulk of the annual turnover of almost £70 million derives from Test cricket. But this money does not primarily go into producing excellence for England at Test level. It goes to counties, who increasingly use their subsidies to hire Australians and the disaffected from other counties.

If a younger Flintoff wants to make the most he can from cricket, he can earn just as much by being a valuable one-day player for his county as by being an excellent member of England's Test team – or more, if he paces himself to last for 10 years and gets a benefit, rather than burning himself out for his country. The system is not so much unhealthy as plain sick.

CHAPTER 7
THE 2000s

INTRODUCTION

The England team celebrated the dawn of the new millennium in South Africa unaware of the fact that they would soon be unwittingly dragged into one of the greatest crises to hit the game.

Just a few weeks after their victory in the final Test at Centurion, Hansie Cronje, the devout Christian captain and symbol of the vibrant new South Africa, was revealed as a man bankrolled by bookmakers.

It soon became clear that match-fixing was not simply the manifestation of the greed and weakness of one man. The whole of the cricketing world would be dragged into the scandal and the ramifications were still being felt at the 2007 World Cup.

For Cronje the fall from grace was spectacular. Little more than two years after confessing to receiving gifts and money from bookmakers, he died in a plane crash in South Africa. Here we do not reprint Cronje's obituary. There is no lasting tribute to the fallen hero. Instead we have the words of the man himself. His attempts to justify his behaviour and plans for redemption were spoken in an interview with the *Sunday Telegraph*'s Owen Slot, a few months before his death in 2002. The piece reflects the man. Charming, articulate but ultimately flawed. Cronje's battle with the truth permeates every word of this fascinating piece.

Quite what E.W. Swanton would have thought of it all is easy to imagine. The betrayal of the basic tenets of a game he loved would have led to a forthright column in the *Telegraph*. But Swanton passed away on 24 January 2000, with his last column appearing in the paper the previous summer. His output obviously declined over the years but he still enjoyed his visits to the newspaper's offices in Canary Wharf and his dealings with the desk are still talked about today. When one sub-editor named Jazz queried his copy, Swanton said: 'Good Lord, Jazz, is that your name ... I once had a dog called Jazz.' On another occasion one of the *Telegraph*'s current cricket columnists was pulled up for his lack of respectable attire. When the writer said he was leaving the office for Waterloo Station Swanton said to him: 'Good to see you today but when you are at Waterloo you might find time to pop into their branch of Tie Rack.'

Swanton's passing was soon followed by those who filled his many columns. Peter May, Colin Cowdrey, Brian Statham and Sir Donald Bradman. Giants of the game, all given suitable send-offs by the *Telegraph*'s team of writers.

By the turn of the century the *Telegraph* had a new cricket correspondent following Christopher Martin-Jenkins's departure to *The Times*. Michael Henderson inherited the role and brought a new vigour to the position. His views did not always find favour with the *Telegraph*'s readers but then again it 'twas ever thus for the cricket correspondent.

Dear Sir
Don't you think the time has arrived for your cricket correspondent to be quietly disposed of, stuffed, and placed in the Long Room with the curved bats, the sparrow and other freaks of the game.

That letter was sent to E.W. Swanton in 1956 but nearly fifty years later we see a *Telegraph* correspondent receiving similar tidings.

Henderson's stint was brief and eventful. In 2002 the former England all-rounder Derek Pringle was poached from the *Independent* to fill the role vacated by Henderson's departure.

Moreover, the presence of Mark Nicholas, by now the anchor for Channel 4's innovative television coverage, and the self-styled analyst Simon Hughes meant that the *Telegraph* enjoyed unrivalled international cricket commentary.

By this time Mike Atherton's writing had matched the heights of his cricket career and his columns in the *Sunday Telegraph* had become essential reading within the game. His poignant and revealing piece on the proliferation of cricket suicides is given added weight by his interview with one player who had decided to end his own life.

Atherton and Pringle, friends and ex-team-mates, had shared in England ups and downs of the previous decade. The steady regeneration under Duncan Fletcher and Nasser Hussain is celebrated and culminates in the regaining of the Ashes in 2005. A souvenir supplement and book were published to mark the occasion and cricket enjoyed a new-found popularity with the public and the media.

That victory was soon followed by the decision for the *Telegraph*'s daily sport section to change its format. The new tabloid section was launched in October 2005.

That was quickly followed by further evolution at the newspaper. Towards the end of 2006 the *Daily Telegraph* moved from its Canary Wharf offices into a new multi-media 'hub' in London's Victoria. The move coincided with a new approach, combining newspaper production and online content, and the Ashes tour of 2006 was to be the first major sports event to be covered across the new media spectrum.

Simon Hughes's daily podcast was combined with blogs by Simon Briggs and Derek Pringle. A blog by Briggs is reproduced here and contains an ominous message. His story about the murder rate in Jamaica was published just five days before Bob Woolmer was found dead in his Kingston hotel room. After a long investigation, Woolmer's death was proved to be from natural causes.

---

24 JANUARY 2000

Ted Dexter

If Jim Swanton, who died on Saturday aged 92, had been an American, he might well have been called by his initials, E.W. Everyone in cricket knew who E.W. was. He was the establishment voice of the summer game both on radio and through the columns of the *Daily Telegraph*.

I don't remember how long it took me to call him Jim but it was certainly Mr Swanton in the early years. He would have been aware of Dexter, the schoolboy cricketer both at Radley College and in the representative matches at Lord's, mainly as a close friend and subsequently the biographer of 'Gubby' Allen, who helped me so much in my career.

My first real awareness of this impressively large man was when he wrote a letter to the editor of the *Telegraph* after my omission from the tour to Australia in 1958. I had scored 50 on the eve of the selectors' meeting and when they passed me over it was Jim who castigated them most strongly with the memorable description of 'thrice-blinded moles'.

As I grew to more senior positions as a player at county level and for England, it was definitely fashionable to disparage the Swanton column as the work of a dinosaur who still viewed the game in terms of MCC, I Zingari, Free Foresters, Authentics and indeed his own creation, The Arabs. Eton v. Harrow was certainly on his agenda, as also was Gents v. Players.

He had quite a stentorian voice at the microphone and it was the known practical joker Peter Richardson who brought a county game at Canterbury to a halt while the umpires investigated a 'peculiar booming sound' coming from above and behind the pavilion sightscreen – ie from the radio commentary box.

Jim defied everyone's opinion of him as a confirmed bachelor by marrying late in life. Though he never had children, my wife, Susan, has never forgotten the charming way that he played with our two little youngsters in the mid-'60s on one of those balmy days at Arundel.

When I did my near five-year stint as chairman of England selectors, I have to say that I crossed swords with his opinions on various occasions and a letter to the *Telegraph* during that period, this time from me, did its best to tear a strip off him.

Not to be put off, he invited me to dinner and reinforced his opinions with a decent bottle of Bordeaux. When, once again, I interrupted by saying that 'I couldn't agree less' with half of what he was saying, there was that familiar 'harrumph' which meant that we had agreed to differ.

Not that Jim was a man to cross, because he always had influence in cricket, through a variety of committees, both for MCC and for his home county, Kent, quite apart from his powerful position within the media. When he retired from full-time journalism, he was able to indulge his considerable enjoyment of the game of golf and I remember his loyal support when I was chasing amateur honours at Royal St George's, Sandwich.

Aged 90, there were two remarkable demonstrations of his undiminished senses. Across a noisy dining table at a charity dinner, the current sports editor of this paper asked him when his first column was due. Jim gave the day and date without even a pause from his conversation.

He was then the main speaker at the jubilee dinner of the Cricket Writers' Association in the same year. It was a tour de force, witty, comprehensive and all of it elegantly constructed in simple English. I began to think that I should have given his opinions more credit in those earlier years.

---

12 JUNE 2000

Michael Henderson

Please excuse this intrusion into the death of a much-loved public performer but if I offer a private reflection on Brian Statham, who died yesterday a week before his 70th birthday, it is because he played in the first cricket match I saw, and is one of the reasons I learnt to love the game. His passing is a reminder of how much has gone of life.

A young boy growing up in Lancashire absorbed the greatness of 'George' Statham as he understood the huge public affection for Tom Finney or, in a different field, Kathleen Ferrier. It was a 'given'. Like them he came from a modest background and went on to conquer the world. Like them he never imagined that fame separated him from his fellows.

Statham was approaching the end of his career when I first saw him bowl, against Derbyshire, in 1967. He was 38, a great age by today's standards, when he took 6 for 34 to bowl out Yorkshire for 61 a year later. So I can at least boast that I saw him run through the champions.

That was his last fling. He retired at the end of the season and Fred Trueman, who played against him in that match, did not delay his own retirement long. Trueman and Statham: they went together like Lennon and McCartney, and it was no surprise to hear the great Yorkshire bowler leading the tributes yesterday.

How far removed the lion-hearted Statham was from the world of players trotting off to see psychologists 'to get their minds right'! The abiding image of this lean, wiry man with the double-jointed action was of a fast bowler who ran in, rain or shine, and took his pleasures in the saloon bar with a fag or two and several pints of bitter, or mild. He wasn't choosy.

Times change quickly, and reputations fade. The generation growing up today may not be familiar with men like Statham. Indeed, on England's tour of South Africa last winter, one (admittedly young) member of the party failed to recognise Colin Cowdrey in a group portrait. Laugh if you like, but it's true.

Players can be unreceptive to the achievements of the past. David Green, who grew up under Statham at Old Trafford and who writes about cricket for this paper, was once talking to a young English bowler who took a dim view of previous generations, and wondered, in particular, whether Statham was fast.

'How fast do you think he was, then?' Green asked. 'About as sharp as Neil Foster,' was the reply. 'I'll tell you how fast he was,' said Greeny. 'Roy Marshall reckoned that if he could push George through mid-off for a couple in his fifth over he was doing pretty well. And Roy Marshall could play a bit. Ne'then, lad, shall we look at your figures?'

That chastened young shaver, incidentally, never played for England. Statham did, 70 times, and took 252 wickets, often with Trueman at the other end. Whereas Trueman was fast and, on occasions, wild, Statham was the model of accuracy, operating on the premise of 'you miss, I hit'. As Neville Cardus wrote: 'Did Statham ever send down a wide?'

There were times when he came off the field with blood in his boots but, privately and publicly, there were no grumbles. He belonged to a generation that had seen real hardship at first hand, and such experience tends to put things like cricket into a clearer perspective. When one considers the longevity of his career, and the peaks he scaled along the way, nobody can question his claim to greatness, though this modest man would never press his own case.

The England players who gather at Birmingham today may well read his obituary and pass on, as they have a Test on Thursday. But they would do well to reflect on a good man and a great career. Statham brought to the game that most precious of human qualities: glory, lightly worn. He added a verse to the eternal chorus, and must be remembered.

---

10 JULY 2000

Michael Parkinson

They auctioned Jack Fingleton's baggy green the other day, the one he wore during the 1935–6 tour of South Africa when he scored three Test centuries. He made it four in a row – the first cricketer to do so – against England in the first Test of their 1936–7 tour of Australia.

Anyway, I bought the cap because Jack was an old and dear friend and because I always wanted to own a baggy green. It is the most famous cricket cap in the world, and the best looking. There is no more defining and thrilling sight in cricket than the Aussies turning out in that distinctive headgear. It is both a trademark and a declaration that the men wearing it have earned it the hard way.

It will go nicely with the Aussie sweater Keith Miller gave me. He turned up for lunch in Oz carrying a plastic bag. After the meal, as he stepped into a taxi home, he thrust the bag into my hands. 'I want you to have this, it doesn't fit me any more,' he said. When I looked inside I was choked. I nearly burst into tears. I'm just an old-fashioned romantic, really, and the older I get the more reason I find to be so.

The cap arrived two days ago badly abused in transit. The plastic case it travelled in had been smashed and the peak of the cap was broken. I'm not sure if this was caused by the journey or a Harold Larwood bouncer. Harold told me that Jack never flinched from the short stuff. In fact, what he said was: 'He was a tough little bugger. You couldn't knock him down'.

I worked with Jack on a Sunday newspaper in the '60s and early '70s, but really got to know him after he had retired. I was making a speech at the National Press Club in Canberra and invited questions. Pretending he didn't know me, Jack stood up and reduced the formality of the proceedings to a rubble.

His question (it lasted five minutes) included the observation that although I was a Pom I was at least a Yorkshire Pom, which wasn't so bad, although I came from Barnsley which, as everyone knew, had the highest illegitimacy rate on the planet and, what is more, was the birthplace of the groundsman who prepared the wicket at Headingley where Fred Trueman twice bowled out the Aussies to win a Test match which was clearly a fix, since the only way we could ever beat the Aussies was by cheating, and on, and on, and on.

All this was delivered out of the corner of the mouth and with twinkling eyes. He was a funny, cantankerous, wise and argumentative man. Like his great friend, Bill O'Reilly, he was afeared of no man, including Bradman.

He was a fine cricketer. In the first-class game he scored nearly 7,000 runs at 44. In Test cricket he averaged 42. He was also a marvellous observer of the game. Like Richie Benaud, he was a journalist by training and instinct. The best kind. In my list of favourite cricket writers he is among the top half-dozen.

Fingleton's laconic manner made him a television natural. The first time I interviewed him he overdid the dental fixative required to stop his teeth clacking and spent an agonising hour in his hotel bathroom experimenting with various solvents so that he might unclamp his jaws. As he explained, it would have been embarrassing, to say the least, had he arrived on the set with appropriate fanfare only to say 'G'Gay Gichael'.

He was such a success we invited him back. He worried how he could top his first appearance. The night before he rang me. 'I've been thinking about what I might do tomorrow,' he said. 'Tell me, has anyone ever croaked on your show?'

He died a year later. I miss him but not in a sad way. Whenever I think of Jack Fingleton I hear the echo of remembered laughter.

---

5 SEPTEMBER 2000

AUSSIES ALERTED BY OVAL EUPHORIA

Martin Johnson

Modern television camerawork gets in so close to the crowd these days, that it is a brave man indeed who phones in sick on a Monday morning and then takes himself off to the cricket. 'Come in Smith. Now then, can you explain exactly how, a few hours after phoning in with an apparently terminal case of influenza, you managed to make such a marvellous recovery that somebody looking remarkably like you was seen sprinting across the outfield at the Oval planting slobbery, germ-ridden kisses all over Nasser Hussain?'

Thirty-one years without a series victory over the West Indies is, of course, an interminably long time to wait, but it was still hard to believe the size of yesterday's crowd. The fifth day of a Test match normally produces one of those Scottish Second Division football attendances. Supporter phones club. 'What time's the kick-off?' Club tells supporter. 'What time can you get here?'

Under normal circumstances, the height of inconvenience for an Oval security guard on Test Match Monday is an occasional interruption to the crossword to issue directions to the appropriate turnstile. Yesterday, though, the Hobbs Gate was resembled the portcullis of the Bastille, with the Surrey committee only just stopping short of having vats of boiling oil sent up to the ramparts.

The last time England filled the ground on the fifth day of a Test match was at the same venue, against the same opponents, in 1991. On that occasion, though, it filled up gradually, the excitement generated by England inching towards victory in the match diluted by the knowledge that it meant nothing more than a 2-2 draw in the series.

Several fans were in tears at their failure to get in, as they were when they were teething, or requiring a nappy change, on the last occasion England won a series against this opposition. In 1969, Concorde was making its maiden flight, the cell doors were clanging shut on the Krays, Tony Jacklin was winning the Open golf championship, and the two captains were tossing up with pre-decimal coinage.

One of them was Raymond Illingworth, but the last man to captain England to a series win against the West Indies was not around yesterday to comment on then and now. If he had been, you wouldn't have ruled out Raymond (never one to knowingly relegate his own achievements in the historical pecking order) snorting: 'When I were captain, West Indies were a bloody sight 'arder to beat than this lot.'

And, if you are looking for a qualifying clause to this summer, so they were. Australia will not be arriving in around eight months time trembling with fear, but neither will there be any early injury problems for them as a result of slipping over in their own saliva. At the risk of prompting an outbreak of guffawing in Wollongong and Wagga Wagga, England appear to have a team, and more importantly a newly acquired collective 'bottle', to make a real series of it.

A cautionary note, however, is that the West Indies arrived here on the back of 10 consecutive away Test defeats, and while they shortly depart for a tour of Australia by aeroplane, a more appropriate mode of transport would be a tumbrel. Their bowling will be desperate without Curtly Ambrose and Courtney Walsh, and their batting technique is abysmal. The pad is either nowhere near the bat, or else thrust half forward in a way that gives the blade nowhere to go — like watching someone trying to run the 100 metres with their trousers round their ankles.

Ambrose and Walsh both walked to the crease yesterday to a standing ovation and an England players' guard of honour. It's a fair assumption that Walsh's batting has never been compared to Bradman's, but both of them were out for a second ball duck in their final Test innings, allegedly unable to see through the tears in their eyes. If Walsh's batting has brought tears to anyone's eyes down the years, it's been the spectators'.

There has been talk about feeling sorry for the West Indies in their present state, but let's not forget that we once felt sorry for the Australians. When Mike Gatting was invited to consider that Australia's consolation victory in the 19867 series was 'good for Test cricket', he emitted a strange choking noise, and a look you might reserve for someone newly arrived from Mars. He was right too. Let's not just beat the arrogant sods next time, let's whitewash them.

---

11 DECEMBER 2000

Michael Henderson

Karachi

Although they are becoming harder to beat, England do not know how to win many Test matches. Unless there is a bizarre sequence of events today, they will leave Pakistan tonight with a third successive draw. But they may wonder, when they are unwrapping their Christmas presents, whether a bolder approach here would have brought them greater reward.

By taking three wickets yesterday, England opened the door slightly. Should Pakistan, who lead by 88, lose five more wickets before lunch, as they did on the second morning, English nostrils may sniff an unlikely victory. It is far more likely, though, that the game will meander to a close with honour more or less satisfied.

Being a side of limited means, England could argue that they have done their best. But have they? Remember what Nasser Hussain, the captain, said before the game. 'I've told the boys we'll be absolute mugs if we don't give it absolutely everything in the next five days.'

Is it asking too much of these players to make more than 388 in 180 overs? The main feature of England's innings was a century of character- istic self-denial and, to be frank, monumental tedium by Michael

Atherton. On Friday night and for much of Saturday morning, he batted wonderfully. But oh, how hard he made it look as he crawled, session by session, from 76 to 94, then to 117 by stumps before he was eventually out yesterday morning, all but strokeless, for 125.

Atherton has many outstanding qualities, and he has played very well in this series for 314 runs. His 16th Test hundred was also his first against Pakistan, and it took him past Wally Hammond (7,249) in the list of England run-makers. Now Atherton has only four more peaks to conquer: Gooch, Gower, Boycott and Cowdrey.

But really for almost a whole day his batting made for insufferable viewing. In 9hrs 35mins, in which time one could hear the whole of *Götterdämmerung* twice and still nip out to the pub for last orders, he failed to score off no fewer than 350 balls. It was, in its own way, admirable. It was also stultifying and, one could argue, counter-productive.

Occupation of the crease is fine, but not for its own sake. If they are honest, England may admit that they missed a trick on Saturday. A remarkable fact emerged yesterday morning, when the scorers notched the 5,000th 'dot ball' of this series. In plain English it meant that, out of 13 days and one session of play, 10 whole days had been runless. The slow pitches have had something to do with that but those are not figures to convince spectators, here or elsewhere, that they have spent their money wisely.

When Atherton was out, caught behind as he tried to run a single down to third man, he had batted for 13 hours since his dismissal in the first innings at Faisalabad, where he was unbeaten in the second innings. In his defence he might well say that he had to dig in because two members of the top six are desperately out of form. But, deary me, it was tough sledding.

Hussain, despite making his first half-century of the year, remains in bad nick. His was a horrible innings, though it may prove an important one. The other struggler, Graeme Hick, gifted his wicket to Waqar Younis in the first over yesterday when he pulled a feeble shot to that most unusual position, square-leg. Did he not know a man was there?

England's lack of ambition extended to the way they set about Pakistan's second innings. They began well, Gough having Imran Nazir caught behind off the glove and Graham Thorpe holding a superb catch over his shoulder at long-leg when Saeed Anwar hooked Andrew Caddick.

Ashley Giles, tempting Inzamam to sweep a ball that pitched in the rough outside leg stump, baffled the batsman when it turned past his withdrawn bat to hit the top of off stump. That was the bowler's 15th wicket, more than any other England bowler has taken in a series here.

Salisbury has taken only one wicket and it has cost him the little matter of 193 runs. Hussain publicly rebuked him last night, first admonishing him for conceding a boundary behind point when he had been instructed to bowl defensively outside the leg stump, and then taking him off. Don't worry, Solly. One more day, and you're a free man.

---

16 DECEMBER 2000

Sir — I hope the cooks at the *Telegraph* have a recipe for humble pie. If not there is still time to master it before you sit your increasingly irritating cricket correspondent Michael Henderson down to lunch on his return from Pakistan.

He wasted his column unsubtly suggesting Mike Atherton should be dropped instead of pointing out Atherton had laid the foundations for a possible victory. Even though England have started winning Test matches and series, Henderson cannot bring himself to write anything other than the most grudging praise. He is no doubt sharpening his pencil now for an assault on the team's failings in the run-up to the Ashes.

Andrew Capon
London

---

17 DECEMBER 2000

Mike Atherton

At around 5.30 p.m. on that final day in Karachi, the sirens sounded from the local mosque to indicate that the sun had gone down and that the fast that Muslims religiously adhere to in Ramadan was over for the day. England still needed a dozen or so runs to complete a famous victory and time was running out.

The physio's room where I was sitting was a northern enclave as with me were Michael Vaughan and Darren Gough, all of us aware of the cricketers' superstition, which dictates that you can't move seats when things are going well. The mood was tense, in a kind of will we, won't we way, but also light-hearted. Vaughan was running a book on how long each over would take and Gough had the dollar signs whizzing in front of his eyes announcing that this victory would put a good few grand on his benefit year.

The moment of victory approached: Graham Thorpe was playing what looked like shadow shots as no one could see the ball, least of all Inzamam-ul-Haq at deep cover, who decided not to show us his athleticism in the deep for one last time and failed to move to the ball at all. Thorpe then executed his trademark Chinese cut and we all congregated on the balcony for the ritual celebrations.

Soon there were tears running down my eyes. Not through happiness or emotion, as you might think, but because in the celebrations 'Chalky' White had forgotten to put his bat down, and instead brandished it around like a madman and clobbered me on the end of the hooter. It necessitated a quick visit to the toilet to check for damage, which meant that again, as at the Oval at the end of last summer, I missed out on being on the victory photo in the changing-room.

Mayhem in the dressing-room for some time. Andrew Caddick replicated the victory moment, in the absence of any champagne, by releasing a bottle of pop.

There was much back slapping and hugging and then a ridiculous dog chant initiated by the physio Dean Conway that still baffles me. The 'David May' award was given. The award, in remembrance of the fine Manchester United defender, is given to the 12th man or substitute who finds himself at the front of the victory celebrations, or nearest the trophy most often. Paul Nixon and Matthew Hoggard were the recipients.

Then the match presentations took place, in complete darkness, to remind us of how close we were to not finishing the game. The Pakistan team came out and graciously shook our hands and congratulated us. Moin Khan looked distraught and I felt for him because I have enjoyed playing against him, and in particular enjoyed his chat behind the stumps.

It was gratifying to receive the man-of-the-match award for my first-innings hundred. I am aware of the criticism of slow batting and I am sure it was not the most riveting passage of play. Above all, however, as a batsman you have to play according to the situation and the needs of the team. If I had scored an eight-hour hundred batting first, criticism would have been entirely justified as I would not have been giving the team time to bowl the opposition out twice and win the match.

But the situation was that we were batting second and facing a big first-innings score. To have any chance of getting anything out of the game we had to get close to or past their score. We knew that if we did, Pakistan had such a proud record at Karachi and so much hinged on the match, that they were bound to be nervous second time around.

I know that without the innings we would not have won the match, and could well have lost it, so in its way I view it among the best of the match-winning innings I've played for England. Off the field the tour was no different from any other I've been on for England. Team spirit was pretty good, though inevitably there were the usual cliques and irritations that occurred. Some players were curious about Pakistan and others less so. Some enjoyed the country and one or two found the tour extremely hard going. We won simply because we played good cricket and have been doing so for most of the previous six months.

There are four fairly straightforward reasons for this. Most important is the contract system introduced last year: it enables England's strike bowlers to rest more often and makes sure the players' focus is primarily on England and not their counties. Second is the important partnership between Nasser Hussain and Duncan Fletcher which gives the team clear leadership. Third is selection, which, after the shemozzle of South Africa, is picking by and large the best players in England. And fourth is the age group of the senior and influential players within the team; these players are at the peak of their powers and should remain so for a short while yet.

---

27 FEBRUARY 2001

Peter Fitzsimmons

The news broke in Australia at 7.15 a.m. yesterday, Sydney time. Bradman was dead. He had died in his bed on Sunday morning, at the modest home in Adelaide where he had lived for the last 76 years.

Within minutes every media organisation in the country scrambled to get details as car drivers pulled over to the side of the road the better to listen, and people everywhere formed into small groups to talk it over. Only a short time later, the Prime Minister, John Howard, released a statement lauding the cricketer as 'the most dominant figure in Australian life for decades', and the 'best Australian sportsman in the last 100 years'.

Within hours, both the *Sydney Morning Herald* and the *Sydney Daily Telegraph* had hit the streets with special editions, the latter trumpeting on the front page: 'Bradman is dead. Nation mourns greatest hero.'

Though the South Australian government offered a state funeral, the family is preferring to have a small private one this Thursday, with a big and public memorial service in three weeks' time in the church that overlooks his beloved Adelaide Oval. His death is not being viewed as a tragedy, for he was, after all, 92 years old and had suffered so many recent illnesses that it was not unexpected, but all acknowledge it as a significant moment in our country's history.

Of course, no single epitaph could hope to do Sir Donald Bradman justice, but in terms of his pure cricketing ability, I nominate the words of one of yours, English cricket writer, R.C. Robertson-Glasgow: 'Poetry and murder lived in him together. He would slice the bowling to ribbons, then dance without pity on the corpse.'

Ne'er a truer word written, and in the wake of his death many stories have been recalled to demonstrate the extraordinary grandeur of his domination. A personal favourite is the occasion when the Don scored 334 runs in a 1930 Test at Leeds, and a London newspaper finally trumpeted just two grateful words on posters around the city: 'HE'S OUT!'

Of his later years, of course, far fewer stories are told simply because Sir Donald became such an enigmatic and distant figure that there are only a handful who were intimate enough with him to be able to tell any such stories. Nevertheless, I think I have a beauty. It was told to me by the great Australian batsman, Dean Jones, who positively swore on the head of his daughter it happened, and I have since been told that Merv Hughes also confirms its truth.

The scene is set at a Test match between Australia and the West Indies at Adelaide Oval back in February 1989. These were the days when the Windies were the greatest power the cricketing world had ever seen, the days when they used to select 11 fast bowlers in the team and a 12th man who was a fast bowler just to be on the safe side.

And it was into just such a furnace that the young bowler Mervyn Hughes walked – with bat in hand. Figuring fortune favoured the brave, Hughes wielded the willow like an axeman his axe, and somehow – after snicking fortutiously, connecting full-bloodedly, and missing entirely – he finished the day's play at 72 not out.

The tradition in Test cricket is that the batting side take a few beers into the fielding side's dressing-room afterwards, but not on this evening. Instead, Merv took an ice-box full of bottles, so keen was he to give the men of the Windies the full blow-by-blow account of every run he'd made. So it was that half-an-hour later, Jones – who himself had contributed 216 – and Hughes and several other Australian players were in the Windies dressing-room, when a sudden hush fell upon the gathering.

They looked to the door and there was Sir Donald Bradman himself, being ushered into the room by several South Australian cricket officials. The Don had expressed a desire to meet this mighty team, and now here he was.

For the next 15 minutes or so, the great man was introduced to the visiting players, with each West Indian standing up well before Sir Donald got to their position on the bench. Then, when their time came, they warmly shook his hand and had a few words.

This all proceeded splendidly until Sir Donald got to the last man on the bench, Patrick Patterson – the fastest bowler in the world at that time. So the story goes, not only did Patterson not stand, he simply squinted quizzically up at the octogenarian. Finally, after some 30 seconds of awkward silence, Patterson stood up, all two metres of pure whip-cord steel of him, and looked down at the diminutive Don.

'You, Don Bradman!?!' he snorted. 'You, Don Bradman?!?! I kill you, mun! I bowl at you, I kill you! I split you in two!'

In reply, Sir Donald, with his hands on his hips, gazed squarely back at Patterson and calmly retorted: 'You couldn't even get Merv Hughes out. You'd have no chance against me, mate!'

Fare thee well, Sir Donald. True or not, we will all still be fondly recalling stories of your life to our own dying day.

19 MARCH 2001

Michael Henderson

Colombo

There are days in the life of a sportsman, and they are exceedingly rare, when he can hear the mermaids singing. Saturday in Colombo was one of them. Transformed by the diaphanous light of victory, the England players could for one voluptuous afternoon share a moment of mutual rapture that they may never know again.

At the end of an emotional day, when tears were not far away, they had won a Test match, and with it a series, in a way that strained credulity. The swift disposal of Sri Lanka, who were bundled out for 81 in a single breathless session of play, left the 5,000 English followers rubbing their eyes in disbelief, and when England got home by four wickets shortly after 6 p.m., their joy was unconfined.

England have now won four series in a row, and one must go back 22 years to find an achievement that matches it. If the victory against Zimbabwe last summer was a hillside scramble, and the one against the West Indies was a hike of Helvellyn, then the win in Pakistan before Christmas represented the scaling of a minor Alpine peak and this latest success was like conquering the Eiger.

This has not been an easy tour, for all sorts of reasons. England lost the toss in each Test, and had to endure heat and humidity that, for Europeans, was almost unbearable. They lost the first Test by an innings in a way that still leaves a foul taste in the mouth, and yet never once did the players complain, privately or in public.

Simply put, they rolled up their sleeves and seized two matches by the force of their personality, which is why this performance must be considered the finest by an England touring side since Mike Gatting's team won in Australia 14 winters ago. In fact it might be better than that. Never before have Sri Lanka gone one-up at home and lost a series. South Africa couldn't win here last year. Australia were beaten the year before. Just think about that.

Before reflecting on Saturday's extraordinary events, when 22 wickets fell, it is worth dwelling on that defeat in Galle, because it was the way that England responded that enabled them to hit back so strongly. They could have moaned and groaned about the poor decisions they got there but, on the final evening, the players were drinking and laughing in their hotel bar, swapping tall tales and even going for a midnight swim! That was not the reckless behaviour of men who didn't care. Rather, it was their way of winding down after a fraught five days. 'It's not that we lost!' one of them said. 'We might have gone down anyway. It's that we were denied the chance to save the game.'

Having cleared their heads that night, and having banished all thoughts of the way they lost, the players immediately looked ahead to the second Test, which they won with a superb display of attacking cricket. It was the finest all-round England performance for years. They then carried that momentum into the final Test, and when they opened their final assault on Saturday afternoon they found that the Lankans, gifted as they are, offered pitiful resistance.

It was a day for real men, just as it has been a tour for real men, and England have a few. The victory was a personal reward for three men in particular: captain, opening bowler and star batsman. Nasser Hussain went into the game about 25 per cent fit and captained them superbly, Darren Gough tore in with his customary panache, and, as for Graham Thorpe, he can write his own notices and nobody will quibble.

Thorpe has enjoyed a magnificent winter, and this was his finest hour. He made 145 undefeated runs in the match and saw England home despite feeling so tired that he went dizzy and nearly threw up in the middle, unsettled by the sheer physical exhaustion of being out there for nearly three whole days. It was a feat of bravery as well as class.

Twice last summer, at Lord's and Leeds, England ran through the West Indies in a session. Now lightning has struck three times. Gough, as ever, led the way and his world-class credentials are now beyond dispute.

Later, when the crowd swarmed round the pavilion, and the sun-touched spectators supped deep into a balmy night, Gough's was the name everybody chanted. Is there, one wonders, a more popular – as opposed to famous – sportsman in England? True, he doesn't wear his wife's clothes or give his children batty names, but one mustn't hold that against him.

There is something Dickensian about his spirit, in the way that people respond warmly to what they perceive, rightly, as chivalry and a bigness of heart. In Pakistan and now here he has bowled with fire and ice, and England could not have won either series without his wickets, and the example he has set. He has filled out as a man and a cricketer, and he returns to England a hero.

It is hard to think of many better days for English cricket than Saturday. England, we are told, has been a horrible place in the last two months. If this win offers any compensation, or makes even one person walk a little taller, then these cricketers may have performed a useful service.

This was a great victory, one in a hundred, as somebody else once said, in a different context altogether: rejoice!

---

2 APRIL 2001

GREAT MAN REMEMBERED AS CRICKET WORLD PAYS TRIBUTE TO COLIN COWDREY

Robert Philip

Well, did you evah, what a swelegant, elegant party this is ...

So you thought Oscars night was a pretty impressive gathering of A-list celebrities, did you? Well that was nothing compared to the bash the Cowdreys arranged on Friday. Prepare yourself while I name-drop from a very great height. I began the round of festivities with breakfast at The Ritz in the company of Sir Gary Sobers; repaired to Westminster Abbey where 2,500 people, including John Major, Ted Heath and William Hague, plus a veritable Who's Who from the world of cricket, attended a thanksgiving service in memory of the sorely missed Colin Cowdrey; and ended the day sipping white wine on the terrace of the House of Lords where friends and family watched the Thames flow gently past with fond reminiscences of the great man.

But let us begin in the Palm Court of The Ritz where Sir Garfield, still recovering from the effects of jet-lag following his flight from Barbados the previous evening, overcame his suspicion of newspapermen to explain why he missed the recent funeral of Sir Donald Bradman in Adelaide so he could come to London to pay homage to a man officially known as Lord Cowdrey of Tonbridge but who always preferred to be addressed simply as 'Colin'.

'Donald Bradman was a great, great cricketer but Colin was a great, great man,' Sobers said with tangible affection. 'My eyes aren't as good as they once were and my hands and legs give me a bit of bother these days so I couldn't make both trips. But it wasn't a difficult decision to reach. I had to be here to say farewell to a good friend and a true gentleman.'

The figures are impressive enough – 114 Tests for England at an average of 44.06 – but that was not the reason Colin Cowdrey was so beloved by everyone who knew him: he was painfully modest – habitually fending off compliments in the manner he formerly blocked the fearsome deliveries of Dennis Lillee and Jeff Thomson – seductively charming, a passionate supporter of minorities and charities, and blessed with the most mischievous sense of humour.

'I don't think Colin ever appreciated what a truly great cricketer he was,' Sobers continued. 'He was a team man from the peak of his cap to his bootlaces, so although he could be as elegant as anyone who has ever played the game, he frequently subdued his own instincts for the good of his team.

'Everyone in Barbados remembers him as an incredibly sporting opponent; he was always a thorn in our side but at the same time he was always very gentle on the pitch, very quiet. Being Colin, of course, he could never resist making a little joke here and there.

'We played in the same Commonwealth eleven once in India where we both made hundreds and Colin's innings that day was one of the greatest I have ever seen. When he completed his century I shook hands with him in the middle and said "why don't you play like this more often?" and he gave me this shy smile and replied "because I only learned to play like this from watching you at the other end". That was Colin; no matter what he achieved he remained completely unassuming.

'He loved Barbados like a second home and Barbados, in turn, loved him. I get invited to hundreds of cricket dinners and celebrations all over the world most of which, sadly, I have to refuse. But nothing would have kept me away today.'

The feeling was reciprocal. 'The three people dad most respected in cricket were Wally Hammond, The Don and Sir Garfield here,' explained Graham Cowdrey, who followed his father and his brother, Chris, into the Kent side.

'They had some great battles and Sir Gary always says they ended up even, but I think if dad was here today he'd tell you he probably lost 21 in injury time. I know dad would be very upset that Gary has wasted three or four days in London when he could be out on the golf course under the Barbados sun.'

To Westminster Abbey where Albinoni's Adagio filled the air as the great and good took their seats; Sir Garfield from the West Indies, Ted Dexter representing England, John Reid from New Zealand, Ali Bacher from South Africa, Asif Iqbal from Pakistan, the Maharajkumar Raj Singh of Dungarpur from India; Botham and Gower; Colin's team-mates from Kent's 1970 championship winning side; politicians; cricketing comics Brian Rix and Ronnie Corbett; Michael Stoute and Walter Swinburn, chums from his love of horse-racing; wife Ann, sons Graham, Chris and Jeremy, daughter Carol, and his nine beloved grandchildren.

There were hymns and prayers, pomp and ceremony, but as with any occasion involving Colin Cowdrey, there was laughter amid the tears. 'I remember watching him pack his suitcase before heading off to Australia in 1974,' Chris told the congregation. 'What on earth are you doing, dad?' I asked him. 'The might of Lillee and Thomson. You're 42 years old now.' And he looked at me with that small smile of his and replied: 'I think it will be rather fun, don't you?'

'How thrilled he would be to see the turn-out here today, for he loved cricket and cricket people. And yet such was his consideration for others he would ask me: "Why would anyone want to come to London on a Friday? Try to hurry things along so everyone doesn't get caught up in the rush-hour".'

'When I was old enough to appreciate what it all meant – I suppose I was about seven at the time – I remember dad taking me to Lord's one day. "This", said dad, "is the home of cricket. The home of the MCC." Aware that dad's initials also happened to be M.C.C., I confess that as I looked around the thought crossed my childish mind "one day, all this will be mine…"

'We all have great memories of our blissfully happy childhood but perhaps my most vivid when he had the opportunity of watching me play centre-forward for Wesley House in a local school derby against Selby. I had been put in the Second eleven for disciplinary reasons – 14 black marks being something of a school record. My father watched me score all five goals in a 5–0 thrashing, whereupon my mother, Penny, hardly a disciplinarian herself, told him to give me a strict talking-to. Nervously I climbed into the back seat of the car and dad turned round to face me. "Do you know?" he said, "I particularly enjoyed that second goal…"

'Dad couldn't say "no"; was there a church fete he hadn't opened, a charity he hadn't supported or a school at which he hadn't spoken?'

In a moving address, John Major spoke with deep affection of his many nights in the flat above No. 10 Downing Street where Colin would drop by for a chat and a large tumbler of whisky. 'When the phone rang bringing me news of Colin's death, there was a prickling in my eyes and millions felt exactly the same. To many of those millions who had never met him, Colin was one of he world's greatest cricketers; to those who knew him, he was one of the world's loveliest men. I will forever remember listening to the broadcasts in the middle of the night, when Colin was batting in Australia, with my ear pressed to the radio so my parents wouldn't know I was awake. Lovely people my parents, but no understanding of what Colin Cowdrey meant to an eight-year-old. My prophecy is this: heaven's bowlers beware, that great firm, Cowdrey and May, are about resume their partnership.'

Before the final prayers, the choir of Westminster Abbey enjoined in the following: music by Gilbert and Sullivan, new words sung by 'Colin' penned by Sir Tim Rice:

As some day it may happen that a victim must be found,
I've got a little list, I've got a little list,
Of some cricketing offenders I would banish from the ground,
And who never would be missed, who never would be missed;
Such as coaches who would rather run 10 miles than hold a net,
And chaps whose innings end because some blighter placed a bet,
I used to think that sledging was a sport that needed snow,
But now I know it's something else it really has to go,
And how can stretch pyjama cricket trousers still exist?
They'll none of 'em be missed,
They'll none of 'em be missed.

There's the deadly spin of Ramadhin, the blazing speed of Wes,
So rickey to resist, I've got them on the list!

There's running with Sir Geoffrey and no matter what he says,
He's going on the list, young Boycs is on my list;
And then there are selectors who decide the thing to do,
Is make you face some blinding pace when you are forty-two,
Or send you out in fading light in plaster head to toe,
And EGMs at MCC — I bid them cheerio!
And the off-the-field sensation-seeking tabloid journalist,
I don't think he'll be missed — I'm sure he won't be missed…

At the House of Lords the memories flowed as generously as the wine. 'He was the man who invented timing,' observed David Gower. 'As thorough a gentleman as you could wish to meet,' recalled Dickie Bird. 'It was almost the perfect party,' said Sir Garfield by way of farewell. 'What would have made it perfect? Why, if Colin had been here, of course.'

---

2 SEPTEMBER 2001

Mike Atherton

Knowing when to finish is one of the hardest decisions … but I was spot on caught Warne, bowled McGrath. To be dismissed by England's twin tormentors of this and other series was not exactly the greatest way to go, but, as Steve Waugh said, there are not too many fairytale endings in sport. My initial reaction was one of acute disappointment: it wasn't a particularly fearsome delivery, my bat was a little crooked and I had only really unfurled a cut and a pull that were worthy of mention in my final innings. There was the habitual shake of the head (can't remember where that started but it is now an ingrained habit), a few mutterings of disgust behind the chinstrap of my helmet and then I began the long walk back.

Halfway, it suddenly dawned on me that it was my last innings for England: the disappointment flooded away and my overwhelming emotion was one of relief that it was all over. For the last 20 yards I was determined to soak in the atmosphere and try to remember the feeling for a long time to come. I looked up and the magnificent Oval pavilion was packed to the rafters, the sun was shining and I realised that I was being given a standing ovation. It was a touching moment, although there were no tears, and I tried to convey my thanks with some acknowledgement to a crowd that has always been good to me. It will remain a favourite due to the long ovation I received following my hundred against the West Indies last year. Then, it was up the steps for the last time. I remembered to try not to trip up (the Oval steps are peculiarly spaced). Mark Butcher tapped me on the shoulder in acknowledgement as he went out to bat and Nasser and Stewie, my colleagues for the longest time in that team, greeted my entry. I sat in my corner with a towel on my head in a kind of numb trance and when I emerged it was to see a list on television that showed I scored more runs in Test cricket since January 1990 than anyone else. It made me feel slightly better.

I had known for a while that this was to be my last game. After a lengthy innings against Essex earlier in the season I struggled with my back for days afterwards and I knew then that I would not go on beyond this year. It was not just the physical side of things: opening against the best bowlers for a hundred or so games in the short space of a decade can take its toll mentally. Once the Ashes had been lost at Nottingham it was as if the wind had gone out of my sails and the manner of my two dismissals there knocked me back. Try as hard as I might I could not raise my game for the last two Tests.

There was some comment as to why I didn't announce my retirement before the last game. I think that every cricketer has a right to announce his retirement in his own way and I wanted to do it quietly after my last match. I had always said to myself that I would try to go out at the top and under my own terms with some dignity and I hope I achieved that.

Immediately after the public confirmation of my retirement the winter squads were announced. It was a swift reminder that the wheel continues to turn and that no cricketer is indispensable to the team, or bigger than the game. It would be a mistake for anybody to think so and it is not a mistake that I made. That is not to say that I won't miss it. There are obvious things that I will: most of all the challenge of facing the world's best bowlers.

The challenge was always the thing. I was lucky, or unlucky, to have played in an era when there were a high number of great bowlers. Each nation seemed to have a pair of quickies: Ambrose and Walsh; Pollock and Donald; Srinath and Prasad; Wasim and Waqar and McGrath and Gillespie. There were a couple of spinners (Saqlain and Muralitharan) who can justifiably claim to have revolutionalised their art, while Shane Warne revitalised an ancient but nearly forgotten art and was surely the best bowler of my generation.

The camaraderie of the dressing-room is an experience allowed to very few and that I will also miss. There are always one or two that you fall out with along the way but on the whole I think I leave more friends than enemies. I was lucky to have played my county career in a very happy dressing room with a bunch of like-minded players of a similar age who had grown together through the schoolboy ranks and on to the county scene. Lancashire's success was based around a bunch of mates having fun. It is a wrench to leave a dressing room and club that was a wonderful place for a decade or so.

Some of the county games, though, I will not miss, and I say that hoping not to sound arrogant. After a time it becomes difficult to justify playing a professional game in front of so few spectators, especially when that game is also a poor feeder for the national team. I have been, and will continue to be, a critic of the system (not the players) that serves our game poorly and in that sense it would have been hypocritical to continue to play on even if I was fit to do so.

Reading some of the articles following my retirement, I get the feeling that the lows have been dwelt on as much as the highs. That is not the way I feel right now: 7,000-odd runs, 100-odd caps, series wins against every nation bar Australia, and eight domestic trophies with Lancashire. I'll settle for that. And if I could be transported back to one moment, it would be that hundred I scored against the West Indies at the Oval last year. Only one other person got 50 in the match, the ovation from the crowd was something I'll never forget and it saw the Wisden Trophy come to England after a very long time.

Some years ago I asked a couple of former England cricketers about a player who was held in enormous public esteem. They painted a very different picture and throughout my career I hoped for respect from the people closest – that is team-mates and opponents rather than the media or general public. As I looked back on the field of dreams last Sunday for one last time, I saw the Australian team applauding, and the reaction of my own team as well was enough to mean that I leave pretty much satisfied.

Of course, there is always more that could have been done, but it is too late for that now. Once, after seeing a particularly scratchy innings of mine somewhere, Angus Fraser turned to me and said, 'Athers, you're just a natural mistimer of the ball.' That may well have been true but in the matter of my retirement I think my timing was spot on. Knowing when to finish is one of the hardest decisions a sportsman has to make, but, I've had 15 wonderful years and, in truth, I knew my time was up. I haven't had a moment's regret since.

---

8 SEPTEMBER 2001

TOUCHING MOMENT... BUT NO TEARS

Martin Johnson

The venue is Lord's, the occasion is England versus Australia, and the year is 2020. 'Owzat?' yells the bowler as the ball thuds into the batsman's pads, and all eyes swivel towards an android (dressed, for nostalgic reasons only, in a white coat) which begins to hum and whirr while an assortment of silicone chips go through several million computations. 'That's out,' it confirms in a Dalek-style monotone, before handing back – upon receipt of the appropriate retinal recognition scan – the bowler's sweater.

As we know (apart from occasional attempts to start nuclear wars, crash aeroplanes, or send old ladies gas bills for £4 million) computers never make mistakes, which is why the umpire whose bloodline stretches back to anything other than Intel Pentium is slowly but surely being phased out. And cricket, which relies so heavily on human interaction for its enduring romance, will be much the poorer for it.

There are many legendary umpiring stories. Remember the 1971 Gillette Cup semi-final between Lancashire and Gloucestershire, which ran into the BBC's Nine O'Clock News? Jack Bond, the Lancashire captain, complained to Arthur Jepson that it was too dark to carry on, to which Jepson replied: 'You can see the moon, how far do you want to see?'

Or how about India v. England in 1980, when Mike Brearley was the victim of a dreadful decision from one of the home umpires. As the England captain sat eating his lunch, the umpire came over and said: 'Mr Brearley, I am very sorry. I knew it was not out, but I felt my finger going up and I just couldn't stop it.'

This kind of anecdote is disappearing fast, and more stories will vanish as the older umpires — like Ray Julian — depart. In a recent match at Lord's, Phil Tufnell turned to Julian and said: 'I only need one more wicket for 1,000 first-class victims.' 'In that case,' replied Julian, 'you're bowling at the right end. I only need two more myself for 3,000 lbws.'

Being an honest man as well as a popular one (Julian has won the players' award for best umpire for the past three years) Tufnell had to look elsewhere for his 1,000th wicket, but Julian has never been one to worry too much about giving the batsman the benefit of any doubt. If Dickie Bird's biography had been entitled *Not Out*, Julian, should he ever write one, will probably call it *On Your Bike, Son*.

After precisely half-a-century in first-class cricket, beginning as Leicestershire's youngest wicket-keeper debutant and concluding with enforced retirement after 29 years on the umpiring list, Julian is currently standing in his last championship match on his old home ground, Grace Road.

Bowlers all over the country might well have considered marking the occasion with black armbands, given that they will no longer turn around to see that familiar upraised finger, bent almost sideways as the legacy of an old wicket-keeping injury. However, while the finger may be crooked, the man himself is as straight as they come.

It is mildly disconcerting for a batsman to look up and see himself being dispatched by a man with a broad smile on his face, but Julian has never looked anything but blissfully happy on a cricket field. The late Sam Cook was one of the most legendary 'outers' the game has seen and, when he and Julian stood together, sensible counties only ever booked the catering staff for two days.

'Sometimes me and Sam would leave the pavilion together at lunchtime, and Sam would say: "Only six wickets to go, Ray, I've a good chance of being back in Tetbury by 10 o'clock." And sure enough, he'd shoot out nine, ten and eleven with the consoling words: "Sorry, son, I've a train at six o'clock."'

Julian says he would carry on umpiring for half the money if he was allowed to stay on, while acknowledging that the job is nothing like as straightforward as it used to be. 'When I started, everyone accepted the umpire's decision, but nowadays, what with players' attitudes, and all the electronic devices, the umpire is in court every day.'

To some extent, the extra rigours involved are compensated by a decent wage – when Julian began umpiring in 1972, the summer fee was a flat £500. 'I remember Dave Halfyard used to sleep in his van to save on hotels, and Ron Ley would get from Northampton to Leicester on a pedal cycle.'

Julian used to travel around in a second-hand motorhome, and was a player in the days when all his laundry bills were subject to scrutiny from the Inland Revenue. If he broke his one complimentary bat, he had to pay for a replacement himself. 'Attitudes have changed so much,' says Julian. 'Nowadays the first question a young player asks is: 'Where's my sponsored car?' Everything is more or less handed to them on a plate, and there is much less of the after-play camaraderie the old players had.

'I don't know much about modern 'warm-downs', but I warmed down by climbing into my winklepickers, slapping on some Brylcreem, riding off to the local Palais on my Lambretta, and grabbing the first granny I could find.'

---

10 SEPTEMBER 2001

Michael Parkinson

The adage that a successful Yorkshire team is good news for England has been put to bed by Yorkshire winning the County Championship in some style while England lost everything possible against Australia and Pakistan.

Things are not like they used to be, and you can say that again. Nonetheless the White Rose triumph is not without relevance to the future of English cricket.

Yorkshire's academy, and their assiduous trawling of the leagues and schools for young players, sets the example. If the system has so far produced more seam bowlers than batsmen then the reason might be the Headingley wicket, rather than a lack of batting talent.

Any sensible cricketer would want to bowl seam-up at Headingley rather than bat on it. Generally it favours the bowler, which is why one or two of them have struggled when selected for international duty. Matthew Hoggard is the exception and I believe he and James Ormond will provide a substantial amount of England's bowling in future years. The lesson of Headingley – and it is not particular to that ground – is that until our cricketers learn to bowl and bat on good, true surfaces they will nearly always be second-best to players who do.

I am delighted that David Byas has his hands on a trophy at last. No one deserves it more. He has steered himself and his team through the minefield of tribal conflict and petty controversies so beloved by Yorkshire Cricket Club with the rugged common sense required of a farmer.

One imagines that, having dealt with the unpredictable behaviour of beasts and the elements, the eccentricities of Yorkshire CC afforded nothing more than light-hearted relief. If only that were true. Nevertheless his forbearance and determination have paid off and he will deservedly win his place in the annals of the club as the captain who emerged victorious from a long, barren and troubled time. He was greatly assisted by his overseas player. The county have not always chosen wisely in the past but opting for Darren Lehmann was absolutely right. It is to be hoped his present spat with his captain is just that, and is settled amicably.

Yorkshire need him and if Australia continue to ignore his talents then he might find in Yorkshire the recognition, appreciation and respect missing in his native land. They should make him a Freeman of Leeds immediately. So Yorkshire are the champion county and I should be a lot more chuffed than I am. Maybe I'm getting older and more miserable, maybe it's simply that the County Championship doesn't seem as important as it once was. More likely it becomes increasingly difficult to be optimistic about the game's future in this country.

Do enough people care? Are the young given the opportunity to learn the game and love it? Are we all overwhelmed and intimidated by the riches and success of football?

The next 10 years will define the future of cricket in England. The question is not will it change, but how much?

They talk of regional cricket, but where's the spectator attraction in that? There is still a frisson created by Yorkshire against Lancashire, or Yorkshire v. Surrey. It might be diminished, but it is certainly more than would be generated if the North-East played the North-West.

Fewer counties maybe, but don't get rid of the lot. What needs improving is the quality of the player who becomes a professional cricketer. And that leads down a channel that has its source in our schools. Anyone who read Sue Mott's interview on these pages with John Major (4 September) will not be optimistic of radical change in that area. The situation is not hopeless but neither does it give much cause for optimism, which is maybe why I don't feel like turning cartwheels at Yorkshire's triumph. Having said that, I am firmly of the opinion that it is not Yorkshire who are to blame for the present situation but the rest of them. Particularly that lot down south at Lord's.

I have changed. But not that much.

---

23 SEPTEMBER 2001

THE GOSPEL ACCORDING TO HANSIE CRONJE

Owen Slot

Hansie Cronje was standing waiting in the George airport terminal as arranged, looking relaxed, arms folded, leaning against a wall, chatting to one of the terminal staff. Without even saying a word, he had made his first point: he doesn't hide away, as one might have expected, in fear of castigation from the outside world.

He doesn't need to. Strangers queued up wide-eyed for the chance of meeting him, to ask for his autograph, to tell him what a great player he was; not a single word of dissent. Here at home, they have elected to remember the good bits. He is still Cronje the cricket hero.

'Hi,' he said, looking up as he completed another signature. He asked about the flight, helped carry our bags and then drove myself and the photographer to lunch (he insisted on paying) at a beautifully situated lodge overlooking a dramatic coastline. There was even a whale in the bay to complete the picture.

Perhaps it is easy to see why people here like Cronje because on Tuesday, when we met him, he was majestically charming. Maybe he is like this every day now, but certainly I have never had an interview with a sportsman attended to with such hospitality. He talked for two hours and barely shunned a question; he was witty, thoughtful and intelligent (and at times, it seemed, on another planet, but more of that later). He then posed for pictures, gave us a tour of the area round three local schools in which he is involved and the immaculate estate on which he lives, and returned us to our hotel. Early the following morning he was back again to drive us to the airport with a bottle of red as a leaving present.

In the middle of the afternoon drive, he had even stopped the car when hailed by a local black worker he knew, took out his wallet and handed him a crisp 20 rand note. If this seemed too good to be true, he knew it because he made a nice self-deprecating joke about how he hoped that that would look good for his media guests.

Why the head-spinning charm offensive? It might be something to do with his belief that 'the next five, 10, 20 years will probably determine how people remember me. People will remember me for last April [when the match-fixing scandal exploded], but also I hope for the way I have lived my life afterwards, the fact that I was willing to get out in public, to try to make a difference and not hide away.'

It might also be something to do with Wednesday's court case in Pretoria when Cronje's lawyers will challenge the ban that South Africa's United Cricket Board have placed against him ever playing or coaching cricket again. If Cronje's team were to win, then, 17 months on from being exposed as a major player in cricket's worst scandal, all penalties and sentences would be lifted. He could even be back playing cricket for Free State when the season starts next week. So now is the time to look good.

I asked Cronje if he really believed a 17-month suspension from the game was sufficient penalty. He replied that he couldn't be the judge of that, but that 'it's a pretty tough thing when you take someone's livelihood away. I've had that for 17 months; it was also public so I've had a double humiliation. Financially, if you add up all the knocks, it adds up to about 2.5 million rand [about £200,000]. If that's not bad enough, I wouldn't know what is. I carried all my legal costs, I was on my own.'

We should remember here that Cronje also made a considerable amount of money (over £100,000) from subsequently selling his story around the world. That, I suggested, was not necessarily the act of a repentant man. To which he gave one of the most unbelievable responses I have ever heard.

'A lot of people wrote letters of encouragement,' he said. 'My wife and I felt that there had to be some stage where we come out and say to people "thank you for everything". In all those interviews my wife was with me; it was a case of saying we're actually OK, thanks for standing by us. So, do I feel comfortable about it? Yes, I do. It wasn't even enough to cover my legal expenses.'

He added that he has meanwhile turned down five offers from publishers wanting to do a book deal and that he hasn't charged a penny for this interview, which is true. He also stressed the effort he is now putting into charities and local schools and to make his point he drives us afterwards past Kretzenhoop Primary School in a suburb nearby called Blanco.

Next to the school is a newly growing playing field which, he explained, was formerly state-owned scrubland. It was he, he said, who went to the headmaster and persuaded him that it could belong to the school and, he added, he then started lobbying local government to donate it.

The trouble with this lovely tale is that a phone call to the headmaster, Dennis Campher, the following day found it to be deeply flawed. 'He did nothing at all,' he said. 'As a matter of fact, I did it all myself. He did give us a couple of rand which he collected, but it was just a drop in the ocean.'

This is the trouble with this fallen man, as various investigative bodies have found in the last 17 months: working out where the truth ends and his own interpretation of it takes over is not easy. He would have you know, for instance, that whenever he was asked to provide financial documentation to the King Commission, the national inquiry into cricket corruption, he provided it instantly. A call to Shamila Batohi, the Chief Investigator on the Commission, suggests otherwise. 'That's incorrect,' she said. 'We had to issue a subpoena at one stage. When you do that, it generally means you've exhausted other ways.'

He would also have you know that he has 'spoken and apologised on numerous occasions' to Herschelle Gibbs and Henry Williams, the two players he dragged down with him in the scandal. When further pressed on this, though, he conceded that it took him a year to get round to calling Williams. 'In actual fact I didn't have his phone number ... Also I was embarrassed.'

Even on the subject of his history of lying, he has an interesting version of the truth. The whole scandal broke on 7 April last year when Indian police revealed they had taped evidence of Cronje attempting to fix matches. Cronje denied all but the next four days broke him. He says he 'was thinking about jumping out of the hotel window.

'I didn't really sleep, I didn't feel good. If that was what my life was gong to be like, I didn't want it. If I kept quiet, I would probably have got away with it but it would have been baggage that I would have had to carry for the rest of my life and I wasn't able to do that.'

On April 11, the broken captain wrote a confession and gave a tell-all press conference with the Minister of Sport. This tell-all, however, was later proven to be an extremely economical version of the truth, yet Cronje insists he didn't lie that day; he says that with events moving so fast, he just never got the opportunity to tell the whole truth.

'I didn't try to lie to the Minister of Sport,' he said. 'Had we had time, I probably would have told him [the whole truth] as well. There was no platform for me to come out and give my spiel.'

So no one once asked if there was any more to come out? 'No,' he insisted. I told Cronje that this was hard to believe. 'I still find now,' he replied, 'that people say: 'it's very hard to take you at your word'. There's nothing I can do about that.'

What certainly is genuine about Cronje is his contrition and the fact that his exposure led to some extremely hard times. 'I know I was wrong and I've been willing to take the flak,' he said. 'Morally, ethically, from a captain of a country, even suggesting to a fellow player to under-perform is fundamentally wrong. It goes contrary to everything I live for and stand for.'

He went on anti-depressants as a consequence: 'There were times when I would lie in bed and close my eyes and hope that today and tomorrow would go by quicker so I could get on with life. Everyone tells you that there is an end, there is light at the end of the tunnel, but that doesn't help. The toughest part was the embarrassment to friends, family, team-mates.'

These are certainly the people with whom he now surrounds himself: supporters, those who have stood by him, Afrikaners who remain in awe. There is a theory that the reason he appears to believe so fervently his version of events is because there is no one near him to tell him otherwise.

Certainly, on the match-fixing itself, his appears to be a rose-tinted view. He insists repeatedly that 'the only thing that makes me able to face it is the fact that we never did under-perform.' This, in itself, is questionable, as is his contention that, the Gibbs-Williams game (a one-dayer in Nagpur last year) apart, 'the only other time I spoke to anyone about under-performing was in that meeting in 1996 [before a one-dayer in Bombay] when we decided not to.'

So what about the Mandela Trophy game in 1995 when he was made an offer to throw the game and discussed it with Pat Symcox? 'I said to Symmo: "we've been made an offer to under-perform." He said: "don't even think about it".'

What about the Bangalore Test last year when he approached Lance Klusener, Mark Boucher and Jacques Kallis with an offer? 'They would tell you that it was a 30-second joke. That's really what it was, a stupid joke.'

And the approach to Pieter Strydom before the Bombay Test last year? Again, he says, it was a joke: 'If it was so serious, why did he not go and report it? As with Boucher, Kallis, Klusener, the fact that we spoke about it briefly doesn't mean there was anything untoward.'

But what if any of these players had taken him seriously and taken the bait? 'We never really went there,' he replied interestingly. 'I would-n't be able to say, it'd be speculation. I hate to think it would have gone that way [acceptance of the offer]. I don't think it would.' Suddenly these jokes don't seem so funny any more.

If this is all a little hard to take, the good news is that Cronje says he wasn't particularly enjoying it either. When he fixed the Gibbs-Williams deal, he says: 'I was shaking, I was nervous, it was not nice for me. At that stage it was a case of covering my own arse, I had taken $10,000 off this guy [the fixer] earlier and I was trying to get him something back in return. But I never felt comfortable with it. If you look at my entire life, how I played, how I trained, losing didn't come easy to me.'

Again, he repeats that his side never under-performed. 'That is really important. I'm not justifying what I did. I'm not trying to defend myself. But those points need to be out there, otherwise you'll think it was seven years of captaincy as a crook and that's not the case.'

No matter how much of Cronje's words you are prepared to believe, I genuinely think that he has emerged from the last 17 months a better person. His supporters in South Africa are growing in number, but there is a more prevalent view abroad that his every move is selfish and cynically designed to improve his own cause.

His former team-mates appear to be rallying round gradually. He hasn't yet spoken to Daryll Cullinan, but otherwise there appears to be a recent wave of forgiveness. 'The message has been: "it was a big mistake but we're with you,"' he said. 'To me this has been a great lesson. So many times in my life I have been very critical of people; it's been a real eye-opener for me to see this.'

His marriage has got stronger too due to their time together. 'We'd sort of got alienated,' he said. 'If you spend three months a year with your wife, it's hard to forge a friendship and bond that is so strong. There's a level of friendship now that we never had before. For her, the toughest part will be trust again. To a certain extent we've mended that and we've got a wonderful relationship, but you can't blame her if one day she refers back to it.'

But this will be Cronje's eternal problem: people will always refer back to it. 'Some people will never be satisfied that I've paid high enough a price,' he said, and he is right. Expect another tidal wave of wrath if he is cleared in court this week.

For his rehabilitation to become absolutely complete, he should start by accepting one of those book deals and giving every single penny to charity. And he needs to tell all this time, be utterly honest, far more so than I believe he was in our interview.

The legal mess that would clutter South Africa's law courts thereafter would be astonishing and that is one reason why this will never happen. 'People wouldn't want to read it, would they?' said Cronje. That, I'm afraid, is another point on which we disagree.

WHIRLWIND ASTLE STEALS SHOW IN LOSING CAUSE

Martin Johnson

When Australian Stan McCabe was scoring a double century in 232 minutes at Trent Bridge back in 1938, his captain, Don Bradman, ordered those members of his team engaged in the traditional dressing-room pursuits – taking a nap, or doing the crossword – to get out on to the balcony.

'You may never', said the Don, 'see the like of this again.'

Bradman was not to know it then, but Test cricket has changed so radically that McCabe's innings today would be in serious danger of attracting a cry of 'have a go, yer mug!' In the space of three weeks, Ian Botham's 1982 record for balls faced to reach a double century has been beaten by Adam Gilchrist, approached by Graham Thorpe, and now – after an innings of almost unbelievable savagery – annihilated by New Zealand's Nathan Astle.

Before Saturday's extraordinary events, had you mentioned the name Astle in any pub in the land, you would probably have received several blank looks and a 'wasn't he the bloke who played for West Bromwich Albion?' Not now, though. Astle's 153-ball double century wiped out Gilchrist's record with 59 deliveries to spare, and at 217 minutes it ranks second fastest to Bradman (214) at Headingley in 1930.

Astle would have broken that record, too, but for the fact that Bradman's innings wasn't interrupted as many times as his own, once for a drinks break, and twice more because the ball he had just been facing was halfway down Christchurch High Street.

It is hard to imagine the conversation as the umpires inspected the replacement ball box, but it might have gone something like this. 'Er, have you got one that's only six overs old with 89 runs on the clock? Still quite red, but otherwise looks as though it's been chewed by the groundsman's alsatian.'

Eighty-nine runs off six overs – one of which was a wicket maiden – was the immediate result of Nasser Hussain taking the second new ball, presumably with an instruction along the lines of, 'let's get this game over and done with.' And this against Andrew Caddick and Matthew

Hoggard, who are not exactly flight-and-loop bowlers, and at that point had 15 of New Zealand's 19 wickets between them.

Caddick, at one stage, bowled seven consecutive deliveries that went for 4–6–6–4–6–6–6, mostly the result of Astle charging down the pitch to him as though he was facing a club spinner. Astle went from 100 to 200 in 39 balls, and the field set for Hoggard during this carnage was a real collector's item. Three slips and six men on the boundary.

At tea, New Zealand required 280 runs to win, and an hour and a half later, had brought it down to 98. It was then, with England becoming near frantic with worry, that Astle finally edged Hoggard to the wicket-keeper attempting to add to his tally of 28 fours and 11 sixes. All told, 178 of his 222 runs (from 168 balls) came in boundaries. This was not slogging, either. It was clinical destruction.

It was, throughout, an enthralling Test match, which began with batsmen groping at thin air, and then, as the grassy drop-in pitch dried out into 22 yards of QED for the Flat Earth Society, spectators diving for cover as yet another aerial missile was thrown back covered in bits of scotch egg and wooden seat splinters.

The fact that no one in the crowd got injured was largely down to the fact that there wasn't a crowd. Not one worthy of the occasion, anyway. The twists and turns of the longer game (although longer is now anything that gets past the third day) for some reason holds no appeal outside England.

New Zealanders, like Australians, prefer the pyjama stuff, quaffing ale from plastic cups while the standard, formularised plot unfolds. It is their loss, and sad for Astle too that he should finally leave the field to a standing ovation from a smattering of English Barmies and an ice-cream vendor.

It will remain a great imponderable as to what might have happened had Chris Cairns, now ruled out of the rest of the series while he undergoes knee surgery, come in higher than no. 11. He wasn't intending to bat, and, it seems, only did so because the New Zealand captain, Stephen Fleming, didn't want to stop watching Astle bat. Eventually they added 118 in 69 balls for the last wicket.

While adhering to the ridiculous notion that man of the match awards have to be made on the basis of contributions to a victory, the adjudicators could still have chosen Astle for donating 196 runs to England as well as 222 to New Zealand when he dropped Thorpe on four.

In any event, the England player who deserved it most was Nasser Hussain for his first-innings century.

The last time England won a match on an overseas tour without anyone noticing was in Australia in 1990–1, when the headlines were more about David Gower's Flying Circus. It's a good job he wasn't up in the Tiger Moth again when Astle was batting yesterday, as he would almost certainly have have been shot down.

The Don never thought he would see the like of it again, and neither did anyone else who was in Christchurch on Saturday.

---

24 MARCH 2002

Mike Atherton

Those of us who tuned in late on Friday evening in the hope of following England's serene progress in New Zealand's green and pleasant land were confronted instead by images of a black Porsche, literally wrenched in two and cruelly smashed to pieces, and the knowledge of a young life curtailed. It was a profoundly shocking image. As Ben Hollioake's family are left to cope with their tragic loss, so the rest of us, colleagues and friends, are left to our memories.

As captain of England, I recall handing a first one-day international cap to Ben on a glorious day at Lord's in 1997. The series against Australia had already been won and it was a chance to let this precocious young cricketer, straight out of the Under-19s, show off his talent. I asked him if he fancied going in at no. 3, and he shrugged and said, in his laconic way, he'd give it a go.

Give it a go! Against Shane Warne and Glenn McGrath, he scored a breathtaking 63 off 48 balls to justify the selectors' judgment; it sounds violent but the drive for four off his third ball and the swept six into the Tavern Stand off Warne were launched with a languid ease and grace and it earned him the man-of-the-match award in his first game.

His brother, Adam, had already shot to prominence earlier in the summer, and in the spirit of fraternal competition he scored the winning runs in that game, as he had in the first two matches of the series. The Hollioakes were suddenly the talk of the town, part of a brighter future for English cricket, and Ben the new wunderkind of our game.

Ben's initial success, and the manner of it, propelled him into the nation's consciousness and brought immediate adulation, and all its attendant problems. Like others before and after him, he was labelled 'The New Botham' — that king of all albatrosses. And when you are young and lacking in knowledge and guidance, the rise to fame can be so difficult to handle.

The media's voracious appetite for all things black and white, with no room for any shade of grey, creates personalities instead of people and caricatures instead of character. Suddenly expectation is upon you, a cloak that is so difficult to remove and a cup so difficult to fill. There was the odd glimpse of brilliance afterwards. Two man-of-the-match awards in one-day finals for Surrey reinforced the initial belief that he had the temperament to match the big occasion, and he did become the youngest player since Brian Close in 1949 to win a Test cap for England. Mostly, though, after the initial burst, the limelight and success evaded him: he was ill-suited to the backwaters and daily grind of county cricket and the expectation went largely unfulfilled. We are left wondering only what might have been.

For there is no doubting the talent was there. His batting looked casual, and occasionally was casual, but he had a grace and ease of movement and time to play, visited upon only the lucky few. His loose, long limbs enabled him to bowl without apparent effort — quickish with a hint of away swing.

His athleticism was ready-made for the modern game; a captain would always send him to patrol the most important parts of the outfield. He had got back into the one-day international team, and was pushing hard for a place in the World Cup squad. There was still plenty of time.

Yesterday Nasser Hussain was right to emphasise the futility of the game at such a time. Understandably, in the aftermath of Ben's death, there will be those who will overplay his talent and achievements, but what does that, or the reality, matter? What is undeniable, and ultimately more important, is the affection with which he was held by everyone who shared the Surrey and England dressing-rooms with him. Remarkably, only five years after Graham Kersey's death in a road accident, Surrey have lost another.

It is difficult to imagine that he and Adam were brothers, so different were they in character, build and temperament. Adam, short and pugnacious, very physical and fiercely committed – every inch the street fighter. Ben, tall and languid, seemingly at ease with the world and his place in it – not cerebral but quick to smile and easy to laugh. He really was a player you wanted to see succeed, and I cannot imagine that he would have inspired jealousy anywhere within the game. He could be infuriating on the field, but it was quickly forgiven.

Along with his brother he was part of the influx of Australian-born cricketers who came to England throughout the 1990s. With Ben it was easy to see the influence of both his English roots and the land of his birth; most at home in the outdoors and on the beaches of Perth, but without the abrasiveness that characterises so many of his countrymen. Both Australia, where his family is, and England, his adopted home, will feel his loss keenly.

It is in the dazzling light of youth, rather than the decay of old age, that we'll always remember Ben – but that does not make it any easier to bear.

---

11 FEBRUARY 2003

FLOWER AND OLONGA DEFIANTLY SPEARHEAD SPIRIT OF REBELLION

Martin Johnson

Harare

While England continued to dither and dawdle in the city of the timeless Test (if they'd stopped shaving at the start of the great debate, they'd all look like W.G. Grace this morning), two senior Zimbabwean cricketers were, by contrast, issuing a statement from Harare of unparalleled political forcefulness, not to mention bravery.

There are any number of people in Zimbabwe who don't quite share the government's view that they are led by a kindly and benevolent gentleman. However, for Andy Flower and Henry Olonga – on the morning of their country's opening World Cup game – to describe their president as an oppressive dictator who condones rape, murder, beatings, torture, racism and suppression of opinion was quite extraordinary.

We didn't expect Flower to be batting for very long yesterday, and indeed he wasn't, though the real surprise was that he left the field of his own volition rather than under armed arrest. The joint statement by Flower, the team captain until recently, and fast bowler Olonga was last night being examined by the Zimbabwe Cricket Union, and I think we can take it that a copy was sent to the presidential palace, which is next door to the Harare Sports Club.

Olonga was suspended last night by his club, Takashinga, whose chairman, Givemore Makoni, said: 'It is disgraceful what Henry Olonga and Andy Flower have done. Taking politics on to the playing field is something that the ICC and other sporting bodies, including the Zimbabwe Cricket Union, have been avoiding.

'What is most disheartening is that Olonga has been a hero and role model to the black cricketing community. It seems he has decided to enter into the political arena using cricket.'

Makoni said Olonga, the first black cricketer to play in the national team, had breached the club's code of conduct, which stipulates that they are non-political. The stand by Olonga and Flower is hugely damaging to President Robert Mugabe given the international spotlight on the World Cup, and on Zimbabwe in particular. Heath Streak, the captain, said after the game that 'everyone is entitled to their own opinion,' which was the opposite of the point being made by two of his players.

Streak and the other Zimbabwean players were apparently unaware that Flower and Olonga were making their public stand until just before the start of the game, and none of the other home players joined those two in their on-field protest of wearing black armbands to symbolise their 'mourning for the death of democracy in our beloved Zimbabwe'.

However, as Streak's farming father Dennis spent some time in prison not long ago, it is not hard to guess where his sympathies lie, though going public in Zimbabwe, as Flower and Olonga pointed out, is not necessarily a recipe for a long and healthy life. Whether through fear or apathy, it was bizarre to be in the press box when the statement landed and watch the local media react as if they'd been informed that the luncheon interval had been rescheduled for 1.30.

Streak said that he was 'not sure' whether the two players would be disciplined by the Zimbabwe Cricket Union, though a fine or a ban from that organisation would be the least of their worries. Mugabe's undercover police were at the ground, looking so undercover that the pavilion bar manager spotted them immediately and ordered his staff not to serve them. The spirit of rebellion was clearly catching.

Most people at the game were unaware of the statement and if England were watching the game on television in the expectation of a crowd riot, there wasn't one. This was because there wasn't a crowd, or at least not one worthy of the name, and the opposition party's call for 'peaceful demonstration' failed to materialise. In any event, spectators were too occupied being frisked at the entrances to demonstrate, and rarely has there been such heavy security at such a sparsely attended game.

Namibia themselves had arrived the day before to be escorted from the airport by two motorbikes, a truckload of heavily armed militia, a helicopter, and – perhaps to reassure England that all would be well even if one of the guns went off by accident – an ambulance.

---

18 MAY 2003

TUFNELL'S A CELEBRITY – BUT DO WE WANT HIM?

Mike Atherton

That Phil Tufnell is the only England cricketer to have left Australia 'a winner' these past 16 years has not escaped the notice of the England and Wales Cricket Board's ever-vigilant marketing department. Only a cynic, of course, would wonder at the number of viewer votes that flooded in from St John's Wood for the reality television show, I'm a Celebrity, Get Me Out of Here. A vote for Phil is a vote for cricket.

No sooner had the crown nestled on Tufnell's head, and before he was even able to down his first post-programme pint, the ECB had reclaimed him as one of their own.

All the letters from the discipline committee, the tantrums, the boozing, the drug allegations and the fines, were forgotten in an instant as the establishment opened their arms and welcomed him home. Mike Soper, deputy chairman, opined that Tufnell had done more for cricket than anybody in the last 10 years, while John Read, marketing manager, rubbed his hands at the thought of Tufnell promoting this summer's international cricket. Vinny Codrington, Middlesex secretary, wondered aloud what might happen if the summer was a hot one, and the wickets began to turn.

The rest of us, his former team-mates, could only watch in shock and awe as Tufnell transformed himself into the ultimate team player and modern man. Bushtucker trial? No problem. A couple of witchetty grubs for dinner? Yum, yum. When a strange little man accused him of being a 'homophobe', Tufnell recoiled and gave such a startled look, as if to say, 'Homophobic? Me, Phil Tufnell, with my reputation?'

A decade as an England cricketer, of course, prepared him wonderfully well for two weeks of fear, deprivation and humiliation in Australia. He said his final meal of live beetles, worms, red ants and witchetty grubs was the most terrifying experience of his life, but he'd clearly forgotten facing Merv Hughes at Perth in 1991. Both events rendered him ashen-faced and caused him to throw up, but in this instance it was the creepy-crawlies who self-ejected; they took one look at Phil's ravaged stomach-lining, after a decade of alcohol and nicotine abuse, and got the hell out of there.

Now, I know I am naive when it comes to matters of PR, image and marketing, but quite what Tuffers has done for English cricket this last 10 days is beyond me. Will fathers be telling their sons: 'Go play cricket for England, son, 'cos at the end of it all you'll look 37 going on 60 and you can loaf around a former banana plantation 10 minutes from Murwillumbah with a bunch of weirdos, performing silly tasks'?

If that is the kind of publicity cricket needs, the game is in a worse state than we all thought. Tuffers has done a lot for himself, of course. If his agents are to be believed he will soon make up for the penury caused by two divorces and nearly two decades of professional cricket. And I can't imagine that there will be any former colleagues who will resent his 15 minutes, days, months or years of fame or new-found wealth. County cricket no longer provided Tufnell with the attention and the celebrity he craved. He now has it and good luck to him.

The alacrity with which cricket's establishment is milking Tufnell's fame is slightly pathetic, though. Evidently, cricket needs him. Whether

Tufnell now needs cricket, or whether it can afford him, is an entirely different matter.

---

15 JUNE 2003

TWENTY20 OPENS UP A VISION OF THE FUTURE

Mike Atherton

The county ground at Bristol was packed yesterday on a glorious morning, as were five other grounds on Friday evening, as a lost generation of cricket supporters gave a wholehearted thumbs-up to the new Twenty20 Cup. It is early days yet, but the signs are good: the first five Twenty20 games attracted 30,050 supporters compared to 6,295 for the corresponding Benson and Hedges games in 2001.

The ECB's marketing department recognised cricket's profile – white, middle-class and old – to be disastrous for the sport. Apparently, any committee man seen wearing a tie to the game between Gloucestershire and Worcestershire game was liable to be ejected from the ground and this deterrent seemed enough: for the most part, the crowd was young and family orientated. As for middle-class and white, well, one step at a time has always been cricket's way.

The atmosphere at Bristol was slightly more low-key than had been apparent for the opening match at Hampshire. This reflected a Saturday morning start rather than the Friday evening opening extravaganza when spectators were treated to the talents of Alesha, Sabrina and Su-Elise – not Hampshire's new overseas players but the band Mis-Teeq – along with D'Side and the United Colours of Sound.

There were no such musical accoutrements to entice the spectators to Nevil Road, but the spectators seemed happy enough to rely on the talents of the cricketers on display.

Ultimately, it is the cricket that has to win them over. To their credit, the players threw themselves about with total commitment. Matt Windows said he had never been so exhausted, but then he's not often batted at the other end from cricket's Peter Pan, Jonty Rhodes.

Eventually, the cricket will have to stand on its own two feet, once the novelty and the razzmatazz has worn off. But there is every chance it will, because finally the game is being played at a time when people can actually watch (i.e. after work) and in a way that more accurately reflects the times that we live in. You can be in and out in three hours and still be home for *Eastenders* or *Corrie*.

As for the cricket itself, there is no reason why it should be detrimental to the development of our game and our players. The fielding throughout the three frenetic hours was outstanding. Jack Russell took to the new game, as does a dog to a bone.

He stood up to the bowlers from virtually the first ball – scurrying, scampering, snarling and generally at his irritating best. His wicket-keeping wasn't bad either.

All eyes were on Jonty Rhodes, still the world's best fielder, at backward point. He even agreed to wear a microphone, so that he could relay his thoughts to the television commentators. But, by the halfway stage he had only touched the ball three times and was reduced to shouting encouragement to the bowlers, and badgering Dermot Reeve to shut up when he was asked a question as the bowler was running in to bowl.

The bowlers, themselves, must have feared for their futures when this competition was announced in mid-winter. But in this low-scoring match they found that, by using their brains, they could keep one step ahead of the enemy. Gloucestershire decided that slower balls were the way to go. Mark Alleyne led the way with a variety, front of the hand and back of the hand, getting slower and slower and loopier and loopier.

David Taylor, Worcestershire's new recruit from league cricket, looked bemused as Alleyne's deliveries crept past his bat at a slower pace than he would find at his club, High Wycombe, on a Saturday afternoon. He found Mike Smith a tougher proposition at the other end and was soon gone, but any game that promotes a closer association between the recreational game and the professional game must be a good thing. There will be more league players getting a go in this competition.

Although this game was a bit of a canter for Gloucester, there is every chance that Twenty20 matches will, as a rule, be closer than one-day games of late. In the World Cup I reckoned there to be only one game in 10 that was a tight match. A shorter game means less of a chance for star players to turn a match, to play the match-winning innings or bowl a devastating spell. The opening set of matches on Friday confirmed this trend.

Players, then, will be constantly playing in matches where the winning margins are small. Consequently, they will be learning continually how to play under pressure; how to bowl at the death, how to finish a game with the bat and how crucial one piece of brilliance in the field can be.

All in all, Twenty20 should produce more innovative bowling, better fielding, batsmen who can score quicker and off every ball and captains who can make decisions on the hoof rather than sticking to pre-determined plans. All that, and played in front of good crowds too in a cracking atmosphere. I almost wish I'd have played it myself.

The initial buzz surrounding Twenty20 is vindication for those of us who argued for change, and to English cricket's much-criticised administrators we must doff our caps. In the long run, Twenty20 cricket might not work but at least they have tried to shake county cricket out of its undeniable decline – it's just a pity it's taken them so long. Oh, and Gloucester won by six wickets.

---

28 SEPTEMBER 2003

THE TRAGIC SHADOW OF SUICIDE

Mike Atherton

Frank Bruno's sad descent into depression is a further reminder, if any were needed, of the enduring problems that many sportsmen face as retirement beckons. David Frith's latest book, *Silence of the Heart*, shows that in cricket, especially, those consequences can often be fatal. *Silence of the Heart* updates Frith's earlier work of 12 years ago in which he chronicled 80 or so cases of cricketing suicides.

That number, according to Frith, has doubled now. In just 15 years I played against three players who decided that life was not worth living: David Bairstow of Yorkshire, Danny Kelleher (Kent) and Mark Saxelby (Nottinghamshire/Derbyshire). And Shane Clements, of Western Australia, is the latest high-profile cricketing suicide.

This summer, cricket nearly added one more to its list of victims. This week I spoke to a well-known county cricketer who decided to end his own life four months ago. That he is still around to speak about it now is down only to an outrageous piece of good fortune. He agreed to talk to me on the understanding that he would not be named, but in the hope that the problems that many sportsmen face, and the help on offer, could be highlighted.

'I was playing in the first eleven, but things weren't going great and I was in the last year of my contract. I was becoming stressed about my future and this, in turn, was affecting my relationship at home and in the end we split up. Cricket was not the only problem, but it was a big part of it. I bottled everything up; I didn't feel as though I could talk to anyone. I had nowhere to go, nowhere to turn. I felt I was in a big black hole and that there was no way out.'

The solution was a drastic one: one afternoon in June he locked himself in the bathroom of his flat, filled the bath, slashed his wrists and waited for the inevitable. Fortunately, a team-mate arrived in time, smashed down the door and he hauled his friend to safety. The shock for the saviour was profound: he, too, needed professional counselling to get over the trauma although there was a delayed reaction and the shock took days to sink in.

After the incident, the role played by the Professional Cricketers' Association was vital. 'I can't speak highly enough of them. They got in contact straight away. They gave me financial help, found me somewhere to live, organised professional counselling and, most importantly, found time to call and chat on a regular basis.'

The PCA are the obvious port of call for depressed players and those with question marks over their career and future options. The PCA, in partnership with the England and Wales Cricket Board, run two schemes: one called the Placement and Learning Access Network which links cricketers and companies together hoping that cricketers can develop work-related skills while achieving their sporting goals.

The second scheme, called Cricket Ace UK, advises players more effectively on balancing success on and off the field. The ACE UK counsellors offer educational guidance, career planning, transitional support and development programmes. For Richard Bevan, Chief Executive of the PCA, the ACE UK scheme is especially important 'because it creates awareness of lifestyle management at a young age'.

Those two schemes, along with the PCA's offer to their members to fund 50 per cent of the cost of educational and vocational training courses, means that the PCA have, in reality, taken over the duty of care towards players. In the last year the PCA have spent over £80,000 sending players on vocational courses, although Bevan feels a fund of £250,000 is necessary. 'Players are retiring earlier now and they are more aware of the kind of help we offer, so our resources are stretched.'

The role of official bodies like the PCA, and charities such as that set up by Tony Adams for addicted and depressed sportsmen, are crucial because of the widespread misery that retirement can bring. For less well-known players, the problems are often lack of money and/or lack of work opportunities.

The more famous sportsmen are considered the lucky ones. People often said to me towards the end of my career, 'You've no need to worry, you've captained England!' But it is the more well-known faces who can battle the most: think of George Best, Jimmy Greaves, Malcolm MacDonald and Paul Gascoigne. Think of Bruno.

The problem here is not so much the failure to cope financially, but simply the failure to cope with life. With the loss of the limelight and celebrity comes a gaping void. The sight of a former sportsman making a fool of himself on some show or other is a sad one — more often than not it is his way of saying, 'Look at me, I'm still here!'

How can the transition from a sporting life to real life be handled best? I don't hold myself up as an example at all, but here are some thoughts: the timing of retirement (if there is a choice) is important; think ahead and plan a little; avoid the grasping claws of celebrity if at all possible, because it will chew you up and spit you out when you are at your most vulnerable, and try to forge a second career so that you don't spend the rest of your life trying to be someone you once were.

These problems affect performers from all sports. Suicide, as the ultimate consequence of depression, seems a problem more specific to cricket. During his research, Frith could not find a single instance of a golfer or tennis player who had committed suicide, and he found only a handful of footballers and boxers.

Peter Roebuck, in his foreword to Frith's first book, suggested that cricket attracted suicidal types. This must be utter nonsense. Cricket attracts normal people, but has the ability to turn them sour. Who knows why? Maybe, because of the time it takes to play, the game becomes all-consuming: full-on professionalism, for all but the elite, is bad for the soul. Maybe the game plays too many tricks on your mind: can you think of a game that causes more mental stress? Maybe luck plays too big and too random a part (umpiring decisions/the pitch, for example). Maybe because a cricket team is an environment where everything is done for you, the transition to having responsibility for your own life is hard to handle. Who knows? I do know that, thankfully, for the county cricketer in question the future is much brighter.

'I've realised that I'm not alone and that there is a network of help out there. Even if my cricket career doesn't pan out I know now there are other options. Cricket is not everything, although I could not see it at the time. I'm not scared any more. I'm coping and I am facing the future with a greater sense of confidence.'

---

19 JULY 2005

YORKSHIRE GRANDEES FORGET OLD SQUABBLES FOR SAKE OF ART

Simon Briggs

For Englishmen of a certain age, 2005 has been the year of reconciliation. Rock fans have already thrilled to the sight of Cream and Pink Floyd reforming after decades of acrimony. But for many cricket lovers, the most unexpected reunion of the summer happened not in front of 200,000 baby-boomers in Hyde Park, but in an immaculate pub garden in the Miss Marple-ish village of Ripon, West Yorkshire. This was the venue where the Four Greatest Living Yorkshiremen – Geoff Boycott, Fred Trueman, Ray Illingworth and Brian Close – gathered for a portrait sitting in late May.

Strictly speaking, it was not the first time the FGLY had been in one place since their great on-field alliance was disbanded in 1968. Three years ago they all attended the opening of Headingley's new East Stand; but while that was a stuffy Yorkshire committee function, this summer's less formal assembly was proposed by Trueman himself. As art publisher Barry Cox explained: 'The artist John Blakey and I went to see Fred, and he suggested that we should capture the four of them in conversation.

They have had their well-documented friendships and fall-outs, but I think they have recognised that at a certain age you should let bygones be bygones.'

Those without a doctorate in the history of Yorkshire cricket might not realise that some of those bygones make Pink Floyd look like the best of friends. Even in the glory days of the 1960s, it was no secret that Yorkshire fought like cats and dogs behind closed doors. But the parting of the ways brought fresh tensions. When Close and Illingworth collided in the Gillette Cup, as captains of Somerset and Leicestershire respectively, each man accused the other of cheating, sending the whole of Yorkshire into helpless mirth.

And then there was Boycott, the youngest of the group by eight years, and a man described by his biographer Leo McKinstry as a natural focus for discontent. His eight seasons as Yorkshire captain were divisive enough, earning many accusations of selfishness and poor man-management from Trueman in particular. But his most infamous hour came in 1984, when moves to sack him prompted his supporters to rise up, overthrow the Yorkshire committee, and oust Illingworth instead.

When you consider how much poisonous water has flown under this bridge, it was a bold move for Cox and Blakey to press ahead with their group portrait. Especially as, unlike Sir Bob Geldof, they did not have a global TV audience to dangle in front of their feuding foursome.

Blakey had already painted Trueman on a number of occasions, producing one striking canvas that hangs in the dining room of the same Ripon pub. A traditional oil portraitist, he has worked with film stars, politicians and royalty. But this was one of his most daunting assignments.

'Up until the last minute, you have your heart in your mouth,' said Cox, who is publishing Blakey's forthcoming book *Portraits of Yorkshire*. 'You wonder if the Yorkshireness of them all will allow them to converge in the same time and place, or if any of them had woken up in a bad mood whether they would have bothered to turn up.'

The same thought seemed to have occurred to Boycott. Around half-an-hour after the players were due to convene, he was striding around checking his watch like a man waiting for the plumber. 'Fred always does this,' he spluttered. 'This is virtually his bloody local and he still manages to be late. Can't we make a start? The day will get away from us if we're not careful.'

Reclining calmly in the pub's sunlit conservatory, Close and Illingworth were sipping coffee. Despite the odd altercation, these two have always had a strong bond, based on Close's status as godfather to Illingworth's daughter. And now they were chuckling over old stories. 'Do you remember the time he left Jimmy Binks in the car while he went to talk to that barmaid?' said Close. 'Jimmy was waiting an hour before he came back.'

Perhaps 45 minutes had passed when the door finally burst open, and Trueman strode in, shaking his shaggy head like a wet labrador. 'Terrible journey it were,' he announces in his distinctive baritone, much imitated but never equalled. 'I were stuck behind a caravan' – he pronounces it cara-vannh – 'for three miles, then flock of sheep at Grassington.'

And then they were off. Anyone anticipating any lingering froideur between these Yorkshire grandees would have been amazed by the obvious delight they took in each other's company. The atmosphere was less like *Goodfellas* than *Last of the Summer Wine*. Except that the jokes – most of them unprintable – were undeniably funny.

Trueman was at the centre of it all, just as he always was in Yorkshire's heyday. 'When I was starting in the team I would run to mid-on as quickly as I could, just to hear Fred talking,' said Boycott. With the artist's eye for group dynamics, Blakey placed him immediately at the heart of the painting, ignoring Trueman's complaints that the ball he had been given to hold up was only a youth's size.

Though Trueman is 74 now, with a substantial girth, he still cuts a powerful figure. Close is his junior by 18 days, but looked the frailer of the two as he slumped in his chair, endlessly rotating a cigarette packet in his spidery fingers. Their conversation went in circles as well, with the pair of them talking over and around each other like a Yorkshire version of The Muppets' Statler and Waldorf.

The others were quiet by comparison. Butting in with the occasional sardonic aside, Illingworth played his customary role of the wise old bird – the same persona that won him a turbulent 1990s spell as England's selector-cum-coach. And if Boycott was uncharacteristically muted, it was because he will always be the little brother in this company. As with any family reunion, each member slotted immediately back into his traditional role.

Of course, the meeting had hardly been convened before the modern game was under attack. As Blakey propped a set of individual studies against the bar, prompting admiring remarks from Trueman in particular, Close was already railing against Pakistan's claims to have invented the art of reverse-swing.

Illingworth was quick to back him up. 'Donald Waterham showed me how to wet one side of the ball in 1947,' he announced triumphantly. 'Fine bowler, Donald Waterham, took 1,000 Bradford League wickets.'

Over a lengthy pub lunch, there was earnest discussion of how Wes Hall had been timed at 104 mph at Lord's, 'bowling off the back-foot rule which meant he let it go a yard-and-a-half nearer you,' how Duncan Fletcher hasn't a clue about batting technique, and how Ant and Dec do not deserve to be mentioned in the same breath as Morecambe and Wise.

The most vicious criticism was reserved, appropriately enough, for the phenomenon of sledging. 'I think it's an appalling way to carry on,' said Boycott. 'If you said those things in the local pub somebody would smack you on the chin. Yes, Fred used to say things too, but they were funny things that made everybody on the field laugh.'

'Nobody ever abused anyone verbally in our day,' chimed Close, a man who used to pride himself on staring batsmen out from his vantage point at short-leg. 'We used to have so much fun, but we were not kidding when we went on the field, we were hammer and tongs. And if it went wrong, if it didn't go our way, we were the first to go up and say well done.'

And with that, they set off on their separate roads. Despite a few tactful enquiries, none of them had ever really explained why the FGLY had spent more than three decades pointedly avoiding each other. There were mumblings about work and charity commitments, and how difficult it was to get together. But Cox has his own theory about their collective change of heart, which relates to Boycott's recent battle with throat cancer.

'The key catalyst was the friendship that had developed between Geoffrey and Fred, who rang him regularly during his illness to offer support,' said Cox. 'That has broken down a number of psychological barriers. Everyone could see that they were genuinely thrilled and relieved to be together. I think it is no exaggeration to call this a landmark event.'

8 AUGUST 2005

ENGLAND BEAT AUSTRALIA
BY 2 RUNS

Derek Pringle

Edgbaston

Levelling this series should have been a formality for England yesterday but it was typical of this extraordinary Test match that the interested parties were kept on tenterhooks until the last possible moment. Well almost the last possible moment because when Geraint Jones took a tumbling catch off Steve Harmison to dismiss Michael Kasprowicz, England still had two runs in hand, albeit a sweaty one.

The two-run margin is the narrowest yet in an Ashes Test. But while that surely elevates this one to being the greatest between these two old foes, the fact that England have come from behind to level with Australia for the first time since 1981 is far more pertinent.

It was a big moment, at least for England. As umpire Billy Bowden raised his finger, Michael Vaughan and his team became airborne as one, a collective leap of joy counterbalanced by Kasprowicz and his batting partner, Brett Lee, who sank heavily to their haunches in disbelief that their last-wicket heroics should count for nought. Lee cannot have played a better or braver innings – he took a nasty blow to his left hand off Andrew Flintoff – and he was plainly distraught.

The differing reactions of the combatants revealed the draining amounts of emotion and effort invested in this ding-dong Test match. While his team-mates went to mob Harmison, Geraint Jones went what used to be described as ape-jumping, snarling and punching his right glove at a group of Australia fans who had been sledging him from the Wyatt stand.

As at Lord's, Jones has not enjoyed the best of matches with bat or gloves (he let through four byes at a crucial moment yesterday), though to be involved in the dramatic last act of levelling the series will have raised his spirits as the team head for Manchester and the third Npower Test, which starts on Thursday.

Although Kasprowicz would not have known it at the time, he was not out. While there is no doubt the bouncer from Harmison brushed his right glove as he took evasive action, television replays revealed his hand to be about three inches off the handle at the time (it has to be in contact), but it would take a brave and eagle-eyed umpire to spot and call it in a match so finely poised.

Certainly, Australia did not appear to feel cheated by the decision, something they had every right to be the previous day when Lee had a plumb lbw against Simon Jones turned down by the same umpire. Jones and Flintoff, whose last-wicket partnership of 51 was the clinching act of this match, added only two more runs before Shane Warne ended the spree – the same margin as England's victory.

Whittling down the 62 runs the pair needed to just three, before Harmison found the ball with an Aussie name on it, can floor you more effectively than any Mike Tyson uppercut. Yet had the ball gone for 4, or even 3, and England lost the match to go 2–0 down in the series, they would have needed something a lot stronger than smelling salts to revive them.

'I don't think we would have come back from 2–0 down against a team like Australia, the number one side in the rankings. It's fantastic to get back to 1–1,' Vaughan said. 'To get over the line is a real good boost. It sets the series up fantastically well. The most important thing now is to take this momentum into the third Test and start well again on Thursday at Old Trafford.'

Australia's captain, Ricky Ponting, tried to be upbeat about his team's defeat. 'It was probably the most nerve-racking end to a match that I've ever played in, right up there with the World Cup semi-final against South Africa in 1999 [also at Edgbaston]. But we can take as much away from this as England can after the way we fought it out.'

After an amazing Saturday in which 17 wickets fell (not to mention the frenetic cricket on the first two days), yesterday promised to be something of an anti-climax with England expected to wrap up victory quickly, their thunderous fast bowlers knocking over Australia's last two wickets.

Yet, led by Warne, Australia's tail were not about to be bobbed as 24 runs were taken off the opening four overs. Needing 107 to win did not turn them into statues, though that came later once the target got below 10 and the pressure of expectation took hold.

Warne has made two first-class hundreds for Hampshire this season and would have fancied his chances. Ironic then that a batsman's flourish, a flick of the right heel when attempting a clip to leg off Flintoff, should prove his undoing as he trod on his stumps.

Having been England's enforcer with bat and ball in this match, Flintoff was expected to crown an immense personal performance – that saw him score 68 and 73, as well as take seven wickets – by delivering the *coup de grâce*. It did not come and with Lee carving to off and Kasprowicz shovelling to leg, the sell-out crowd began to get fidgety as the runs kept coming. England began to look anxious, too, though Vaughan kept his cool, at least outwardly. Inundated with offers of advice from his team throughout the match, he revealed that none was forthcoming yesterday.

With five runs needed, Lee and Kasprowicz changed their approach, which went from attack to the belief that they could get the runs in singles. Lucky, then, that a juicy full toss from Harmison, which Lee struck hard, was restricted to a single by Ian Bell, as it brought Kasprowicz on strike.

Sensing that this was the last chance saloon, Harmison, who had bowled Michael Clarke the previous evening with an outrageous slower ball, banged in short. The rest, as Kasprowicz parried to Jones, has kept the Ashes and the summer from football's greedy grasp.

The hard bare expanses of Old Trafford beckon next, but while Australia are sure to be without Glenn McGrath, following his ankle injury here, they are talking up Warne's prospects of going well beyond his 600th Test wicket (he is presently on 599). But while Warne can turn it on most surfaces, England should take heart from Old Trafford's reputation as a place for reverse-swing. In this Test, Flintoff and Simon Jones used the skill far better than Australia did and should retain their edge in Manchester.

England's pace bowlers were also more aggressive, though Jones was deemed by the match referee, Ranjan Madugalle, to have overdone the aggro when he showed Matthew Hayden the way back to the pavilion after dismissing him on Saturday. Jones was fined 20 per cent of his match fee (roughly £1,000), but after yesterday's win he will recoup that, and more, the next time he does a photo shoot with his clothes off.

---

13 SEPTEMBER 2005

ENGLAND'S ASHES

Derek Pringle

Edgbaston

It used to be the dream that disappeared on waking, the yearning that had no release, and the trophy that England teams could neither win, borrow nor steal – at least not since 1989. Then, amid tumultuous scenes at the Oval yesterday, the Ashes fell back into English hands, the little brown urn finally secured after an astonishing century by Kevin Pietersen made the final Test safe from one last Australian ambush.

Pietersen's high-octane innings did not prevent the moment being sealed with a whimper though, after Australia openers Justin Langer and Matthew Hayden accepted the offer of bad light.

With the visitors needing an impossible 338 runs from 17.2 overs, the move simply sealed the draw prematurely, though Michael Vaughan, perhaps wanting to savour the moment in front of another capacity crowd, seemed more than a little aggrieved.

Vaughan's annoyance was short-lived and once he had given the replica urn a peck on the cheek and held it aloft to roars of delight, he and the team appeared overjoyed as they did a lap of honour to renditions of Jerusalem and Land of Hope and Glory – a combination that with all the flags and confetti made the occasion feel like a cross between a Wembley Cup final and Last Night at the Proms.

Eight Ashes series had been lost before this 2–1 win. It has been fully deserved too, and after their defeat in the opening Test at Lord's, England's has been the bolder and more persuasive cricket, a combination that has relied on finding the right man at the right time. Yesterday, that man was Pietersen, who ever since he brought his combination of bling and bluster to this England side has threatened to produce something sensational, though thrill-seeker that he is, he left it until the attention of the entire country, as well as the insomniac parts of Australia, were on him before producing it.

In the context of the game, which England needed to make safe by batting out most of the day, it was a reckless but glorious ride, most of it at breakneck speed. By the time Glenn McGrath ended it, clean bowling him with the second new ball for 158, he had struck seven 6s and 15 4s, nearly all whistle clean off the middle of the bat.

Given the extraordinary events of this series, it would be easy to be blase about Pietersen's deeds. But as they have done ever since they got their noses in front during the Edgbaston Test, England once more faltered as the main prize hove into view as McGrath and Shane Warne probed for scar tissue in England's collective psyche one last time.

But Pietersen is wired up differently to most and does not do caution or self-doubt, as he revealed when hooking 93 mph bouncers from Brett Lee high into the crowd at long leg. Although he is more likely to reveal the dark roots in his blond streak than the English ones in his make-up, he clearly cares, though perhaps not to the extent that he chokes up as some of his team-mates have done.

Arriving at the crease after McGrath had removed Vaughan and Ian Bell in successive balls to leave England 69 for three, Pietersen survived the hat-trick ball, but only just as the bouncer missed his glove by a whisker before striking his upper arm. With the whole team appealing for the catch, the pressure on umpire Billy Bowden was enormous, but his intransigence proved to be the right decision – one of several hairline ones the umpires got spot-on during the day.

If that near-miss could be put down to Pietersen's skill, he also enjoyed some luck, being dropped on nought and 15. The first chance came off Warne, as Pietersen edged to Adam Gilchrist, and the second to Warne, as he edged a drive off Lee to first slip. If the first was tricky the second was standard fodder and shouts of 'Warney's dropped the Ashes' echoed around the Oval for the rest of the day.

While it is indisputable that the mistake cost them dear, without Warne Australia would have been pole-axed this summer. Worrying times for Australia then that he and McGrath, who took 3 for 85 yesterday, are into the last phases of their careers. Warne finished with six wickets to bring his tally to 40 for the series. While that is not an Australian record for an Ashes series (Terry Alderman took 42 and 41 in the 1980s and Rodney Hogg 41 before that), he did beat Dennis Lillee's record for the most Ashes victims over a career, now set at 172.

He almost rallied his team for one last attempt to claw back their proud Ashes legacy, following the dismissal of Marcus Trescothick and Andrew Flintoff, caught and bowled after Warne had lured him into an indiscreet drive.

The double strike left England looking distinctly insecure on 126 for 5 at lunch. Fortunately for them Warne's mastery of Pietersen here was limited to the first innings only. While others groped and smothered his spin, the skunk-haired one treated him with disdain, twice sweep-slogging him for 6 over mid-wicket before biffing him straight for another two 6s as the mood took him.

It was the stuff of fantasy, ably abetted by a sturdy 59 from Ashley Giles, who added 109 runs with Pietersen for the eighth wicket, an Oval record against Australia. Although both eventually perished and the team were bowled out for 335, all threat had been defused and the game, and with it the series, was in the bag.

England have won the Ashes – a statement that has a magnificent ring to it.

———

3 JULY 2006

WHAT AN ADDITION TO ANY CELESTIAL XI

Martin Johnson

It is hard to believe he's gone, but he'll be a great addition to the commentary team on the celestial version of Test Match Special. 'And after a word from St Peter, it will be Fred Trueman.' 'Call them Pearly Gates? Tha' must be joking. And as for that harp player, give me the Brighouse and Rastrick Brass Band any day. Three wise men? Know booger all about t'game if tha' ask me.'

'Well thank you Fred, and now we welcome World Service listeners with the news that it's time for the shipping forecast.' There is an entire generation of cricket followers who only associated Fred with his radio commentaries, in which he rarely knew 'what was going off out there' and would dissolve into a paroxysm of outraged harrumphing when Derek Pringle became the first England cricketer to take the field sporting an earring.

He was so entrenched in the past that they assume he must have opened the bowling for the Old Testament eleven ('that Methuselah, he could ruddy play') but not many chroniclers of the game of cricket, charged with compiling a list of England's greatest bowlers, would place Frederick Sewards Trueman any lower than no. 1.

Never the most modest of men, this was a view with which Fred was happy to concur. Many years ago, when invited by Michael Parkinson to think of a working title for an autobiography, Fred didn't even pause for a puff of his pipe. 'Ey up, Parky lad, 'ow about: "T'Definitive Volume of T'Greatest Fast Bowler who ever Drew Breath"?' Tongue in cheek? Probably not.

The 1950 *Wisden Almanack* is a veritable collector's item for the passage in the Yorkshire notes of that year. 'Yorkshire gave a trial to three young players, Lawson, an opening batsman, Close, an all-rounder, and Trueman, a spin bowler.' Well, not many spinners went on to bowl 90 mph out-swingers with a classical side-on action, all the more effective for the batsman being rooted on the back foot having been persuaded by Fred that preservation of his teeth was more important than the preservation of his wicket.

It was the unshakable belief in his own ability which made him the bowler he was, and the conviction that there were two ways of doing things. His way, and the wrong way. Which led to an interesting exchange when England were heading for Australia by boat on the 1962–3 Ashes tour, and the captain, Ted Dexter, discovered that one of the passengers was the athlete Gordon Pirie.

Dexter asked Pirie to organise a daily run around a deck, to which Fred inquired 'why?' 'To keep your legs strong,' Pirie replied. 'Listen here sunshine,' said Fred (he called everyone sunshine), 'I bowled 1,141 overs last summer for 153 wickets at 17.75 apiece. What makes thee think my legs need strengthening.' Followed by a jabbed finger in the direction of Pirie's matchstick lower limbs. 'And tha's not much of an advert for legs art tha'?'

Just about every cricket story told has been attributed to Fred, one or two of which are true. England batsman Peter Parfitt, in his first season with Middlesex, was hit in the mouth attempting to hook the great man, retired hurt, and returned at the fall of the next wicket. 'Have you taken leave of your senses, lad?' Fred inquired when Parfitt reappeared. 'Why's that Fred?' Parfitt asked. ''Cause people don't usually come back after I've 'it 'em, that's why.'

Trueman is even more of a hero to many of us for having played the game in an era when cricket's entry in the Oxford dictionary as a colloquial term for fair play was actually accurate. Batsmen who didn't walk risked becoming dressing-room pariahs (in their own dressing room as well as the opposition's) and were equally happy to take a fielder at his word when claiming a catch. Neither did fielders appeal unless they thought the batsman was out.

And perhaps the most pleasing legacy we have from that period is that old television footage of Fred's magnificently graceful run-up has been preserved without — as will sadly not be the case for the great fast bowlers of the present era — having to watch him glide across a multi-coloured advertisement for a supermarket or an electricity company.

Perhaps the most misleading view of Trueman is that he rarely took the field without first downing a pint of ale, and at close of play would sink a gallon more. In fact he was never a big drinker, and it's probably true to say also that some of his fabled witticisms were not meant to be amusing at all. Ergo, when the Rev David Shepherd suffered a spate of dropped catches in a Test match, and Fred said 'tell us Rev, do you only put your 'ands together on a ruddy Sunday morning?', it was delivered with more of a snort than a chuckle.

Trueman himself was a regular churchgoer and, after he retired, he performed countless unpublicised tasks for charity. It was Fred who organised a fund-raising dinner for Brian Statham when his old bowling partner fell on hard times, and despite having no great affection for Geoff Boycott in the era when Boycott was the catalyst for Yorkshire infighting, it was Fred who phoned him every week when Boycott was fighting his own battle against cancer.

He perfectly fitted the northern stereotype of underprivileged working class, and the Monty Python sketch on that subject might have been written with Fred in mind. 'Lived in a house? Looxury. We were three to a bed in the outside privy.' It made him ideal for the role of presenter, along with Sid Waddell, in Granada TV's *The Indoor League*, which featured pub games like darts, skittles, and shove h'appeny, and always ended with Fred signing off: 'I'll si' thee.'

Hardly surprising, then, that Fred was not entirely comfortable with the idea of becoming related to Raquel Welch. When his daughter married the film star's son, Fred accused Ms Welch of trying to steal the bride's thunder, and when the marriage was over almost before it started, Fred observed: 'My run-up lasted longer.'

Test Match Special hired him for a combination of his celebrity status and his vast experience of the game, but while he had many sound observations to make, they often got lost in a rant about all things modern. I remember tuning in one morning when England were playing Sri Lanka to hear Fred's indignant splutter: 'Sri Lanka? You'll not hear me calling them Sri Lanka. What's wrong with Ceylon? Perfectly good name, Ceylon.'

He upset a few with his moaning, but it was usually unwise to take him on. Once, when he was grumbling about England's batting to some friends in the pavilion, a voice dripping with sarcasm piped up: 'And how many centuries did you make for England, Mr Trueman?' Fred's response was instantaneous. 'One, and it were not out an' all.'

Now, though, the umpiring finger in the sky has gone up on his final innings, and it only remains to bid him a fond farewell. And as they closed the coffin lid, you could almost hear him one last time. 'Funeral? Call that a funeral? Don't get me wrong, er, er, very fine vicar, er, er, one of the best, er, er, but, er, er, in my day, er, now that were a funeral.'

---

29 SEPTEMBER 2006

EXCLUSIVE: SENSIBLE END TO CHAOTIC AFFAIR: THE INZAMAM VERDICT

Simon Hughes

Ranjan Madugalle's verdict at the Oval yesterday did not only declare 20 August a Bad Hair day. It was also a victory for common sense, an entity that had been in short supply at that same venue a month earlier.

It emerged during the hearing that that afternoon was one of allegation, obfuscation, provocation and indignation resulting in the forfeiture of a Test match. There was chaos behind the scenes in the pavilion after tea. At the very moment officials were indulging in desperate brinkmanship with the enraged Pakistanis, the on-field umpires were independently removing the bails to declare the match awarded to England. It is clear that, with a bit of discretion here and a deep breath there, this fiasco would never have come about.

First things first. The ball. Was it tampered with? I first examined it in the London offices of the International Cricket Council's lawyers, Olswang, two weeks ago. It was presented to me in a heavily taped up cardboard box containing much packaging. Deep inside was the ball, wrapped in clear plastic. It was handed delicately to me, as if it were a murder weapon, though I was not asked to wear white gloves.

It surprised me. After 56 overs on a dry, fourth-day Oval pitch, it was in pretty good condition. There were a number of small abrasions on the rough side fairly typical of normal wear and tear on a deteriorating Test pitch. The only thing that looked slightly suspicious was a number of slightly curved striations concentrated on one area. I concluded that those could have been man-made scratches, but there was no way I could be sure. There was no hard evidence of ball tampering.

At the hearing on Wednesday, I briefly took the witness seat to reiterate my uncertainties about the origin of the marks on the ball. This 5½oz lump of leather was exhibit A in the Legends Lounge at the Oval, an L-shaped room decorated with pictures of the greats and used on match days as a sponsors' bar.

The Pakistanis – Inzamam-ul-Haq, his interpreter and the board chairman, Shaharyar Khan – sat behind Mark Gay and his team from elite law firm D.L.A. Piper down one side. The four umpires, the match referee and ICC personnel sat behind their defence counsel, Pushpinder Saini, down the other side, facing adjudicator Madugalle and his legal adviser, David Pannick, an eminent QC. Inzamam and Darrell Hair managed to avoid making eye contact at any point.

Hair was first to be called to sit in the hot seat. This was a separate table at the front, facing at right angles to Madugalle and the others. The ball was produced from its box and he indicated the indentations on the rough side that had not been there four overs earlier and which, he concluded, 'could only be man-made'. He had shown it to the other umpire, Billy Doctrove, who was 'quite surprised' at the marks. Crucially, though, Doctrove had suggested waiting a few more overs to try to identify a culprit before taking the matter further.

Hair, however, argued that if Doctrove agreed that the marks looked irregular they should act. He said he told Inzamam: 'We are changing the ball because its condition has been unfairly altered.' It emerged later that the Pakistan captain, whose English is not particularly good, either had not heard this or had not understood it. He later revealed that the first time he realised that they had been charged with ball tampering and docked five penalty runs was when he was watching the television in the dressing room at tea, more than an hour after the incident.

Under cross-examination from Gay, Hair gave a dignified and resolute defence of the umpires' actions. A stickler for the laws of the game, he argued he couldn't have acceded to a more cautious reaction to the state of the ball 'because law 42.3 does not provide umpires condition for warning the players. We wouldn't have been doing our job'.

'Isn't this an over-legalistic approach?' Gay inquired. 'You'd know all about legal approaches, Mr Gay,' Hair countered. There was a brief outburst of laughter.

It was the crux of the matter, though. Hair applied the law rigorously, as a traffic cop might when overtaken by a driver doing 72 mph on the motorway. The problem was Hair was guessing, using the flimsiest evidence, as the cop might with no radar-gun reading. Fair enough, you'd say, if the bloke had shot past doing about 90. Nick him. But the marks on the ball were not blatant enough for the drastic measures Hair took. The laws of cricket are there to ensure the smooth running of the game, and therefore should be interpreted reasonably — it is why humans umpire the game rather than machines.

Hair would have been better emulating the umpires last year at the Oval, who warned the Surrey captain that they suspected ball tampering was going on before taking action a few overs later when it continued. Hair did not see it that way. Asked by Gay if he would act differently next time, he said: 'Faced with those circumstances I would do the same again.'

The rest of Wednesday morning's formalities revolved around the umpires showing solidarity, though Doug Cowie, the ICC's umpires manager who was at the Oval that day, admitted that as soon as he saw the five penalty runs being awarded, he said: 'Oh s***, there's going to be some trouble now!' The match referee, Mike Procter, also revealed that during the post-tea protests by the Pakistanis he was so caught up behind the scenes in feverish attempts to restore play that he did not see the umpires remove the bails. 'The first I knew the match had been awarded to England was when Darrell was having a shower in the umpire's room,' he said.

Geoff Boycott arrived after a break for lunch and inevitably enlivened proceedings. He greeted Pakistan's first speaker, Shaharyar Khan, to the witness desk with a cheery 'Oopening the battin'! First and last time you'll go in ahead of me!' and later delivered an impassioned and at times hectoring speech about the importance of the spirit of the game. 'You don't just put on a white coat and say, "I'm God, I'm in charge,"' he said. 'You've got to be a bit more humane.'

Boycott was adamant that there was nothing wrong with the ball, and stuck to his guns under cross-examination from Saini, warning: 'He better not try and do some point-scoring or I'll come back at him!' and had to be politely dissuaded by Pannick. 'Why didn't you ever bat like that, Boycs?' I asked at the break. 'Aw, these days they've got covered wickets, big bats, small boundaries. I never had any of that,' he said.

All the Pakistan witnesses – Khan, coach Bob Woolmer and Inzamam through his interpreter – gave accounts of the scene in the dressing room which prevented play from continuing. Poor communication and pigheadedness on both sides exacerbated the situation. After their first sit-in, the Pakistanis claimed they were heading out to play but the umpires were coming off the field and shortly arrived at the dressing room back door. Woolmer let them in.

Accounts differed as to what was said next, but it wasn't particularly civil. Hair apparently asked: 'Are you coming out to play?' To which Inzamam replied: 'Why did you change the ball?' Hair claims he then said: 'We are returning to the field and if you don't accompany us that will be deemed a refusal to play,' but the Pakistanis refute that and say they found Hair's tone 'brusque', which caused further resentment.

By the time they had seen reason it was too late. There is no doubt that lighter handling of the situation, a captain more au fait with the laws and closer proximity of players' and umpires' dressing rooms (they are two floors apart and in a separate building at the Oval) would have brought about a different outcome.

During my evidence I produced two other balls for comparison – one that I'd deliberately and blatantly tampered with, another that was roughed up naturally by my bad bowling. 'Not again!' Madugalle said, smirking.

Umpire John Hampshire was the last witness, and summed it all up by saying: 'I find it incredible that this ball could cause so much controversy.' Impressively though Saini articulated the umpires' stance, Madugalle and Pannick saw reason and sense and announced the decision that had been expected all along. 'Another case, another verdict,'

Saini said ruefully, before adding: 'Actually, Inzamam is one of my favourite players.' When it comes to lawyers, they are a law unto themselves.

---

28 NOVEMBER 2006

Michael Henderson

OH, what is that sound which so thrills the ear
Down Under, drumming, drumming?
Only the Aussie green caps, dear,
The Aussie green caps coming.
Oh, who are those players so full of fear
They run for their lives daily, daily?
Only our toiling batsmen, dear,
Donating their wickets gaily.
Oh, are they so poor, and the foe without peer,
They must submit so meekly, so meekly?
The Aussies have answered that in four days, dear,
And not at all obliquely.
Oh, is there no hope, one Test to the rear:
Have we no Harmy, no Harmy?
If you had seen him bowl, dear,
You wouldn't talk so barmy.
Oh, where is the man to restore our cheer?
Is it the stumper, the stumper?
His gloves are on the floor, dear,
And he's lost the ball up his jumper.
Oh, it must be the spinner who is our panacea,
It must be Gilo, Gilo!
He's done his hip by the pool, dear,
And is coming round on a lilo.
Oh, it may be K.P. who sounds the all-clear,
It may be the hitter, the hitter!
He's writing another book of his life, dear,
To give us all a big titter.

Oh, there's Jimmy, of course, who makes the ball veer,
Surely he will deliver, deliver?
They walloped him out of the ground, dear,
And fished the ball from the river.
Oh, there's Freddie, as well, the star of last year,
He's on our side, thank heaven, thank heaven!
He plays heart and soul, as ever, dear,
But he's only one of eleven.
Oh bother, oh crumbs, you make me feel queer!
Is it worth hanging on to my ticket, my ticket?
The Ashes have already gone, dear,
To Australia: bat, pad and wicket.
(With apologies to W.H. Auden – 1907–1973)

---

28 DECEMBER 2006

Martin Johnson

Melbourne

The MCG is a big ground, as indeed it had to be when Duncan Fletcher assembled the entire England squad – players, coaches, doctors, physios, shrinks, everyone bar the wives and girlfriends – on the outfield before the second day's play. What could it be, we wondered. A pep talk? Surely not. Fletcher has many qualities, but when it comes to stirring oratory, England's taciturn coach could make the shipping forecast sound like Churchill.

More likely, as news filtered out that England's dressing-room battle plans had been leaked in an email to the Australian Broadcasting Corporation, he was trying to find out if there was a mole in the camp. If so, however, the players were entitled to look a little bemused, as England's planning for this tour has suggested a dressing-room not so much resembling the Admiralty War Room as the Tiny Tots Day Nursery.

The ABC may well have passed on the leaks to the Australian version of MI5, who even now are trying to decipher the code. 'I think I've cracked it sir. We're still working on what "babysitter for the Harmisons at 9 p.m." means, but the Enigma machine reports that "organise shopping expedition for the WAGS" is actually a devilish scheme to move silly mid-off a bit straighter for Matthew Hayden.'

So now we know why England have lost the Ashes, and to what unspeakable lengths the Australians have stooped in their desperation to get them back. The gloves are off for 2009. If that's the way they want to play it, the Lord's dressing room attendant will report straight to M for instructions on how to plant a bug in Ricky Ponting's baggy green cap and report any suspicious messages such as: 'Who'll come a waltzing Matilda with me' for decoding.

There is only one clear inference to be drawn, which is that Australia have been able to second-guess England's every move since Operation Ashes was hatched. How else would they have known that every time England arrived at a defining moment in a Test, their plan was to clamber into a hammock for a quiet doze until Australia had re-established their supremacy?

So it was again yesterday, when Andrew Symonds walked out to bat with white zinc cream plastered all over his lips in temperatures that – for Australians at any rate – would have altered the anatomy of a brass monkey. What followed, though, was confirmation of the suspicion that when it comes to playing England, Australian cricketers put this stuff on more as war paint than sun protection.

Symonds's dark complexion made him look like Al Jolson, and his Test batting (average 18.47 until yesterday) has been more of a song-and-dance routine than a serious application of his talent. In fact, had Damien Martyn not decided to retire so completely that he is rumoured to be sharing a tent in the Outback with Lord Lucan, Symonds wouldn't even have been considered.

England will claim that Symonds's mammoth partnership with Hayden would never have got going in the first place but for umpire Rudi Koertzen's apparent belief that the ICC have done away with the lbw law, and England's bowlers are approaching the point where ideal choice of ends has less to do with the conditions than which end Rudi is standing.

In the case of Sajid Mahmood, he'll take any end, so long as he gets to bowl. In Perth, the hosts wasted no time in baiting him when he came into bat. 'Who's this bloke, then? Buggered if I know, but he must be a batsman, as he doesn't seem to bowl.'

Mahmood even claimed he felt 'ignored' in his ghosted newspaper column, which, while breaking new ground in this field by saying something interesting, may not have endeared him to the hierarchy. Yesterday, he was again put out to grass until England had exhausted their other options, and his eventual breakthrough came well after horse-bolting time.

Symonds and Hayden are close mates; one likes angling and the other is a nifty chef. Symonds catches the fish, while Hayden cooks them, although they once came close to being on the menu themselves when their dinghy capsized in waters populated by a dangerous species of shark.

They did, in one way, spoil Australia's reputation as a team oozing testosterone by both using bats with pink handles. The object of the exercise was to draw attention to a breast cancer charity, so at least, with the two batsmen being sponsored for every run, England's bowlers could content themselves with the fact that they were contributing to a worthy cause.

---

5 JANUARY 2007

Derek Pringle

Sydney

Andrew Flintoff's England team suffered only the second whitewash in Ashes history after losing the final Test in Sydney by 10 wickets. The previous occasion such an ignominy occurred was on the 1920–1 tour captained by J.W.H.T. Douglas, though that side were depleted by the First World War. This team had no such excuse and were simply ill-prepared for a potent and highly motivated foe.

As in all but one of their defeats this series, the last rites were administered swiftly after England's last five wickets fell for 45 runs in 15 overs. That left Australia needing 46 runs for victory, a target they achieved before lunch on the final day.

If England were harbouring any thoughts of last-minute heroics, they got off to the worst possible start when Kevin Pietersen was caught behind off the third ball of the morning. Inevitably, as he has done throughout his career, Glenn McGrath supplied the telling ball, a typically precision instrument that drew the batsman forward before taking the edge of the bat.

Pietersen's departure, as throughout the series, exposed England's frail tail and they were still on their overnight score when nightwatchman Monty Panesar was run out by a direct hit from Andrew Symonds. Not the fastest sprinter in the squad, Panesar would have needed Olympic qualifying times to beat the throw after being called for a quick single by Chris Read.

A fine keeper, Read does not possess a cool head and it was always a risky run. Indeed, England did not add to their total until the 23rd minute of play when Sajid Mahmood snicked McGrath through the slips for 4. With Brett Lee dismissing Read for four, swishing at an outswinger, and McGrath bowling Mahmood off his pads, it was time for Ricky Ponting to engineer a farewell wicket for his other retiree, Shane Warne. It did not work, and although Warne had a stumping chance referred to the third umpire when Steve Harmison dragged his foot, he did not add to the 708 Test wickets he has taken over a 14-year career. Instead it was McGrath that improved his final tally to 563 after having James Anderson caught at mid-on by Michael Hussey as he tried to work the ball to leg.

The wicket brought hugs, especially between Australia's bowlers. England paid their own tribute before the start of Australia's innings when they formed a guard of honour on the square for Justin Langer. The certainty of the result did not prevent the Sydney Cricket Ground from being filled close to capacity, many of them England supporters. Although most tickets were pre-sold for the fourth day, the lure of seeing the final act of three stellar talents proved irresistible.

The trio will not be replaced overnight. Langer, who overcame adversity throughout his career as well as dozens of blows to the head, has several already queuing for his spot, but Australia will not easily make good the yawning hole left by McGrath and Warne.

The pair have proved a near-unstoppable force, especially when teamed together, Australia losing just 15 of the 105 Tests in which their names have appeared on the same teamsheet. With a staggering 1,271 Test wickets between them, they will torment batsmen no more, which is about the only succour England can take at the moment.

6 JANUARY 2007

Simon Briggs

Sydney

Test cricket woke up this morning to a world without Shane Warne. For lovers of the sport – especially those with English allegiances – it is a strange and slightly hollow feeling.

As Englishmen, we should probably be celebrating the departure of a man who has broken our teams, abused our players, and brought many promising Test careers to a premature end. Warne has been a scourge of English cricket – an equal, in this respect, to that other great Australian antagonist, Don Bradman. But in our hearts, many of us are still sorry to see him go. Perhaps this is why the French call masochism 'le vice anglais'.

Some will argue that Glenn McGrath has been the greater bowler. The statistics might even back them up. But McGrath has never been so photogenic in his methods, nor so fascinatingly flawed as a human being. He has not commanded the stage with the same elan. It is Warne's mystical (sometimes mythical) bag of tricks, his gift for psychological warfare and his off-field vulnerabilities that have combined to make him the most compelling sportsman of the age.

'I'd like to think I've made cricket entertaining,' Warne said, 'and I'd like to think that I've made it pretty cool.' He has, of course, and that is why we love him. In an age when identikit seamers try to hit 'good areas', nothing has encapsulated the beauty and mystery of Test cricket like Warne's luminous leg-spin.

Warne's duels against the game's leading stroke-players, the Kevin Pietersens or Sachin Tendulkars, have taken the sport to a higher plane. The best passages of this series came when Pietersen tried to collar him. It was like watching a mongoose battle with a cobra – a dazzling dance with death.

When batsmen went in to face Warne, they knew they were sharing a pitch with greatness. Whatever the conditions, whatever the state of the match, runs against him were the most valuable currency in the game. Alastair Cook may have endured a largely unfulfilled tour, but at least he can tell his grandchildren that he scored a century against the best spinner who ever lived.

Without the blond bombshell to blow them away, England's Ashes fortunes can only improve. But victory will never taste as sweet as it did in 2005. The scale of Michael Vaughan's achievement can be judged by the fact that Warne and Bradman both played in eight Ashes series, yet Bradman lost twice and Warne once.

While Warne's physical attributes have waned slightly with age, he has never shown as much passion as he did this winter. His wickets cost over 30 runs apiece, a fortune by his frugal standards, yet his influence was everywhere. He took five catches at slip, shared at least two match-turning partnerships, and led the verbal onslaughts like a man suffering from Tourette's.

On the last day at Adelaide, Warne bowled 27 overs off the reel to skewer an England team who had been ahead of the game for four days. If England had drawn that match, they would have had a foothold. They might even have started believing in themselves. Instead, he sentenced them to the most soul-destroying defeat imaginable. Here was the clutch moment of the highest-profile series in Ashes history. And Warne, inevitably, was the man who clutched it.

By the time he reached Sydney, Warne had bowled so many overs that he could hardly get his arm past the horizontal. Yet he still found a way to ambush England with a helter-skelter innings of 71, fuelling himself with caffeine and some caustic backchat. As he put it afterwards: 'My scriptwriter has been on fire.' Indeed, the story has been so irresistible that the lesser scribes employed by McGrath and Justin Langer have hardly got a word into the papers over the last few days.

By the end, Warne would have been as worthy a recipient of the Compton–Miller Medal for player of the series as Ricky Ponting. But he was happy with what he got, a 5–0 whitewash in his final series. Had Australia lost this match, it would have been easy to see him hanging on for one last tilt at the Poms in 2009.

Now Warne faces perhaps his greatest challenge: life without the oxygen of professional sport. Asked how he would replace international cricket, he replied: 'I'm a pretty competitive person, so playing poker will be up there. A bit of pool or snooker, or the odd wager on the golf course. But nothing can replace the experience of playing for Australia.

'The one thing I won't miss is people camping on my front lawn and following me around in cars. Hopefully that will die down. Maybe I can get my gear off and dance on top of a bar if I want to.'

Perhaps we should try to talk him out of retirement after all.

---

13 MARCH 2007

WORLD CUP BLOG WWW.TELEGRAPH.CO.UK

Simon Briggs

Judging by the tone of the local World Cup coverage over the last few days, the West Indian media are feeling as nervous about the next seven weeks as a young suitor inviting his girlfriend back to meet the parents for the first time. This is the first major tournament to be staged in the Caribbean, and the region's columnists and reporters are worried that its natural beauty and charm will be outweighed, in the eyes of visitors, by the inconvenience of navigating around and the shabbiness of some half-finished stadia.

The tournament is expected to bring in some 100,000 extra tourists – a major figure for an economically depressed area that relies heavily on visitors. So it is important that Mum and Dad don't say anything too embarrassing and frighten the honoured guest(s) away. The probability is that the essentials will be in working order. Pitches will be playable, outfields may even be flat, and spectators should be able to find the seats they paid for.

It is the details that are likely to niggle: the potholed car park that never got its tarmac, or the power cut that shorts out the big screen at the critical moment. The early indications are not all that encouraging, though it is the players – rather than the fans – who had to deal with the inconvenience of Sabina Park's unfinished net facilities.

There are also the crime statistics to consider, especially here in Jamaica. As Tym Glaser wrote in *The Gleaner*, the island's dominant newspaper, 'a couple of mass murders, riots, etc, may just put you off your

googlies and prompt you to tell your pals back home that Baghdad
might be a safer holiday destination next time around.'

While Glaser may be exaggerating for effect, you can be sure that no
one with an interest in the Caribbean's economic future will be relaxing
until this tournament is over. A relatively hitch-free production would
do a great deal for the image of this whole region (which has spent the
past decade being bossed about by the IMF). It might even prove more
valuable to the West Indies than winning the Cup itself.

---

25 MARCH 2007

Scyld Berry

Bob Woolmer, who will be forever remembered for the way he died,
deserves to be remembered for his cricket too.

He batted as he coached and lived. There were no sharp edges, nothing
spikey or confrontational, in his cover-driving or his speech. He was
softly-spoken, smooth and accomplished, an outsider who was accepted
wherever he went because, for a passport, he had his lifelong enthusiasm
for cricket.

He scored three Test centuries for England, coached the most
successful county side of all time – Warwickshire in 1994 – and made
South Africa second only to Australia. But he was at his best as a batting
consultant for it was then, as when he was ICC's High Performance
Manager, that his enthusiasm shone through. And in that lies irony,
because by training up Associate Members like Ireland, he helped to
bring about their defeat of Pakistan, which seems to have resulted in a
fatal pressure on him.

One day in Zimbabwe he took me to the Academy in Harare, which
has since been burned down by the frustrated ex-Test player Mark
Vermeulen. The plan had been for us both to address a group of 20 or so
boys, but once Woolmer had a bat in his hands, the words and strokes
flowed.

He was a 'like pole' with Duncan Fletcher: both of them coaches
domiciled in Cape Town, both fascinated by the theories and practices of
cricket and batting in particular. But Woolmer was as talkative in public

s Fletcher is taciturn. He kept it simple as the best teachers do, limiting himself to a couple of main points, which is as much as the beginner's brain can absorb.

By the time he had finished talking about the left elbow, and the importance of removing the front leg from the line of delivery when hitting to leg, it was not only the Academy boys who felt they could bat for their country. On another occasion we met at one of those impossibly beautiful wineries in the Western Cape, in the hinterland of Cape Town, settled by the Dutch and as manicured as a model's finger-nail.

The second Test between 'his' South Africa and England had just been drawn, owing to the five-session rearguard innings of 185 not out by Mike Atherton. Woolmer acknowledged it was a fine innings, but he was a skilful propagandist too. England, having been set 479 to win, had lost their first four wickets cheaply; yet Woolmer, to deflect criticism from the sterility of his bowlers, said he was surprised England did not go for the win.

A couple of winters ago he showed me round the Pakistan Academy in Lahore where he lived much of the year, when not on tour or with his wife Gill in Cape Town. He had all the creature comforts in his apartment inside the complex, including a chef to indulge him, but it was a place short of light and company except for the chowkidars – the gate-keepers.

He had always been an outsider, which made it easier for him to break away from the pack to join World Series Cricket or the first England rebel tour of South Africa. He was born in Kanpur, where his father was working, and raised a little in Calcutta. He never put down roots after being sent to boarding school in Kent. Yet you could not call him a merce-nary, because he wandered the earth talking about cricket to everyone who would listen, of whatever race.

He had learned only a few words of Hindi when young, but they came in useful when Pakistan's captain Inzamam-ul-Haq strolled in, and the pair embraced and smiled and exchanged greetings with such effusion that it was hard to know how much sincerity was involved.

The last time we talked was 10 days before he died, at the Pakistan team's hotel in Port of Spain. He had moved on mentally as their coach. Three years of politicking – he was particularly unimpressed by the

Board's chief executive Salim Altaf – had got him down. 'When I started I could influence everything,' Woolmer said. 'Now I can influence nothing.'

He was not sad, or depressed, however, let alone suicidal. He was not even resigned to becoming a TV commentator, a lifestyle which I thought would have suited him. 'I want to coach,' he said, as near emphatically as his softness of tone would allow.

He knowingly worked in dangerous waters, with South Africa in the Hansie Cronje years of corruption, then with the team representing a country that is rotten to the political core.

---

22 APRIL 2007

LOYALTY ULTIMATELY PROVED THE UNDOING OF FLETCHER

Mike Atherton

After a winter when most things he touched turned not to gold but dust, Duncan Fletcher got one thing spot on last week. Given that Fletcher has manoeuvred himself into an all-powerful position within English cricket it is only right that a large dollop of accountability has been laid at his door for a winter gone disastrously wrong. The manner of his departure – resignation or sacking – was irrelevant. It was time for a change.

It has been a harrowing six months following the England cricket team. During the Champions Trophy they played with their minds elsewhere, eyeing a greater prize on the horizon, as if the tournament at hand was beneath them. The fug of self-delusion that enveloped them following the Ashes triumph of 2005 was subsequently blown away by an Australian team who were demonstrably better prepared, more focused and more determined (and, it must be said, more talented).

The fag end of the Commonwealth Bank series provided blessed relief, but even that proved to be a curse, encouraging Fletcher and the selectors, as it did, to keep faith with a bunch of players who were clearly out of their depth in one-day cricket. The result was a World Cup in which England appeared as bemused and grumpy onlookers, unable to omprehend a game that had moved on without them. After such a winter, the position of the man responsible had become untenable.

And Fletcher was responsible. He was given more authority than any other figure in recent English cricket history, save for Raymond Illingworth, who enjoyed a brief period of megalomania. The chairman of selectors, David Graveney, was sidelined. To say the relationship between Graveney and Fletcher had broken down would be wrong; there was never much of a relationship in the first place. Dissenters departed (Rod Marsh) or were sent to Siberia (the press). Lieutenants were hand-picked – some on the basis of familiarity and friendship rather than expertise – outsiders were shunned.

Although he often described himself as a consultant to the captain, this was very much Fletcher's ship. When things went well, as they did for much of his first five years in charge, it was right that the skipper of the vessel received much of the praise. And he did. For a long time he was accorded a fair passage by Fleet Street, the Ashes triumph widely reported as the culmination of years of Fletcher's hard work and meticulous planning. A gong, a handsome publishing contract, a rolling ECB contract (from which Fletcher will now benefit with a large pay-off) and public affection were the rewards.

In the aftermath of 2005, a great outcry went up to give Fletcher a British passport; those same newspapers last week called for his deportation. Such is the nature of the job. The winds were bound to turn less favourable – they always do – and so the passage was always going to turn rough in the end. Fletcher had the good grace to accept that after the hosannas comes the cross. Once his mind was made up, as we have seen with his cricketing decisions over a period of time, he was not for turning.

Given Fletcher's overriding influence over selection, strategy and the make-up of the back-room staff, it is certain that his departure will have a destabilising effect. For the England team have lost more than a coach. They have lost a mentor. There is not one survivor from the pre-Fletcher era (apart from Graveney, and his future might be short-lived if certain members of the Schofield Review have their way). All the players have bought into Fletcher's habits. The good – such as the discipline, the hard work, the forward press, the sweep and reverse sweep – and the bad – such as the insularity, narrow-mindedness and suspicion of those with a broader-minded, more generous view of life.

In that sense, as well as having a destabilising effect, it might also hav a liberating one for players who are good enough to force themselves into a new era. It became increasingly evident to outsiders, and this process accelerated as the criticism of Fletcher increased, that players were discouraged from seeking out a fresh view or a different take on things. It didn't say much for the strength of mind of the majority of players that they acquiesced, and it said much about the insecurity of the management group. The relationship between the players and the coach should never be servile.

It is inconceivable that there will not be further changes. One such should be announced with immediate effect. The blame for England's woeful one-day performances over the last four years should be shared equally with Michael Vaughan. Graveney, last week, announced that Vaughan is likely to lead England into the first Test against the West Indies in three weeks' time. Fair enough, but it is inconceivable that Vaughan can carry on as one-day captain. At some stage the figures cannot be ignored: England do not win many one-day games under his leadership, and he doesn't score enough runs to warrant a place in the side. You can have as many good nets as you like, but ultimately you have to score some runs in the middle. For the best part of 90 matches, Vaughan has been accorded due deference. His time as a one-day player has run out.

At some stage England will have to come to grips with one-day cricket. It is not true to say that England have not produced any decent one-day cricket in the last 15 years. When they were intermittently successful, though, it was by playing a brand of cricket − gradually increasing the impetus when batting because of the absence of field restrictions and defensive bowling − that is no longer relevant in the modern game.

England need to discover some power players of their own, and a wicket-taking bowler or two. The first will be easier to find than the second.

I believe that not only should England have split captains now that Vaughan no longer warrants a place in the team, but split coaches too. The job is too demanding, physically and technically, for one man to do well. There could be problems if two coaches are telling the same set of players different things, but I would envisage two coaches working in tandem for the benefit of each other, able to keep players fresher and ore motivated by dint of the fact that they themselves would be fresher and more motivated.

Much of the analysis last week of Fletcher's mistakes in the past 18 months has focused on the coach's misplaced loyalty. Loyalty was one of Fletcher's greatest virtues, and it also proved to be his undoing at the start of this winter's Ashes series, but I also think that many of the mistakes can be put down to mental weariness. Think of the amount of time a coach spends away from home with the same set of players. It becomes difficult to step back and view things with detachment.

Fletcher looked increasingly burdened and tired this winter. Two coaches would result in greater periods of rest and recuperation (important in itself for men who are normally older and less fit than the players) and would allow them a chance to step back from the melee and organise their thoughts.

That won't happen now that the ECB have rushed to replace Fletcher with Peter Moores. It is a missed opportunity. Although the Davids, Morgan and Collier, have repeatedly said this week that Moores's name has been inked in for a while, two members of the Schofield Review group told me last week that Fletcher sounded like a man who wanted to carry on for some time yet. So how much thought have the ECB given to how the England teams of the future should be coached? In any case, wasn't this supposed to be part of Schofield's brief? It is messy.

I have no idea whether Moores is the best man for the job. The ECB don't know either. How can they when they haven't talked to any other candidates? Sometimes the inside replacement is not necessarily the best thing, as the Football Association are finding out with Steve McClaren. Besides, Moores is linked to an Academy that is failing English cricket right now, producing decent cricketers but human beings who are so one-dimensional and so narrow-minded, unable to do little more than grunt in public, that they became an object of derision this winter among Australian cricket reporters.

Had the ECB appointed cosily from within, instead of going through a thorough process designed to get the best man for the job, they would never have appointed Fletcher in the first place. And although inevitably recent weeks have homed in on Fletcher's failings in the last 18 months, and in one-day cricket, it should be stressed that Fletcher was the best appointment the ECB ever made.

Unwilling to face his tormentors, Fletcher issued a statement that indicated he had much to be proud of during his time as England's coach. He is right. Stability in selection, clear-sighted planning, inspired selections of some under-performing cricketers from county cricket, victories on the sub-continent and, of course, against Australia, were all accomplishments of which Fletcher can be justifiably proud.

Ironically, things had come full circle by the end. Fletcher arrived just after an England captain had been booed, and he leaves with the same sound ringing in Vaughan's ears. But, and it is a big but, Fletcher leaves the English cricket team in a far healthier state than he found it. In between the jeers there was plenty of joy.

---

30 APRIL 2007

Mark Nicholas

The World Cup finished much as it began, in disarray. From the very real tragedy of Bob Woolmer's death to the superficial one of a final played out in pitch black to a full house that could no longer identify the players, never mind understand the revised rules, cricket has appeared as a fool too often to be funny.

Someone, somewhere, must be accountable, but won't be. The International Cricket Council are not a federation governing the game; they are a holding company who facilitate the egos of each member nation. In time, there will be a meeting, some platitudes, even a promise about the future, but the truth is that everyone is in it for themselves, not for the greater good. One day this will come home to roost, for cricket is on a collision course with a world that offers myriad simpler options. For the moment, we are left to celebrate one exceptional team while reflecting on the incompetence that surrounds them.

The Australians gave the tournament every last drop of themselves and thus received the most back. Not once were they taken to their limit by the opposition so instead they pushed their own boundaries, improving almost daily to the point at which they exposed the South Africans, who occupied the top spot in the world rankings, as impostors.

Only Sri Lanka had the gumption to look Ricky Ponting's team in the eye and run their race. That they came second was no disgrace. A good fist was made of a daunting cup-final target in conditions that turned on them, most particularly when the umpires took the players off in the 25th over because of the drizzle. At this point there was rhythm to the batting and the suggestion that Mahela Jayawardene had the measure of the Australian attack, but when the players returned, the theatre of the absurd kicked in.

Nobody, not umpires on the field or off it, not the match referee, nor the players and spectators, commentators or officials had a clue about the revised target. Two overs were deducted but no mention was made of the runs required. Jayawardene pulled away after a ball or two, disgusted by the confusion. How could he pursue a figure that was not there? Could he, or any of us, believe this was the World Cup final?

Suddenly, painfully, it had become the final that the ICC deserved: ill-conceived and ill-fated. Through the wet morning there was sympathy to be heard – could the Barbados weather really scupper the game it so reveres? But now sympathy was overrun by ridicule.

Eventually, Jayawardene was given the information he needed but so diverted was he that he missed a ball from Shane Watson that was missing leg stump. Steve Bucknor missed that too and upheld the lbw appeal. Game over.

By taking the players off, the umpires had extracted any last semblance of soul from the tournament. Here was chance to throw the letter of the law aside and apply common sense. Had the show gone on, with the players slipping and sliding, the darkness descending, the run-rate fluctuating and the crowd riveted, we would have forgiven a deal of what had gone before. The match might even have finished in soft twilight, not dense black, so allowing a natural conclusion instead of the farce that replaced it.

The more one thinks about it, the more one recalls two long months of heavy-handed officialdom, both on and off the field. The ICC are good at the stuff that doesn't matter, issues such as Michael Clarke running on the pitch after his first ball and being penalised his run, but not so good at the big picture. If they do not deal with this mis-direction – some would say ineptitude – the big picture will lose its appeal.

Enough! To Adam Gilchrist we must turn, the man Richie Benaud calls the cleanest striker of a cricket ball he has seen. Given Benaud was on the wrong end of Garry Sobers too often for comfort, this is high praise.

In December, Gilchrist made a Test hundred against England in 57 balls, just a single ball outside the world record. On Saturday, he took 72 balls for his first World Cup hundred, just six balls outside the World Cup record set by Matthew Hayden a month ago. From the Ashes to the World Cup final, it is clear Gilchrist is not fazed by the grand occasion. Rather the opposite, he is inspired by it. His batting is the material of comic book strips, of dreams rarely realised, of fantasies that few sportsmen get to live out.

The freedom of his strokes sets the tone for a team who are far beyond their contemporaries in every facet. The medical men even saw Andrew Symonds to full fitness from an injury some felt would take six months to heal safely. Attention to detail clears the way for the players to make the most of their gifts. If sometimes this is achieved without charm, it is because we live in an increasingly charmless world. The Australians win well and entertain while doing so. Only the churlish begrudge them.

From the buccaneering spirit of Gilchrist to the extraordinary disciplines applied by Glenn McGrath, Australia prove that cricket in any format is a game for all people, all styles, all temperaments. McGrath's farewell robs us of a patience and subtlety not often seen among fast men. He made batsmen play his game rather than their own by examining minds and breaking hearts. The cold assassin to Shane Warne's mesmeric sorcerer, this man of the bush was a part of the greatest bowling partnership that ever lived.

It took seven weeks to find out Australia are the greatest one-day team on the planet. Actually, we already knew. The ICC's coup de grace was that Percy Sonn, their president, made a windy speech and then presented Ponting with the trophy. Sir Garry was on that podium too for goodness sake, ready and willing but not asked. Really, enough said.

---

7 JULY 2007

SIR – If I were Simon Briggs I should glance nervously upwards every time I ventured out for fear of being struck down by a thunderbolt from

n high. Why? Because he described Fred Trueman as 'probably the
.inest fast bowler England ever produced'. Probably?

Richard Green
Swanage

---

31 JULY 2007

Martin Johnson

Trent Bridge

ENGLAND'S cricket team have been searching for a fielding coach for
quite some time, but have so far failed to approach the obvious candidate. With the accent moving less towards how to hold a catch and
more towards how to hold a conversation, Michael Parkinson is not
only passionate about his cricket, he also knows a thing or two about
chat shows.

Matt Prior, the England wicketkeeper, said on Sunday night that the
verbal side of fielding was an important part of 'creating intensity',
which is presumably why he is apparently intent on making a career out
of trying to convince everyone within a five-mile radius of his irritating
banshee that every ball England send down is actually a live hand
grenade. If it were, it would at least explain some of his juggler's glove-
work.

With all this sledging going on, maybe a toboggan would be a more
suitable England crest than three lions, but whenever they do locate a
new fielding coach, let's hope he can come up with something a bit less
juvenile than planting a jelly bean on the pitch.

Now we know why batsmen do all that prodding. They're trying to
flatten out all those sugary sweets.

It's schoolboy stuff, it really is. Tee hee, what a wizard jape. Jelly and
blancmange will doubtless be on the menu at England's end-of-season
dinner, and if England lose this match, Michael Vaughan's worried
expression at the press conference will have less to do with the result
than wondering whether someone might have planted a whoopee
cushion on his chair.

There is an argument that the jelly bean business was all a bit of harmless fun, as it might have been had Mike Gatting been batting instead of Zaheer Khan. Gatt would simply have picked it up and eaten it. However, it certainly got up the Indians' collective nose, and Zaheer had so much to say to the England batsmen yesterday he was more in need of a throat lozenge than a jelly bean.

Just about the only time he wasn't chuntering away was when he had a mouthful of food down on the boundary. All this sledging clearly gives a chap an appetite, as quite apart from the unusual sight of the 12th man running on to the field to deliver a sandwich, there were only 15 minutes to go before tea.

Zaheer's new-ball partner, Shantha Sreesanth, took a slightly different view, and decided to let the ball do the talking. The beamer (beaner?) he fired at Kevin Pietersen's head must have caused Pietersen's life to flash before his eyes — a life so action-packed, incidentally, Kev has modestly recorded it in hardback — £ 18.99 at all good bookshops.

This did not go down especially well with either Pietersen or Vaughan, especially as the latter had earlier been minding his own business at the non-striker's end when Sreesanth's shoulder gave him a not insubstantial nudge.

The England captain came pretty well out of the day, and not just for his batting. Zaheer's constant attempts to eyeball Vaughan met with such a lack of response that he might just as well have been trying to hold a conversation with the speaking clock, but when the match referee sorts all this out tonight, there is only one possible verdict: both teams sent straight to bed with no supper (having first had their jelly beans confiscated), and no ragging in the dorm.

Test cricket has got to move with the times, and even the scorers will soon be turning their attention to more important matters than leg byes and dot balls. You can imagine Bill Frindall interrupting Henry Blofeld's animated description of a pigeon pecking on the outfield to inform Test Match Special listeners: 'That's the 15th sledge between lunch and tea, which is the second highest for a Test between England and India, and a record for Trent Bridge.'

'Thank you Bearders, and after another word from Vic, it will be CMJ.'
